Topics in Applied Economics

The Editors

G. Mythili is Associate Professor at the Madras School of Economics, Chennai. Currently she is visiting Indira Gandhi Institute of Development Research at Mumbai. Having obtained Ph.D. in Econometrics discipline, she visited University of California at Berkeley during 1990-91 as a Ford Foundation Post Doctoral Fellow. She was associated with many research projects including Farm Management Studies, Farm Production Risk, Globalisation of Indian Agriculture and Environmental Problems related to Energy Sector. She has co-authored a book on Farm Production Decision under Uncertainty. Recently she visited University of Peradeniya at Sri Lanka for nine months as a Visiting Fellow in Environmental Economics. She was a member of Course Curriculum Committee of World Bank/MOEF Capacity Building in Environmental Economics. She has to her credit many journal articles and research reports.

R. Hema is Associate Professor at the Madras School of Economics. Her Doctoral dissertation was on optimal pricing in the electricity sector. Subsequently she has been working on various topics relating to the electricity sector – financial performance, regulatory mechanisms, institutional restructuring. She visited the University of California at Berkeley during 1991-92 as a Ford Foundation Post-Doctoral Fellow. Was associated with a programme on International Comparison of Electricity Regulation at the Energy Institute there. She has been on the faculty of Tata Energy Research Institute, New Delhi, Madras Institute of Development Studies, Chennai and adjunct faculty at DePaul University, Chicago. She has been associated with many studies on the power sector that were sponsored by the Asian Development Bank, Power Finance Corporation, Tamil Nadu Electricity Board, Planning Commission *etc.* and also with a study on Social Exclusion, sponsored by the International Labour Organisation. She has made contributions to the Vision 2020 Document for the Union Territory of Pondicherry and the Tamil Nadu State Development Report.

Topics in
Applied Economics
Tools, Issues and Institutions

A FESTSCHRIFT VOLUME FOR PROF. U. SANKAR

Editors

G. MYTHILI AND R. HEMA

ACADEMIC FOUNDATION
NEW DELHI

First Published in 2005 by

ACADEMIC FOUNDATION

4772-73 / 23 Bharat Ram Road, (23 Ansari Road),
Darya Ganj, New Delhi - 110 002.
INDIA.

Phones : 23245001, 02, 03, 04.
Fax : +91-11-23245005.
e-mail : academic@vsnl.com
www : academicfoundation.com

Topics in Applied Economics : Tools, Issues and Institutions
edited by G. Mythili and R. Hema

ISBN 81-7188-365-6

Designed and typeset by Italics India, New Delhi
and printed at Print Perfect, New Delhi.

Contents

Authors / Contributors

Arnold Zellner is H.G.B. Distinguished Service Professor Emeritus of Economics and Statistics at the Graduate Business School of the University of Chicago. He also spends considerable time as Professor at the Department of Agriculture and Resource Economics of the University of California at Berkeley. Zellner has made very significant contributions in the area of Econometrics and Statistics, and is an authority in Bayesian techniques. He was elected President of the American Statistical Association in 1991 and he is the Founder and first elected President of the International Society for Bayesian Analysis. He is the co-founder and co-editor of the Journal of Econometrics. He was the founding editor of the ASA Journal of Business and Economic Statistics. He has served on the Editorial Board of Journal of Economic Literature. He has published over 20 books and he has to his credit about 250 papers published in a wide range of leading journals and edited volumes.

Raja J. Chelliah is the Founder-Chairman, of the Madras School of Economics. He is a fiscal economics expert and his authority and contributions in this area are such that his name is immediately associated with taxation in India. He was Chairman of the Tax Reforms Committee set up by the Government of India in 1991 and was Chairman of the Tax Reforms and Revenue Augmentation Commission set up by Government of Tamil Nadu in 2002. He was fiscal adviser at the Ministry of Finance, GoI, in 1993, was a member of the Union Planning Commission and a member of the Ninth Finance Commission. He has been chief of the Fiscal Affairs Division at the Fiscal Affairs Department of the International Monetary Fund and was a consultant to the Government of Papua New Guinea on Centre-Provincial Financial Relations. He was the Founder-Director of the National Institute of Public Finance Policy, New Delhi and subsequently became its Chairman. His book on fiscal economics was a popular textbook in Indian colleges and recently he has prepared a primer on VAT.

Paul P. Appasamy is Professor at Madras School of Economics and Member-Secretary of the Centre of Excellence in Environmental Economics under the Ministry of Environment and Forests. His areas of specialisation and research interests are in technological and environmental planning, natural resource economics and urban economics. He was Director at Madras School of Economics and has been Director at the Madras Institute of Development Studies. He has done consulting work for the U.S. Environmental Protection Agency in Washington D.C., Indian National Trust for Art and Cultural Heritage, Chennai, UN Centre for Human Settlements, Nairobi, Swedish International Development Cooperation Agency, and the United Nations Development Programme. He is an expert on water, environment and urban studies and has completed several projects in these areas, funded by national and international agencies. He has 27 publications in Indian and foreign journals.

V.K. Chetty is a statistician/economist. He is currently a health economist at the Boston Medical Center. He has been Professor of Economics at Columbia University, New York and the Indian Statistical Institute, New Delhi. His current research interests are in medical decision-making, taking appropriate costs into account and reducing medical errors. At present, he is working on cost-effective management of Diabetes, using sequential statistical methods and complex adaptive systems approach. He has been a consultant to the United Nations and the World Bank. He has published many papers in leading journals and prepared about nine technical reports.

Nagesh S. Revankar is Professor of Economics and Director of Graduate Studies at the State University of New York at Buffalo, where he joined the Department of Economics as Assistant Professor in 1967. His early work is in the area of production theory and consumer analysis, and his subsequent research interests have been in the area of econometrics. He has several contributions to his credit which have appeared in various leading journals. He holds a Master's degree in Statistics from the University of Pune, India.

M. Salih is currently Director of Decision Science for Digital Matrix Systems. This group is primarily devoted to developing credit scores for lending institutions throughout the US. He did his Ph.D. work under the supervision of Prof. Revankar in the State University of New York at Buffalo. Shortly after his graduation in 1993 he worked as Adjunct Faculty there and taught several economics and statistics courses. In 1996, he moved to Dallas, Texas, to work for FirstPlus Financial, which is a second mortgage lending company, in the risk management area. He was primarily doing loss and prepayment forecasting and developing default and pricing scores. Subsequently, he worked for Digital Matrix Systems, Ocwen Financial Corporation, The Associates and Citigroup in the statistical modeling and credit scorecard development areas.

K.L. Krishna headed the Delhi School of Economics for many years and is currently an Honorary Research Advisor at the Centre for Development Economics, Delhi School of Economics. Also a long-term professional associate of U. Sankar, he has been instrumental in developing the curriculum for "Econometrics" in India. He is noted for his significant contribution in the application for Econometrics to industry, trade and macroeconomics. He has served on the Editorial Board of journals like Indian Economic Review and was the Founder Managing Editor of Journal of Quantitative Economics. He has also served on many national and international committees. He was the President of the Indian Econometric Society in early 1990s.

A. Vaidyanathan is Emeritus Professor at the Madras Institute of Development Studies, Chennai. He is a leading authority in India on irrigation issues. He has made notable contributions in the area of water pricing, water resource management, irrigation pricing etc. He has been serving as the President of Indian Society of Agricultural Economics. He has visited the Institute of Development Economics, Tokyo, as a Research Fellow. He was a National Fellow of the Indian Council of Social Science Research during 1996-97. He has served as a Member of the National Planning Commission, the Prime Minister's Economic Advisory Commission and also on many committees of national and international importance.

Gopal K. Kadekodi is currently Director of the Institute for Social and Economic Change. He has been Research Professor at the Centre for Multi-Disciplinary Development Research, Dharwad and a Professor at the Institute of Economic Growth, New Delhi. He was Visiting Professor at Erasmus University, Rotterdam. His areas of research include Common Property Resources Valuation, Energy, Natural Resource Accounting and Economic Development. He has been the President of the Indian Society for Ecological Economics. He is Editor, Journal of Social and Economic Development, and on the Editorial Boards of Environment and Resource Economics, The Pacific and Asian Journal of Energy and Journal of Quantitative Economics. He has published over 10 books and more than 100 articles in national and international journals.

S. Subramanian is Professor at the Madras Institute of Development Studies, Chennai. His principal areas of research concern are collective choice theory, aspects of social and economic measurement, and development economics. He is the editor or co-editor of four books, and his work has been published in journals like *Social Choice and Welfare, Theory and Decision, Journal of Development Economics*, and *Economics and Philosophy*.

Taradas Bandyopadhyay is Professor of Economics at the University of California, Riverside, U.S.A. He taught in various universities in the U.S., U.K., Canada and India. His main area of expertise is economic theory, particularly the analysis of individual and social choice, and mathematical economics. He has a long list of publications in the leading professional journals such as Review of Economic Studies, Journal of Economic Theory, Economic Journal, Economic Theory, Journal of Mathematical Economics, Social Choice and Welfare, Mathematical Social Sciences and Journal of Mathematical Psychology.

Kaliappa Kalirajan is currently a Professor at the Foundation for Advanced Studies on International Development and the National Graduate Institute for Policy Studies, Tokyo. He also holds an adjunct professorship at the Australian National University, Sophia University, and the Madras School of Economics. His areas of specialisation are Econometrics, Development Economics and Macroeconomics. He has made original contributions in the field of Econometric Analysis of the Frontier Production Function and its application in many areas. He has developed disequilibrium models using frontier production functions and applied to macro-econometric modeling. He has to his credit several books and papers in international refereed journals.

Sreejata Banerjee is a Visiting Professor of Great Lakes Institute of Management at Chennai and also teaches Economics and Finance for Herriot Watt University's MBA programme offered at International Institute of Business Management, Chennai. She is an alumni of Jadavpur University. She was Prof. Sankar's student for her Ph.D. programme at the University of Madras. She has taught financial economics at some of the leading colleges in Chennai and has published research articles in India and abroad on capital markets and international finance. She is currently working on issues of empowerment in Microfinance.

V. Anuradha is currently working for a multinational company in Bangalore. She worked for her Ph.D. under the guidance of Prof. Sankar and is a product of the Madras School of Economics. She has collaborated with Prof. Sankar on projects funded by World Resources Institute, UNDP and the World Bank. She worked as Business Analyst at GE Capital International Services at New Delhi.

G. Mythili is Associate Professor at the Madras School of Economics, Chennai. Currently she is visiting Indira Gandhi Institute of Development Research at Mumbai. Having obtained Ph.D. in Econometrics discipline, she visited University of California at Berkeley during 1990-91 as a Ford Foundation Post Doctoral Fellow. She was associated with many research projects including Farm Management Studies, Farm Production Risk, Globalisation of Indian Agriculture and Environmental Problems related to Energy Sector. She has co-authored a book on Farm Production Decision under Uncertainty. Recently she visited University of Peradeniya at Sri Lanka for nine months as a Visiting Fellow in Environmental Economics. She was a member of Course Curriculum Committee of World Bank/MOEF Capacity Building in Environmental Economics. She has to her credit many journal articles and research reports.

R. Hema is Associate Professor at the Madras School of Economics. Her Doctoral dissertation was on optimal pricing in the electricity sector. Subsequently she has been working on various topics relating to the electricity sector – financial performance, regulatory mechanisms, institutional restructuring. She visited the University of California at Berkeley during 1991-92 as a Ford Foundation Post-Doctoral Fellow. Was associated with a programme on International Comparison of Electricity Regulation at the Energy Institute there. She has been on the faculty of Tata Energy Research Institute, New Delhi, Madras Institute of Development Studies, Chennai and adjunct faculty at DePaul University, Chicago. She has been associated with many studies on the power sector that were sponsored by the Asian Development Bank, Power Finance Corporation, Tamil Nadu Electricity Board, Planning Commission *etc.* and also with a study on Social Exclusion, sponsored by the International Labour Organisation. She has made contributions to the Vision 2020 Document for the Union Territory of Pondicherry and the Tamil Nadu State Development Report.

Preface

A person with an untiring quest for learning and an unshakeable commitment to his teaching and research pursuits in economics - that is quintessential Prof. Sankar. The breadth and depth of his academic achievements and contributions stand testimony to this fact.

He completed his undergraduate programme in Economics at St. Xavier's College, Palayamkottai and his B.A. (Honors) programme at Annamalai University and was a rank holder at both places. After a brief spell as Lecturer at Annamalai University and as a Research Associate at the Gandhian Institute of Studies at Varanasi, he went to the United States of America to pursue a Ph.D. programme in economics. He was at the University of Wisconsin, Madison and was fortunate to work for three years as a Research Assistant to Prof. Arnold Zellner, the renowned econometrician. Before he went to the U.S., Prof. Sankar had no formal training in mathematics or quantitative techniques. His close association with Prof. Zellner enthused and enabled him to get a good grasp of quantitative economics and especially econometrics. It was Prof. Zellner's influence and expert advice that transformed Prof. Sankar from a descriptive economist into an applied economist and shaped his academic career. At Madison, Prof. Sankar also worked with Prof. Robert Baldwin, a well-known expert in international economics. While pursuing his Ph.D. work, he was a recipient of the Ford Foundation Doctoral Dissertation Fellowship. He also got the prestigious CIC Scholarship, which enabled him to visit the University of Chicago as a traveling scholar and complete his thesis work under Prof. Zellner, who had moved there. At Chicago, he also interacted and worked with other leading econometricians like Grilliches, McFadden, Mundlak, and Theil.

On completing his doctoral work he joined the University of Wisconsin at Milwaukee in 1967 as an Assistant Professor and within nine years became a full Professor. His papers were published in journals like Review of Economic Studies, Bell Journal of Economics and Management Science, International Economic Review, Journal of Economic Theory, Southern Economic Journal and Review of Economics and Statistics. In 1978, when the eminent educationalist Dr. Malcolm Adiseshiah, who was then Vice Chancellor of Madras University, invited him to join the Economics Department of University of Madras, he decided to come back to India. He was serving as Chairman of the Graduate Studies Committee at the University of Wisconsin, Milwaukee, at that time. The University was reluctant to let him go and kept his position open for two years.

There was however, no looking back for Prof. Sankar. Studying economic problems relating to the Indian economy has always been his main focus and devoting his time and efforts to the cause of teaching economics and providing economic inputs for policy making in India had now become his priority. He, along with Prof. Nalla Gounden, was instrumental in establishing the Department of Econometrics at the University of Madras. His efforts to promote a teaching and research programme of high quality at this Department paid off and many of the students who passed out from here have proved themselves both at the national and at the international level.

While for most people retirement would be a time when they ease up on their career pursuits, start reminiscing and resting on their laurels, for Prof. Sankar it was a time of rededicating his time and effort to academics with renewed vigour. On the verge of retiring from the University of Madras, he teamed up with Prof. Raja Chelliah on a major initiative – the setting up of the Madras School of Economics. He has provided and continues to provide invaluable support in this venture and is the chief architect of the high caliber economics graduate programme offered here. He is a Founder Member of the School, was its first Director and now is an Honorary Professor.

Prof. Sankar's teaching and research cover an enviable expanse of areas and issues. The range of graduate courses he has taught includes microeconomics, macroeconomics, advanced microeconomic theory, mathematical economics, econometrics, applied econometrics, econometric theory, economics of public utilities, agricultural economics, welfare economics and environmental economics.

During his early years of research in the U.S. he was analysing production functions in the Indian manufacturing sector – their implications for economic development, Bayesian methods of estimating them and understanding and tackling errors in the variables. He then moved on to study investment behaviour in network industries like electricity and telephones in the U.S, which are subject to regulatory constraint. AT&T, Ford Foundation and National Science Foundation were among the sponsors for the projects he undertook or worked on. After he returned to India he worked in two broad areas. One was concerning agricultural production, productivity and farm level decision-making under uncertainty. The other was relating to pricing policies in multi-product public sector enterprises, which included the electricity and the telecom sectors. Ministry of Agriculture of Government of India, University Grants Commission, Indian Council of Social Science Research and Bureau of Industrial Costs and Prices sponsored the projects he undertook in these areas. He then took up the task of preparing the Input-Output transactions table for the agriculture and manufacturing sectors in Tamil Nadu, for the State Government.

In the early nineties Prof. Sankar got interested in working on environmental economics. He worked on various projects sponsored by World Health Organisation, World Resources Institute, UNDP and the Netherlands Embassy. He analysed the relative merits of using economic incentives *vis-à-vis* regulation for pollution abatement, looked at fiscal reforms needed for sustainable development, carried out an economic evaluation of the environmental damages caused by the tanning and textile dyeing industries and made suggestions for policy. The start of the twenty first century saw Prof. Sankar embarking on a research journey that carried out a techno-economic analysis of the Indian space programme for ISRO. The remarkable aspects about Prof. Sankar's work in these two areas are that he ventured into these new areas when he was nearing retirement and a few years after retirement. He had to spend considerable time and effort learning many new things because his inter-disciplinary approach demanded an effective blending of economic principles with scientific and technical information. This was also the time when he was shouldering the academic and administrative responsibilities of building up the Madras School of Economics. Yet the proficiency he gained in environmental economics within a short span of time got him to be appointed in 1997 as the National Programme Coordinator for the Environmental Economics component of the World Bank's Environmental Capacity Building Programme in India.

Between 1996 and 1999, Prof. Sankar also carried out a study on the growth impacts of globalisation on Indian agriculture, in collaboration with the Australian National University. His current project is a study of trade and environment issues in the context of the Indian leather industry.

The long list of publications that Prof. Sankar has to his credit includes eleven books and monographs, twenty papers presented at international conferences, twenty five at national conferences and innumerable articles in various journals and edited volumes. As a mark of recognition for the very significant and substantial contributions made by him, the Indian Council of Social Science Research offered Prof. Sankar a National Fellowship for the years 2003 and 2004.

Prof. Sankar's contributions through his active involvement as a member of various professional associations, editorial boards, academic councils, executive councils, governing councils, boards of trustees and expert advisory committees are immense. An amasing range of institutions seeks his advice, guidance, expert opinion and prescriptions for policy and governance. He was a member of the Council of the Indian Econometric Society for many years and then served as its Vice President and President. He was also elected President of the Tamil Nadu Association of Economists. He was a member of the Executive Committee of the Indian Association of Social Science Institutions. He has been a member of the Board of Trustees of the Indian Economic Association Trust for Research and Development for many years now. He has played an important role in designing the curriculum and syllabi for teaching economics in India. He was a member of the UGC Panel on Quantitative Economics for recommending syllabi, the UGC Curriculum Committee for drafting Economic Syllabi, and the UGC Panel in Economics. He was the Chairman of the Environmental Economics Course and Curriculum Committee under the World Bank-Ministry of Environment and Forests programme. He is on the Editorial

Boards of *Journal of Quantitative Economics* and *Environment and Development Economics*. He is a member of the Editorial Advisory Boards of *Review of Development and Change* and the *Journal of Social and Economic Development*.

The Ministry of Environment and Forests draws on his expertise and advice as a member of its Expert Committee on Environmental Economics, Think Tank in Environmental Economics, Core Group on Sustainable Development and Expert Group on Coastal Regulation Zone Management. He was on its Sub-Group for Environmental Impact Assessment during the Ninth Plan and is on its Advisory Committee for Preparation for the World Summit on Sustainable Development.

Prof. Sankar has made contributions to the planning process in India in various capacities. He was a member of the Tamil Nadu Planning Commission between 2001 and 2004. At the Union Planning Commission he was a member of the Working Groups on Environment and on the Space Programme, the Committee on Air Traffic and the Evaluation Advisory Committee. Given his expertise on statistical databases he was appointed a member of the Governing Body of the National Sample Survey Organisation and as Chairman of Tamil Nadu Statistical Committee. The Madras Chamber of Commerce and Industry has nominated him a member of their General Committee and the Confederation of Indian Industry had him on their Tamil Nadu State Council. Most recently he has been made a member of the Research Advisory Committee of the Competition Commission of India.

The persistent and innumerable demands on his time due to his varied commitments notwithstanding, Prof. Sankar always finds time for his students. He is ready to share his knowledge and wisdom with anyone who seeks it. At the same time he ensures that his students do not become completely dependent on him. He values individual independence and believes in individual responsibilities. Fifteen students have successfully completed their doctoral programme under his guidance and twenty students have received their M.Phil. Degree.

Above all, Prof. Sankar is a man of noble principles. He is a true Gandhian at heart and in his ways. His concern for the causes that he is committed to comes before his personal interests. A small example of this is the fact that he has donated the entire amount of his two years' ICSSR National Fellowship to the Madras School of Economics. His simplicity and modesty are to be seen to be believed. He is always forthright in his views and very democratic in his decision-making. He never forces his views or his ways on others. His closest friend is his wife, Thilagavathy, with whom he has been sharing his life for 36 years now. She has contributed to his success in no small measure. She has beautifully complemented his personality, shouldered a significant part of their domestic responsibilities in raising two children and been a source of strength and moral support.

We are proud and extremely privileged to have had the opportunity to be among his students, to have worked under his research guidance, to have been able to derive from his experience and wisdom and most importantly to have had a long-term association with such a noble person. This volume is a token of appreciation for the invaluable contributions he has made as an academician. We wish that his contributions would continue for many more years to come and we wish Prof. Sankar and his family much happiness and peace.

— G. MYTHILI
and R. HEMA

In Honour of Professor Ulaganathan Sankar

ARNOLD ZELLNER

It is indeed a pleasure to contribute to this volume honouring Professor Sankar, my long-time friend, professional colleague and former student. In 1988 and 2000 I had enjoyable visits with him and his family in Madras and appreciated greatly the warm hospitality accorded to me. I was favorably impressed by his wonderful family and many professional achievements. He has worked with many graduate students and published many papers and books dealing with important theoretical and applied problems, particularly relevant for helping to promote India's economic progress. A few of the research areas in which he has worked include public sector pricing, uncertainty and farm production decisions, elasticities of substitution and returns to scale in Indian manufacturing industries, investment behavior in the electric utility industry, methodology of applied econometric and economic research and formulation and modification of hypotheses in economics. His research on these and other important topics has been a most fruitful blend of methodological and applied work, a great achievement that has been widely recognised and appreciated. Indeed, he has been selected to serve as President of the Indian Econometric Society, 1993-94. and as President of the Association of Economists, Tamil Nadu, 1991-92, in recognition of his work that has had a substantial impact on agricultural, environmental, public pricing policies and economic and econometric methodology in India and elsewhere. In addition to these fine research and policy contributions, he has been Head of the Department of Econometrics at the University of Madras and Director of the Madras School of Economics.

That Sankar has been so active and successful in many different areas, namely, family, research, teaching, administration, etc. is the result of his strong determination, strength of character, fine intellect, willingness to work very hard and excellent judgment in choice of research topics and other matters. When I first met Sankar in the early 1960s when he was a doctoral student in the Department of Economics, University of Wisconsin in Madison on a very cold winter day, I was amazed to see his positive attitude and strong determination in spite of the below zero Farenheit, cold winter weather. And when he attended my courses and served as my research assistant, I learned more about his great intellect, determination, willingness to work hard and his devotion to India and its well being. Between periods of work, we would discuss India's problems and his plans to return to India to help solve them. One such problem, that he analysed in his doctoral dissertation, was the effects of limiting the scale of enterprises in Indian manufacturing industries on economic efficiency. In his thesis and published article, "Elasticities of Substitution and Returns to Scale in Indian Manufacturing Industries," International Economic Review, Vol. II, October, 1970, he used data relating to Indian manufacturing industries to analyse this important policy problem, an example of the important policy problems that he analysed later on his return to India after receiving his doctoral degree.

It was a pleasure being associated with Sankar when he was working on his significant doctoral dissertation. We both appreciated the importance of having good data to analyse problems and were shocked at the quality of some publicly available data that many used in economic research. These concerns led us to review the econometric and statistical literature on "errors in the variables" models, the topic of our joint paper, "On Errors in the Variables" that is included in this volume. Sankar was quick to understand the intricacies of this difficult class of models and the strengths and weaknesses of various econometric and statistical methods for analysing it. In addition to theoretical analyses, the paper includes an analysis of a set of international data that had been utilised to test the Friedman proportionality hypothesis, namely that the ratio of permanent consumption to permanent income is independent of the level of permanent income, or equivalently that the savings ratio is independent of permanent income. An earlier analysis of these data by a leading econometrician led to the conclusion that the proportionality hypothesis could not be rejected. Since I had an earlier disagreement with Friedman about whether those with extremely low permanent incomes save the same percentage of permanent income as those with high or very high levels of permanent income, it was of great interest to me to reanalyse this set of data that had been used to test the proportionality hypothesis. Sankar and I discovered that not only are errors of measurement important but, equally important, the earlier investigator had used an inappropriate functional form for his relation. On nesting the proportionality hypothesis in a more suitable function and taking account of measurement errors, we were able to reject the constant proportionality hypothesis with these data. That is, very low-income countries in our sample saved about 5 per cent of income while high-income countries saved about 10 per cent of income. Needless to say, Sankar and I were very pleased to see that our alternative model for the observations, an errors in the variables model, produced reasonable results.

In closing, it has been a pleasure to know and work with Sankar and I congratulate him for his many outstanding accomplishments. My wife and I send him and his family our warmest regards and best wishes for the future.

Professor Ulaganathan Sankar

Sankar — A Profile

RAJA J. CHELLIAH

Dr. U. Sankar is a man of many talents. His winsome personality and quiet dignity embellish his deep scholarship and many notable academic achievements. As a person, a scholar, a research colleague and a teacher he has endeared himself to the academic community of three generations.

After a very creditable educational career, terminating in a Degree of Doctor of Philosophy in Econometrics awarded by the University of Wisconsin at Madison USA, Dr. Sankar settled down to teach at the University of Wisconsin at Milwaukee in 1967. He rapidly rose from the level of Assistant Professor to become Professor in 1976. By all standards he was doing well in the academic world of USA. However, in response to an invitation from the University of Madras, Prof. Sankar returned to India and joined the faculty of the University of Madras as Professor of Econometrics in 1977. In 1990 he became the Head of the Department of Econometrics which position he occupied with distinction till 1995.

Making the University of Madras his main location of work for the next twenty years or so, Prof. Sankar rendered yeoman service to students and to the profession of economics through his teaching, guidance of research, undertaking of many important research projects, publishing research papers and rendering policy advice to governments and educational institutions.

Prof. Sankar could be said to be mainly responsible for introducing the quantitative approach and element in the study of economics in the University of Madras.

Prof. Sankar's research interests have covered a wide field. His main contributions have been in public enterprises pricing, input-output analysis, impact of globalisation on Indian agriculture, environmental economics and cost-benefit analysis of the Indian space programme.

The third major phase of Prof. Sankar's career-started when he joined the efforts to found Madras School of Economics and became its first Director in 1995. Building up the Madras School of Economics (MSE) as a first-rate teaching and research institution, from scratch, is in itself an outstanding achievement and a great contribution to the pursuit of post-graduate studies in economics in the country. Along with his work related to the building up of MSE, Prof. Sankar has been pursuing his research activities and has also been overseeing the implementation of a large capacity-building project in environmental economics funded by the World Bank.

In this period starting from 1995, Prof. Sankar has concentrated on two major areas of research : environmental economics and techno-economic analysis of the Indian Space programme. In both these new areas of research for economists in India, Prof. Sankar is making a pioneering contribution. In the area of environmental economics he has conducted policy oriented studies on pollution abatement, environmental damage by tanneries, use of market-based instruments, etc. He is now engaged in a substantial study on trade and environment (with reference to leather) sponsored by the Ministry of Environment and Forests. In relation to Space, Prof. Sankar has been working with Indian Space Research Organisation carrying out a project on Techno-Economic Analysis of the Indian Space Programme. He has now been asked to develop a long-term relationship between MSE and ISRO. He would be in charge of that extended programme.

In recognition of his long and meritorious contribution to economics the Indian Council of Social Science Research has awarded Prof. Sankar the National Fellowship in Economics for 2003 and 2004. As one of the leading economists of the country, Prof. Sankar has been called upon to advise the government through membership in important commissions and committees. He was a member of the State Planning Commission, Tamil Nadu between 2001 and 2004. He was the Chairman, State Statistical Committee, Tamil Nadu. He is the Secretary of the Steering Committee of the Centre of Excellence in Environmental Economics at MSE sponsored by the Ministry of Environment and Forests. He was also a member of the Kelkar

Committee to Assess the Socio Economic Benefits Arising from CSIR's R&D Activities.

As teacher, scholar, researcher, institution builder and policy adviser, in each capacity, Prof. Sankar has distinguished himself by making invaluable contributions. Pursuit of excellence and service to society can be said to have been the guiding motives in all his work. Like a true Indian seer, he has sought little but given much. His colleagues, collaborators and students respect and admire him - and also learn from him the principles of conduct of an intellectual leader.

May Prof. Sankar be given a long life to continue his service to the profession and to society.

Prof. U. Sankar – A Tribute

PAUL P. APPASAMY

Prof. U. Sankar has been a friend, philosopher, and guide to me for more than a decade. I came to know Prof. Sankar when I was a faculty member and later Director, Madras Institute of Development Studies. He was associated with MIDS as a member of the Academic and Governing Councils and used to visit the Institute frequently for seminars, workshops, and various academic activities. My association with him became closer when I succeeded him as Director, Madras School of Economics in January 2000 and he continued as Honorary Professor and National Programme Coordinator of the World Bank Capacity Building Programme in Environmental Economics. There have been numerous occasions when I have sought his advice on both administrative and academic matters relating to the School. Although his preference has been for academic work, his keen grasp of administrative issues and procedures always made his guidance invaluable. He would rarely volunteer his views on administration, and generally provide his opinion only when asked.

Prof. Sankar's clarity of thought and expression make him a very good teacher and researcher. He has the ability to intervene effectively in seminars or lectures even on arcane topics in economics. He continues to read widely and has a phenomenal memory for journal articles and books in economics. A large number of students at Madras University benefited from his years of teaching and guidance there. Despite his teaching requirements, Prof. Sankar found time to carry out research projects, guide scholars for the Ph.D. degree, and carry out various administrative duties, both at the University and at Madras School of Economics.

Prof. Sankar is one of the most versatile economists in the country, whose abilities have been recognized by policy-makers both at the Centre and at the State level. Given his solid grounding in economic theory, he has been able to apply the tools of economics to diverse aspects of public policy such as agriculture, energy, telecommunications, environment, and most recently space. His forte is his ability to transcend disciplines, and learn whatever is needed for economic decision-making. His keen intellect as well as his devotion to work have made him a multi-faceted economist, who is equally at home with academics and administrators.

In his academic and administrative work, Prof. Sankar is known for his professional integrity. His insistence on meeting procedural requirements and deadlines ensured that the World Bank programme proceeded smoothly and remained on course. The conduct of the programme was commended by the World Bank and by the Ministry of Environment and Forests, and resulted in MSE being designated as a Centre of Excellence in Environmental Economics. His contributions to the economics profession have been recognised by professional societies like the Indian Economic Society and the Indian Econometric Society. The fact that Prof. Sankar served as a member of the Tamil Nadu State Planning Commission and is an adviser to the Tamil Nadu State Electricity Regulatory Commission is indicative of the recognition that he has received in the public sphere.

Despite all his professional accomplishments, Prof. Sankar is known for his simplicity and his dislike of ostentation. His early years with Jayaprakash Narayan and other Gandhians have had a lasting impact on his life-style and values. His constant willingness to be of assistance to others is a hallmark of his life of service to the profession and to society. I hope and pray that he will continue to enjoy good health and find fulfillment in the years to come.

Introduction

G. MYTHILI and R. HEMA

When we started work on this festschrift volume for U. Sankar, we realised that a set of papers written on a particular theme would really not capture the diversity of topics he has deeply delved into and the variety of tools he has been able to master and apply in his illustrious career. Hence, the heterogeneity of contributions to this volume, made by some of his long-term professional associates – his teacher, his graduate days colleagues, his academic associates in India and his students, is deliberate in order to reflect the breadth and depth of Sankar's interests and contributions.

An interesting and very unusual feature that may be noticed in this volume is that it contains a paper that has been authored by Sankar himself ! We want to give you the story behind this. When we approached his teacher Zellner for a possible contribution to this volume he sent us a copy of this paper. He said he and Sankar jointly wrote this in the sixties but they never got it published. However, at a Bayesian conference that Zellner attended in recent years the importance of the kind of issues they had raised in their unpublished paper was being recognised. Hence, appreciating the relevance of this contribution even today and as a tribute to Sankar's intellect he sent it for inclusion in this volume.

Although the papers in this volume deal with different themes they all share a strong commonality. Each contribution is either an effort at refining and expanding the existing tool kit available to understand economic phenomenon, be it through better conceptualisation of issues or better measurement methods, or an effort at suggesting refinements in existing delivery mechanisms and in the institutions in which they are embedded, or both. We have however, broadly grouped the twelve papers in this volume into three categories: *Tools, Issues and Institutions,* depending on the relative emphasis given to these aspects. The papers by Zellner and Sankar, by Chetty and by Revankar and Salih fall under the first category – *Tools*.

Much, if not all, economic data contain measurement errors. People working with economic data are all too familiar with the fact that measurements on the same variable derived from alternative sources sometimes reveal large discrepancies. Proceeding blithely with analyses either by ignoring or by assuming away the implications of such errors would obviously lead to erroneous inferences. Zellner and Sankar were seized of this issue when they were working with some publicly available data and were shocked to notice such measurement errors. This stimulated them to reconsider available methodology for analysing economic data containing measurement errors, particularly the classical "errors in the variables" model (EVM). Recognising the limitations of the classical EVMs, the most significant being the need for strong prior information, the authors present a Bayesian approach that would enable an investigator to start with a looser prior information structure and then to learn how sample information modifies the prior information.

The classical EVMs are quite versatile, as Zellner and Sankar point out, since they could be employed not only to compare pairs of economic measurements that purport to measure the same variable but could also be used in analyses that might want to understand the relationship between the estimated values of two different variables. In the context of measurement errors, these models obtain the expected value based on the sample observations from each source and test for 'consistency' of these expected values by testing for a relationship between them. A well known analysis of the second type is in the context of Friedman's consumption function hypothesis. Permanent income and permanent consumption may be estimated based on sample observations of actual income and actual consumption and then using the linear functional form for the logarithm of these values it would be possible to test Friedman's hypothesis of unit elasticity.

The problem with estimating the EVMs, however, is that the number of parameters is incidental on the number of sample observations and hence the parameters are not identified. Moreover,

Zellner and Sankar argue that even if prior information is available to identify the model's parameters, available estimation procedures would, at best, produce estimators that are weakly consistent and the maximum likelihood method can even produce inconsistent estimators. In this paper they provide a Bayesian alternative and suggest a suitable 'non-informative' set of prior *pdfs*, which they believe are rich enough to represent many practical situations.

The robustness of the approach suggested by Zellner and Sankar is effectively brought out when they demonstrate its application to data analysis. Both by using Monte Carlo methods and by applying their model to test the Friedman consumption function hypothesis, the authors demonstrate the superiority of their Bayesian approach.

Moving on from errors in the variables, Chetty addresses the issue of errors in estimation and their implications for the 'costliness' of decision-making, when the outcomes of actions are random variables with unknown parameters. Typically, to inform decision-making in a situation when the relationship between actions and outcome is not deterministic, a two-step procedure has been followed. First, the parameters of a probability distribution of the outcomes are estimated, using some criterion like minimising the squared errors or maximising the likelihood. Then, taking these parameters as given, the optimal action is chosen so that the expected gain is maximised or expected loss is minimised. Chetty points out that such an approach, which separates the problem into one of estimation and then prediction, introduces two sources of errors because the choice of the estimation rules and the prediction rules are based on two different loss functions. Hence, a method that would jointly take care of estimation and prediction, based on a common loss function would be preferable. While Bayesian procedures have been developed to address this joint estimation and prediction problem, Chetty argues that these have to make assumptions about the distributional form and this would be a constraint in some cases. In this paper, Chetty sets out to develop a non-parametric method that is a frequentist's analogue to the Bayesian approach for problems of simultaneous estimation and prediction.

Chetty argues that there is really no "true" estimate because the criteria on the basis of which the estimate is chosen is not independent of the purpose for which it is ultimately used. He indicates that the tradition of using a symmetric, quadratic loss function (the least squares of errors) had its origin in astronomy and geodesy problems and was introduced by Legendre in 1805, which was later developed by Gauss and Laplace into a formal statistical theory of errors. The method was basically developed to deal with experimental errors in the physical sciences where positive and negative errors are equally bad and large errors are particularly bad. It was also subsequently found to have some desirable properties, particularly that of being an unbiased estimator. In many social and biological problems, however, unbiasedness is not necessarily a virtue and can in fact lead to grave consequences since the cost of negative errors and the cost of positive errors could be asymmetric. Management of diabetes is one such problem, as elaborated by the author.

The physician's problem in managing the health of a diabetic patient is to make the optimal choice of the insulin dosage, so that the patient's blood sugar level is maintained close to the recommended optimum. The blood sugar level is not a deterministic function of the insulin dosage alone but a stochastic function of various other factors like age, weight, stress level, exercise and food habits and so on. Moreover, costs of a blood sugar level that is too low are different from the costs of a level that is too high. In a problem of this kind the estimator should be one that minimises the expected loss based on the probabilities and costs of the negative and positive errors.

If the probability distribution of the blood sugar levels is known then the optimal value that minimises the expected loss function can be determined. However, for the case where the probability distribution is not known, Chetty develops a non-parametric method, which he labels "c-min", that would minimise the expected loss of prediction using the historical sample data to simultaneously estimate the probability distribution and the prediction rule. This approach does not require any prior on the distribution of the error terms too. However, if there is information on the error distribution, then this could be incorporated and the "parametric c-min" estimator developed.

Using theoretical arguments, small sample Monte-Carlo experiments and results of empirical studies carried out on data relating to diabetic patients in Northern Illinois, the author demonstrates that the "c-min" estimator weakly outperforms the least squares estimator, *on an average*, in small samples; has significantly lower error costs compared to ordinary least squares method; percentage of more costly negative errors are significantly lower and the "c-min" estimator asymptotically attains the lower bound for expected loss function.

Revankar and Salih concur with the view expressed by Bergstrom, more than half a decade ago, that price and quantity indexes should be assigned a more activist role than being viewed as nothing more than just descriptive measures of general movements in prices and quantities over time. Bergstrom indicated that these indexes could be effectively used to estimate group price elasticity. Bergstrom essentially formulated a group demand function and treating the price and quantity vectors as endogenous to this structural equation he searches for an optimal price-quantity vector combination that would provide the best fit to the structural equation by minimising the residual variances.

Extending this basic framework, Revankar and Salih consider 'm' interrelated markets each with its own pair of demand and supply equations and in equilibrium. Then they seek to deduce the price-quantity indexes concurrently through linear aggregation of all the demand equations as well as all the supply equations. The advantage of such an approach is that it is based on a structural formulation that captures some underlying economic theory and hence would not end up with 'measurement without theory' as is often the criticism. It would also permit estimation of the group elasticities with respect to the predetermined vector used in the model, where elements of this vector are likely to be policy variables. The indexes that are derived are also independent of the units of measurement.

The unique feature of the model developed here is that it imposes a Consistent Aggregation Condition (CAC) in the linear grouping of the 'm' demand equations and 'm' supply equations. This imposes certain restrictions on the weights that could be attached to the prices and quantities of the individual component markets. The optimal choice of these weights is made using the criterion of maximum correlation between the indexes. The authors develop appropriate estimators for the optimal weights, and discuss their asymptotic properties. They also provide some theoretical insights based on their formulation.

Revankar and Salih indicate that the approach adopted here differs from Waugh's indexes in that while Waugh's approach also follows the standard canonical correlation technique, his formulation ignores the CAC. On the other hand, Theil's indexes are developed by minimising the squares of the discrepancies between the index-constructed and actual values of each price-commodity bundle. The authors also demonstrate an application of their model by using it to analyse the red meat market in the US between 1965 and 1990 and compare their results from this study with Waugh's and Theil's indexes computed for the same data.

The next five papers are grouped under the category – *Issues*. Two of them are review papers. Krishna reviews the literature on the patterns and determinants of economic growth particularly focusing on those dealing with comparisons across space and time, while Vaidyanathan provides a critical appraisal of the various quantitative techniques applied to understand growth in agriculture. Mythili estimates the fall in marginal productivity of land due to an exploitative cropping culture and Kadekodi suggests the need and a methodology for valuing community labour expended on common property resources. Subramanian is concerned about the distributional benefits that accrue from economic growth and development. He criticises the existing conceptual framework and the delivery mechanism based on it to be biased in favour of the 'richer groups' among those in the impoverished category. He therefore suggests an alternative approach to conceptualising the issue so that income transfers to the poor are directly related to their degree of poverty.

Since the time of Adam Smith's classic Inquiry into the Nature and Cause of Wealth of Nations in 1776, economists have paid considerable attention to the issue of understanding economic growth as is evidenced by the large body of literature that exists on this topic. K.L. Krishna's critical look at this body of literature echo's the sentiment expressed by Soludo and Kim that "we know as much as we don't in terms of what determines the differences in cross-national growth performances".

K.L. Krishna first takes a look at the literature that uses the aggregate growth accounting framework, which emphasises the role of total factor productivity (TFP) following Abramovitz's and Solow's contributions in the mid-fifties. He focuses on the recent literature in this area that is an outcome of the Global Research Project on "Explaining Growth", which attempts a comprehensive assessment of growth experiences of seventy developing and transition economies belonging to six geographical regions of the world. The stylised facts that emerge from this body of literature indicate that TFP, rather than factor accumulation account for most of the differences in the levels and growth rates of income across different countries. These facts have however, to be qualified by the fact that the data on capital input is not very satisfactory and that the empirical work does not decisively distinguish among the different theoretical conceptions of TFP growth.

Reviewing the body of literature that have their theoretical foundations in the neoclassical model of Solow-Swan-Ramsey, which hypothesises that economies converge to the steady state where growth depends only on TFP growth, K.L. Krishna agrees with Soludo and Kim that many of these empirical studies lack clear guidance from economic theory, have specification uncertainty, problems with the estimation techniques and lack of robustness of the parameter estimates. One of the reasons for these could be that growth variability and volatility are central issues to most developing countries and these have somewhat been ignored so far, as pointed out by Pritchett. The existence of variability and volatility would particularly create problems when yearly panel data is used in conjunction with country-specific fixed effects to investigate long run growth correlates. Such panel data analysis would result in dynamic misspecification, endogeneity, greater measurement error and lower statistical power. Moreover, the results of this approach can also not be compared with those based on time-averaged cross section regressions, because the nature of difference between these cannot be predicted *a priori*. K.L. Krishna opines that there is considerable scope for exploring the new approaches as suggested by Pritchett in that episodes of growth acceleration or the onset of deceleration along with the accompanying economic, political, institutional and policy conditions should be examined. Cross sectional analysis of changes in growth rates over time may be looked at.

K.L. Krishna then takes a detailed look at the literature on patterns of economic growth in Indian states from 1960 to 2000.

With the quality and comparability of data for Indian states leaving a lot to be desired there is much work to be done in building continuous and comparable data series on growth correlates, states K.L. Krishna. He also indicates the need for more detailed analysis of this kind at the level of various sub-sectors – agriculture, industry, services, and social capital – to understand the underlying dynamics.

Going from the macro level to the sectoral level, Vaidyanathan takes a critical look at the various techniques applied for quantitative analysis of the agriculture growth phenomenon, ranging from simple regressions to optimisation models of complex systems, and discusses their merits and limitations. He indicates the need for a rethink on our approach to understanding this sector and provides an alternative paradigm.

Vaidyanathan discusses the complexities that are inherently involved in designing appropriate tools for analysing the agricultural sector given the nature of inputs and processes specific to this sector. This is compounded in no small measure by the lack of reliable data. Though there exists a nationwide system to compile such data, they are of low quality and insufficient coverage, lack consistency and hence restrict comparability over time and across space.

Vaidyanathan points out that the trend analysis implicitly assumes that the systematic changes in production over time are a result of the systematic changes in inputs and technology. Weather is a crucial input here and while it is not systematically changing in a particular direction, it is not absolutely random either so that its effects would be subsumed in the 'error' term. It tends to have a cyclical pattern and this also has a complex synergy with various other inputs like soil moisture, supply from irrigation system, cropping pattern and so on. Attempts have been made to correct for this weather factor and the weather corrected trends significantly differ from uncorrected trends. However, constructing a meaningful, composite weather index is fraught with difficulties.

Vaidyanathan analyses the models that seek to understand the underlying factors that contribute to growth in terms of two categories, one that uses multivariate regressions that attempt to decompose the impact of separate factors and the other that uses the production function approach. While the poor quality of data is a major constraining factor for both these types of analyses, the production function approach has deeper conceptual and estimation problems, he argues. Land, as an input in agriculture, is different from other types of capital. Area is not a satisfactory measure of this input because quality is highly variable. Part of these qualitative differences may be due to irrigation or other land development inputs, which could be captured under 'capital'. However, some innate differences in terms of depth, texture, composition and so on affect productivity and these are difficult to capture by a single index. The other issue regarding the capital stock is that part of it is yield augmenting (e.g., irrigation) while part of it is a substitute for human or animal input. In terms of the functional form, the linear form implies that the yield increment per each incremental unit of input is constant and is independent of its level or the level of other inputs. This does not reflect reality. The Cobb-Douglas form on the other hand assumes that all inputs are substitutable over the entire range of application, when, in fact, we know that is not the case. The complex synergy among the various inputs is not really captured in these models, which then exhibit strong multicollinearity. Faced with the situation, analysts tend to drop variables that are not significant. Under these circumstances it becomes difficult to interpret the results and even more difficult to accept the interpretation that the residuals capture the total factor productivity.

In the light of the above appraisal, the author builds a case for a rethink on the nature of the production process in agriculture. Vaidyanathan argues that it would help to view it as a biochemical process rather than as a primary factors centered process as has been conventionally done till now. While these two are certainly interrelated, this interrelationship could be studied as a separate exercise. Viewing yield as a function of soil moisture regime and the local composition of nutrients would provide a more meaningful concept of production function. He then discusses a basic methodology and the intuition on which it is built, for carrying out the analysis using this approach. He points out that data reliability would still be an important issue, though this approach would economise on the data required. Vaidyanathan recognises that a lot of wrinkles have to be ironed out. Nonetheless, the methodology would be founded on a more realistic representation of the agricultural processes, in his opinion.

The model used by Mythili, to assess the fall in the marginal productivity of land, goes some way in absolving the production function approach in studies on Indian agricultural analysis of Vaidyanathan's criticism, that the synergy between weather and other inputs is often not captured in the models. The objective of the paper is to assess the magnitude of environmental quality that has been sacrificed in the quest for rapid increase in agricultural production. The environmental price paid is reflected in the loss of natural vegetation, loss of bio-diversity, surface and ground water depletion, soil erosion and land degradation. Mythili's paper attempts to measure the fall in soil productivity that is brought about by exploitative cropping cultures and cautions about the unsustainable nature of such an approach. The methodology adopted here explicitly recognises that, in order to arrive at fairly reliable estimates of the marginal productivity of agricultural inputs, it is important to carefully specify the random factor in looking at the input-output relation. Introducing the random terms in an *ad hoc* manner, as is often done, will not vest the interpretation of parameters with the desired level of confidence. This study therefore not only assumes that the random factors depend on the 'state of nature' but also allow for their being non-neutral with respect to different inputs and hence with respect to their marginal productivities. In other words, it allows for the weather induced random factor to affect different inputs differently.

Mythili rejects the conventional method of introducing the random term in a multiplicative form in the input-output relation by arguing that this assumes the random term to be neutral with respect to marginal productivities and with respect to marginal rates of substitution. Moreover, if variance in output is taken to capture the level of risk then this specification implies that risk always rises with increase in input levels. As regards the Cobb-Douglas form, it cannot accommodate zero inputs. Attempts to modify the model to accommodate zero inputs, as was done by Rudra, impose increasing returns to scale. The elasticity coefficients in the Cobb-Douglas specification are also neutral with respect to 'state of nature'.

Mythili uses the quadratic functional form that was developed earlier by Sankar and Mythili. This specification helps to separate the mean effect from the variance effect, so that a distinction can be made between protective inputs and non-protective inputs. A protective input would be one whose increase results in reduction of output variance. Mythili's model explicitly allows for input responses to be related to the random effect.

The above model is employed to estimate the change in the marginal productivity of land in the North and South Arcot districts in the state of Tamil Nadu that has been largely employed in the cultivation of groundnut. Groundnut cultivation is a high-risk proposition with seed costs alone accounting for 40 per cent of the total cost, so that when weather factors are adverse, the loss would be high. On the other hand, it is a cash crop that fetches a good price in the market. Thus, there is a trade off between mean return and risk. The analysis is carried out on farm level sample data, for three consecutive years each, during the eighties and the nineties.

It emerges from Mythili's study that the marginal productivity of the land allocated for groundnut production in these two regions, measured in constant value of output, has definitely declined. Moreover, the selected region had earlier enjoyed productivity levels that made it the most suitable and most preferred for this crop and now the productivity here is lower than for the state as a whole. The decadal decline in land productivity worked out to about 35 per cent. These results clearly indicate the need for moving towards a more bio-friendly approach to cultivation.

Talking about sustainable development, Kadekodi and Agarwal address this issue in the context of the inter linkages between private property resources and common property resources. Traditionally, voluntary labour that is expended on developing common property resources has been treated in economic literature either as part of leisure or as social work or even as a prestige good. Hence, the opportunity cost of such labour is implicitly assumed to be zero. Kadekodi and Agarwal argue that the asymmetry in the valuation of labour that is expended on private property resources (PPR) *vis-à-vis* the community labour that is spent on developing common property resources (CPR) would result in sub-optimal levels of development of the CPR. Given a strong complementary relationship between the growth in CPR and PPR, an imbalanced relative growth in PPR at the cost of neglecting the CPR would not be sustainable in the long run.

Kadekodi and Agarwal point out that traditional economic thinking has largely been built on the notion of substitutability and issues of complementarities have been dealt with only in a marginal fashion. However, ecologists, environmentalists, social scientists and policy makers are increasingly recognising the significance of the contributions of CPR to the productivity of PPR. In this paper, the authors develop a model to capture the structural characteristics of labour inputs into PPR and CPR with the ultimate objective of arriving at a method to value labour devoted to managing common property resources.

The model is constructed as an inter-temporal optimisation problem, where the rate of consumption is maximised subject to the conditions that the growth rates in PPR and CPR are optimal. The share of labour that is allocated between managing PPR and managing CPR and the rate of savings are the two choice instruments in this optimisation problem. The conditions for optimisation would require that the shadow prices of labour employed in the production of normal goods and in the management of CPR be the same. This would enable us to impute an appropriate value for the voluntary labor spent on CPR.

Kadekodi and Agarwal point out that an economy could already be in a steady state, or it could reach the steady state from either of two possible initial conditions. The initial condition could have been one where the stock of PPR is quite high or it could have been one where the stock of PPR is relatively very low. The authors demonstrate that in each of the three situations, under an optimal growth path scenario, the CPR will continue to grow implying a positive shadow price for voluntary labour. This reiterates the complementary nature of CPR and emphasises the need for recognising and rewarding community labour spent on it so that better CPR management could be promoted.

Conceptualising poverty and developing an appropriate index to measure it has always been a complex exercise. The predominant approach has been to identify the dividing line that separates the poor from the non-poor in society and then to aggregate information on all those falling under the poor category so as to inform policy making. Much of the discussion in the poverty literature has focussed on identifying the dividing line and a popular approach to this exercise is founded on the 'basic needs' principle, which is also the method currently adopted by Indian policy makers.

A considerable amount of debate has been generated regarding the merits of this '*absolutist*' approach to poverty. It has been argued that everyone need not have the same basic needs, everyone does not have the same tastes and everyone does not face the same kind of opportunities and constraints. Therefore, treating a single income level as the dividing line would in fact cause a lot of injustice, it has been argued, and the need for a '*relativist*' approach has been emphasised.

Subramanian and Bandhyopadhyay point out that the lucid exposition provided by Sen on this concept would help evaporate much of the confusion surrounding the '*absolutist-relativist*' debate. Sen conceptualises poverty as an absolute notion when it comes to capabilities and a relative notion in terms of the resources needed to achieve the specified level of minimum capabilities. As an example, Subramanian and Bandhyopadhyay elaborate that the need to avoid undernourishment is an absolute need but the calorific resources needed by different individuals to meet this need would be different, based on their age, gender, work status, body mass index and so on.

In this paper, Subramanian and Bandhyopadhyay suggest a method to develop suitable indices that would help translate the 'relative view' of 'absolute poverty' into working tools to enable measurement and aid policy interventions. They use the family of poverty indices developed by Foster, Greer and Thorbeck (FGT) as a starting point for their model, because these satisfy a number of desirable axioms that poverty measures are expected to satisfy, like monotonicity, decomposability, transfer-sensitivity and so on. The approach in this paper is based on the recognition that all individuals do not have the same ability to transform incomes into capabilities and therefore, as a logical extension, instead of working with a single poverty line, as is done in the FGT indices, they work with a set of individual specific poverty lines. The authors demonstrate that the extension of the FGT indices to the individual-specific minimum requirement scenario suggested by them not only satisfies all the desirable axioms that FGT indices satisfy but also additional axioms like the equity-sensitivity axiom. In fact, the FGT indices would be a special case of the more generalised set of indices suggested here.

Based on the poverty indices developed here, Subramanian and Bandhyopadhyay also suggest an optimal set of rules for income transfer, given constraints in the total budget available for transfer. The authors demonstrate that unlike the conventional approaches, which would intrinsically be biased in terms of favouring a random subset of the poor at best and the 'richer' subset of the poor at worst, the optimal rules suggested here could effectively be translated into relatively more help to the poorest among the poor. Subramanian and Bandhyopadhyay do recognise that identifying individual-specific minimum requirements would not be feasible in practice, but suggest that it would be possible and worthwhile to identify relatively homogeneous subgroups and then work out the group-specific minimum requirements.

Of the four papers that focus on the efficacy of institutional arrangements and their policies in translating economic goals into realities, three of them are concerned with the implications of the structural reforms that started in India during the early nineties. Kalirajan's quest is to find out how 'open' is India's liberalised trade policies, while Sreejata seeks to assess the impact of the changes in the financial sector's regulatory environment on the primary capital market by analysing investors' behaviour and firms' performance in both the old and new regimes. Hema takes a critical look at the ongoing reforms in the power sector and given the issues and constraints faced in the Indian context, suggests a desirable institutional reform. The last paper by Anuradha demonstrates how the institute of collective action could be efficiently utilised to tackle pollution control when the units involved are small and financially constrained. She stresses the need for appropriate rules of the game to ensure that the institution is sustainable and develops such mechanisms.

Having set itself the goal of self-sufficiency and with a view to protect its fledgling industries, independent India had virtually closed its economy from international trade, by raising tariffs and non-tariff barriers, for nearly half a century. In 1991, as part of the structural reforms that were introduced in fiscal, monetary, industry and exchange rate policies to stimulate the economy and pull it out of a debt crisis, trade policies also underwent drastic changes. India was beginning to reorient itself and integrate with the global economy.

Kalirajan traces the trade policy changes that have been made since 1991 and seeks to understand how open India's trade has been after a decade of reforms.

Kalirajan discusses the confluence of international and national developments that motivated India to initiate the long overdue economic reforms. Policies of liberalisation adopted by China, Vietnam and other communist countries and the disintegration of the Soviet Union followed by the collapse of India's bilateral trade arrangements with it, dramatised the need for liberalisation in India. The culmination of India's long-term fiscal indiscipline, brought on by inefficient interventionist domestic policies, into a debt crisis in the early nineties precipitated the urgent need for reforms. While the government interventions have been credited with India's achievement of self-sufficiency in cereal grains and with minimising the impact of uneven income distribution on the incidence of poverty, they were not carried out in a sustainable manner and hence led to the debt crisis.

Import substitution had been the cornerstone of India's trade policy and for the first time, in 1992, the policy was given an export bias. Import was also liberalised. Since then, several measures have been introduced to reduce or eliminate regulatory and discretionary controls. Kalirajan however points out that this march towards free trade has been a relatively slow one, facing some stumbling blocks on the way and characterised by a few steps backwards at times. While India has had to abide by the WTO agreements in terms of removing quantity restrictions and licenses, it has substituted these with tariff barriers. WTO allows tariffs up to a certain ceiling and India has been hovering close to the ceiling rates in many cases and very often, which does not augur well. It has vested the right to import certain agricultural products exclusively with the State Trading Corporations. Although these corporations are expected to work on commercial principles it is still a form of non-tariff barrier.

It is understandable that the government policy on international trade is concerned about ensuring adequate availability of food items at reasonable prices to a large section of the population. Also, being a democratic nation that has to obtain a certain amount of consensus across different interest groups before policy changes can be implemented, the slow pace of reforms is to some extent inevitable, argues Kalirajan. At the same time, when tariff or non-tariff barriers are erected as a result of pressure from producer lobbies it would only reduce social welfare. Trade barriers should not be an instrument to protect inefficiencies in agriculture, industry, public sector and small-scale sector. These domestic failures should be corrected through appropriate domestic policies. Thus, while India has set itself on the right path and made some progress, it still has a long march ahead in terms of its trade policies.

The reforms that were initiated in the Indian financial sector, during the early nineties, as part of the overall structural reforms in the economy, transformed the regulatory regime from a tightly controlling one to a more market-oriented approach. Sreejata Banerjee sets out to analyse the implications of the change in the regulatory philosophy and mechanisms for the primary capital market. The focus of the study is to understand the major factors that influence demand for public issues, to evaluate the subsequent performance of firms and to ascertain the degree of asymmetric information in the primary market, under both the regulatory regimes.

The Controller of Capital Issues (CCI), which was the regulating authority under the former regime, did not permit firms to freely price their public issues. The level of premium, if any that could be charged, would have to be approved by the CCI. Issues being offered at a premium were more an exception than the norm. This being the case, the issues were considerably under-priced and over subscribed. In 1996, the Securities Exchange Board of India (SEBI) revised the guidelines and allowed firms that had a good record of financial performance to freely price their public issues.

Sreejata Banerjee carries out the analysis for two time frames – between 1986 and 1991 to capture the regulatory effect under the CCI regime and between 1992 and 1998 to evaluate the effect of the SEBI regime. Data pertaining to a sample of firms that are listed in the Madras Stock Exchange are used for the analysis. For the post-reforms phase a similar analysis is also carried out for a sample drawn from the Bombay Stock Exchange so as to capture the national perception. Issue specific, firm specific, securities related and macroeconomic data are the four major types of data used in the empirical analysis.

Using multivariate regression models Sreejata Banerjee identifies the major factors that influenced investor decision-making in both the regimes. The interesting results that emerge from the analysis indicate that while the issue price was perceived to reflect the quality of the issue under the earlier tightly controlled regime, it did not have any significant impact on the investors' decision-making in the latter regime. The promoters' stake in the new issue was the most significant factor to influence investors' decision-making in both the regimes. The size of the firm, captured by its net worth had a significant effect in both the regimes though in the earlier one it had a negative but low impact on the subscription ratio. Sreejata Banerjee's analysis for the Bombay Stock Exchange sample under the liberalised regime indicates that the issue price is not a significant factor in this case also. The important factors are promoters' stake, size of the firm and the overall market sentiment.

In terms of the post-issue performance of the firms and whether these measure up to projections and promises made in their offer documents, Sreejata Banerjee finds that about 60 per cent of the firms could not achieve their projected levels of net profit and 40 per cent out of these could not even reach 50 per cent of their target. On the other hand, about 30 per cent of the firms were able to achieve net profits that were beyond their own projections. Such under-performance in the post-issue phase is not uncommon and is observed even in well developed financial markets as some studies have shown. Some of the possible reasons for this could be that the firm's accounts are window-dressed prior to going public, the issue offers are timed to coincide with a period of unusually good performance, the agency costs rise after a firm makes the transition from private to public holding and so on. Nonetheless, when over 50 per cent of the companies are unable to attain their targets, it is bound to erode investor confidence, Sreejata Banerjee suggests.

The empirical exercise undertaken by the author to examine whether the investors' expectations were fulfilled by the firms' performance reveals that the market information has been highly asymmetric in the former regulatory framework and continues to remain asymmetric even in the liberalised regime. Sreejata Banerjee observes that while the primary capital market in India might have the enabling conditions of the existence of supply, demand and instruments, it will fail to achieve the optimal outcome if the sufficient conditions of investor confidence and information transparency do not exist.

Over a decade of efforts now to reform the rapidly deteriorating Indian power sector have not been able to achieve a significant turnaround in the performance of this sector. Inadequate availability of power continues to seriously constrain the growth potential of the economy and the quality of life it can afford. Hema takes a critical look at the ongoing reforms and, based on theoretical underpinnings and on required ground realities, tries to understand the reasons for their inefficacy. Lessons are drawn from the ongoing reforms in many other countries to identify the combination of factors and the type of reform mechanisms that contribute to the success or the failure of process. Then, given the ground realities in the Indian context and the priorities faced, she suggests a possible approach to institutional reforms. Hema argues that the suggested approach would enable a smoother transition, would involve lower transaction costs and is likely to be more sustainable. More importantly, it would involve a gradualist approach to institutional change unlike the ongoing approach that may complicate subsequent improvements and may be too costly to reverse.

The dominant approach to reforms has been based on unbundling the existing state-owned, vertically integrated, monopoly entities into smaller privately owned entities and allowing them to compete. This reflects a rethink on the natural monopoly argument for the electricity supply industry and the idea that natural monopoly features do not characterise all segments of the industry. Hence, it is now considered more efficient to introduce competition in those segments where feasible. However, Hema argues that introducing effective competitive forces is not possible right away when the sector is characterised by significant excess demand combined with huge financial losses. And transferring the ownership from public to private would not by itself lead to more efficiency unless there is real competition. Competitive forces would provide the needed incentives for efficiency. She emphasises that the incentive mechanisms provided by the institutional arrangement is the important factor rather than ownership *per se*.

Hema suggests that a private investor owned, vertically integrated, monopolistic entity that is regulated by an independent and efficient regulatory authority might be an optimal choice under the circumstances. This would be more or less akin to the investor owned regulated utilities that have characterised the electricity supply industry in the US for many years. Designing the appropriate incentive mechanisms and ensuring independent and efficient regulation would be the key issues here and the author provides suggestions for these. The basis on which regulatory prices could be determined and enforced is also elaborated. Hema recognises that subsidies to the really deserving users will have to continue for a few more years. However, she strongly urges that the regulatory authority must have the final authority on the *manner* in which such subsidies are given and should also be able to specify a ceiling for it, since the costs of the incentive distortions and negative externalities created by the subsidy schemes are much higher than the direct costs and overwhelm any distributional benefits.

In his Logic of Collective Action, Mancur Olson had stated that unless the individuals in a group are quite small or unless there is coercion or some other special device to make individuals act in their common interest, rational and self-interested individuals will not act to achieve their group interests. Recognising this, Anuradha suggests a set of 'special devices' that would sustain collective action in the context of Common Effluent Treatment Plants (CETP) for the leather industry in India.

The leather industry in India has been a major source of employment generation and export earnings. In the early seventies, the growing real wages combined with stringent environmental regulations in the developed countries ended up exporting these industries to developing countries. This turned out to be a mixed blessing for India. While the industry witnessed rapid expansion, which meant greater employment opportunities and higher foreign exchange earnings on the one hand, its negative impact on the local environment was exponentially rising. The shift in the tanning technology from the eco-friendly vegetable tanning method to chrome tanning, which releases a lot of toxic chemicals in the wastewater, had a severe negative impact on the environment.

Anuradha points out that in recent years, with environmental regulations being tightened in India and with the industry also facing stiffer competition from other developing countries, the financial health of many of these firms is precarious. Given that many of the leather-tanning units are in the small-scale sector and located in clusters, it would be cost-effective for these units to meet the mandatory requirement of cleaning up their wastewater by setting up Common Effluent Treatment Plants. Instituting and maintaining the CETP is essentially a collective action exercise.

Anuradha, however, argues that the existing institutional arrangement for the CETPs and the incentive structure created by it may not ensure the sustainability of the collective action because it could violate the individual rationality constraint. The main reason for this is the current mechanism for cost allocation, which is based on an equal sharing principle. Using the cooperative game-theoretic approach, she demonstrates that an individual will have an incentive to stay in the coalition as long as the share of the individual's cost in this arrangement is lower than his or her stand-alone cost. In order to ensure that the opportunities and constraints afforded by the institution of collective action are in tune with the individual's incentive structure, the cost burden that is imposed on each member should be equal to the Shapley Value, Anuradha states. Hence, given that the firms that join the CETP venture have different production capacities, use different techniques of production and raw material combinations, their pollution impact would also be different. Their cost burden in the venture should reflect these differences.

Anuradha substantiates her argument with a study of the CETP that has been established in the North Arcot district of Tamil Nadu. The appropriate cost shares for firms located in four different zones that participate in this venture have been worked out using the Shapley Value principle. Compared to the existing cost sharing arrangement, where each member of the coalition has an equal share, the Shapley values indicate that two of the zones are being subsidised while the other two zones are overpaying. This might encourage the firms that are currently over-paying to leave the coalition.

The author also points out that this sustainable cost-sharing mechanism should also be backed up by appropriate exit penalties. The existing arrangement has not provided for any penal actions for a member leaving the coalition. Unless a stiff exit cost is imposed the sustainability of the collective action could be fragile. Finally, effective monitoring and enforcement is a prerequisite.

1

On Errors in the Variables

ARNOLD ZELLNER and U. SANKAR

1. INTRODUCTION

Many, including Morgenstern (1963), Ferber (1966), Modigliani and Ando (1960), and others, have for long emphasised the importance of measurement errors in economic data. In our past and recent work ... cf. Galenson and Zellner (1957), Zellner (1958), Zellner and Sankar (1966), we have been struck by the large discrepancies between measurements on the same variable derived from alternative sources. In fact, it was our interest in comparing pairs of economic measurements purporting to measure the same quantity which stimulated us to reconsider certain aspects of the available methodology for analysing economic data containing measurement errors. In particular, since the classical "errors in the variables" model (EVM) seemed appropriate for some of our analyses, attention is directed herein at methods for making inferences about the parameters of this model.

As is evident from previous work on the EVM— see e.g. Lindley (1947), Reiersol (1950), Kiefer and Wolfowitz (1956), Madansky (1959), Jeffreys (1961), Kendall and Stuart (1961), Malinvaud (1964) — this model is far from simple. Among the most salient problems arising in the analysis of it are the following. First, in order to identify the parameters of the functional equation form of the model in the "classical" or "sampling theory" approach, strong prior information is required. That is, for example, one has to know the ratio of the error terms' variances or alternatively one or both of the variances. Unfortunately, we often do not have such precise prior information and thus cannot proceed with analyses. Second, even when we do have the prior information to identify the model's parameters, it is the case that most currently available procedures produce estimators with just the weak property of consistency. Third, the previous statement has to be qualified since the well known method of maximum likelihood can produce inconsistent estimators for parameters of this model, an aspect of the problem of incidental parameters brought to the attention of econometricians by Neyman and Scott (1948). Fourth, in the multi-parameter problem, it appears that certain conventional estimators are probably not admissible in the statistical sense in the light of the work of Stein (1956) and James and Stein (1961). Fifth, in the Bayesian approach to the analysis of the functional equation form of the model, it is necessary to be quite careful in the choice of "diffuse" or "non-informative" prior probability density functions. Sixth, in our work, we note, some interesting similarities between the sampling theory approach to the analysis of the structural form of the model and the Bayesian approach to the functional form of the model. Such similarities may indeed be general when sampling theory analyses of random parameter models are compared with Bayesian analyses of fixed parameter models.

In what follows the above points will be spelled out in detail. Further, we shall show that it is possible to analyse the model using weaker prior information about unknown variances in the Bayesian approach than in the usual maximum likelihood approach. This feature of the Bayesian approach is indeed appealing in situations in which information about error terms' variances is far from certain.

The plan of the paper is as follows. In, Section 2, we specify the model which we are analysing and indicate several specific situations in economics where it has been used or could be used. Then in Section 3, we provide a review of the maximum likelihood approach. In addition, we describe a simple method for generating consistent estimators which are identical to the corrected maximum likelihood estimates (corrected to make them consistent) and which does not involve a normality assumption. Section 4, is devoted to the development of Bayesian methods for analysing the model. In Section 5, certain of the methods presented in Sections 3 and 4 are applied in analyses of data. Last, in Section 6, we provide some concluding remarks.

2. SPECIFICATION AND INTERPRETATION OF THE MODEL

The model which we analyse initially is the one that Kendall and Stuart (1961) call the functional equation form of the "errors in the variables" model. That is, we have observations x_α and y_α,

$\alpha = 1, 2, ..., n$, which are assumed to be generated as follows:

$$y_\alpha = \eta_\alpha + u_\alpha \qquad ...(2.1)$$

$$x_\alpha = \xi_\alpha + v_\alpha \qquad ...(2.2)$$

$$\eta_\alpha = \beta_0 + \beta \xi_\alpha \qquad ...(2.3)$$

where u_α and v_α are random error terms, β_0 and β are parameters of the functional equation in (2.3), and $\eta_\alpha = Ey_\alpha$ and $\xi_\alpha = Ex_\alpha$, $\alpha = 1, 2, \ldots, n$, which implies, $Eu_\alpha = Ev_\alpha = 0$ for all α. We further assume that the error terms, u_α and v_α are normally and independently distributed with constant variances σ_u^2 and σ_v^2, respectively, for all α. Note that the model contains $2n + 4$ parameters and that each additional pair of observations brings in two additional parameters, namely, another η and another ξ.

This model can be employed to compare pairs of economic measurements purporting to measure the same quantity, say cross section demand deposits as in Ferber's (1966) study. If $\beta_0 = 0$ and $\beta = 1$, then from (2.3) $\eta_\alpha = \xi_\alpha$, that is $Ey_\alpha = Ex_\alpha$, which implies that the pairs of measurements are "consistent." Of course, this equality of means does not rule out the possibility, for example, that both sets of measurements contain an equal additive bias; however, this may be considered to be unlikely. Thus, being able to make inferences about β_0 and β will enable us to compare pairs of measurements on the same economic variable in situations in which means vary from observation to observation.

A second well known interpretation of the model within the context of Friedman's (1957) consumption function model follows. For the αth household in a cross section sample, regard y_α and x_α as the logarithms of measured consumption and measured income, respectively η_α and ξ_α as the logarithms of permanent consumption and permanent income, respectively, and u_α and v_α as transitory consumption and income, respectively. Then we might wish to investigate whether β, the elasticity of permanent consumption with respect to permanent income, is equal to one as predicated by Friedman's theory. In addition, estimates of the parameters ξ_α, $\alpha = 1,2, \ldots, n$, will provide us with valuable information regarding the distribution of households with respect to permanent income.

Unfortunately, it is not possible to proceed with estimation of the model as specified above since, as is well known, the model's parameters are not identified. If one were to overlook this fact and proceed to derive "maximum likelihood estimates," he would obtain the absurd result $\hat{\beta}^2 = \hat{\sigma}_u^2 / \hat{\sigma}_v^2$, a fact apparently first pointed out by Lindley (1947). To identify the model more prior information is needed. It has been customary to assume that either or both σ_u^2 and σ_v^2 are known exactly or that the ratio $\lambda = \sigma_u^2/\sigma_v^2$ is known exactly. Alternatively, one can identify the model if he knows the value of β_0 or β. However, there are many situations in which such sharp prior information is not available. Below, we relax the need for such precise prior information by the use of prior probability distributions for the parameters in the Bayesian approach.

Above, we have considered the functional equation form of the EVM. In some situations, it may be appropriate to consider the ξ vector stochastic. With this assumption Kendall and Stuart (1961) refer to the model as the structural equation form of the EVM. For example, it may be used in connection with Friedman's consumption function model if it is assumed that consumers' permanent incomes are random variables. As is pointed out below, the complete unconditional analysis of the structural form of the EVM from either the sampling theory or Bayesian approaches requires that consideration be given to the form of the distribution of the ξ's. Thus, within the context of Friedman's consumption function model, considerations regarding the distribution of consumers with respect to permanent income enter in the analysis of their consumption behavior if one wishes to make inferences not conditional upon the values of permanent income associated with consumers in a single sample.

3. MAXIMUM LIKELIHOOD ESTIMATION

Since the maximum likelihood (ML) approach to the analysis of the EVM has been considered extensively in the literature — see e. g. Lindley (1947), Kiefer and Wolfowitz (1956), Madansky (1959),

Kendall and Stuart (1961), page 383, Johnson (1963), Ch. 6, and Malinvaud (1964), Ch. 10 — we shall present just a brief review of some of the main results, some clarifying comments, and a few extensions of the model to show how certain kinds of prior information can be introduced within the sampling theory framework. We first take up the classical EVM with the ξ vector assumed nonstochastic. Then we proceed to consider cases in which the ξ vector is stochastic.

Maximum Likelihood Estimation: ξ Vector Nonstochastic

As mentioned above, prior information about the variances σ_u^2 and σ_v^2 is required in order to identify β_0 and β — see e.g. Reiersol (1950).[1] Here we review the case in which

$\lambda = \sigma_u^2/\sigma_v^2$ is known. For this case the likelihood function is given by:

$$(\underline{\beta}, \underline{\xi}, \sigma_u \mid \underline{x}', \underline{y}', \lambda) \propto \sigma_u^{-2n} \exp\left\{\left(-1/2\sigma_u^2\right)\left[\sum(y_\alpha - \beta_0 - \beta\xi_\alpha)^2 + \lambda\sum(x_\alpha - \xi_\alpha)^2\right]\right\} \qquad ...(3.1)$$

where $\underline{\beta}' = (\beta_0, \beta)$, $\xi' = (\xi_1, \xi_2, \ldots, \xi_n)$, $\underline{x}' = (x_1, x_2, \ldots, x_n)$, $\underline{y}' = (y_1, y_2, \ldots, y_n)$, and all summations extend from $\alpha = 1$ to $\alpha = n$. The ML estimates are given in the following expressions:

$$\hat{\beta} = \frac{m_{yy} - \lambda m_{xx} + \sqrt{(\lambda m_{xx} - m_{yy})^2 + 4\lambda m_{xy}^2}}{2m_{xy}} \qquad ...(3.2)$$

$$\hat{\beta}_0 = \bar{y} - \hat{\beta}\,\bar{x}, \qquad ...(3.3)$$

$$\hat{\xi}_\alpha = \frac{\hat{\beta}(y_\alpha - \hat{\beta}_0) + \lambda x_\alpha}{\hat{\beta}^2 + \lambda} \qquad \alpha = 1, 2, \ldots\ldots, n \qquad ...(3.4)$$

1. See Appendix A for a discussion of the information matrix for the case of unknown σ_u^2 and σ_v^2. Even though β_0 and β are not identified, the information matrix is found to be non-singular, indicating that there is some information in the data relating to parameters of the model.

$$\hat{\eta}_\alpha = \hat{\beta}_0 + \hat{\beta}\,\hat{\xi}_\alpha, \qquad \alpha = 1, 2, ..., n \qquad ...(3.5)$$

and

$$\hat{\sigma}_u^2 = (1/2n)\left\{ \lambda\sum(x_\alpha - \hat{\xi}_\alpha)^2 + \sum(y_\alpha - \hat{\beta}_0 - \hat{\beta}\hat{\xi}_\alpha)^2 \right\} \qquad ... (3.6a)$$

or, on substituting from (3.4),

$$\hat{\sigma}_u^2 = \frac{\lambda}{2n(\lambda + \hat{\beta}^2)}\sum(y_\alpha - \hat{\beta}_0 - \hat{\beta}x_\alpha^2) \qquad ...(3.6b)$$

where $\bar{y} = n^{-1}\sum y_\alpha$, $\bar{x} = n^{-1}\sum x_\alpha$, $m_{xx} = \sum(x_\alpha - \bar{x})^2$, $m_{yy} = \sum(y_\alpha - \bar{y})^2$ and $m_{xy} = \sum(x_\alpha - \bar{x})(y_\alpha - \bar{y})$.

The expression for $\hat{\beta}$ in (3.2) arises as the solution of the following quadratic equation:

$$\beta^2 m_{xy} + \beta(\lambda m_{xx} - m_{yy}) - \lambda m_{xy} = 0. \qquad ...(3.7)$$

Kendall and Stuart (1961) and Madansky (1959) present clear arguments for selecting the root shown in (3.2) as the ML estimate. In addition, Kendall and Stuart (1961) show that the estimators in (3.2)-(3.5) are consistent but that the ML estimator in (3.6) is seriously inconsistent. In fact, plim $\hat{\sigma}_u^2 = (1/2)\,\sigma_u^2$, a result appearing in Lindley (1947). This is an example of a breakdown of the ML method when "incidental parameters" (here the elements of ξ) are present — see Neyman and Scott (1948). Kendall and Stuart (1961, p. 387) explain this breakdown of the ML method in the following terms, "The inconsistency of the ML estimator is therefore a reflection of the small-sample bias of ML estimators in general." What they are suggesting is that in situations in which the number of parameters grows with the sample size, it may be that the finite sample bias of ML estimators does not disappear. They then use the following "degrees of freedom" argument to patch up the ML estimator for σ_u^2 to make it consistent. There are 2n observations to estimate n + 2 parameters, namely n ξ's, β_0 and β; thus there are 2n - (n + 2) degrees of freedom left for the estimation of σ_u^2. They then suggest the following estimator $\tilde{\sigma}_u^2 = [2n/(n-2)]\,\hat{\sigma}_u^2$ which is a consistent estimator.

We do not think that this explanation of the inconsistency of the ML estimator for σ_u^2 gets to the heart of the difficulty even though the solution is probably acceptable in large samples. The main problem is that the ML estimator for σ_u^2 depends on the unknown parameters $\underline{\xi}' = (\xi_1, \xi_2, \ldots, \xi_n)$ and $\underline{\beta}' = (\beta_0, \beta)$. By inserting sample estimates for these parameters, as is done in (3.6), we obtain a *conditional* estimator for σ_u^2, that is an estimator conditional upon $\underline{\xi} = \hat{\underline{\xi}}$ and $\underline{\beta} = \hat{\underline{\beta}}$. Note from (3.6a) that the probability limit of $\hat{\sigma}_u^2$, conditional upon $\underline{\xi} = \hat{\underline{\xi}}$ and $\underline{\beta} = \hat{\underline{\beta}}$ is indeed σ_u^2 if the conditioning information is valid. However, when $\hat{\sigma}_u^2$ is viewed as an unconditional estimator, the error which is committed is that no allowance has been made for the fact that sample information has been used to estimate $\underline{\xi}$ and $\underline{\beta}$. In situations in which the number of parameters does *not* grow with increased sample size, the *proportion* of sample information used to estimate *unknown* parameters appearing in an expression for a ML estimator usually decreases toward zero as the sample size increases. However, when the number of parameters does increase with increased sample size, the aforementioned proportion does not necessarily decrease to zero. Thus, incorrectly viewing (3.6) as an unconditional estimator for σ_u^2 is for us the essential reason for the inconsistency of the ML estimator. Below, with random $\underline{\xi}$, it will be seen, in line with the general results of Kiefer and Wolfowitz (1956), that when the unknown ξ vector is treated properly, ML estimates are indeed consistent.

Since ML estimation is rather complicated, we are stimulated to develop a simpler "old fashioned" heuristic approach, which without a normality assumption yields the same estimates, as does the ML method. As above, we assume that $\lambda = \sigma_u^2/\sigma_v^2$ is known. We regard

$$y_\alpha = \beta_0 + \beta\xi_\alpha + u_\alpha \qquad \alpha = 1, 2, \ldots, n$$

as a simple regression model, which it would be except for the fact that the ξ_α are unknown and have to be estimated. Pursuing the simple regression analogy, we estimate β_0 as follows:

$$\begin{aligned}\beta_0 &= \bar{y} - \beta\bar{\xi} \\ &= \bar{y} - \beta\bar{x}\end{aligned} \qquad \ldots(3.8)$$

wherein we take $\bar{\xi} = \bar{x} = n^{-1}\sum_{\alpha=1}^{n} x_\alpha$ as an estimator for $\xi = n^{-1}\sum_{\alpha=1}^{n}\xi_\alpha$

and $\tilde{\beta}$ is an estimator for β given by

$$\tilde{\beta} = \frac{\sum(\tilde{\xi}_\alpha - \bar{x})(y_\alpha - \bar{y})}{\sum(\tilde{\xi}_\alpha - \bar{x})^2} \qquad \text{...(3.9)}$$

In (3.9) the estimates of the ξ_α, denoted by $\tilde{\xi}_\alpha$ appear. These estimates are obtained as follows. From (2.1)-(2.3), we have

$$x_\alpha = \xi_\alpha + v_\alpha \qquad \text{...(3.10)}$$

and

$$\frac{y_\alpha - \beta_0}{\beta} = \xi_\alpha + \frac{u_\alpha}{\beta} \qquad \text{...(3.11)}$$

Then on averaging x_α and $(y_\alpha - \beta_o)/\beta$, with the reciprocals of their respective variances as weights, we obtain:

$$\xi^*_\alpha = \frac{\frac{\beta^2}{\sigma_u^2}\left(\frac{y_\alpha - \beta_0}{\beta}\right) + \frac{1}{\sigma_v^2}x_\alpha}{\frac{\tilde{\beta}^2}{\sigma_u^2} + \frac{1}{\sigma_v^2}} = \frac{\beta(y_\alpha - \beta_0) + \lambda x_\alpha}{\beta^2 + \lambda} \qquad \text{...(3.12)}$$

On inserting estimates of β and β_0, this becomes

$$\tilde{\xi}_\alpha = \frac{\tilde{\beta}\left(y_\alpha - \tilde{\beta}_0\right) + \lambda x_\alpha}{\beta^2 + \lambda} \qquad \alpha = 1, 2, ..., n \qquad \text{...(3.13)}$$

We then substitute (3.13) into (3.9) and use (3.8) to obtain an equation in $\tilde{\beta}$ which is in exactly the same form as (3.7). The solution, shown in (3.2), is our estimator $\hat{\beta}$ which when substituted in (3.13) yields estimates of the ξ_α. Then, pursuing the regression analogy, σ_u^2 is estimated by

$$\tilde{\sigma}_u^2 = \frac{1}{n-2}\sum_{\alpha=1}^{n}\left(y_\alpha - \hat{\beta}_0 - \hat{\beta}\hat{\xi}_\alpha\right)^2 \qquad \text{...(3.14)}$$

with the divisor roughly justified by the "degrees of freedom" argument explained above. These estimates, except for that in (3.14), are identical to the maximum likelihood estimates.[2]

2. In (3.12) we are estimating n means, the ξ_α, and in the light of the work of Stein (1956) and Stein and James (1961), it is probably the case that the estimator in (3.13) is inadmissible for a quadratic loss function. Whether use of a better estimator for ξ would produce a better estimator for $\underline{\beta}$ is at present an open question.

Maximum Likelihood Estimation: ξ Vector Stochastic

The model with the ξ vector stochastic is often referred to as the "structural form" of the EVM. Perhaps the most basic general result for this case is due to Kiefer and Wolfowitz (1956) who prove that if the parameters are identified, then ". . .under the usual regularity conditions, the maximum likelihood estimator of a structural parameter is strongly consistent, when the (infinitely many) incidental parameters are independently distributed chance variables with a common unknown distribution function" (p.887). Among other examples, they provide the following result for the EVM. If the ξ_α are independently distributed and each has a non-normal distribution,[3] then ML estimates are consistent. The condition of non-normality is required to identify β_o and β when nothing else is assumed known — see Reiersol (1950).

If additional information is available, for example if $\lambda = \sigma_u^2/\sigma_v^2$, is known, the model is identified even if the ξ_α are normally distributed. Below we shall consider a few interesting cases.

With the incidental parameters, the elements of $\underline{\xi}$, regarded as random, we have the following joint pdf to consider:

$$p(\underline{x}, \underline{y}, \underline{\xi}\,|\,\underline{\theta}) = p_1(\underline{x}, \underline{y}\,|\,\underline{\xi}, \underline{\theta}_1)\; p_2(\underline{\xi}\,|\,\underline{\theta}_2) \qquad \text{... (3.15)}$$

where $\underline{\theta}$ denotes all the parameters of the joint pdf, $\underline{\theta}_1$ the subset of parameters appearing in the conditional pdf for $\underline{x}$ and $\underline{y}$ given $\underline{\xi}$, and $\underline{\theta}_2$, the subset of parameters appearing in the marginal pdf for $\underline{\xi}$, namely $p_2(\underline{\xi}\,|\,\underline{\theta}_2)$. If we specify the forms of p_1 and p_2 in (3.15), we can integrate (3.15) over the elements of $\underline{\xi}$ to obtain the marginal pdf for $\underline{x}$ and $\underline{y}$ which, when viewed as a function of its parameters, is the likelihood function associated with the observations $\underline{x}$ and $\underline{y}$. That is, with the forms of p_1 and p_2 in (3.15) specified, we perform the following integration

---

3. The results of Reiersol (1950) indicate that, if nothing else is assumed known, non-normality of the ξ_α is both necessary and sufficient for identification of the structural parameters. This apparently strange condition may be due to the fact that of all proper distributions with given mean and covariance matrix, the normal distribution is the one which minimizes Shannon's measure of information — cf. Shannon (1949, p.56). Thus the condition of non-normality implies that additional information is available (relative to the assumption of normality) which identifies the model's parameters. Shannon's results apply just to proper distributions with finite first and second moments. Further work is required to extend the argument to distributions whose moments do not exist.

$$g(\underline{x}, \underline{y} \mid \underline{\theta}) = \int p(\underline{x}, \underline{y}, \underline{\xi} \mid \underline{\theta})\, d\underline{\xi} \qquad \text{...(3.16)}$$

$$= \int p_1(\underline{x}, \underline{y} \mid \underline{\xi}, \underline{\theta}_1)\, p_2(\underline{\xi} \mid \underline{\theta}_2)\, d\underline{\xi}$$

to obtain the pdf for $\underline{x}$ and $\underline{y}$ which, when viewed as a function of the elements of $\underline{\theta}$, is the likelihood function for these parameters, that is $L(\underline{\theta} \mid \underline{x}, \underline{y})$. This function can be maximized with respect to $\underline{\theta}$ to obtain ML estimates. Below we take up this approach with varying assumptions regarding the distribution $p_2(\underline{\xi} \mid \underline{\theta}_2)$, shown in (3.15), and regarding our state of prior information about σ_u^2 and σ_v^2.

Case 1: We assume σ_u^2 and σ_v^2 unknown and

$p_2(\xi \mid \underline{\theta}_2) \propto$ constant. $-\infty < \xi < \infty$, $\alpha = 1, 2, \ldots, n$. ...(3.17)

In (3.17), we are assuming that the elements of $\underline{\xi}$ are uniformly and independently distributed.[4] On inserting (3.17) in (3.15) and writing out the expression for $p_1(\underline{x}, \underline{y} \mid \underline{\xi}, \underline{\theta}_1)$, we have

$$p(\underline{x}, \underline{y}\ \underline{\xi} \mid \underline{\theta}_1) \propto \frac{1}{\sigma_u^n\ \sigma_v^n} \exp\left(-\frac{1}{2\sigma_u^2} \sum (y_\alpha - \beta_0 - \beta\xi_\alpha)^2 - \frac{1}{2\sigma_v^2} \sum (x_\alpha - \xi_\alpha)^2 \right) \qquad \text{...(3.18)}$$

we then integrate over the elements of ξ to obtain

$$g(\underline{x}, \underline{y} \mid \underline{\theta}_1) \propto \frac{\lambda^{\frac{n}{2}}}{\sigma_u^n (\lambda + \beta^2)^{\frac{n}{2}}} \exp\left[-\frac{\lambda}{2\sigma_u^2 (\lambda + \beta^2)} \sum (y_\alpha - \beta_0 - \beta x_\alpha)^2 \right] \qquad \text{...(3.19)}$$

with $\lambda = \sigma_u^2 / \sigma_v^2$. The function in (3.19), viewed as a function of the parameters $\theta_1 - (\beta \mid \sigma_u^2, \lambda)$, is the likelihood function. On maximising this function with respect to β_0 and β, we find the ML estimators:

$$\hat{\beta} = \frac{\sum (y_\alpha - \bar{y})(x_\alpha - \bar{x})}{\sum (x_\alpha - \bar{x})^2} \quad \text{and} \quad \hat{\beta}_0 = \bar{y} - \hat{\beta}\, \bar{x}. \qquad \text{...(3.20)}$$

---

4. Note that (3.17) is non-normal and thus β_0 and β will be identified according to Reiersol's (1950) results.

In this case, perhaps surprisingly, the ML estimators of β_0 and β are identical to those obtained from a least squares regression of y on x. The explanation for this result is that the form of (3.17) is such as to imply that the variance of the ξ_α is infinite, a condition which insures the consistency of the estimators shown in (3.20).[5] Thus the ML method results accurately reflect the prior information brought in to specify the form of $p_2\ (\underline{\xi}|\underline{\theta}_1)$ in (3.17).[6]

Case 2: We assume $\lambda = \sigma_v^2/\sigma_u^2$ known, σ_u^2 unknown and $p_2(\xi|\theta_2)$ given by (3.17).

On performing the same operations as in Case 1, we are led to the following ML estimates:

$$\hat{\beta} = \frac{\Sigma(y_\alpha - \bar{y})(x_\alpha - \bar{x})}{\Sigma(x_\alpha - \bar{x})^2}, \quad \hat{\beta}_0 = \bar{y} - \hat{\beta}\,\bar{x}, \text{ and} \qquad \text{...(3.21)}$$

$$\hat{\sigma}_u^2 = \frac{\lambda}{n(\lambda + \hat{\beta}^2)}\,\Sigma\left(y_\alpha - \hat{\beta}x_\alpha\right)^2 \qquad \text{...(3.22)}$$

Here, as in Case 1, ML estimators for β and β_0 are identical to least squares estimators and are consistent, given the form of (3.17). Also, in contrast to (3.6b), the estimator for σ_u^2 in (3.22) is a consistent estimator. The fact that the divisor in (3.22) involves n rather than 2n, as in (3.6b), is produced automatically by the integration over the n elements of $\underline{\xi}$.

Case 3: Here we assume that

$$p_2\ (\underline{\xi}|\underline{\theta}_2) \propto (1/n)\ \exp\{-1/2\tau^2\ \Sigma\ (\xi_\alpha - \mu)^2\}, \qquad \text{...(3.22)}$$

that is the elements of $\underline{\xi}$ are normally and independently distributed, each with mean μ and variance τ^2. As noted above, β_0 and β will not be identified unless we introduce additional prior information. Analyses of this case when $\lambda = \sigma_u^2 / \sigma_v^2$ is known are presented in e.g. Kendall and Stuart (1961), Johnston (1963) and

---

5. As is well known, plim $\hat{\beta} = \beta\left(\frac{1}{1+(\sigma_v^2/\sigma_\xi^2)}\right)$ where $\hat{\beta}$ is the slope estimator shown in (3.20). Thus if σ_ξ^2 is infinite, plim $\hat{\beta} = \beta$.

6. It does not appear possible to obtain ML estimates of σ_u and λ for this case.

Birch (1964). The main problem in applying the results of these analyses in practice is that the ratio of error terms' variances is seldom known precisely. In the next section, this problem is considered from a Bayesian point of view with the introduction of a prior pdf for the variances and their ratio.

4. BAYESIAN ESTIMATION

As in the treatment of ML estimation, we shall consider the non-random and random ξ vector cases separately. With the ξ vector non-random, we require a prior pdf for the elements of ξ as well as for other parameters of the model. It will be seen that results for this case are similar in certain respects to some of those presented above for the ML analysis with the ξ vector assumed random. Also, by introducing a prior pdf for the variances σ_u^2 and σ_v^2, we are able to analyse the model without exact knowledge regarding the variances and/or their ratio. Then we go on to treat the random ξ case.

Bayesian Estimation with ξ Vector Non Stochastic[7]

The present problem with the n elements of ξ, β_0, β, σ_u^2 and σ_v^2 as parameters is indeed a multi-parameter problem and thus care must be exercised in the choice of a prior pdf in order to avoid putting some information into the analysis which we may not wish to include. For example, suppose we attempt to be "non-informative" or "diffuse" by using the following prior pdf:

$$p\,(\xi, \underline{\beta}, \sigma_u, \sigma_v) \propto 1/\sigma_u\,\sigma_v \qquad \ldots(4.1)$$

with $-\infty < \xi < \infty$, $-\infty < \underline{\beta} < \infty$, $0 < \sigma_u < \infty$ and $0 < \sigma_v < \infty$.

In (4.1) we are assuming that the elements of ξ and $\underline{\beta}$, $\log \sigma_u$ and $\log \sigma_v$ are independently and uniformly distributed. Diffuse improper prior pdfs such as (4.1) have been used widely and successfully in analysis of many problems — e.g. Jeffreys (1961), Box and Tiao (1962), Geisser (1965), and Lindley (1965). Let us see, what results we obtain when (4.1) is used as a prior pdf in the analysis of the

7. As H.V. Roberts has pointed out, this terminology, used by Kendall and Stuart (1961), is not appropriate for all situations. In many situations, it would be better to use the phrase "conditional upon given $\underline{\xi}$" rather than non-stochastic $\underline{\xi}$.

EVM. Using Bayes' Theorem to combine (4.1) with the likelihood function for the model and integrating over the elements of ξ and σ_v, we obtain the following expression for the joint posterior pdf for $\beta' = (\beta_0, \beta)$ and $\lambda = \sigma_u^2 / \sigma_v^2$:

$$p\left(\underline{\beta}, \lambda \mid \underline{x}, \underline{y}\right) \propto \frac{1}{\lambda}\left\{vs^2 + \left(\underline{\beta}-\underline{\hat{\beta}}\right)' M\left(\beta-\hat{\beta}\right)\right\}^{-\frac{n}{2}} \qquad \text{...(4.2)}$$

where v = n - 2,

$$\underline{\hat{\beta}} = \begin{pmatrix} \hat{\beta}_0 \\ \hat{\beta} \end{pmatrix} = M^{-1} \left(\underline{\ell} : \underline{x}\right)'\underline{y} \qquad \text{...(4.3)}$$

$\underline{\ell}'$ is a 1 x n row vector with all elements equal to one, that is $\underline{\ell}' = (1, 1, \ldots, 1)$, $M = (\underline{\ell} : \underline{x})'(\underline{\ell} : \underline{x})$ and

$$vs^2 = \left[\underline{y} - (\underline{\ell} : \underline{x})\underline{\hat{\beta}}\right]'\left[\underline{y} - (\underline{\ell} : \underline{x})\underline{\hat{\beta}}\right]$$

It is seen from (4.2) that λ and $\underline{\beta}$ are independently distributed with the marginal distribution for λ being improper. The posterior pdf for $\underline{\beta}$ is in the Student bivariate form with mean given by (4.3). As is clear from (4.3), the mean of the posterior pdf for $\underline{\beta}$ is just the least square estimate obtained from the regression of y on x, a result which parallels that obtained in the ML approach with random ξ vector assumed to be distributed according to (3.17). The reason for obtaining the least squares quantity as the mean of the posterior pdf appears to be the same as discussed in connection with (3.20), above. The prior pdf, $p(\underline{\xi}) \propto$ constant implies that $\underline{\xi}'\underline{\xi} >> n$ with high probability, a fact noted by Stein (1962, p. 280) in connection with his analysis of means. That is, $p(\underline{\xi})\ d\underline{\xi} \propto d\underline{\xi}$ implies $p(z)dz \propto z^{\frac{n-1}{2}}\ dz$, where $z = \left(\underline{\xi}'\ \underline{\xi}\right)^{\frac{1}{2}}$ which is far from "diffuse" on this quantity, a quantity which plays a key role in the analysis of the EVM.

To indicate that the result in (4.2) is not very sensitive to what is assumed known about the error variances, we carried through the above analysis with $\lambda = \frac{\sigma_u^2}{\sigma_v^2}$ assumed known and with prior pdf $p\left(\sigma_u, \underline{\beta}, \underline{\xi}\right) \propto \frac{1}{\sigma_u}$. The marginal posterior pdf for β_0 and β is found to be

$$p(\beta_0, \beta \mid \text{data}, \lambda) \propto \left\{ \Sigma (y_\alpha - \beta_0 - \beta x_\alpha)^2 \right\}^{-n/2} \quad \ldots(4.4)$$

$$\propto \left\{ vs^2 + (\underline{\beta} - \hat{\underline{\beta}})' M (\underline{\beta} - \hat{\underline{\beta}}) \right\}^{-n/2}$$

which is exactly the same result for $\underline{\beta}$ as in (4.2).

The prior pdf which we consider useful for a broad range of circumstances is explained below. We write the joint prior pdf as follows :

$$p(\sigma_u, \sigma_v, \underline{\beta}, \xi, \mu) = p_1(\sigma_u)\, p_2(\sigma_v) p_3{}^* (\underline{\beta} \mid \xi, \sigma_u, \sigma_v) p_4 (\xi, \mu) \quad \ldots(4.5)$$

$$= p_1(\sigma_u)\, p_2(\sigma_v) p_3 (\underline{\beta}^* \mid \xi, \lambda, \sigma_u) p_4 (\xi, \mu)$$

where $\lambda = \dfrac{\sigma_u^2}{\sigma_v^2}$ and μ is the common unknown mean of the elements of ξ. Note that *a priori* information about $\underline{\beta}$ is not assumed independent of information about ξ, λ and σ_u.

For the parameters σ_u and σ_v, we use the following "informative" inverted gamma pdf's — see Raiffa and Schlaifer (1961, p. 228) for properties of this pdf:

$$p_1(\sigma_u \mid v_1, s_1) \propto \frac{1}{\sigma_u^{v_1+1}} \exp\left(-\frac{v_1 s_1^2}{2\sigma_u^2} \right) \quad 0 < \sigma_u < \infty \quad \ldots(4.6)$$

and

$$p_2(\sigma_v \mid v_2, s_2) \propto \frac{1}{\sigma_v^{v_2+1}} \exp\left(-\frac{v_2 s_2^2}{2\sigma_v^2} \right) \quad 0 < \sigma_v < \infty \quad \ldots(4.7)$$

with v_1, v_2, s_1 and s_2 being parameters of these prior pdf's to be assigned by an investigator to reflect the state of his information about σ_u and σ_v — see section 5 for examples. It is interesting to observe that when we make a change of variables from σ_u and σ_v to σ_u and $\lambda = \dfrac{\sigma_u^2}{\sigma_v^2}$, the joint prior pdf for σ_u and λ is :

$$p(\sigma_u, \lambda \mid v_1, v_2, s_1, s_2) \propto \frac{\lambda^{\frac{v_2-2}{2}}}{\sigma_u^{v_2+v_1+1}} \exp -\frac{1}{2\sigma_u^2} \left[v_1 s_1^2 + \lambda v_2 s_2^2 \right] \quad \ldots(4.8)$$

Then on integrating (4.8) with respect to σ_u, the marginal prior pdf for λ is found to be:

$$p(\lambda \mid v_1, v_2, s_1, s_2) \propto \frac{\dfrac{s_2^2}{s_1^2}\lambda^{\frac{v_2-2}{2}}}{\left(v_1 + v_2 \dfrac{s_2^2}{s_1^2}\lambda\right)^{\frac{(v_1+v_2)}{2}}}, \quad 0 < \lambda < \infty \qquad \text{...(4.9)}$$

It is thus seen that the marginal prior pdf for $(s_2^2/s_1^2)\lambda$ is in the form of an F distribution with v_2 and v_1 degrees of freedom — see e.g. Kendall and Stuart (1961, p. 377).[8] We believe that these prior pdfs for σ_u and σ_v or, alternatively, for σ_u and λ are rich enough to represent prior information in many practical situations.

With respect to the factor $p_3(\beta \mid \underline{\xi}, \lambda, \sigma_u)$ appearing in (4.5), we utilised Jeffreys' (1961, p. 179) invariance theory by taking it proportional to the square root of the determinant of the conditional information matrix for $\underline{\beta}$ given $\underline{\xi}$, λ and σ_u — see Appendix B for details. This leads to

$$p_3(\beta \mid \underline{\xi}, \lambda, \sigma_u) \propto \frac{\lambda}{\sigma_u^2(\lambda+\beta^2)}\left[(\underline{\xi}-\bar{\xi}\underline{\ell})'(\underline{\xi}-\bar{\xi}\underline{\ell})\right]^{\frac{1}{2}} \quad -\infty<\beta<\infty \qquad \text{...(4.10)}$$

with $\bar{\xi}=n^{-1}\Sigma\xi_\alpha$, the unknown mean of the elements of $\underline{\xi}$.

Finally, with respect to the last factor of (4.5), namely

$p_4(\underline{\xi}, \mu) = p_5(\underline{\xi} \mid \mu)\, p_6(\mu)$, we take

$$p_6(\mu) \propto \text{constant} \quad -\infty < \mu < \infty \qquad \text{...(4.11a)}$$

and

$$p_5(\underline{\xi} \mid \mu) \propto \left[(\underline{\xi}-\underline{\mu})'(\underline{\xi}-\mu\underline{\ell})\right]^{-\left(\frac{n-1}{2}\right)} \quad -\infty < \underline{\xi} < \infty \qquad \text{...(4.11b)}$$

In (4.11a) we are "diffuse" on μ while in (4.11b) we are using a prior pdf on $\underline{\xi}$ which is very close to the one which Stein (1962, p. 281) indicates can be used to produce his estimator for n means.

---

8. As is well known, the cumulative distribution function for $(s_2^2/s_1^2)\lambda$ can be obtained from tables of the incomplete beta function by making the following transformation: $\phi = 1+\lambda\left(\dfrac{v_2 s_2^2}{v_1 s_1^2}\right)^{-1}$.
Then $p(\phi) \propto \phi^{\frac{v_1-2}{2}}(1-\phi)^{\frac{v_2-2}{2}}$ with $0 < \phi < 1$.

Stein (1962, p. 281) mentions that D. Wallace and I. J. Good have provided the following geometric interpretation of (4.11b). Consider an n-dimensional hyper-space with the variables $\xi_\alpha - \mu$, $\alpha = 1,2, \ldots.n$, measured on the axes. Then if for a given radius vector equal to $\left[(\underline{\xi}-\mu\underline{\ell})'(\underline{\xi}-\mu\underline{\ell})\right]^{\frac{1}{2}}$, we assume the $\xi_\alpha - \mu$ uniformly distributed over the surface of a hypersphere with this radius and then take a uniform marginal pdf on the radius vector, we are led to a pdf precisely in the form of (4.11b).

On combining the prior pdfs in (4.6), (4.7), (4.10) and (4.11) with the likelihood function for the model, we have the following posterior pdf for the unknown parameters after integrating over μ :

$$p(\underline{\beta}, \sigma_u, \sigma_v, \underline{\xi}, | \underline{x}, \underline{y}) \propto$$

$$\frac{\exp\left\{-\frac{1}{2}\left(\frac{v_1 s_1^2}{\sigma_u^2}+\frac{v_2 s_2^2}{\sigma_v^2}\right)\right\}\exp\left\{-\frac{1}{2}\left[\Sigma(y_\alpha-\beta_0-\beta\xi_\alpha)^2+\frac{\sigma_u^2}{\sigma_v^2}\Sigma(x_\alpha-\xi_\alpha)^2\right]\right\}}{\left(\frac{\sigma_u^2}{\sigma_v^2}+\beta^2\right)\sigma_u^{n+v_1+1}\sigma_v^{n+v_2+3}[(\underline{\xi}-\bar{\xi}\underline{\ell})'(\underline{\xi}-\bar{\xi}\underline{\ell})]^{\frac{n-3}{2}}} \quad \ldots(4.12)$$

To obtain the marginal posterior pdf for $\underline{\beta}$, σ_u and σ_v , complete the square on the ξ's in the exponential and use properties of the non-central χ^2 distribution to perform the integration over the elements of $\underline{\xi}$. This operation yields the following result:[9]

$$\frac{\exp\left\{-\frac{1}{2}\left(\frac{v_1 s_1^2}{\sigma_u^2}+\frac{v_2 s_2^2}{\sigma_v^2}\right)\right\}\exp\left\{-\frac{1}{2\sigma_v^2(\beta^2+\sigma_u^2/\sigma_v^2)}\Sigma(y_\alpha-\beta_0-\beta x_\alpha)^2\right\}}{\sigma_u^{n+v_1-2}\sigma_v^{n+v_2+3}\left\{\beta^2+\left(\sigma_u^2/\sigma_v^2\right)^{5/2}\right\}} \quad \ldots(4.13)$$

on integrating with respect to β_0,[10] we obtain

$$\frac{\exp\left\{-\frac{1}{2}\left(\frac{v_1 s_1^2}{\sigma_u^2}+\frac{v_2 s_2^2}{\sigma_v^2}\right)\right\}\exp\left\{-\frac{Q(\beta)}{2\sigma_v^2(\beta^2+\sigma_u^2/\sigma_v^2)}\right\}}{\sigma_u^{n+v_1-2}\sigma_v^{n+v_2+2}\left\{\beta^2+(\sigma_u^2/\sigma_v^2)\right\}^2} \quad \ldots(4.14)$$

---

9. See Appendix C for details.
10. If interest centers on β_0, then we would not integrate over β_0 at this point. The subsequent steps would be exactly the same but the result shown in (4.16) would be a trivariate pdf involving the variables β_0, β and λ which can be analysed numerically.

where $Q(\beta)=\Sigma[y_\alpha-\bar{y}-\beta(x_\alpha-\bar{x})]^2$.

We now change variables from β, σ_u and σ_v to β, σ_u and $\lambda=\sigma_u^2/\sigma_v^2$ which yields

$$p(\beta,\sigma_u,\lambda\,|\,\underline{x},\underline{y},)\propto\frac{\lambda^{\frac{n+v_2-1}{2}}}{\sigma_u^{2n+v_1+v_2-1}(\beta^2+\lambda)^{\frac{1}{2}}}\exp\left\{-\frac{1}{2\sigma_u^2}\left[v_1s_1^2+v_2s_2^2\lambda+\frac{\lambda}{\beta^2+\lambda}Q(\beta)\right]\right\}$$

...(4.15)

Then on integrating with respect to σ_u , the resulting bivariate posterior pdf for β and λ is:

$$p(\beta,\lambda\,|\,\underline{x},\underline{y})\propto\frac{\lambda^{\frac{n+v_2-1}{2}}(\beta^2+\lambda)^{\frac{2n+v_1+v_2-6}{2}}}{\{(v_1s_1^2+\lambda v_2s_2^2)(\beta^2+\lambda)+\lambda Q(\beta)\}^{\frac{2n+v_1+v_2-2}{2}}}\qquad ...(4.16)$$

Lastly, it is useful to express (4.16) in terms of β and $\gamma=1/\lambda$, where $\gamma=\sigma_v^2/\sigma_u^2$. In terms of β and γ, the posterior pdf is:

$$p(\beta,\gamma\,|\,\underline{x},\underline{y})\propto\frac{\gamma^{\frac{n+v_1-1}{2}}(1+\gamma\beta^2)^{\frac{2n+v_1+v_2-6}{2}}}{\left\{\left(\gamma v_1s_1^{\,2}+v_2s_2^{\,2}\right)(1+\gamma\beta^2)+\gamma Q(\beta)\right\}^{\frac{2n+v_1+v_2-2}{2}}}\qquad ...(4.17)$$

$$\propto\frac{(1+\gamma\beta^2)^{\frac{2n+v_1+v_2-6}{2}}}{\gamma^{\frac{n+v_2-1}{2}}\left\{(v_1s_1^2+v_2s_2^2/\gamma)(1+\gamma\beta^2)+Q(\beta)\right\}^{\frac{2n+v_1+v_2-2}{2}}}$$

Bivariate numerical integration techniques can be used to evaluate the normalising constant of (4.17). Then the normalized bivariate pdf can be employed to make joint inferences about β and γ. Further, using numerical integration techniques, the marginal posterior pdfs for β and γ can be computed and used to make inferences about β and γ individually. In Section 5, numerical examples illustrating these operations are presented.

It is interesting to note from the second line of (4.17) that the conditional pdf for β given γ close to zero (that is, $\sigma_v^2 << \sigma_u^2$), is approximately in the univariate Student t form, centred approximately at $\hat{\beta} = m_{xy} / m_{xx}$, the least squares quantity, given that $v_2 s_2^2 << m_{xx}^2$. When γ is not small, aside from the factor in the numerator of the second line of (4.17), the conditional pdf would be in the univariate Student t form. The mean of this Student t form is pushed away from the origin by the presence of the factor $(1+\gamma\beta^2)^{\frac{2n+v_1+v_2-6}{2}}$ in the numerator. In a rough sense, this is a correction for the bias toward zero of the least squares quantity $\hat{\beta}$ viewed as a sampling theory estimator. Of course, we usually do not know γ in practices and thus the marginal pdf for β will be used in practical analyses to make inferences about β. This is reasonable since, as is well known, a marginal posterior pdf can be viewed as an average of conditional posterior pdfs with the weight function being the marginal posterior pdf for the conditioning variable. In the present context we can write $p(\beta \mid \underline{x}, \underline{y}) = \int h(\beta \mid \gamma, \underline{x}, \underline{y}) g(\gamma \mid \underline{x}, \underline{y}) d\gamma$ where $h(\beta \mid \gamma, \underline{x}, y)$ is the conditional pdf for β given γ and $g(\gamma \mid x, y)$ is the marginal posterior pdf for γ.

Bayesian Estimation with ξ Vector Stochastic[11]

As in Section 3.2, we have to consider the joint pdf for $\underline{x}$, $\underline{y}$ and $\underline{\xi}$, namely

$$p(\underline{x}, \underline{y}, \underline{\xi} \mid \underline{\theta}) = p_1(\underline{x}, \underline{y} \mid \underline{\xi}, \underline{\theta}_1) p_2(\underline{\xi} \mid \underline{\theta}_2) \qquad \ldots(4.18)$$

where $\theta_1 = (\beta, \beta_0, \sigma_u, \sigma_v)$ and θ_2 represents the parameters of the marginal pdf for ξ which we take in the following form:

$$p_2(\xi \mid \theta_2) \propto \frac{1}{n} \exp\left\{-\frac{1}{2\tau^2}(\xi - \mu\ell)'(\xi - \mu\ell)\right\}; \qquad \ldots(4.19)$$

that is, we assume the elements of ξ to be normally and independently distributed, each with mean μ and variance τ^2. Thus in (4.19), $\underline{\theta}_2 = (\mu, \tau)$.

Now we can integrate p ($\underline{x}$, $\underline{y}$, ξ | $\underline{\theta}$) with respect to the elements of ξ to obtain the marginal pdf for $\underline{x}$ and $\underline{y}$. This pdf when combined

11. Jeffreys (1961, pp. 216-217) treats this case with known error variances and a uniform marginal pdf for ξ. That is, in (4.18) Jeffreys takes $p_2(\xi \mid \underline{\theta}_2) \propto$ constant. Since this pdf may not be satisfactory in general and since he assumes known error variances, his results, while extremely interesting, appear to have limited applicability.

with prior pdfs for the parameters will yield the joint posterior pdf. Further integrations will yield the marginal posterior pdfs for parameters of interest. Alternatively, we can bring in the prior pdfs and change the order of the integration — specifically, integrate over τ first and then over the elements of ξ to obtain exactly the same results as obtained by first integrating with respect to the elements of ξ and then with respect to τ. The expression to be integrated is

$$\frac{\Pi_1(\underline{\beta},\sigma_u,\sigma_v)\Pi_2(\mu,\tau)}{\sigma_u^n\sigma_v^n\tau^n}\exp\left\{-\frac{1}{2\sigma_u^2}\Sigma(y_\alpha-\beta_0-\beta\xi_\alpha)^2-\frac{1}{2\sigma_v^2}\Sigma(x_\alpha-\xi_\alpha)^2\right\}$$
$$\exp\left\{-\frac{1}{2\tau^2}(\underline{\xi}-\mu\underline{\ell})'(\underline{\xi}-\mu\underline{\ell})\right\}$$

where $\Pi_1(\underline{\beta},\sigma_u,\sigma_v)$ and $\Pi_2(\mu,\tau)$ are prior pdfs. If we take $\Pi_2(\mu,\tau)\propto$ constant and perform the integration over τ, $0<\tau<\infty$, we obtain

$$\frac{\Pi_1(\underline{\beta},\sigma_u,\sigma_v)}{\sigma_u^n\sigma_v^n\left[(\underline{\xi}-\mu\underline{\ell})'(\underline{\xi}-\mu\underline{\ell})\right]^{\frac{n-1}{2}}}\exp\left\{-\frac{1}{2\sigma_u^2}\Sigma(y_\alpha-\beta_0-\beta\xi_\alpha)^2-\frac{1}{2\sigma_v^2}\Sigma(x_\alpha-\xi_\alpha)^2\right\} \quad ...(4.20)$$

On comparing (4.20) and (4.12), it is seen that they are in exactly the same form, after integration over μ, if the prior $\Pi_1(\underline{\beta},\sigma_u,\sigma_v)$ is taken as the product of (4.6), (4.7) and (4.10). Thus, with ξ normally distributed, as shown in (4.19), and with the prior distributions we have introduced, the analysis of the random ξ case is exactly the same as the analysis of the non-random ξ case. In particular, the posterior pdf in (4.17) is applicable for both cases. It should be emphasised that this will not be the case if ξ is not assumed normally distributed.

5. APPLICATION OF METHODS IN THE ANALYSIS OF DATA

To illustrate application of the methods discussed above, we first generated n=20 pairs of observations, (x_α, y_α), from the following model :

$$y_\alpha = 2.0 + 1.0\,\xi_\alpha + \mu_\alpha \qquad \alpha = 1, 2, \ldots 20 \qquad ...(5.1)$$

$$x_\alpha = \xi_\alpha + v_\alpha\,. \qquad ...(5.2)$$

In (5.1), we have taken $\beta_0 = 2.0$ and $\beta = 1.0$. Further, the error terms u_α and v_α were independently drawn from normal distributions with zero means and variances 1 and 4, respectively. The ξ_α were independently drawn from a normal distribution with mean 5 and variance 16. These conditions are summarised below :

$$u_\alpha : NID(0,1) \ ; \ v_\alpha : NID(0,4) \ ; \text{ and } \xi_\alpha : NID(5,16). \quad ...(5.3)$$

A plot of the generated data is shown in Figure 1.1, while the data are given in Appendix D.

Figure 1.1

Plot of Generated Data

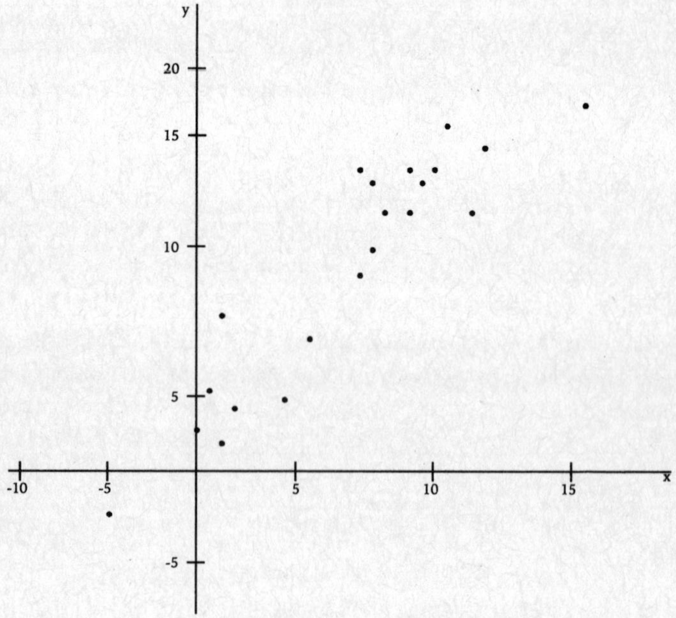

For our prior pdfs for σ_u and σ_v we used the inverted gamma functions shown in (4.6) and (4.7) above with the following prior parameter values:

$$s_1 = 1.0, \ s_2 = 2.0 \text{ and } v_1 = v_2 = 40. \quad ...(5.4)$$

With these values for the parameters of our prior pdfs for σ_u and σ_v we have from properties of the inverted gamma function — (see Raiffa and Schlaifer 1961, p. 228) :

Prior pdf for	*Modal Value**	*Mean**	*Variance**
σ_u	0.988	0.510	0.793
σ_v	1.975	1.190	2.794

* For an inverted gamma pdf of the kind shown in (4.6) with parameters v and s, the expressions for the modal value, mean and variance are :

Modal Value $= s\sqrt{v/(1+v)}$

Mean $= s\sqrt{v/2\Gamma\left(\frac{v-1}{2}\right)}\Big/\Gamma(v/2)\quad v>1$

Variance $= [s^2v/(v-2)] - (\text{Mean})^2 \qquad v > 2$

where Γ denotes the gamma function.

The prior pdfs for σ_u and σ_v imply the following prior pdf for $\gamma = \sigma_v^2/\sigma_u^2$:

$$p(\gamma \mid v_1, v_2, s_1, s_2) \propto \frac{\left(\frac{s_1^2}{s_2^2}\gamma\right)^{\frac{v_1-2}{2}}}{\left(v_2 + v_1\frac{s_1^2}{s_2^2}\gamma\right)^{\frac{v_1+v_2}{2}}} \qquad \text{...(5.5)}$$

From (5.5), $(s_1^2/s_2^2)\gamma$ is distributed as F_{v_1, v_2}. Using properties of the F distribution, we have:

Variable	*Modal Value**	*Mean** $(v_2 > 2)$	*Variance**$(v_2 > 4)$
$\frac{s_1^2}{s_2^2}\gamma$	0.929	1.053	0.120
γ	3.714	4.210	0.480

* Expressions for the modal value, mean and variance of γ are:

Modal Value $= \dfrac{s_1^2}{s_2^2}\dfrac{(v_1-1)}{v_1}\dfrac{v_2}{(v_2+2)}$

Mean $= \dfrac{s_2^2}{s_1^2}\dfrac{v_2}{(v_2-2)} \qquad (v_2 > 2)$

Variance $= \dfrac{s_2^4}{s_1^4}\dfrac{2v_2^2(v_1+v_2-2)}{v_1(v_2-2)^2(v_2-4)} \qquad (v_2 > 4)$

Thus we have selected our prior parameters so as to give γ a modal value = 3.714, a mean = 4.210, and a variance = 0.480. As regards β_0 and β, we employ the prior pdf shown in (4.10), while for the elements of ξ we use the prior assumptions in (4.11). Alternatively, we could use the assumptions of Section 4.2 above and arrive at the same posterior pdf for β and γ.

With the above prior pdfs and our generated data, we used the computer to evaluate the normalising constant of the posterior pdf for β and γ shown in (4.17). In Figure 1.2, we present the contours of this bivariate pdf. The mode is located rather close to the values of β and γ, 1.0 and 4.0, respectively, which we used to generate our data. Also shown in Figure 1.2 are the loci of the conditional modal

Figure 1.2

Contours and Conditional Modes of Joint Posterior pdf for β and γ (Generated Data)

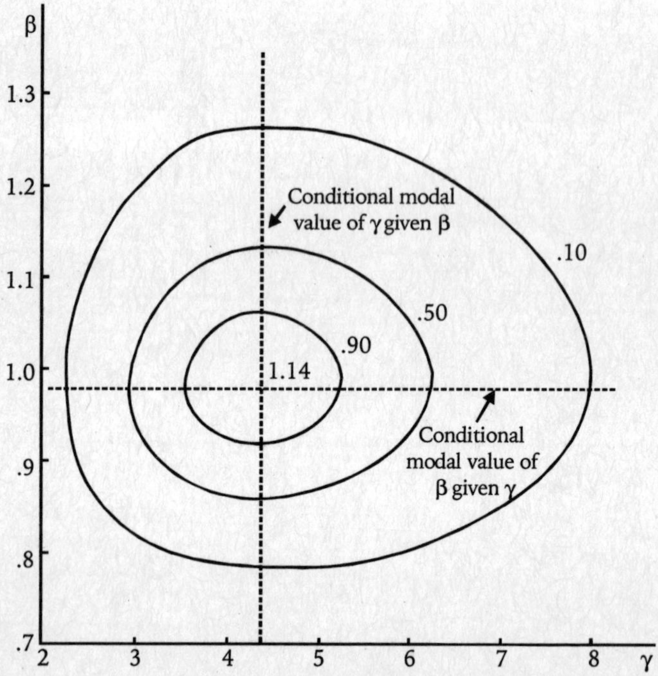

values for β given γ and for γ given β. It is seen that the conditional modal values of β are somewhat insensitive to the conditioning values of γ, at least over the range of γ values considered. Further, it should be realized that the joint posterior pdf for β and γ can be used to make point inference about β and γ.

That is, by using bivariate numerical integration techniques we can evaluate the posterior probability that β and γ lie in a particular region of the parameter space,[12] for example the probability that $0.7 < \beta < 1.2$ and $3.5 < \gamma < 4.5$.

In Figures 1.3a and 1.3b, we present the marginal posterior pdfs for β and γ. It is seen that the posterior pdf for β is centred near the value of β used to generate the data, namely 1.0. In fact the mean of the posterior pdf for β is 1.013 while the variance of this pdf is 0.01357. It is interesting to contrast these results with what is obtained from a least squares regression of y on x for our generated data, namely,

$$\underset{}{\hat{y}_\alpha} = \underset{(0.674)}{2.893} + \underset{(0.948)}{0.876}\ x_\alpha$$

where figures in parentheses are "conventional" standard errors. The least squares estimate of β, 0.876, is seen to be below the posterior mean for β. With respect to the posterior pdf for γ, shown in Figure 1.3b, the information contained in the given sample of data combined with our information has resulted in a posterior mean for γ equal to 4.907 and variance of γ equal to 2.025. With this large variance, the results do not appear inconsistent with the hypothesis that γ is equal to 4.0, the value used to generate our data.

As a second illustrative example of application of the above methods, we consider data on per capita real consumption (C) and per capita real disposable income (Y) relating to 28 countries[13] which Houthakker (1962) presented and analysed in an effort to determine

12. In Zellner (1965) such an approach is applied in the analysis of a bivariate posterior pdf involving the coefficients of a second order autoregressive scheme to make probability statements regarding properties of its solution.

13. For each country, the variables C and Y are each averages of about five to seven annual observations. Houthakker used official exchange rates to express C and Y in common units, namely, U.S. 1955 dollars.

Figure 1.3a

Marginal Posterior pdf for β

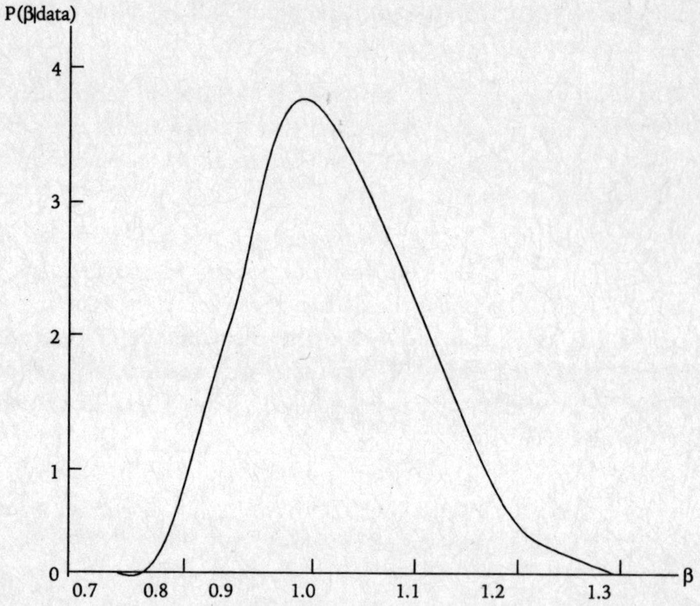

Figure 1.3b

Marginal Posterior pdf for γ

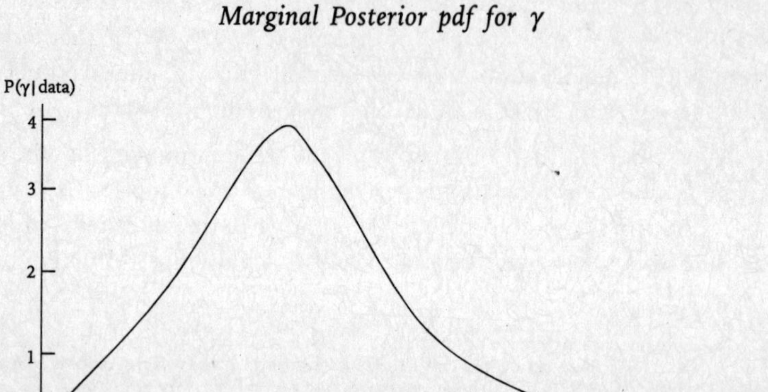

whether the average propensity to consume, C/Y, depends on the level of income, Y. With respect to this issue, some earlier theoretical analysis in Zellner (1960) relating to the behavior of C/Y at low permanent income levels suggests that an alternative to the hypothesis C/Y = constant should be a nonlinear relationship.[14] In particular, this work suggests that as permanent income falls to low values, the average propensity to consume should approach one, that is as $Y \to 0$, $C/Y \to 1$. One function which has this property is the following one:

$$w_\alpha = \ln\left(\frac{C_\alpha / Y_\alpha}{1 - C_\alpha / Y_\alpha}\right) = \beta_0 + \beta \ \ln \ Y_\alpha + u_\alpha \qquad \alpha = 1,2,\ldots,n \qquad \ldots(5.5)$$

with the subscript α, denoting an observation for the αth country and ln denoting natural logarithms. In (5.5) with $\beta<0$ as $Y_\alpha \longrightarrow 0$, $(C_\alpha / Y_\alpha) \longrightarrow 1$. Further if $\beta = 0$, then (5.5) is in agreement with the hypothesis that the, consumption-income ratio does not depend on the level of income.

To begin with, we first ignored possible measurement errors and regressed w_α on ln Y_α. This yielded the following result:[15]

$$\hat{w}_\alpha = \underset{(0.6339)}{3.7745} - \underset{(0.1063)}{0.2074} \ \ln \ Y_\alpha \qquad \alpha = 1, 2, \ldots, 26. \qquad \ldots(5.6)$$

where figures in parentheses are "conventional" standard errors. We see that the coefficient of ln Y_α is negative but accompanied by a fairly substantial standard error. Of course if measurement errors are

14. Note that if we use $C = a + bY$ as an alternative hypothesis to constancy with $a > 0$, then at low levels of Y, $C/Y > 1$ which can hardly be considered reasonable given that C and Y are "permanent" variables. Also, if $C = kY^{1-\delta}$ is entertained as an alternative hypothesis with $\delta > 0$, this implies that $C/Y \to \infty$ as $Y \to 0$ which is certainly an unreasonable formulation of the alternative hypothesis. In fact, Houthakker's analyses resulted in rejection of both these alternatives. However, a visual inspection of Houthakker's residuals suggests that a departure from constancy may be present in the data which he examined.

15. In this computation and those reported below, data for two countries, Panama and Peru, which had consumption-income ratios larger than one, have been omitted. Thus, our sample size is n = 26. Further, using (5.6), the following is the behaviour of C/Y as a function of Y:

Y:	$50	100	200	300	500	1,000	2,000	3,000	5,000	10,000
C/Y:	.951	.944	.936	.930	.923	.912	.900	.892	.882	.866

present in ln Y_α, the estimate of this variable's coefficient may be biased toward zero.[16]

On the problem of possible measurement error in the present data and analysis, we note *at least* the following possible sources of error: (1) errors in Houthakker's proxies for permanent income and consumption, (2) errors associated with the use of exchange rates to express variables in common units, and (3) errors in the underlying national income data for many countries. Obviously, these errors may be systematic and/or random. Given this complicated error situation, we regard the following computations merely as illustrating methods and not necessarily representing an optimal analysis of this complicated body of data.

For present purposes, we shall assume that Houthakker's ratios C_α/Y_α measure what they purport to measure without error. To the extent that C_α and Y_α have *common* random and/or systematic proportional errors, these will cancel when we form the ratio C_α/Y_α. The disturbance term, u_α in (5.5), will be interpreted as a random "country effect" with mean zero and variance σ_u^2, the same for all countries. Further the u_α are assumed normally and independently distributed. We also assume that ln Y_α has an associated random measurement error v_α with zero mean and variance σ_v^2 for $\alpha = 1, 2, \ldots, n$. The v_α are assumed normally and independently distributed. With these assumptions, the analysis of (5.5) reduces to that of the models considered in previous Sections.[17]

In Table 1.1, we present conditional maximum likelihood estimates of β_0 and β in (5.5) for various assumed values of $\gamma = \sigma_v^2/\sigma_u^2$ — see Section 3.1. The results in Table 1.1 can be compared with that shown in (5.6) which assumes $\gamma = 0$. From Table 1.1 it is seen that for $\gamma = 1.0$, the estimate of β is -0.2790 (with stand error 0.1043) which is substantially more negative than the estimate -0.2074 associated with the assumption that $\gamma = 0$. Further it is interesting to observe that the "large sample" standard errors in Table 1.1, computed from the inverse of the information matrix, are not very sensitive to variation in the assumed values for γ.

16. Here we abstract from possible "simultaneous equation" complications and other possible specification errors.

17. Note that if errors in C_α and Y_α were considered separately, the nonlinear form of the dependent variable in (5.5) presents new problems which are under consideration.

Table 1.1

Conditional ML Estimates of Parameters in Equation (5.5) and Associated Standard Errors

Assumed Values for γ	Estimate of β_0	Standard Error for $\hat{\beta}_0$	Estimate of β	Standard Error for $\hat{\beta}$	Estimate of σ^*_u
0.1	3.8085	0.6325	-0.2132	0.1061	0.4570
0.2	3.8441	0.6311	-0.2192	0.1059	0.4559
0.3	3.8813	0.6298	-0.2255	0.1056	0.4548
0.4	3.9204	0.6285	-0.2322	0.1054	0.4536
0.5	3.9613	0.6273	-0.2391	0.1052	0.4524
0.6	4.0041	0.6261	-0.2463	0.1050	0.4511
0.7	4.0490	0.6649	-0.2540	0.1048	0.4497
0.8	4.0960	0.6238	-0.2619	0.1046	0.4483
0.9	4.1452	0.6228	-0.2703	0.1045	0.4468
1.0	4.1968	0.6219	-0.2790	0.1043	0.4453
1.1	4.2506	0.6212	-0.2881	0.1042	0.4436
1.2	4.3070	0.6205	-0.2977	0.1041	0.4419
1.3	4.3658	0.6200	-0.3076	0.1040	0.4400
1.4	4.4271	0.6197	-0.3180	0.1040	0.4382
1.5	4.4909	0.6196	-0.3288	0.1040	0.4362
1.6	4.5574	0.6196	-0.3401	0.1040	0.4341
1.7	4.6263	0.6199	-0.3518	0.1041	0.4320
1.8	4.6978	0.6205	-0.3639	0.1042	0.4297
1.9	4.7716	0.6212	-0.3764	0.1043	0.4274
2.0	4.8478	0.6223	-0.3893	0.1045	0.4249

* Corrected ML estimate — see Section 3.1 above.

Next we turn to a Bayesian analysis of the model in (5.5) with the assumptions about its measurement errors introduced above. In Table 1.2, we present the values for parameters of our prior pdf's which were used to compute posterior pdf's for β and γ using (4.17) above. Also shown in Table 1.2 are some summary measures relating to our pdf's. For example, the posterior mean for β is –0.234 and its variance is 0.00911. From the plot of the posterior pdf for β, shown in Figure 1.4a, we see that the posterior probability that β is positive is quite small. With respect to γ, its posterior mean is equal to 0.431, modal value approximately equal to 0.400, and variance equal to 0.0159. Thus the sample information, when combined with the prior information, has led to a posterior mean for γ somewhat lower than the prior mean.[18] These posterior results for γ suggest that σ_u^2, the variance of the "country effect", may be larger relative to σ_v^2, the variance of the random measurement error in ln Y_α, than our prior assumptions indicate.

Table 1.2

Measures Associated with Prior and Posterior Pdfs for Analysis of Equation (5.5)

Pdf	*Mean*	*Modal Value*	*Variance*
Prior for γ**	1.071	0.875	0.171
Posterior for β	-0.234	-0.238	0.00911
Posterior for γ	0.431	0.400	0.0159

** The parameters of the prior pdf for γ were assigned the following values: $v_1 = v_2 = 30$ and $s_1^2 = s_2^2 = 0.100$.

Figure 1.4a

Marginal Posterior pdf for β Using Houthakker's Data

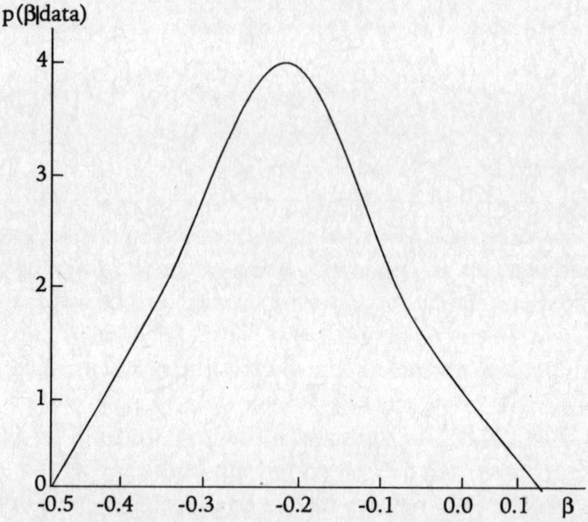

18. As an aside, it is interesting to observe that if we enter Table 5.1 with γ equal to its posterior mean, the conditional ML estimate of β is very close to the mean of the posterior pdf for β.

Figure 1.4b

Marginal Posterior pdf for γ using Houthakker's Data

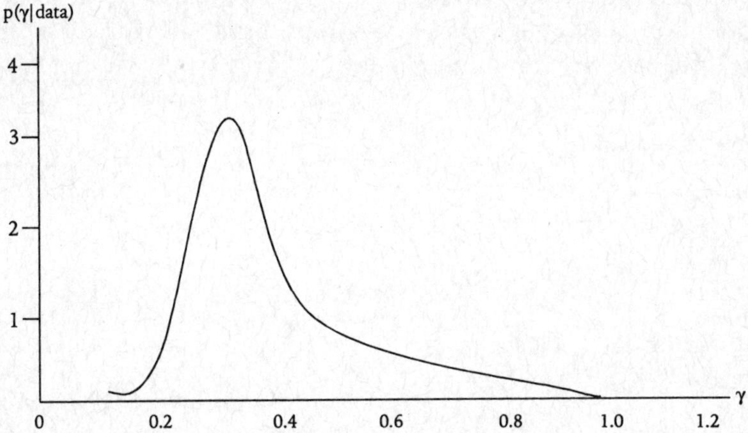

6. CONCLUDING REMARKS

In this paper we have presented a Bayesian approach to the analysis of the classical EVM which has involved a loosening of the prior information required concerning error variances. In fact, the present approach enables an investigator to learn how sample information modifies his prior information about error variances. Further, while we have gone forward above using a "diffuse" prior on the slope and intercept parameters, β and β_0, it would not be difficult to introduce informative prior pdfs for these parameters in the above analysis. In this connection, while the mathematical analysis may appear complex, it is the case that numerical analyses of a bivariate posterior pdf, such as (4.17), can be performed quite easily with a high speed electronic computer. For example, it took just about 0.4 minutes of IBM 7094 computer time to compute the normalising constant for (4.17), the marginal pdf's for β and γ their first two moments, and to list the output. That this numerical analysis can be performed without great difficulty is fortunate given that the outputs are exact finite sample results.

In closing, we note again that much, if not all, economic data contain measurement errors. To proceed blithely with analyses assuming that such errors do not exist may often lead to erroneous inferences. Hopefully, the techniques presented above will be found useful in practice and can be developed further to apply to more general models.

• Research financed in part by the National Science Foundation under grant GS-1350. The comments of S.J. Press, H.V. Roberts and D.L. Wallace were very helpful. Naturally, the authors remain solely responsible for what is presented.

APPENDIX A

In this appendix we present the information matrix for the classical EVM and evaluate its determinant. The information matrix, $I_{\underline{\theta}} = \left\{ -E \dfrac{\partial^2 \log \ell}{\partial \theta_\alpha \partial \theta_\ell} \right\}$, where $\log \ell$ is the logarithm of the likelihood function and θ_α denotes the αth element of the parameter vector

$\underline{\theta}' = (\beta_0, \beta, \xi_1, \xi_2, \ldots, \xi_n, \sigma_u, \sigma_v)$, is, with $\lambda = \sigma_u^2 / \sigma_v^2$:

$$
\begin{array}{ccccccccccc}
 & \beta_0 & \beta & \zeta_1 & \zeta_2 & \cdot\ \cdot\ \cdot & \zeta_n & \sigma_u & \sigma_v & \\
\end{array}
$$

$$
I_{\underline{\theta}} = \frac{1}{\sigma_u^2} \left[\begin{array}{ccccccccc}
 & & & & \cdot\ \cdot\ \cdot & & & & \\
n & \Sigma\xi_\alpha & \beta & \beta & \cdot\ \cdot\ \cdot & \beta & 0 & 0 \\
\Sigma\xi_\alpha & \Sigma\xi_\alpha^2 & \beta\xi_1 & \beta\xi_2 & \cdot\ \cdot\ \cdot & \beta\xi_n & 0 & 0 \\
\beta & \beta\xi_1 & \beta^2+\lambda & 0 & \cdot\ \cdot\ \cdot & 0 & 0 & 0 \\
\beta & \beta\xi_2 & 0 & \beta^2+\lambda & \cdot\ \cdot\ \cdot & 0 & 0 & 0 \\
\cdot & \cdot & \cdot & \cdot & \cdot & \cdot & \cdot & \cdot \\
\cdot & \cdot & \cdot & \cdot & \cdot & \cdot & \cdot & \cdot \\
\cdot & \cdot & \cdot & \cdot & \cdot & \cdot & \cdot & \cdot \\
\beta & \beta\xi_n & 0 & 0 & \cdot\ \cdot\ \cdot & \beta^2+\lambda & 0 & 0 \\
0 & 0 & 0 & 0 & \cdot\ \cdot\ \cdot & 0 & n & 0 \\
0 & 0 & 0 & 0 & \cdot\ \cdot\ \cdot & 0 & 0 & n\lambda
\end{array} \right]
\begin{array}{l} \\ \beta_0 \\ \beta \\ \xi_1 \\ \xi_2 \\ \cdot \\ \cdot \\ \cdot \\ \xi_n \\ \sigma_n \\ \sigma_v \end{array}
\qquad \ldots(A.1)
$$

or

$$
I_{\underline{\theta}} = \frac{1}{\sigma_u^2} \begin{bmatrix} A_{11} & A_{12} & 0 \\ A_{21} & A_{22} & 0 \\ 0 & 0 & A_{33} \end{bmatrix} \qquad \ldots(A.2)
$$

Then

$$
|I_{\underline{\theta}}| = \frac{1}{\sigma_u^2 (n+4)} \left| A_{11} - A_{12} A_{22}^{-1} A_{21} \right| \, |A_{22}| \, |A_{33}|
$$

$$= \frac{n^3\lambda^3(\beta^2+\lambda)^{n-2}\Sigma(\xi_\alpha-\bar{\xi})^2}{\sigma_u^{2(n+4)}}$$

which, as stated in the text, will generally be different from zero even though β_0 and β are not identified. Note that $|I_{\underline{\theta}}|$ grows in value as $\Sigma(\xi_\alpha-\bar{\xi})^2$ and /or β^2 increase in value. Also, for given σ_u^2, smaller the σ_v^2 and thus larger the λ, larger the $|I_{\underline{\theta}}|$.

APPENDIX B

Here we evaluate the square root of the determinant of the conditional information matrix for $\underline{\beta}' = (\beta_0,\beta)$ given ξ, σ_u and σ_v. We rewrite equation (A.2) of Appendix A as follows:

$$I_{\underline{\theta}} = \frac{1}{\sigma_u^2}\begin{bmatrix} C_{11} & C_{12} \\ C_{21} & C_{22} \end{bmatrix} \qquad \text{...(B.1)}$$

where $C_{11} = A_{11}, C_{12} = (A_{12} : 0), C_{21} = C'_{12}$, and

$$C_{22} = \begin{pmatrix} A_{22} & 0 \\ 0 & A_{22} \end{pmatrix}$$

Then the leading submatrix of $I_{\underline{\theta}}^{-1}$, denoted by C^{11}, is given by

$$C^{11} = \sigma_u^2(C_{11} - C_{12}C_{22}^{-1}C_{21})^{-1}. \qquad \text{...(B.2)}$$

The inverse of C^{11}, is the conditional information matrix for $\underline{\beta}$ given ξ,σ_u and σ_v. Then

$$\left|C^{11}\right|^{-\frac{1}{2}} = \frac{n^{\frac{1}{2}}}{\sigma_u^2}\frac{\lambda}{\lambda+\beta^2}\left[\Sigma(\xi_\alpha-\bar{\xi})^2\right]^{\frac{1}{2}}$$

is the square root of the determinant of the conditional information for $\underline{\beta}$ given ξ, σ_u and σ_v which is used in the text in forming our prior pdf.

APPENDIX C

In this appendix we take up the problem of integration over the elements of ξ in arriving at the joint posterior pdf for β and γ, shown in equation (4.17) of the text. On completing the square on the elements of ξ in (4.12) we obtain:

$$p(\underline{\beta}, \underline{\xi}, \sigma_u, \sigma_v \mid \underline{x}, \underline{y}) \propto \qquad \text{...(C.1)}$$

$$\frac{\exp\left\{-\frac{1}{2\sigma_u^2}\left[v_1 s_1^2 + \lambda v_2 s_2^2\right]\right\}\exp\left\{-\left(\frac{\lambda+\beta^2}{2\sigma_u^2}\right)(\underline{\xi}-\underline{\delta})'(\underline{\xi}-\underline{\delta})\right\}\exp\left\{-\frac{\lambda}{2\sigma_u^2(\lambda+\beta^2)}\Sigma(y_\alpha-\beta_0-\beta x_\alpha)^2\right\}}{(\lambda+\beta^2)\sigma_u^{n+v_1+1}\sigma_v^{n+v_2+3}\left[(\underline{\xi}-\bar{\xi}\underline{\ell})'(\underline{\xi}-\bar{\xi}\underline{\ell})\right]^{\frac{n-3}{2}}}$$

where $\lambda = \sigma_u^2/\sigma_v^2$ and $\underline{\delta}$ is an $n \times 1$ vector with elements

$\delta_\alpha = [\beta(y_\alpha - \beta_0) + \lambda x_\alpha]/(\lambda+\beta^2)$, $\alpha = 1,2,\ldots,n$. Now make the following change of variable, α = 1,2 ..., n,

$$z_\alpha = (\xi_\alpha - \delta_\alpha)(\lambda+\beta^2)^{\frac{1}{2}}/\sigma_u \qquad -\infty < z_\alpha < \infty \qquad \text{...(C.2)}$$

or

$$\xi_\alpha = \frac{\sigma_u}{(\lambda+\beta^2)^{\frac{1}{2}}}\left[z_\alpha + \frac{(\lambda+\beta^2)^{\frac{1}{2}}}{\sigma_u}\delta_\alpha\right] \qquad \text{...(C.3)}$$

$$= \frac{\sigma_u}{(\lambda+\beta^2)^{\frac{1}{2}}}(z_\alpha + q_\alpha)$$

where $q_\alpha = (\lambda+\beta^2)^{\frac{1}{2}}\delta_\alpha/\sigma_u$, σ = 1, 2, ..., n. From (C.3) we have

$\Pi d\xi_\alpha = \left[\sigma_u^n/(\lambda+\beta^2)^{\frac{n}{2}}\right]\Pi dz_\alpha$. Thus (C.1) can be written as

$$p(\underline{\beta}, z, \sigma_u, \sigma_v \mid \underline{x}, \underline{y}) \propto \qquad \text{...(C.4)}$$

$$\frac{\exp\left\{-\frac{1}{2\sigma_u^2}\left[v_1 s_1^2+\lambda v_2 s_2^2\right]\exp\left\{-\frac{1}{2}\underline{z}'\underline{z}\right\}\exp\left\{-\frac{\lambda}{2\sigma_u^2(\lambda+\beta^2)}\Sigma(y_\alpha-\beta_0-\beta x_\alpha)^2\right\}\right.}{(\lambda+\beta^2)^{\frac{5}{2}}\sigma_u^{n+v_1-2}\sigma_v^{n+v_2+3}\left[(\underline{z}+\underline{q})'(I_n-\underline{\ell}\underline{\ell}'/n)(\underline{z}+\underline{q})\right]^{\frac{n-3}{2}}}$$

where $\underline{z}'=(z_1,z_2,\ldots,z_n),\underline{q}^1=(q_1,q_2,\ldots,n)$ and I_n denotes an $n\times n$ unit matrix.

Now we wish to show that integrating (C.4) with respect to $\underline{z}$, $-\infty<\underline{z}<\infty$, results in a constant not involving the parameters $\underline{\beta}$, σ_u and σ_v, and this yields equation (4.13) in the text. To do this, we concentrate attention on the factors of (C.4) involving $\underline{z}$, namely,

$$\frac{\exp\left\{-\frac{1}{2}\underline{z}'\underline{z}\right\}}{\left[(\underline{z}+\underline{q})'(I_n-\underline{\ell}\underline{\ell}'/n)(\underline{z}+\underline{q})\right]^{\frac{n-3}{2}}}d\underline{z}. \qquad \ldots(C.5)$$

Let $\underline{w}=\underline{z}+\underline{q}$. Then (C.5) becomes

$$\frac{\exp\left\{-\frac{1}{2}(\underline{w}-\underline{q})'(\underline{w}-\underline{q})\right\}}{\left[\Sigma(w_\alpha-\overline{w})^2\right]^{\frac{n-3}{2}}}d\underline{w} \qquad -\infty<\underline{w}<\infty \qquad \ldots(C.6)$$

Where $\overline{w}=n^{-1}\Sigma w_\alpha$. Now use Helmert's transformation — see Kendall and Stuart (1958, p. 250) — to transform from $\underline{w}$ to $\underline{c}$, that is

$$\begin{aligned}
c_1 &= (w_1-w_2)/\sqrt{2}\\
c_2 &= (w_1+w_2-2w_3)/\sqrt{6}\\
c_3 &= (w_1+w_2+w_3-3w_4)/\sqrt{12}\\
&\ldots\ldots\ldots\ldots\ldots\ldots\\
c_{n-1} &= \left[w_1+w_2+w_3+\ \ldots\ +w_{n-1}-(n-1)w_n\right]/\sqrt{n(n-1)}\\
c_n &= (w_1+w_2+\ \ldots\ +w_n)/\sqrt{n}
\end{aligned} \qquad \ldots(C.7)$$

or $\underline{c} = B\underline{w}$ when B is defined by the relations in (C.7) and is known to be an orthogonal matrix. Then $E\underline{c} = BE\underline{w} = B\underline{q}$ and $\underline{c} = E\underline{c} = B(\underline{w}-\underline{q})$. Therefore $\underline{w} - \underline{q} = B^{-1}(\underline{c} - E\underline{c})$ and

$$(\underline{w}-\underline{q})'(\underline{w}-\underline{q}) = (\underline{c}-E\underline{c})'(B^{-1})'B^{-1}(\underline{c}-E\underline{c}) \quad \text{...(C.8)}$$

$$= (\underline{c}-E\underline{c})'(\underline{c}-E\underline{c}).$$

From properties of Helmert's transformation,

$$\sum_{\alpha=1}^{n}(w_\alpha - \bar{w})^2 = \sum_{\alpha=1}^{n-1} c_\alpha^2. \quad \text{...(C.9)}$$

Thus, in terms of $\underline{c}$, the expression in (C.6) becomes:

$$\frac{\exp\left\{-\frac{1}{2}(\underline{c}-E\underline{c})'(\underline{c}-E\underline{c})\right\}}{\left\{\sum_{\alpha=1}^{n-1} c_\alpha^2\right\}^{\frac{n-3}{2}}} d\underline{c} \qquad -\infty < \underline{c} < \infty \quad \text{...(C.10)}$$

$$= \frac{\exp\left\{-\frac{1}{2}\sum_{\alpha=1}^{n-1}(c_\alpha - \bar{c}_\alpha)^2\right\}}{\left\{\sum_{\alpha=1}^{n-1} c_\alpha^2\right\}^{\frac{n-3}{2}}} \exp\left\{-\frac{1}{2}(c_n - \bar{c}_n)^2\right\} d\underline{c}$$

where $Ec_\alpha = \bar{c}_\alpha$, $\alpha = 1, 2, \ldots, n$. Now the integration with respect to c_n can be performed using properties of the univariate normal pdf while the integration with respect to the remaining c's can be performed using properties of the non-central χ^2 pdf — see Kendall and Stuart (1961, p. 227 ff.) — to yield a constant independent of $\underline{\beta}$, σ_u and σ_v.

In summary then, when (4.12) in the text, or (C.1) in this appendix, is integrated with respect to $\underline{\xi}$, the result is equation (4.13) in the text.

APPENDIX D

The data which we generated under the conditions described in Section 5 are shown below:

Observation Number	*X*	*Y*
1	1.420	3.695
2	6.268	6.925
3	8.854	8.923
4	8.532	14.043
5	-5.398	-0.836
6	13.776	16.609
7	5.278	4.405
8	6.298	9.823
9	9.886	12.611
10	11.362	10.174
11	1.964	4.987
12	1.406	6.647
13	0.002	2.873
14	3.212	4.015
15	9.042	10.204
16	1.474	1.953
17	8.528	10.672
18	7.348	9.157
19	6.690	8.552
20	5.796	10.250

References

Birch, M.W. (1964). "A Note on the Maximum Likelihood Estimation of a Linear Structural Relationship", *Journal American Statistical Association*, 50, 1175-78.

Box, G.E.P. and G.C. Tiao (1962). "A Further Look at Robustness via Bayes Theorem", *Biometrika*, 49, 419-33.

Ferber, R. (1966). "The Reliability of Consumer Surveys of Financial Holdings: Demand Deposits", *Journal of American Statistical Association*, 61, 91-103.

Friedman, M. (1957). *A Theory of the Consumption Function*, Princeton : Princeton University Press.

Galenson, W. and A. Zellner (1957). "International Comparison of Unemployment Rates", in the National Bureau of Economic Research Volume, *The Measurement and Behaviour of Unemployment*, Princeton : Princeton University Press, 439-581.

Geisser, S. (1965). "Bayesian Estimation in Multivariate Analysis", *Annals of Mathematical Statistics*, 60, 150-59.

Houthakker, H.S. (1962). "On Some Determinants of Saving in Developed and Underdeveloped Countries", presented to International Economic Association's International Congress on Economic Development, Vienna, 1962, and reprinted in E.A.G. Robinson (ed.), *Problems of Economic Development*, New York: Macmillan Co., 1965.

James, W. and M.C. Stein (1961). "Estimation with Quadratic Loss Function", in J. Neyman (ed.), *Proceedings of the Fourth Berkeley Sumposium on Mathematical Statistics and Probability*, Berkeley and Los Angeles: University of California Press, 1, 361-79.

Jeffreys, H. (1961). *Theory of Probability* (3rd ed.), Oxford: Clarendon Press.

Johnston, J. (1963). *Econometric Methods*, New York: McGraw-Hill Book Co.

Kendall, M.G. and A. Stuart (1958). *The Advanced Theory of Statistics*: *Volume 1*, Distribution Theory, London: Charles Griffen & Co., Ltd.

————. and ————. (1961). *The Advanced Theory of Statistics*: *Volume* 2, Inference and Relationship, London: Charles Griffen & Co., Ltd.

Kiefer J. and J.Wolfowitz (1956). "Consistency of the Maximum Likelihood Estimator in the Presence of Infinitely Many Incidental Parameters", *Annals of Mathematical Statistics*, 27, 887-906.

Lindley, D.V. (1947). "Regression Lines and the Linear Functional Relationship", *Journal of Royal Statistical Society* (Supplement) 9, 218.

————. (1965). *Introduction to Probability and Statistics from a Bayesian Viewpoint (Part II)*, Cambridge: University Press.

Madansky, A. (1959). "The Fitting of Straight Lines when Both Variables are Subject to Error", *Journal of American Statistical Association*, 54, 173-205.

Malinvaud, E. (1964). *Methodes Statistiques de l 'Econometric*, Paris : Dunod.

Modigliani, F. and A. Ando (1960). "The 'Permanent Income' and the 'Life Cycle' Hypothesis of Saving Behaviour: Comparison and Tests", in I. Friend and R. Jones (ed.) *Proceedings of the Conference on Consumption and Saving, Vol. II*, Philadelphia: University of Pennsylvania, 49-174.

Morgenstern, O. (1963). *On the Accuracy of Economic Observations*, Princeton : Princeton University Press.

Neyman, J. and E.L. Scott (1948). "Consistent Estimates Based on Partially Consistent Observations", *Econometrica*, 16, 1-32.

Raiffa, H.A. and R.S. Schlaifer (1961). *Applied Statistical Decision Theory*, Boston: Graduate School of Business Administration, Harvard University USA.

Reiersol, O. (1950). "Indentifiability of a Linear Relation between Variables which are Subject to Error", *Econometrica*, 18, 375-89.

Shannon, C.E. (1949). "The Mathematical Theory of Communication", Bell System Technical Journal, July-October, 1948, reprinted in Shannon, C.E. and W. Weaver, *The Mathematical Theory of Communication*, Urbana: University of Illinois Press, 3-91.

Stein, C.M. (1956). "Inadmissibility of the Usual Estimator for the Mean of a Multivariate Normal Distribution", in J. Neyman (ed.), *Proceedings of the Third Berkeley Symposium on Mathematical Statistics and Probability*, Berkeley and Los Angeles: University of California Press, 1, 197-206.

————. (1962). "Confidence Sets for the Mean of a Multivariate Normal Distribution", *Journal of the Royal Statistical Society*, (Series B), 24, 265-85.

Zellner, A. (1958). "A Statistical Analysis of Provisional Estimates of Gross National Product and Its Components", *Journal of the American Statistical Association*, 53, 54-65.

————. (1960). "Tests of Some Basic Propositions in the Theory of Consumption", *American Economic Review* (Proceedings), 50, 565-73.

————. (1965). "Bayesian Inference and Simultaneous Equation Econometric Models", paper presented to the *First World Congress of the Econometric Society*, Rome, Sept., 1965.

2

Profit Maximising Estimators and Medical Decision Rules

V.K. CHETTY

1. INTRODUCTION

When the relationship between actions and outcomes is deterministic, choosing an optimal action is conceptually simple: evaluate the profit of each action and choose the one that maximises the objective function. Given the limits of current knowledge, causal relations in behavioural and biological sciences are at best stochastic. Treatments can result in a variety of outcomes, each of which occurs with some probability. If the relevant probability distribution is known for each treatment, an optimal action could again be chosen by evaluating the expected profit of each action and choosing the best one. When the probability distribution is not known, however, the problem is more complex. Here the physician or the policy maker faces two sub-problems: (1) Figure out the properties of the probability distribution using available experimental or observational data. (2) Choose an optimal action given this information.

A popular and intuitive approach to choice under uncertainty addresses this problem in two corresponding steps: (1) Estimate the parameters of a probability distribution using some criterion such as minimising the sum of squared errors or maximum likelihood. (2) Choose an action to minimise the expected loss (or maximise expected profit) using the original criterion relevant for the outcome of the action. This approach, which attempts to separate the problem into one of estimation and prediction, first develops a "good" estimate (one that is supposed to be useful for many problems) and then chooses an optimal action, pretending that the estimate is known with certainty in this second stage.

Economists have long recognised that this approach is theoretically sub-optimal: Chetty (1968) noted that "it seems desirable not to introduce the estimate of a parameter as known with certainty when one is not really so certain about it." Bayesian procedures for joint estimation and prediction that make assumptions on distributional forms have since been introduced. But a non-parametric method that avoids this conceptual difficulty has not been clearly formulated or tested from a frequentist point of view. In this paper, we propose such a method of computing an optimal decision rule, which outperforms the conventional procedure in both small and large samples. This method, which we label "c-min", directly computes the optimal decision rule that will minimise error costs using historical data. The criterion that is of relevance to outcomes is used to simultaneously choose the probability distribution as well as in computing the optimal action. This one step approach to solving decision problems under uncertainty takes the view that there is no "true" estimate that should be obtained before prediction; rather, the estimate should be chosen based on the purpose for which it is ultimately used.

This paper contrasts the properties of these two approaches to estimation in the context of diabetes management. Specifically, we study the problem of choosing the optimal insulin dosage for a patient whose blood sugar follows an *unknown* stochastic process. The cost of a blood sugar that falls below a given level (set by the American Diabetic Association) is hypoglycemia, which may result in extreme exhaustion or even death; the cost of high blood sugar is an increased potential for long run complications such as blindness and kidney failure. The loss due to an improper dosage is therefore asymmetric, and is a function of the absolute deviation from the target set by the ADA.

We focus on diabetes as an application of the c-min approach for three reasons: first, in human and economic terms, diabetes is one of the most costly diseases: 16 million or 6 per cent of Americans have diabetes, generating more than $100 billion annually in health-related expenditures (ADA *Facts and Figures*). In fact, the President's Quality Commission has selected diabetes and depression as the first two areas for which it will mount an effort to improve clinical quality of care. Second, there is substantial evidence of the existence of avoidable medical errors in diabetes. In a large representative sample of 168,000 people with diabetes in the Medicare fee-for-service group, only about 40 per cent received an annual eye exam and 20 per cent received the recommended two specialised blood tests per year to monitor diabetes control (General Accounting Office, Health, Education and Human Services Division Report). A third advantage of studying diabetes is one of practicality: it is easier to measure outcomes and define errors in the management of diabetes than for other diseases. There is a specific evidence-based process of care recommended by the American Diabetic Association (ADA) and there are reliable quantitative measures of outcomes, such as glycated haemoglobin (HbA1*c*) and fasting and postprandial plasma glucose.

The plan of the paper is as follows: Section 2 briefly reviews the statistical literature on estimation with various loss functions. Section 3 presents the details of the blood sugar management problem in a statistical framework. Section 4 begins with a derivation of the optimal rule when the distribution of blood sugar levels for a given patient is known. It then derives and explains the motivation for four feasible estimation methods: (1) Ordinary least squares, where the "good" estimate is obtained and is used as a predictor, (2) "Corrected" least squares, where the OLS estimate and an assumed distributional form are treated as known and an optimal action given the loss function for the blood sugar outcomes is chosen, (3) Non-parametric c-min, where a one step procedure is used to find the best target without any assumption on distributional form, (4) Parametric c-min, where information on distributional form is taken as known in computing the best estimate. In Section 5, small sample and asymptotic properties of these estimators are compared analytically and using Monte-Carlo methods. It is shown that the corrected LS estimate is outperformed both in small samples and asymptotically by non-parametric c-min when the distributional form is not known and by parametric c-min when it is known. Section 6 describes preliminary results from an application of c-min to real data from diabetic patients. Section 7 concludes.

2. A REVIEW OF ESTIMATION METHODS

There is an implicit cost of errors in any method of estimation. Loss functions are used to evaluate the consequences of any statistical decision. Wald (1939) remarked that:

> "The question as to how the form of the weight [loss] function should be determined is not a mathematical or statistical one. The statistician who wants to test certain hypotheses must first determine the relative importance of all possible errors, which will depend upon the special purposes of his investigation."

The method of least squares originated in astronomy and geodesy in the context of combining repeated measurements. This symmetric, quadratic loss function was introduced by Legendre (1805), who made the following categorical remarks supporting his method:

> "Of all the principles that can be used for this purpose, I think there is none more general, more exact, or easier to apply than that which we have used in this work; it consists of making the sum of squares of the errors a minimum. By this method, a kind of equilibrium is established among the errors which, since it prevents from dominating, is appropriate for revealing the state of the system which most nearly approaches the truth."

Legendre's method was in fact suitable for his particular problem – defining a standard international unit of length, the meter, to replace the arbitrarily measured yard, defined as the distance from the middle of a British King's chest to the tip of his extended arm. This task required estimating the distance between Montjouy and Dunkirk along the meridian. The problem was to estimate the true distance as accurately as possible, implying that positive and negative errors are equally bad and that large errors were particularly undesirable. Hence, a symmetric quadratic loss function was an intuitive and appropriate choice for the task.

A formal statistical theory of errors that supported the use of least squares was later developed by Gauss (1809) and Laplace (1810). The least squares estimate of a linear predictor was shown to possess desirable statistical properties: it coincides with the conditional mean for normally distributed variables and is the best linear unbiased estimator for random variables with any distribution. Computational ease and the exact sampling theory of least squares estimators further increased its popularity. Thus, a method invented to deal with experimental errors in the physical sciences has gained universal acceptance over the past 200 years, leading to its use with little or no modification in biological and social sciences.

Unfortunately, the assumption of symmetric, quadratic error costs is not always reasonable in social and biological problems, as illustrated by the grave consequences of ignoring the sign of the error in diabetes. Moreover, the problems in such fields may not call for an unbiased estimate of the mean. Though alternative methods had been proposed even before Legendre's work, these methods are gaining popularity only in recent years. The median, or the least absolute deviations method (LAD), was used by Galilee (1632), Boscovich (1757), and Laplace (1793) but its computational difficulties made it unpopular. Several biased estimates have also been proposed to deal with outliers. These include resistant regression (Rousseeuw and Leroy 1987), trimmed mean, M-estimates (Huber 1964), ridge regression (Hoerl and Kernard 1970), and shrinkage estimates (Mayor and Wilke 1973). In recent years, statisticians have started investigating the advantages of using biased estimators (Rao and Toutenburg 1995, Toutenburg and Trenkler 1990, Trenkler and Toutenburg 1990).

A few studies have examined the joint problem of estimation and prediction posed above, and some of these have made use of asymmetric loss functions from the Bayesian point of view. Varian (1975) introduced the asymmetric linex loss function for estimating real estate values. Under assessment results in an approximately linear loss of revenue while over assesment often results in appeals with addendant, substantial litigation costs. The Challenger episode is a dramatic example of the serious consequences of using symmetric loss functions to evaluate the reliability of a system (see Dalal *et al.*, 1989, Thompson and Basu 1996). Fisher (1962) and Zellner and Chetty (1965) provided methods for joint estimation and decision for regression models with squared-error loss functions. Prediction and control problems in a simple regression model with asymmetric cost functions have been studied by Zellner and Geisel (1968) and Zellner (1986).

An important advantage of ordinary least squares relative to the Bayesian methods developed to deal with estimation and prediction jointly is that it is non-parametric. Least squares coefficients can be computed without making any assumptions about the distributional form of the random variables involved. The desirable properties of consistency and unbiasedness obtain without these assumptions as well. The Bayesian models rely on knowing the distributional forms of the random variables involved in order to develop formulae to update prior beliefs given new information. The theoretical contribution of the present study is a frequentist, non-parametric counterpart to least squares for the problem of joint estimation and prediction with a generic loss function.

3. THE PROBLEM OF INSULIN DOSE CHOICE

One major problem that a diabetic patient may face is that his pancreas does not produce enough insulin to metabolise the sugars he consumes. Such a patient's blood sugar level at any time t, y_t, is typically higher than the level y^* recommended for normal individuals by the guidelines of the ADA. This excess blood sugar affects vital organs such as eyes and kidneys in the long run. He must therefore supplement his pancreatic function by taking insulin. The reduction in blood sugar level due to an increase in insulin dose, d, has been well studied; we denote this relationship by a monotonic increasing function $b(d)$. If the blood sugar level of a patient was constant at y over time, the choice of insulin dose would simply be d s.t. $b(d) = y - y^*$.

Unfortunately, the blood sugar levels of these diabetic patients fluctuate considerably over time. The reason is simple: "meetings and events could occur without warning, work hours may vary, meals are delayed or missed, and eating is commonly done on the run....Different people exercise more or less and at different times of the day." (Walsh and Roberts, 1994). In general, the distribution of blood sugar levels at time t will be a stochastic function of various factors observable at time t–1, such as a sample of past blood sugar readings and weight, height, cholesterol, etc, which we label x_{t-1}. Hence, the physician can view blood sugar levels as following an unknown stochastic process, where y_t follows some cumulative distribution function $F(y_t | x_{t-1})$ that depends on the patient's genetic makeup, exercise and meal patterns, etc.

Recognising that there will necessarily be some deviation of y_t from y^*, regardless of the level of insulin, the physician's problem is to prescribe an insulin dose that keeps y_t close to y^*. An important point that must be taken into account is that the costs (for patients or providers) of a blood sugar level that is too low are different from the costs of one that is too high; that is, the loss function is asymmetric. Excess insulin can result in severe hypoglycemia, that is, $y_t << y^*$, leading to potential comas or seizures, and possibly death.

In 1997, there were 12,440 admissions for serious hypoglycemia, with an average charge of $7,332 (data from HCUP). This implies an estimated cost of $91.2 million for admissions for hypoglycemia per annum for payors. On the other hand, as we have noted above, hyperglycemia, that is $y_t > y^*$, is also undesirable from a long-run perspective both for payors, who must incur increased healthcare costs, and the patient, who may experience a deterioration in the quality of life. Studies find that tight glycemic control can result "in a gain of 920,000 person-years of sight" (Aiello *et al.*, 1998), and "a 50 per cent reduction in 86,000 diabetes-related amputations each year, with a saving of $360 million"(CDC *Diabetes At A Glance*, 2000). Safe diabetic management thus requires a delicate balance between excessive and inadequate therapies.

After weighting the probability of undesirable events such as hospital admissions or retinopathy by their costs, one can formulate the cost of a blood sugar level that is too low (a negative error), c_n, and the cost of a blood sugar level that is too high (a positive error), c_p. A larger deviation from y^* leads to a larger probability of an undesirable event; we assume here that the costs increase linearly with the size of the deviation. Given the costs, the insulin dose choice problem in period T can be formally stated as:

$$\min_d L(d) = E_{F(y_T|x_{T-1})}[c_n(y^* - (y_T - b(d))^+ + c_p((y_T - b(d)) - y^*)^+]$$

with the notation $a^+ = a$ if $a > 0$; 0 else.

Letting $\hat{y} = b(d) + y^*$, this problem can be rewritten as

$$\min_{\hat{y}} L(\hat{y}) = E_{F(y_T|x_{T-1})}[c_n(\hat{y} - y_T)^+ + c_p(y_T - \hat{y})^+]$$

where the dose choice can be recovered by finding d^* s.t. $b(d) = \hat{y} - y^*$.

In the reformulated problem, $\hat{y}$ can be interpreted as the physician's target blood sugar level, which would lead to the ideal outcome given insulin dose d^*. Deviations above and below this target $\hat{y}$ map linearly into deviations above and below y^* for a fixed dosage d^*. The problem of choosing $\hat{y}$ is hence equivalent to choosing the dose itself. As the latter formulation allows us to avoid going into the details of the relationship $b(d)$ between insulin and blood sugar levels, we work with this objective function below.

The physician's problem is complicated by the fact that he does not know the $F(y_t|x_{t-1})$ used in taking the expectation needed to compute $L(\hat{y})$. He does, however, have some past observations of $\{(x_{t-1}, y_t)_{t=1,\ldots,N_H}\}$ pairs for the patient that can help him estimate this distribution. His problem is thus one of joint estimation and prediction: he must estimate $F(y_t|x_{t-1})$ and use this information to prescribe an insulin dosage d (by choosing $\hat{y}$).

To make the problem more concrete, let us consider a realistic example. Suppose a patient is currently on 49 units of regular insulin and has three fasting blood sugar readings of y = 50, 55 and 216 mg/dL in the past three weeks. According to accepted norms, a patient is hyperglycemic, if her blood sugar is above 105 mg/dL and hypoglycemic if it is below 60 mg/dL. With a target sugar level of y^* = 100, should the physician increase or decrease the patient's insulin dosage for the next week? What is the size of the change in insulin dosage that should be made in light of these blood sugar readings?

4. SOLVING THE DOSAGE CHOICE PROBLEM

Prediction when the Parameters are Known

It is useful to begin by finding the optimal dosage when the probability distribution of the patient's blood sugar, $F(y_T|x_{T-1})$, is known. As all the distributions in this section are conditioned on x_{T-1}, we denote the conditional distribution simply by $F(y_T)$ below. We can rewrite the expected loss of choosing $\hat{y}$ as

$$L(\hat{y}) = c_n \int_0^{\hat{y}} (\hat{y} - y)dF + c_p \int_{\hat{y}}^{\infty} (y - \hat{y})dF. \qquad \ldots(1)$$

Differentiating w.r.t. $\hat{y}$, we have,

$$c_n F(\hat{y}) - c_p(1 - F(\hat{y})) = 0 \qquad \ldots(2)$$

$$\Rightarrow \hat{y} = F^{-1}\left(\frac{c_p}{c_n + c_p}\right)$$

Since $\dfrac{\partial^2 L}{\partial \hat{y}^2} = (c_n + c_p) f(\hat{y}) \geq 0$, where $f(y_t)$ is the density of y_t, $\hat{y}$ minimises the expected loss.

Note that when $c_n = c_p$, the error costs are equal and the optimal predictor is the median. More generally, the optimal predictors are the percentiles corresponding to $\frac{c_p}{c_n + c_p}$. As the relative cost of positive error (hyperglycemia) increases, the predicted value of $\hat{y}$ decreases because the physician is more inclined to keep blood sugar low and avoid long-run complications.

If y is normally distributed with mean μ and standard deviation σ, the formula reduces to

$$\hat{y}_{Truth} = \mu + \sigma\Phi^{-1}\left(\frac{c_p}{c_n + c_p}\right) \quad \ldots(3)$$

where Φ denotes the distribution function of the standard Normal distribution. This estimator, which is the ideal (but infeasible) estimator for the Normal case, will be used as a benchmark below. Note that if $c_n = c_p$, $\hat{y} = \mu$ since the mean and median coincide for the Normal.

Using the necessary condition (2), the minimum expected loss is given by

$$L = L(F_y^{-1}(\tfrac{c_p}{c_n+c_p})) = -c_n\int_0^{\hat{y}} ydF + c_p\int_{\hat{y}}^{\infty} ydF$$

$$= -c_n\int_0^{\hat{y}} yf(y)dy + c_p\int_{\hat{y}}^{\infty} yf(y)dy$$

$$= -c_n\int_0^{\hat{y}} (y-\mu)f(y)dy + c_p\int_{\hat{y}}^{\infty} (y-\mu)f(y)dy - c_n\mu F(\hat{y}) + c_p\mu(1-F(\hat{y}))$$

$$= -c_n\int_0^{\hat{y}} (y-\mu)f(y)dy + c_p\int_{\hat{y}}^{\infty} (y-\mu)f(y)dy - c_n\mu\tfrac{c_p}{c_n+c_p} + c_p\mu(1-\tfrac{c_p}{c_n+c_p})$$

$$= -c_n\int_0^{\hat{y}} (y-\mu)f(y)dy + c_p\int_{\hat{y}}^{\infty} (y-\mu)f(y)dy$$

If y is normally distributed with mean μ and standard deviation σ, this reduces to

$$L_{Truth} = \frac{\sigma}{\sqrt{2\pi}}(c_n + c_p)\exp\left\{\frac{-1}{2\sigma^2}(\hat{y}-\mu)^2\right\}$$

$$L^* = \frac{\sigma}{\sqrt{2\pi}}(c_n + c_p)\exp\left\{\frac{-\left[F^{-1}\left(\frac{c_p}{c_n + c_p}\right)\right]^2}{2}\right\} \text{using}(3).$$

If blood sugar levels are normally distributed with some mean and variance, L^* provides a lower bound on the expected loss that can be attained by the four feasible estimators discussed in the next section.

Joint Estimation and Prediction

Now suppose that the probability distribution of $y_t|x_{t-1}$ is not known. Suppose the true model controlling blood sugars is the following:

$$y_t = \alpha + \beta x_{t-1} + \varepsilon_t \qquad \text{...(4)}$$

where $\varepsilon_t \overset{iid}{\sim} F[0, \sigma^2]$

In the previous section, we essentially assumed that the physician knows $\gamma = \{\alpha, \beta\}$ for the patient he is treating. We now analyse the methods of choosing insulin dosage when she does not know γ and must use a data from the patient's history $\left\{H = (x_{t-1}, y_t)_{t=1,\ldots\ldots,N_H}\right\}$ to estimate the stochastic process that his blood sugar is following. For example, x_{t-1} could be the fasting plasma glucose observed in period t-1.

There are now two sources of errors in choosing a dosage: those made in estimating γ and those made in predicting y_t. When the estimate is used for prediction, estimation errors will contribute to prediction errors. One intuitive possibility is to first come up with an unbiased, consistent estimate of γ either by ordinary least squares or postulating a probability distribution for the random variables and maximising the likelihood function. Either of these estimates, $\hat{\gamma}_{OLS}$ or $\hat{\gamma}_{ML}$, can then be treated as known and used to derive the expected cost or risk-minimising prediction using the formula above,

$\hat{y} = F_{\hat{\mu}}^{-1}\left(\frac{c_p}{c_n + c_p}\right)$ after making a distributional assumption about the form of *F*.

As a reference point, note that one could predict future blood sugar simply using the unbiased estimate obtained by least squares and ignore the asymmetric loss function for the outcomes completely. Since it is an unbiased, consistent estimate of the next blood sugar reading, this predictor may be of some value in and of itself. This predictor is:

$$\hat{y}_{OLS} = \hat{\alpha}_{OLS} + \hat{\beta}_{OLS}\, x_{T-1}$$

The OLS predictor can be corrected to take into account the asymmetric, absolute deviation loss function using the formula above using $\hat{\mu} = \hat{\alpha}_{OLS} + \hat{\beta}_{OLS}\, x_{T-1}$ as the "true" mean. In this case one must make an assumption on the distribution form of *F*, the probability law governing the error terms, in order to calculate $F_{\hat{\mu}}^{-1}(\bullet)$. One natural choice is to assume Normality, in which case the estimator takes the form given in (3), with μ replaced by $\hat{\mu}$. This motivates the following estimator, which we call *Corrected LS* (CLS):

$$\hat{y}_{CLS} = \hat{\alpha}_{OLS} + \hat{\beta}_{OLS}\, x_{T-1} + \sigma\Phi^{-1}\left(\frac{c_p}{c_n + c_p}\right)$$

The key question is whether it is optimal to separate estimation and prediction, as above. One problem with these two step procedures is that the implicit loss function (squared error loss) used to evaluate the estimation errors in coming up with an unbiased estimator of γ is different from the loss function used for the prediction errors. Ideally, one may conjecture that the choice of *both* the estimator $\hat{\gamma}$ and predictor $\hat{y}$ should be made simply to minimise the *expected* cost or risk given in (1), associated with the ultimate costs of having deviations in blood sugar from *y**. A second problem with the two-stage technique is that the correction stage (prediction) is feasible only if the probability distributions are known or can be estimated with reasonable accuracy.

Both problems can be solved by another method, "c-min", which minimises expected loss of prediction using the historical sample data to simultaneously estimate the probability distribution and the prediction rule. The basic idea is that a predictor that minimises the observed cost of predicting the sample values in the patient's history should also do well in minimising the costs associated with predicting the future values of *y*, since these follow the same stochastic process. The algorithm can best be described iteratively. Pick any value for the parameter γ, say $\gamma_0 = \{\alpha_0 + \beta_0\}$, and consider the associated prediction rule:

$$\hat{y}_t = \alpha_0 + \beta_0 x_{t-1} \qquad \ldots(5)$$

The *historical* cost of this rule is

$$L_H(\gamma_0) = \sum_{t=1}^{N_H} c_n(\alpha_0 + \beta_0 x_{t-1} - y_t)^+ + c_p \max(y_t - (\alpha_0 + \beta_0 x_{t-1}))^+$$

We can choose $\hat{\gamma}_{c\ min} = \arg\min_\gamma C(\gamma)$ by numerical methods or (in some special cases) analytically. The target blood sugar is then

$$\hat{y}_{c\ min} = \hat{\alpha}_{c\ min} + \hat{\beta}_{c\ min} x_{T-1}$$

As in ordinary least squares analysis, there is no need to make any assumptions about the form of *F* to obtain some desirable properties. As discussed in the next section, the desirable property here is that the loss of the c-min estimator approaches the lower bound on expected loss, *L**, asymptotically. However, if one does know the form of error distribution, *F*, one can reduce the expected loss by taking this information into account and imposing this form on *F*. This motivates the "parametric c-min" estimator. For instance, if $\varepsilon_t \overset{iid}{\sim} N[0, \sigma^2]$, we can define the historical cost as

$$L_H(\gamma_0) = \sum_{t=1}^{T} c_n \left(\sigma\Phi^{-1}\left(\frac{c_p}{c_n + c_p}\right) + \alpha_0 + \beta_0 x_{t-1} - y_t \right)^+$$

$$+ c_p \left(y_t - \left(\sigma\Phi^{-1}\left(\frac{c_p}{c_n + c_p}\right) + \alpha_0 + \beta_0 x_{t-1} \right) \right)^+$$

and choose $\hat{\gamma}_{c\ min\ p} = \arg\min_{\gamma} C(\gamma)$ and $\hat{\gamma}_{c\ min} = \hat{\alpha}_{c\ min} + \hat{\beta}_{c\ min} x_{T-1}$

$$+\sigma\Phi^{-1}\left(\frac{c_p}{c_n + c_p}\right).$$

We thus have four feasible choices for the target blood sugar level $\hat{y}$, in period T: $\hat{y}_{OLS}$, $\hat{y}_{CLS}$, $\hat{y}_{c\min}$, and $\hat{y}_{c\min p}$. These estimators are compared with each other and the benchmark estimator $\hat{y}_{Truth}$ in the following section.

5. SMALL-SAMPLE AND ASYMPTOTIC PROPERTIES

Small Sample Analytics

C-min does not introduce any auxiliary loss functions beyond the original one specified by the nature of the problem. If the patient's history is indeed reflective of his future, one expects that it should outperform the CLS technique in small samples because it essentially imposes fewer constraints on the minimisation problem.

To show this formally, we write

$$\hat{y}_{c\min} = \arg\min_{\hat{\gamma},\hat{y}} L_H(\hat{y})$$

$$\hat{y}_{CLS} = \arg\min_{\hat{\gamma},\hat{y}} L(\hat{y};\mu,F)$$

$$\text{s.t. (1) } \hat{\gamma} = \arg\min \textstyle\sum_{t=1}^{N_H} \left(y_t - \hat{\alpha} - \hat{\beta}x_{t-1}\right)^2$$

$$\text{(2) } \mu = \hat{\alpha} + \hat{\beta}x_{T-1}$$

$$\text{(3) } \varepsilon_t \overset{iid}{\sim} F = N\left[0,\sigma^2\right]$$

Since $E_H L_H(\hat{y}) = L(\hat{y};\mu)$ by the assumption that on average history reflects the truth, under some regularity conditions (allowing us to interchange the order of differentiation and integration), $EL_{c\ min} = \min_{\hat{\gamma},\hat{y}} L(\hat{y};\mu) \leq EL_{CLS} = \min_{\hat{\gamma},\hat{y}} L(\hat{y};\mu)$ s.t. $(1-3)$ because the former method searches over a larger domain.

The argument above implies that c-min (weakly) outperforms CLS in small samples *on average*. For particular draws of *H*, it is quite possible that CLS will in fact do better (of course, whether this will happen can only be determined ex-post). The driving force for the result is that c-min does not impose restriction (1), which yields unbiasedness of the estimators at the expense of constraining the choice of the predictor, which is of ultimate interest to the physician and patient.

Note that if condition (3) in the CLS procedure is in fact true, then imposing it can only help in the prediction procedure, as noted above. This is one force that helps CLS outperform least squares in certain draws of *H* – if the draw is unreflective of the true distribution, this added restriction in CLS helps bring the prediction closer to what it would be if the historical loss function were more reflective of the true loss function. However, it remains true that c-min will outperform CLS on average because *H* is reflective of the truth on average. As noted above, the parametric c-min estimator can be used when the form of *F* is known, where condition (3) is imposed on the c-min problem as posed above and this advantage of CLS is eliminated.

If condition (3) is imposed but is *not* true, the CLS estimator performs worse because an improper restriction has been placed on the problem. In this case, c-min is even more likely to outperform CLS. Knowing the distributional form with considerable accuracy is therefore crucial for using CLS successfully.

Small Sample Monte-Carlo Experiments

To get a sense of the magnitude of the difference in performance of these estimators, we conduct numerical simulations when the assumed form of *F* is correct and when it is not. In each experiment, a sequence of historical samples $\left\{ (x_{t-1}, y_t)_{t=1,\ldots,N_H} \right\}$ are generated for increasing values of N_H. Each estimator is computed for the given sample data, and is used to predict blood sugars in a fixed test sample of size N_P = 10,000 generated in the same way as the historical samples. The average loss of each of the predictors is then computed for the test sample; given the large value of N_P, it can be assumed that the mean losses on the test sample are approximately the expected losses of the estimators conditional on the history sample observed. Throughout, we assume that the true parameters controlling the evolution of blood sugar levels are $\alpha = 0$ and $\beta = 1$.

In the first exercise, the costs of positive and negative errors are taken as $c_n = 4$ and $c_p = 1$. The explanatory variables, x_{t-1}, are drawn from a Normal distribution with mean 100 and standard deviation 10. The error terms are generated from a Normal distribution with mean 0 and standard deviation 10. The values of y_t are obtained as specified by the model: $y_t = x_{t-1} + \varepsilon_t$. The results of this experiment are shown in Figure 2.1.

Figure 2.1

Small Sample Costs for Prediction Rules

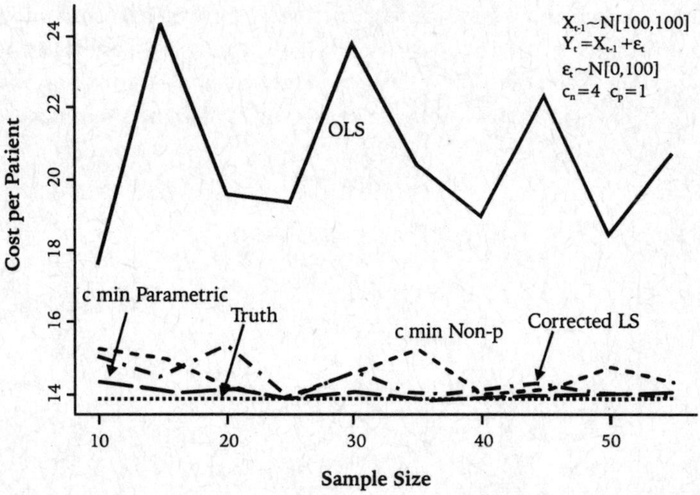

The average loss for the benchmark predictor $\hat{y}_{\text{Truth}}$ is constant with respect to the size of the historical data because the history does not affect this prediction rule, which takes the true parameters as known. As anticipated, the loss of $\hat{y}_{\text{Truth}}$ (13.85) provides a lower bound for the loss of the other estimators. OLS has significantly higher costs (20.55) because it does not take the relative costs of the errors into account in choosing blood sugar targets. The other three estimators, however, all come very close to the lower bound even when historical information is very limited. The non-parametric $\hat{y}_{c\,min}$ (avg. cost 14.38) is outperformed by $\hat{y}_{CLS}$ (avg. cost 14.38) and $\hat{y}_{c\,min-p}$ (avg. cost 14.02) in small samples because it does not take advantage of the information that the error terms are normally distributed. As expected, $\hat{y}_{c\,min-p}$ outperforms $\hat{y}_{CLS}$ on average, especially when the historical data is particularly small and the quadratic loss constraint affects the estimates significantly. It is also interesting to note that the c-min methods lead to much smaller variations in average cost than the other feasible methods.

Figures 2.2 and 2.3 investigate the source of these results by presenting the average magnitude of the errors and the average magnitude of the more costly negative errors for each predictor. Since it is an unbiased predictor of the average blood sugar level, $\hat{y}_{OLS}$ yields errors of the smallest magnitude on average. The biased estimators, which take the asymmetric costs of errors into account, all produce more errors overall, with $\hat{y}_{c\,min}$ producing slightly fewer total errors than $\hat{y}_{c\,min-p}$ and $\hat{y}_{CLS}$. The benefit of the higher error rate is shown in Figure 3, where it is shown that the percentage of

Figure 2.2

Average Magnitude of Errors

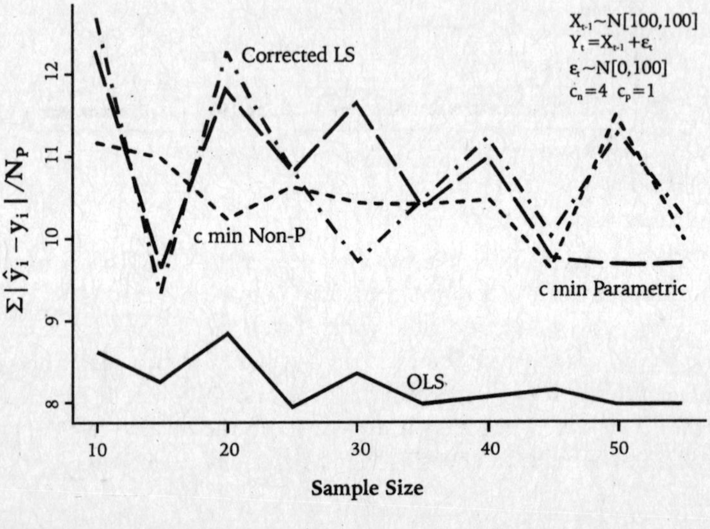

more costly negative errors is significantly lower for the latter predictors than for OLS. The ranking of the estimators in terms of average loss corresponds directly with their propensity to make negative errors. Note that $\hat{y}_{c\,min-p}$ minimises losses by avoiding negative errors more frequently in the beginning, when it has limited historical data and cannot make very accurate predictions, and increasing the rate of negative errors in order to decrease the overall error rate once more information is available.

Figure 2.3

Percentage of Negative Errors

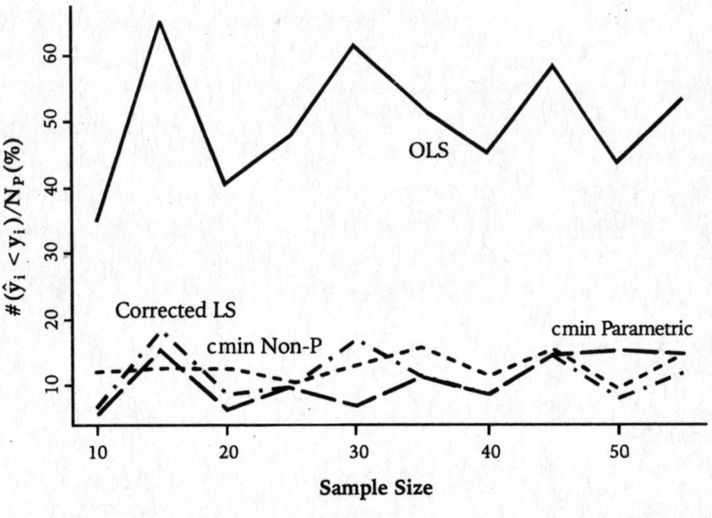

The next experiment studies the effects of misspecifying the distributional form of *F* on the corrected least squares procedure. In both the historical and test samples, errors are now drawn from a Gamma distribution with a shape parameter 1 and scale parameter 10, i.e. with mean 10 and standard deviation 10. The explanatory variables, x_{t-1}, are still drawn from a normal distribution and the values of y_t are still obtained as specified by the model: $y_t = x_{t-1} + \varepsilon_t$. The estimators are all still computed by the formulae above — the parametric procedures are now misspecified because they assume that *F* is Normal when in fact it is Gamma.

The only other change is that costs of positive and negative errors are now equal. This is done to illustrate the fact that the c-min procedure can improve upon conventional methods even when loss functions are symmetric. The reason that $c_n = c_p$ would not have demonstrated the benefits of c-min when errors are distributed Normally is that the mean and median coincide for this distribution, causing the optimal predictor under our absolute deviation loss function and the least squares (quadratic) loss function to coincide. Hence, OLS, CLS, and c-min would always coincide in this case. When the error term follows a Gamma distribution, however, the mean and median are different; CLS and c-min yield different blood sugar targets, even if *F* is specified correctly for the parametric procedures.

Figure 2.4 shows that using the wrong distributional form significantly compromise the quality of the CLS procedure. In this case, the CLS and OLS procedures coincide because the correction term, $\Phi^{-1}\left(\frac{1}{2}\right)$, equals 0. Since the true distribution of *F* is a Gamma, there should in fact be a significant correction to move the unbiased estimate of the mean from OLS closer to the optimal

Figure 2.4

Small Sample Costs with a Misspecified Distributional Form

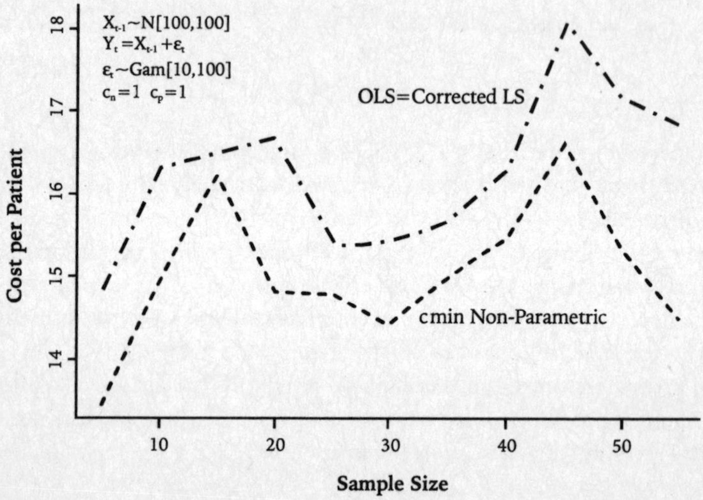

predictor, which is the median under the absolute deviation loss function. The misspecification causes $\hat{y}_{c\,min}$ (avg. cost 15.04) which ignores distributional form completely, to consistently outperform $\hat{y}_{CLS}$ (avg. cost 16.28).

Asymptotic Results

Under weak regularity conditions, $\hat{y}_{c\,min}$ attains the lower bound for expected loss asymptotically: $L_{c\,min} \xrightarrow{P} L_{Truth}$ as $N_H \longrightarrow \infty$. This result can be obtained as a special case of the asymptotic results shown for the class of *M*-estimators by Chen and Wu (1988) and Theorem 9.3 in Rao and Toutenberg (1995). It can be shown that the rate of convergence is exponential. If the assumed form of *F* is in fact its true form, then the expected loss of $\hat{y}_{c\,min-p}$ and $\hat{y}_{CLS}$ also converge to the expected loss of $\hat{y}_{Truth}$ under suitable regularity conditions. The OLS predictor yields consistent estimates of the parameters, but ignores the asymmetric costs; hence its blood sugar target generates higher average loss even in the limit. Details of these arguments are left to the reader.

Figure 2.5 illustrates the convergence of the expected losses to the lower bound when the distributional form of *F* is correctly specified, with asymmetric costs and other features as specified in the first experiment discussed above. The loss for $\hat{y}_{c\,min-p}$ converges most rapidly, which is expectable since it imposes fewer unnecessary constraints than $\hat{y}_{CLS}$ and can therefore take greatest advantage of accumulating historical data. The loss for $\hat{y}_{c\,min}$ converges most slowly because this procedure must estimate not only the parameters and target but also the distribution form of the error term.

The advantage of $\hat{y}_{c\,min}$ is that it attains minimum cost asymptotically even when the distributional form is not known. Figure 2.6 shows that the CLS procedure with misspecified *F* does not fare any better than it did in the small sample experiment when errors are drawn from a Gamma distribution. The same inconsistency result would emerge if the distributional misspecification were less severe, e.g., if error terms are drawn from a Gamma with probability ε close to 0. Thus, the physician must have great confidence in his knowledge of the distributional form of the errors to apply CLS successfully.

Figure 2.5

Asymptotic Costs of Prediction Rules

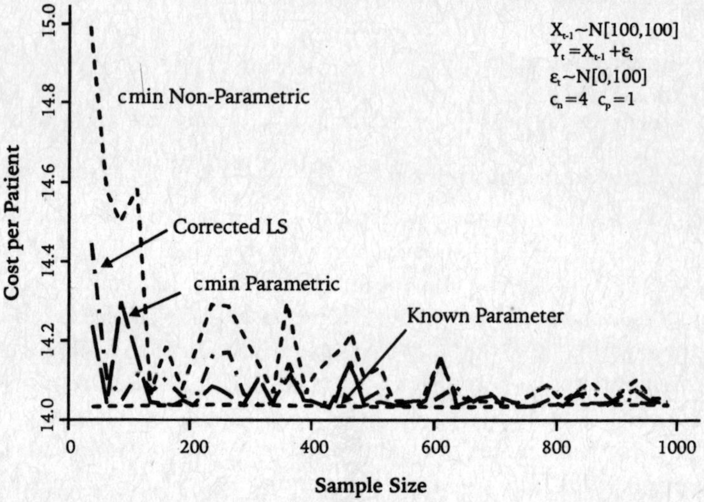

Figure 2.6

Asymptotic Costs with Misspecified Distribution

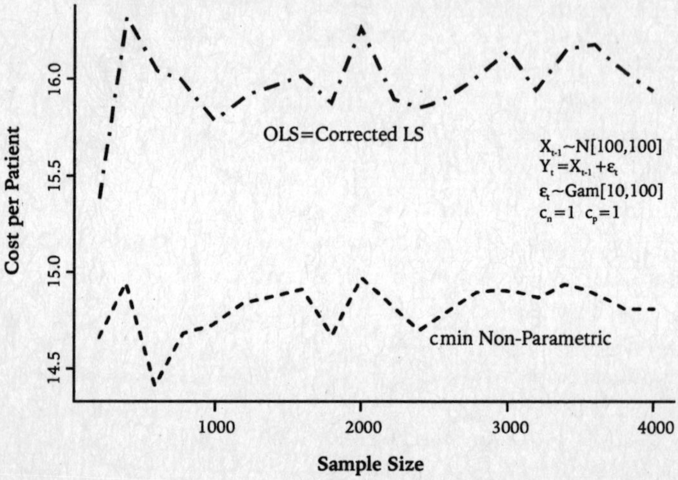

In summary, both the small sample and asymptotic results indicate that $\hat{y}_{CLS}$ is dominated by $\hat{y}_{c\,min-p}$ when F is known and by $\hat{y}_{c\,min}$ when it is not.

6. AN APPLICATION

This Section presents some preliminary empirical results on the choice of insulin doses for diabetic patients that indicate the suboptimality of CLS procedures in practice. We analyse data from an eight quarter retrospective audit of 151 charts of diabetic patients in Northern Illinois. The cross-sectional data is pooled, based on the assumption that the patients' conditional distributions of blood sugar are similar. In view of the severe short run consequences of a negative error, costs are set at $c_n = 3$ and $c_p = 2$. The model is essentially that derived above, with the explanatory variables x_i as specified in the table below. Using the one-to-one correspondence $b(d)$ between insulin dose and blood sugar targets, we use insulin doses as the dependent variable in the regression in order to directly estimate a relationship between a patient's history, x, and the dose that should be prescribed.

The mean insulin dose in the sample was 49 units, mean FPG was 209 mg/dL, and average weight was 90 kg. For a college-educated 60 year old patient with the average FPG and weight who exercises regularly and gets counseling for diet and weight, the recommended insulin doses at the mean are 21 by both OLS and c-min.

	OLS Estimates			*c-min*
	Value	*Std. Error*	*t value*	
Intercept	1.1089	7.9101	0.1402	0.9692
AGE	-0.3294	0.0747	-4.4093	-0.5122
COLLEGE	-23.6963	4.7370	-5.0024	-24.7079
WEIGHT	0.2418	0.0527	4.5878	0.1331
FPG	0.0948	0.0173	5.4755	0.2143
EXERCISE	3.4597	0.8025	4.3109	0.6237
CW.REF	18.6498	1.7172	10.8604	18.4154

Notes: College = 1 if the patient has some college education, 0 otherwise; Exercise = 1 for regular heavy exercise, 0 otherwise; CW.REF = 1 if patient is referred to a diet/weight counselling clinic, 0 otherwise.

Now suppose the fasting plasma glucose of this patient drops to 50 mg/dL, i.e., the patient becomes severely hypoglycemic. The logical treatment in this case is to eliminate insulin, and increase the patient's sugar level by giving him glucose. After the drop in FPG, c-min would decrease the insulin dose by 159 × 0.21 units, yielding a dose of –13 units. In other words, c-min recommends asking the hypoglycemic patient to increase his consumption of sugar. OLS, which ignores the higher cost of a negative error, reduces insulin only by 159 × 0. 0948, yielding a new dose of 6 units. OLS will continue to reduce blood sugar while the patient is hypoglycemic in order to keep blood sugar close to the recommended level on average.

One would expect that the CLS procedure would come closer to matching the physician's likely decision than OLS. Assuming a Normal distribution for errors, the correction factor applied to the OLS predictor is $-.2533 \times \sigma$. Estimates of the standard deviation of FPG are highly unstable across groups, and range from 8 to 55. Even when the standard deviation is quite large, the insulin dose recommended by CLS remains positive or close to 0. The second-stage correction does not change the OLS estimate sufficiently to avoid the dire consequences of prolonged hypoglycemia.

We would expect the CLS procedure to fail in this large dataset only if the Normality assumption were inaccurate. We verify this using data from the National Health and Nutrition Examination survey (for 30,818 participants). Figure 2.7, which presents the frequency distributions of FPG for mild ($115 < \text{FPG} < 140$ mg/dL) and severe (FPG >140 mg/dL) diabetics, confirms this intuition. The marginal distribution of FPG does not appear Normal; and, not surprisingly, neither do the conditional densities. Moreover, the shapes of the distributions are sufficiently non-standard that an analytic formula for the correction is hard to construct. In addition, the instability of the standard deviations across groups suggests that efforts to estimate the appropriate correction using the empirical distribution may also yield suboptimal results. The validity of CLS in formulating guidelines for diabetic management thus appears questionable; the evidence for c-min is more favourable.

Figure 2.7

Marginal FPG Distributions for Diabetics

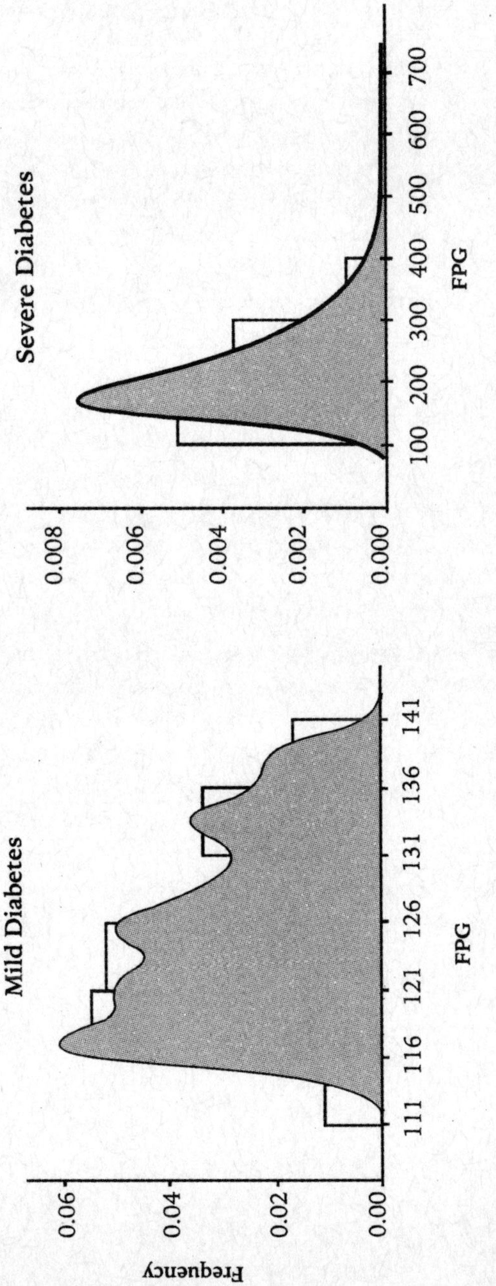

7. CONCLUSION

This paper has presented an estimation technique, c-min, that outperforms the conventional two-stage procedure in problems of joint estimation and prediction. These estimators were contrasted in the context of a real problem faced by physicians — the choice of insulin doses for patients based on their past history. Analytical methods, Monte-Carlo experiments, and preliminary empirical analysis of data from patients indicate that the advantages of using c-min in formulating guideiines for diabetes management may be significant.

The idea of c-min estimation and prediction has potential applications well beyond diabetes. Problems of joint estimation and prediction are implicit in the diagnosis and treatment of almost all chronic diseases, where physicians observe patïents' histories over time and try to choose optimal treatments conditional on current information. Outside the realm of health services, the c-min approach may have implications for business decisions under uncertainty such as the choice of investment projects or loan applicants.

We have attempted to demonstrate that the division of labour between statisticians and economists for choosing an optimal action is in general suboptimal. When there is a well defined "truth", as in the case of the length of the French meridian, perhaps we should seek an unbiased estimate of the true value and weight errors by a symmetric, quadratic loss function. But in other situations, where laws may be stochastic and costs of errors non-quadratic or asymmetric, it seems more efficient to use the ultimately relevant loss structure in the estimation problem.

References

Aiello, L., Gardner, G., King, G., Blankenship, G., Jerry, D., Ferris, F. and Klein, R. (1998). "Diabetic Retinopathy", *New Eng. J. Medicine* 21(1)143-56.

American Diabetic Association. *Diabetes Facts and Figures*, http://www.diabetes.org/ada/facts.asp#costs.

Bascovich, R. (1757). "De litteraria expeditione per pontification dictionem, et synopsis amplioris operis", *Bononiensi Scientiarum et Artum Instituto atque Academia Commentarii*, 4:353-396.

Chen, X. and Wu, Y. (1988). "Strong consistency of M-estimators in Linear Models", *J. Multivariate Analysis*, 27:116-130.

Chetty, V.K. (1968). "Pooling of Cross-section and Time Series Data", *Econometrica* 36(2): 279-90.

Dalal, S.R., Fowlkes, E.B. and Hoadley, B. (1989). "Risk Analysis of the Space Shuttle: Pre-Challenger Prediction Failure", *J.Am. Stat. Assoc.* 84: 945-957.

Fisher, W. "Estimation in the Linear Decision Model." *International Econ. Rev.* 3:1-29.

Galilee, G. (1632). *Dialogo Die Misimi Sistemi.*

Gauss, C. (1809). *Theoria Motus Corporum Celestiam*, Perthes et Besser, Hamburg.

General Accounting Office, Health, Education and Human Services Division. "Most Beneficiaries do not Receive Recommended Monitoring Services", *Report 97-48 B-270222.*

Hoerl, A. and Kennard, R. (1970). "Ridge Regression: Biased Regression for Non-orthogonal Problems", *Technometrics* 12:55-67.

Hubeer, P. (1964). "Robust Estimation of a Location Parameter", *Ann. Math.Statistics*, 35:73-101.

Laplace, P. (1793). "Sur quelques pointw du systeme du monde", *Ouevres* 11:477-558.

———. (1810). "Memoire sur les approximations des formulae qui sont fonctions de tres grands nombreset sur leur application aux probabilities", *Memoires del'Academie des sciences de Paris.*

Legendre, A. (1805). *Nouvelles methods pour la determination des orbites descomets*, Paris: Courcier.

Mayer, L. and Wilke, T. (1973). "On Biased Estimation in Linear Models", *Technometrics*, 15:497-508.

Neyman, J. and Pearson, E. (1933). "On the Problem of the Most Efficient Tests of Hypotheses", *Philosophical Translations of the Royal Society* 231:289-337.

O'Hagan, Anthony. (1994). "Kendall's Advanced Theory of Statistics" Volume 2B, *Bayesian Inference*. London: Edward Arnold.

R and, S., Chetty, V.K., Prost, R., Houghton, V. Mark, L. Strainer, J. Johansen, J., Kim, T.A., and Mueller, W., Meyer, G. and Krouwer, H. (1997). "The Diagnostic Accuracy of Single Voxel Proton MRS", *American Journal of Neuroradiolgy* 18, 1695-1704.

Rao, C. and Toutenburg, H. (1995). *Linear Models: Least Squares and Alternatives*. New York: Springer-Verlag.

Robert, C. (1997). *The Bayesian Choice*. New York: Springer-Verlag.

Thompson, R. and Basu, A. in Berry, D., Chaloner, K., and Geweke, J., eds. (1996). *Bayesian Analysis in Statistics and Econometrics*, 471-482. New York: John Wiley.

Rousseeuw, P.J. and Leroy, A.M., *Robust Regression and Outlier Detection*. New York: John Wiley and sons.

Toutenburg, H. and Trenlkler, G. (1990). "Mean Square Error Matrix Comparisons of Optimal and Classical Predictors and Estimators in Linear Regression", *Computational Statistics and Data Analysis* 10:297-305.

Trenkler, G. and Toutenburg, H. (1990). "Mean-square Error Matrix Comparisons Between Biased Estimators - An Overview of Recent Results", *Statist. Papers* 31:165-17.

Varian, H. (1975). "A Bayesian Approach to Real Estate Assessment", in Fienberg, S. and Zellner, A., eds. *Studies in Bayesian Econometrics and Statistics: In Honor of Leonard J. Savage*, 195-208. New York: North Holland.

Venables, W. and Ripley, B. (1998). *Modern Applied Statistics with S-Plus*. New York: Springer Verlag.

Wald, A. (1939). "Contributions to the Theory of Statistical Estimation and Testing Hypotheses", *Ann. of Math. Stat.* 10(4):299-326.

Walsh, J. and Roberts, R. (1994). *Pumping Insulin*. Torrey Pines Press: San Diego.

Zellner, A. (1986). "Bayesian Estimation and Prediction Using Asymmetric Loss Functions", *J. Am.Stat. Assoc.* 81(394):446-451.

Zellner, A. and Chetty, V.K. (1965). "Prediction and Decision Problems in Regression Models from a Bayesian viewpoint", *J Amer Stat Assoc* 60(310):608-16.

Zellner, A. and Geisel, M. (1968). "Sensitivity of Control to Uncertainty and Form of the Loss Function", in *The Future of Statistics*, New York: Academic Press.

3

Price-Quantity Indexes Through Consistent Aggregation of Markets

NAGESH S. REVANKAR and M. SALIH

1. INTRODUCTION

In an interesting (but largely overlooked) article written more than forty years ago, Bergstrom (1954-1955) urged that the price index (P) and the quantity index (Q) be assigned a more activist role than commonly done. Traditionally, the indexes are viewed as no more than descriptive measures of general movements of component prices and quantities over time. Bergstrom, on the other hand, held that a more important role for the indexes is to be serviceable in obtaining the aggregate demand function for the commodity group in question. What prompts him to take this position, essentially, is his view that formulation of P and Q is not an end in itself, but rather a means for measuring the group price elasticity of demand: $\beta = \dfrac{\partial Q/Q}{\partial P/P}$

Two aspects of the way Bergstrom implements his proposal empirically merit attention. First, using (generated) time series values of P and Q, and also the time series data on the relevant predetermined variables 'x', he considers estimation of the group demand function in the form—his equation (17):

$$\log Q = \beta \log P + x'\gamma + \text{residual}. \qquad \text{...(1.1)}$$

The slope coefficient β, which is the group price elasticity of demand, is a key parameter "which is the object of statistical demand analysis" (p. 23); the coefficient is also a structural (behavioral) coefficient as he essentially viewed (1.1) as a "structural equation" (p. 21) in which P and Q are both endogenous. Second, he experiments with some of the known types of indexes (such as

Laspeyres, Paasche, etc.) in search of an optimal type of P and Q for which (1.1) has minimum residual variance. These two elements of Bergstrom's empirical strategy suggest that his framework may be extended for use in more general settings. This is the main objective in the present paper.

We work with a set of 'm' interrelated markets, each with its own pair of demand and supply equations, and each in equilibrium. Let p_i= price and q_i= quantity in the ith market, and let $\underline{p}' = (p_1, \ldots, p_m)$ and $\underline{q}' = (q_1, \ldots q_m)$. We assume that the market group is governed by the conventional 2m-equation structural system, given by

$$\underline{q}'B_{qq} + \underline{p}'B_{pq} + x'\Gamma_q = u'_q \quad \text{(micro demand)} \qquad \ldots(1.2a)$$

$$\underline{q}'B_{qp} + \underline{p}'B_{pp} + x'\Gamma_p = u'_p \quad \text{(micro supply)} \qquad \ldots(1.2b)$$

in which: (1.2a) stacks the 'm' demand equations and (1.2b) stacks the respective supply equations; B's, Γ's are structural coefficients with B_{qq} (mxm), B_{pp} (mxm) non-singular; 'x' is a predetermined vector; and the u's are the structural disturbances. Following convention, the demand (supply) equations have quantities (prices) as the left-hand side variables. Linearly aggregating (1.2a) using an aggregator vector a_q(mx1), and also (1.2b) using a vector a_p(mx1), we obtain, respectively:

$$Q + \underline{p}'B_{pq}a_q + x'\Gamma_q a_q = u'_q a_q \quad \text{(Aggregate Demand)} \qquad \ldots(1.3a)$$

$$\underline{q}'B_{qp}a_p + P + x'\Gamma_p a_p = u'_p a_p \quad \text{(Aggregate Supply)} \qquad \ldots(1.3b)$$

$$Q = \underline{q}'B_{qq}a_q, \quad P = \underline{p}'B_{pp}a_p, \qquad \ldots(1.3c)$$

to be formally referred to as the *aggregate* demand-supply system.

We develop a Bergstrom-type framework in (1.3) by subjecting it to a two-step specialisation. First, we require that (1.3) constitute a *consistent aggregate* system, by which is meant a two-equation conventional structural system in which P and Q are the only two endogenous variables. This is achieved by positing

$$\underline{p}'B_{pq}a_q = cP, \quad \underline{q}'B_{qp}a_p = dQ \qquad \ldots(1.4)$$

where 'c' and 'd' are scalars. The system (1.3) then emerges as a consistent aggregate system:

$$Q + cP + x'\Gamma_q a_q = u'_q a_q \quad \text{(Group Demand)}, \quad c>0 \qquad \ldots(1.5a)$$

$$P + dQ + x'\Gamma_p a_p = u_p' a_p \quad \text{(Group Supply)}, \quad d<0 \qquad ...(1.5b)$$

to be referred to as the *group* demand-supply system. Condition (1.4) implies a restriction on (a_p, a_q) in terms of the B-coefficients, which we refer to as the consistent aggregation condition (CAC); details in Section 2. The key parameters *a la* Bergstrom are formally 'c' and 'd', involved in the group price elasticities of demand and supply, though we prefer to take them as (c, d; a_p, a_q).[1] Second, following Bergstrom's suggestion, we seek an optimal pair of P and Q, i.e., of the aggregator vectors a_p and a_q, or equivalently of the *weight* vectors

$$\lambda_p = B_{pp} a_p [\Rightarrow P = \underline{p}' \lambda_p], \quad \lambda_q = B_{qq} a_q [\Rightarrow Q = \underline{q}' \lambda_q]; \qquad ...(1.6)$$

deviating from Bergstrom and following Waugh (1942), we choose λ_p, λ_q so as to maximise

$$\mu^2 = [\text{Corr}(P, Q)]^2 \equiv [\text{Corr}(\underline{p}'\lambda_p, \underline{q}'\lambda_q)]^2 \qquad ...(1.7)$$

subject to the CAC. The indexes proposed here correspond to the optimal λ_p, λ_q, and emerge naturally as the equilibrium 'price' – 'quantity' outcomes in a market that 'best fits' individual markets.

The sole purpose of the CAC (which originates with (1.4)) is to secure the coefficients c and d related to the price slopes (hence price elasticities) of the group demand and supply; the condition is expendable if one is interested in the indexes alone. A CAC of some sort is implicit in Bergstrom's analysis as well.

We offer two formulations of the optimal choice problem, both being of independent interest. In each, the optimal λ_p, λ_q are eigen vectors corresponding to a specific root of a pair of matrices with identical roots; unlike in multivariate practice, the matrices are asymmetric. One of these formulations (Approach II, section 2) serves to exhibit the choice problem as essentially a constrained canonical correlation problem which, when the CAC is lifted, is seen to reduce to its traditional counterpart familiar in multivariate analysis — see, e.g., Dhrymes (1970), Hooper (1959) and Hotelling (1936).

---

1. Define: $l_n\underline{q}' = (l_n q_1, ..., l_n q_m)$ and $l_n\underline{p}' = (l_n p_1, ..., l_n p_m)$. If $l_n Q = \lambda_q' l_n \underline{q}$ and $l_n P = \lambda_p' l_n \underline{p}$ replace Q and P (respectively) in (1.5), which is ordinarily the case when the individual demand-supply equations are specified in terms of logarithmic quantities and prices, then of course the entities (-c) and (-1/d) themselves are the group demand and supply elasticities, respectively.

The framework employed here has some advantages. First, to the extent that a structural system depicts some underlying economic theory, our indexes will be above the oft-voiced criticism that indexes generally amount to "measurement without theory" — see Koopmans (1947); also see Auerbach (1982). Second, it permits one to evaluate the effects $\partial P / \partial x_j$ and $\partial Q / \partial x_j$ where x_j is an element of the predetermined vector x; x_j is more likely to be a policy variable. Third, it provides indexes which are invariant to units of measurement. Last, but not least, it affords *concurrent* derivation of the price and quantity indexes in a given application. As with most indexes derived under the 'statistical' (model-based) approach, however, our P and Q fail to meet some of the "tests" discussed in connection with the indexes deduced under the economic approach.[2]

Some or all of these features are lacking in previous model-based studies on the subject, excepting Bergstrom's to a degree; nor do these studies seek out the activist role for the indexes. The primary reason for these outcomes is the fact that they employ (specific) *regression* models rather than a *structural* model of the type (1.2). See, e.g., Clements and Izan [(1981), (1987)], Giles and McCann (1991), Kloeck and DeWitt (1961), Rao and Selvanathan (1992), Selvanathan [(1989), (1991)], Selvanathan and Rao (1992), Theil (1960) and Waugh (1942); also see Anderson, Jones and Nesmith (1997) and Barnett, Hinich and Yue (2000) addressed to the problem of constructing monetary aggregates.

The plan of the paper is as follows: Section 2 derives the CAC and treats the optimal choice problem. Section 3 works out the asymptotic distribution theory for the estimators of the key parameters $(c, d; \lambda_p, \lambda_q)$; the estimators make use of the 3SLS results for the market system. Section 4 implements the analysis in the context of the U.S. red meat market, comprised of beef and pork markets. We also present a comparative picture of the indexes obtained here and those proposed in Theil (1960) and Waugh (1942). Section 5 concludes the paper. Proofs of some results are collected in Appendix A and Appendix B.

---

2. Authoritative accounts of these tests can be found in Diewert and Nakamura (1993, Chs. 2 and 5), Diewert (1995), and Samuelson and Swamy (1974).

2. OPTIMAL INDEXES AND PROPERTIES

We first deduce the CAC and then proceed to the optimal choice problem.

The CAC

The CAC originates with the restrictions (1.4):

$$\underline{p}'B_{pq}a_q = cP, \quad \underline{q}'B_{qp}a_p = dQ\,.$$

Using (1.6) to replace the aggregator vectors (a_p, a_q) by the weight vectors (λ_p, λ_q), these restrictions may be recast as

$$\underline{p}'B_{pq}B_{qq}^{-1}\lambda_q = c\underline{p}'\lambda_p, \quad \underline{q}'B_{qp}B_{pp}^{-1}\lambda_p = d\underline{q}'\lambda_q,$$

in view of which the CAC may be set forth as

$$B_{pq}\ B_{qq}^{-1}\lambda_q = c\lambda_p, \quad B_{qp}B_{pp}^{-1}\lambda_p = d\lambda_q; \qquad \text{...(2.1)}$$

or equivalently as

$$(C_{pp} - gI)\lambda_p = 0, \quad (C_{qq} - gI)\lambda_q = 0, \quad g = c.d, \qquad \text{...(2.2)}$$

$$C_{pp} = B_{pq}B_{qq}^{-1}B_{qp}B_{pp}^{-1}, \quad C_{qq} = B_{qp}B_{pp}^{-1}B_{pq}B_{qq}^{-1}.$$

The CAC restricts the admissible λ_p's, λ_q's to be the eigen vectors of the matrices C_{pp}, C_{qq} which have identical roots and are generally asymmetric. The 'corresponding' vectors (λ_p, λ_q) are associated with the same root, and provide a pair of 'corresponding' indexes $P = \underline{p}'\lambda_p$ and $Q = \underline{q}'\lambda_q$; only such index pairs merit attention. Interestingly, the eigen root 'g' is a product of the key coefficients 'c' and 'd' related to the price slopes of the group demand and supply functions (1.5).

We assume:

Assumption 1[3]

All roots of C_{pp}(mxm) and C_{qq}(mxm) are real, distinct and non-zero. The assumption signals that we choose to avoid situations where some roots of C_{pp}, C_{qq} are possibly complex. It also ensures that there are 'm' distinct pairs of the corresponding vectors (λ_p, λ_q) with real elements.

---

3. The assumption appears to be adequately borne out by the empirical results of section.

Remark 1

The CAC becomes more transparent when viewed from the perspective of the reduced forms of the micro system (1.2) and of the group demand-supply system (1.5). Suppose for the moment that $\lambda_p = B_{pp}a_p$ and $\lambda_q = B_{qq}a_q$ are arbitrary m-vectors with $P = \underline{p}'\lambda_p$ and $Q = \underline{q}'\lambda_q$. The thrust of the CAC is that if λ_p, λ_q satisfy the condition (2.1), then the reduced form of the group system is equivalent to that of $\underline{q}'\lambda_q$ and $\underline{p}'\lambda_p$ implied by the micro reduced form for $\underline{p}, \underline{q}$; the condition is also necessary for the equivalence. This result is established in Salih (1993, Theorem 1).

Optimal Indexes

We offer two approaches to locating the optimal pair of corresponding vectors (λ_p, λ_q); we begin by developing some preliminaries.

Let $v_q = \underline{q} - E(\underline{q} \mid x)$ and $v_p = \underline{p} - E(\underline{p} \mid x)$ be the reduced form disturbances of the micro system (1.2), with zero means and a finite covariance matrix:

$$V\begin{bmatrix} v_q \\ v_p \end{bmatrix} = \begin{bmatrix} \Omega_{qq}, \Omega_{qp} \\ \Omega_{pq}, \Omega_{pp} \end{bmatrix} \equiv \Omega; \qquad \Omega_{qp} \neq 0.$$

Then we have (conditional on x)

$$\begin{aligned} \mu = \mathrm{Corr}(\underline{p}'\lambda_p, \underline{q}'\lambda_q) &= \mathrm{Corr}(v_p'\lambda_p, v_q'\lambda_q) \qquad \text{...(2.3)} \\ &= \lambda_q'\Omega_{qp}\lambda_p \,/\, \sqrt{\lambda_p'\Omega_{pp}\lambda_p}\,.\sqrt{\lambda_q'\Omega_{qq}\lambda_q} \\ &= \lambda_q'\Omega_{qp}\lambda_p, \end{aligned}$$

adopting the normalisations,

$$\lambda_p'\Omega_{pp}\lambda_p = 1, \qquad \lambda_q'\Omega_{qq}\lambda_q = 1 \qquad \text{...(2.4)}$$

familiar in the traditional canonical correlation problem.

Approach I

Let $(\lambda_p^i, \lambda_q^i)$ be the pairs of corresponding eigen vectors in (2.2), given by

$$C_{pp}\lambda_p^i = g_i\lambda_p^i, \quad C_{qq}\lambda_q^i = g_i\lambda_q^i, \qquad \text{...(2.5)}$$

and duly normalised by (2.4); also compute the correlations,

$$\mu_i = \text{Corr}(\underline{p}'\lambda_p^i, \underline{q}'\lambda_q^i) = \lambda_q^{i\prime}\Omega_{qp}\lambda_p^i \equiv \mu(g_i), \quad \text{say, } i = 1,\ldots,m.$$

We assume (somewhat generously) that,

Assumption 2

All μ's are distinct and non-zero.

One then obtains a unique pair of optimal vectors ($l_p \equiv \lambda_p^j$, $l_q \equiv \lambda_q^j$) corresponding to the root $g_* \equiv g_j$ for some $j \in [1,2,\ldots,m]$ such that

$$\max_i (\mu_i^2) = \mu^2(g_*) \equiv \mu_*^2 (\text{say}). \qquad \text{...(2.6)}$$

Clearly,

$$C_{pp}l_p = g_* l_p, \quad C_{qq}l_q = g_* l_q; \quad l_r'\Omega_{rr}l_r = 1 \ (r = p, q). \qquad \text{...(2.7)}$$

There is no presumption that the root g_*, associated with the maximum squared correlation μ_*^2, is necessarily the maximum or the minimum root.

The indexes we propose are based on l_p and l_q, given by

$$P_c = \underline{p}'l_p, \quad Q_c = \underline{q}'l_q; \quad [\text{Corr}(P_c, Q_c)]^2 = \mu_*^2. \qquad \text{...(2.8)}$$

(The subscript 'c' on the indexes stands for 'constrained' — the indexes obey the CAC). Also in view of (2.1) and the normalisations (2.4), we recover the coefficients 'c' and 'd' as

$$c = l_p'\Omega_{pp}B_{pq}B_{qq}^{-1}l_q, \quad d = l_q'\Omega_{qq}B_{qp}B_{pp}^{-1}l_p. \qquad \text{...(2.9)}$$

Theorem 1

The indexes P_c, Q_c are independent of the units of measurement. Proof is provided in Appendix A.

Approach II

An alternative formulation is also available, in which one proceeds directly to maximise $\mu = \lambda_q'\Omega_{qp}\lambda_p$ subject to the normalisations (2.4) and the CAC (2.2). This formulation makes it at once obvious that our optimal choice problem is essentially the standard canonical correlation problem, duly modified to incorporate the CAC; the constraint, however, makes for several points of divergence between the two problems.

To begin, we maximise

$$f = \lambda_q'\Omega_{qp}\lambda_p + \frac{1}{2}\mu_q(1-\lambda_q'\Omega_{qq}\lambda_q)+\frac{1}{2}\mu_p(1-\lambda_p'\Omega_{pp}\lambda_p) + \theta_p'\bar{C}_{pp}\lambda_p + \theta_q'\bar{C}_{qq}\lambda_q$$

where we have set

$$\bar{C}_{pp} = C_{pp} - gI, \qquad \bar{C}_{qq} = C_{qq} - gI;$$

the scalars μ_q, μ_p and the vectors θ_q, θ_p are the Lagrange parameters. The first-order conditions are:

$$\partial f / \partial\lambda_q = 0 \Rightarrow \Omega_{qp}\lambda_p - \mu_q.\Omega_{qq}\lambda_q + \bar{C}'_{qq}\theta_q = 0 \qquad \text{...(2.10a)}$$

$$\partial f / \partial\lambda_p = 0 \Rightarrow \Omega_{pq}\lambda_q - \mu_p.\Omega_{pp}\lambda_p + \bar{C}'_{pp}\theta_p = 0 \qquad \text{...(2.10b)}$$

$$\partial f / \partial\theta_q = 0 \Rightarrow \bar{C}_{qq}\lambda_q = 0, \; \partial f / \partial\theta_p = 0 \Rightarrow \bar{C}_{pp}\lambda_p = 0. \qquad \text{...(2.10c)}$$

Note first from (2.10c) that λ_p, λ_q are again the eigen vectors of C_{pp}, C_{qq} as expected. Next, premultiplying (2.10a) by λ_q' and (2.10b) by λ_p' we find, in view of (2.10c), that

$\mu_q = \mu_p = \lambda_q'\Omega_{qp}\lambda_p = \mu$, whereupon (2.10a) and (2.10b) simplify to

$$\Omega_{qp}\lambda_p - \mu.\Omega_{qq}\lambda_q + \bar{C}'_{qq}\theta_q = 0 \qquad \text{...(2.11a)}$$

$$\Omega_{pq}\lambda_q - \mu.\Omega_{pp}\lambda_p + \bar{C}'_{pp}\theta_p = 0. \qquad \text{...(2.11b)}$$

For our purposes, it is convenient to deduce a version of (2.11) which is free of the nuisance parameters θ_q, θ_p, for which purpose we follow Rao (1973, p.50). The step needed involves use of g-inverses of the singular matrices $\bar{C}_{rr}\Omega_{rr}^{-1}\bar{C}'_{rr} (r = p, q)$,[4] and

---

4. The assumption that the asymmetric matrices do not have complex roots is a reasonable one, in as much as 'c' and 'd' are invariably real and g=c.d. The assumption of distinct roots ensures that the eigen vectors are unique. The assumption of non-zero roots may be inadequate in some applications, as it implies that B_{pq} and B_{qp} are also non-singular. Severe problems arise, however, if one relaxes the assumption of distinct and non-zero roots — especially in working out the asymptotics of the eigen vectors and roots.

The singularity obtains because the (mxm) matrices $\bar{C}_{rr}$ are of rank m-1.

premultiplication of (2.11a) – (2.11b) by the matrices shown in the square brackets [ ] in (2.12) below. We arrive at

$$\left[I-\bar{C}'_{qq}(\bar{C}_{qq}\Omega_{qq}^{-1}\bar{C}'_{qq})^{-}\bar{C}_{qq}\Omega_{qq}^{-1}\right]\Omega_{qp}\lambda_p-\mu\Omega_{qq}\lambda_q=0 \quad \text{...(2.12a)}$$

$$\left[I-\bar{C}'_{pp}(\bar{C}_{pp}\Omega_{pp}^{-1}\bar{C}'_{pp})^{-}\bar{C}_{pp}\Omega_{pp}^{-1}\right]\Omega_{pq}\lambda_q-\mu\Omega_{pp}\lambda_p=0 \quad \text{...(2.12b)}$$

or equivalently,

$$(S_{qq}-\mu^2 I)\lambda_q=0, \quad (S_{pp}-\mu^2 I)\lambda_p=0, \quad \text{...(2.13)}$$

where

$$S_{qq}=\Omega_{qq}^{-1}[I-\bar{C}'_{qq}(\bar{C}_{qq}\Omega_{qq}^{-1}\bar{C}'_{qq})^{-}\bar{C}_{qq}\Omega_{qq}^{-1}]\,\Omega_{qp}$$
$$\times\,\Omega_{pp}^{-1}[I-\bar{C}'_{pp}(\bar{C}_{pp}\Omega_{pp}^{-1}\bar{C}'_{pp})^{-}\bar{C}_{pp}\Omega_{pp}^{-1}]\,\Omega_{pq},$$
$$S_{pp}=\Omega_{pp}^{-1}[I-\bar{C}'_{pp}(\bar{C}_{pp}\Omega_{pp}^{-1}\bar{C}'_{pp})^{-}\bar{C}_{pp}\Omega_{pp}^{-1}]\,\Omega_{pq}$$
$$\times\,\Omega_{qq}^{-1}[I-\bar{C}'_{qq}(\bar{C}_{qq}\Omega_{qq}^{-1}\bar{C}'_{qq})^{-}\bar{C}_{qq}\Omega_{qq}^{-1}]\,\Omega_{qp}.$$

It is now evident from (2.13) that λ_p and the corresponding λ_q are the eigen vectors of S_{pp} and S_{qq} (respectively) associated with the same root μ^2, and since μ is the correlation coefficient between $\underline{q}'\lambda_q$ and $\underline{p}'\lambda_p$, the root to consider is the largest; again, as in Approach I, the matrices have identical roots and are generally asymmetric. The set up in (2.13) mimics the standard canonical correlation problem — see, e.g., Dhrymes (1970).

There are in fact 'm' pairs of eigen value problems in (2.13), the ith corresponding to the root $g = g_i$ of C_{pp} and C_{qq}:

$$(S^i_{qq}-\mu^2 I)\lambda_q=0, \quad (S^i_{pp}-\mu^2 I)\lambda_p=0, \quad i=1, ..., m, \quad \text{...(2.14)}$$

where S^i_{qq} is S_{qq} at $g = g_i$, etc. For given i, let μ_i^2 be the maximum root and λ^i_q, λ^i_p be the associated eigen vectors in (2.14). The optimal pair (l_p, l_q) of the weight vectors is associated with $\mu_*^2 = \max_i (\mu_i^2)$. Needless to say, this approach is computationally less attractive than Approach I.

The eigen value problems in (2.14) may be simplified in light of Theorem 2 (subsection 2C). The theorem implies that, when $\Omega_{pq} \neq 0$, the matrices S^i_{qq} and S^i_{pp} have a single non-vanishing root, which obviously is the maximum root μ_i^2. Moreover, the root is computed effortlessly, as simply the trace of these matrices.

The balance of this subsection is addressed to two other indexes which, like our P_c and Q_c, are model-based and derive from some optimality criteria; we propose to compare these indexes with our's in the empirical section below.

(a) *Waugh's Indexes.* Waugh (1942) proposes indexes following the standard canonical correlation approach, which maximises the correlation μ ignoring the CAC. Taking $\theta_p = \theta_q = 0$ in (2.11) or, equivalently, dropping terms involving $\bar{C}_{pp}, \bar{C}_{qq}$ in (2.13) and rearranging the results, one finds that the weight vectors $(\bar{\lambda}_p, \bar{\lambda}_q)$ are the eigen vectors corresponding to the same root in

$$(\Omega_{qp}\Omega_{pp}^{-1}\Omega_{pq} - \bar{\mu}^2\Omega_{qq})\bar{\lambda}_q = 0 \qquad \text{...(2.15a)}$$

$$(\Omega_{pq}\Omega_{qq}^{-1}\Omega_{qp} - \bar{\mu}^2\Omega_{pp})\bar{\lambda}_p = 0 \qquad \text{...(2.15b)}$$

— the eigen value problems familiar in the traditional canonical correlation theory — see, e.g., Dhrymes (1970, section 2.1); $\bar{\mu} = \text{Corr}(\underline{p}'\bar{\lambda}_p, \underline{q}'\bar{\lambda}_q)$. The optimal vectors $(\bar{l}_p, \bar{l}_q)$ correspond to the largest root $\bar{\mu}_*^2$, and the Waugh indexes are given by

$$P_{uc} = \underline{p}'\bar{l}_p,\ Q_{uc} = \underline{q}'\bar{l}_q;\ [\text{Corr}(P_{uc}, Q_{uc})]^2 = \bar{\mu}_*^2. \qquad \text{...(2.16)}$$

(The subscript 'uc' on the indexes stands for 'unconstrained' — the indexes ignore the CAC.)

Remark 2.

Waugh (1942) works with the *unrestricted* reduced form of some structural equation system; he does not employ a micro system of the type in (1.2). We view the Waugh type indexes as unconstrained even when they make use of the *restricted* reduced form of a system like (1.2) but ignore the CAC.

(b) *Theil's Indexes.* Let P^+, Q^+ be (nxm) matrices whose t^{th} rows are (respectively) the m-vectors of observed prices and quantities in period t (t = 1, . . . , n). Also, let $p_T = P^+\lambda_p^T$ and $q_T = Q^+\lambda_q^T$ be the n-vectors of values of the proposed price-quantity indexes based on the weight vectors $(\lambda_p^T, \lambda_q^T)$. Finally, let $E = p_T q_T' - P^+ Q^{+'}$ be the 'discrepancy' matrix, whose (t, s)th element is the difference between the index-constructed and actual values of the s-period commodity bundle at the t-period prices. Theil's (1960) so-called 'symmetric best linear' indexes minimise tr(EE′) which is the sum of squares of the discrepancies. He shows that the weight vectors $(\lambda_p^T, \lambda_q^T)$ are the eigen vectors in

$$(Q^{+'}Q^+P^{+'}P^+ - \varphi^2 I)\lambda_p^T = 0, \; (P^{+'}P^+Q^{+'}Q^+ - \varphi^2 I)\lambda_q^T = 0, \quad \text{...(2.17)}$$

and that the trace is minimised for the pair (l_p^T, l_q^T) corresponding to the maximum root φ_*^2. The indexes are thus

$$P_T = \underline{p}' l_p^T, \quad Q_T = \underline{q}' l_q^T. \quad \text{...(2.17b)}$$

It is no longer true that φ^2 is interpretable as a squared correlation coefficient; unlike in the cases of constrained and unconstrained indexes, therefore, the maximum root φ_*^2 is not the square of the correlation coefficient between P_T and Q_T.

Some Theoretical Results

We collect here some insightful results pertaining to the indexes, exploiting the development under Approach II. In this, it is convenient to work with a transformed version of (2.13), and to this end we define:

$$G_{rr} = I - \Omega_{rr}^{-1/2}\bar{C}'_{rr}(\bar{C}_{rr}\Omega_{rr}^{-1}\bar{C}'_{rr})^{-}\bar{C}_{rr}\Omega_{rr}^{-1/2} \quad \text{...(2.18)}$$

where $\bar{C}_{rr} = C_{rr} - gI$, it is being understood that 'g' is a root of C_{rr}; also let

$$\lambda_r^* = \Omega_{rr}^{1/2}\lambda_r, \quad H_{rs} = \Omega_{rr}^{-1/2}\Omega_{rs}\Omega_{ss}^{-1/2}$$

so that

$$\lambda_r^{*'}\lambda_r^* = 1, \; \mu = \lambda_r'\Omega_{rs}\lambda_s = \lambda_r^{*'}H_{rs}\lambda_s^*,$$

(r,s = p,q). Then (2.13) may be recast as

$$(\bar{S}_{qq} - \mu^2)\lambda_q^* = 0, \quad \bar{S}_{qq} = G_{qq}H_{qp}G_{pp}H_{pq} \quad \text{...(2.19a)}$$

$$(\bar{S}_{pp} - \mu^2)\lambda^*_p = 0, \quad \bar{S}_{pp} = G_{pp}H_{pq}G_{qq}H_{qp}. \qquad ...(2.19b)$$

It is easily verified that

$$G_{rr} \text{ is idempotent with rank} = 1 \ (r = p,q). \qquad ...(2.19c)$$

Also, since $G_{rr}\lambda^*_r = \lambda^*_r$ (using $\bar{C}_{rr}\lambda_r = 0$), we may write

$$G_{rr} = \lambda^*_r\lambda^{*\prime}_r \quad (r = p, q). \qquad ...(2.19d)$$

Theorem 2

Suppose $\Omega_{pq} \neq 0$. Then for any root g of C_{rr}, S_{rr} in (2.13), or equivalently $\bar{S}_{rr}$ in (2.19a – 2.19b), is of unit rank (r = p,q).

Proof

Follows from the fact that both $\bar{S}_{rr}$ and

$$S_{rr} = \Omega_{rr}^{-1/2} G_{rr}H_{rs}G_{ss}\Omega_{ss}^{-1/2}\Omega_{sr}$$

entail the unit rank matrix G_{rr} (r=p,q).

Theorem 3

Suppose $\Omega_{pq} \neq 0$. Then for any root g of C_{rr}, the root μ^2 of S_{rr} (2.13) or S_{rr} (2.19a-2.19b) is real (r = p,q).

Proof[5]

For any root g, by Assumption 1, G_{rr} is a real matrix, which is also symmetric. Hence its eigen vector λ^*_r corresponding to its only unit root — see (2.19d) — is real. But λ^*_r is also an eigen vector of $\bar{S}_{rr}$, which, by Theorem 2, corresponds to its only non-vanishing root μ^2. This establishes the theorem.

Next, though we know that $\mu = \lambda_q'\Omega_{qp}\lambda_p$ is a correlation coefficient with the property: $0 \leq \mu^2 \leq 1$, this property nonetheless has to be established for μ^2 when considered as a root of $S_{rr}/\bar{S}_{rr}$, which is the objective of the following theorem.

Theorem 4

Suppose $\Omega_{pq} \neq 0$. Then, for any root g of C_{rr}, the non-vanishing root μ^2 $S_{rr}/\bar{S}_{rr}$ has the property that $0 \leq \mu^2 \leq 1$.

---

5. Salih (1993) offers an alternative proof of Theorem 3.

Proof

It follows from Theorem 5 (and Corollary to Theorem 5) below that $\mu^2 \leq 1$; accordingly, we need to prove only that $\mu^2 \geq 0$. The latter is true since, considering $\bar{S}_{qq}$ for any root g of C_{rr},

$$\mu^2 = \text{tr}\bar{S}_{qq} = \text{tr}[G_{qq}H_{qp}G_{pp}H_{pq}] \quad \text{(from (2.19a))} \qquad ...(2.20)$$

$$= \text{tr}[\lambda_q^* \lambda_q^{*'} .H_{qp}.\lambda_p^* \lambda_p^{*'} .H_{pq}] \quad \text{(from (2.19d))}$$

$$= \lambda_q^{*'} H_{qp}\lambda_p^* .\lambda_q^{*'} H_{qp}\lambda_p^* \quad (\text{using } H'_{pq} = H_{qp})$$

$$= (\lambda_q^{*'} H_{qp}\lambda_p^*)^2 \geq 0.$$

Similarly, $\mu^2 = \text{tr}\bar{S}_{pp} \geq 0$. Hence the theorem.

Corollary to Theorem 4

$$\mu_*^2 = [\text{Corr}(P_c, Q_c)]^2 \geq 0.$$

Finally, we show that the correlation coefficient between the constrained indexes is less (in absolute value) than that between the unconstrained indexes. One certainly expects this result to hold but the proof is non-trivial.

Theorem 5.

$$\mu_*^2 = [\text{Corr}(P_c, Q_c)]^2 \leq [\text{Corr}(P_{uc}, Q_{uc})]^2 = \bar{\mu}_*^2.$$

Proof is provided in Appendix A. It is known — e.g., Dhrymes (1970, section 2.1) — that $0 \leq \bar{\mu}_*^2 \leq 1$. Hence we have

Corollary to Theorem 5

$$\mu_*^2 \leq \bar{\mu}_*^2 \leq 1.$$

Finally, Corollary to Theorem 4 and Corollary to Theorem 5 together lead to

Theorem 6

$$0 \leq \mu_*^2 \leq \bar{\mu}_*^2 \leq 1.$$

3. ESTIMATION AND ASYMPTOTICS

The key parameters of interest in this study are (c,d; l_p, l_q), which we estimate using estimates of the structural coefficients B and the reduced form covariances Ω:

$$B = \begin{bmatrix} B_{qq}, B_{qp} \\ B_{pq}, B_{pp} \end{bmatrix} \equiv (B_{rs});\ \Omega = \begin{bmatrix} \Omega_{qq}, \Omega_{qp} \\ \Omega_{pq}, \Omega_{pp} \end{bmatrix} \equiv (\Omega_{rs}).$$

The asymptotic distribution theory we develop for the key parameter estimators will naturally draw on the asymptotic distribution of the estimators $(\hat{B}, \hat{\Omega})$ of (B,Ω).

We understand the following with reference to the market system (1.2). The system is a conventional structural equation system. The sample consists of 'n' independent realisations on all variables/ disturbances in question. In particular, the sample realisations on the structural disturbance vector (u'_q, u'_p) are NID $(0,\Sigma)$, and those on the reduced form disturbances (v'_q, v'_p) (introduced in section 2B) are NID $(0,\Omega=(\Omega_{rs}))$. $\hat{B} = (\hat{B}_{rs})$ is the 3SLS estimator of $B=(B_{rs})$, based on the instrument set X whose rows are the observations on the predetermined vector x'. Standard regularity conditions apply so that, in particular, $\sqrt{n}\,(\hat{B}-B)$ has an asymptotic normal distribution. $\hat{\Omega}_{rs} = \hat{V}_r'\hat{V}_s/n$ is the m.l.e. of Ω_{rs}, where $\hat{V}_q(\hat{V}_p)$ denotes the *unconstrained* reduced form residuals, i.e., the residuals in the regression of the quantity (price) observations on X, and $\sqrt{n}(\hat{\Omega}-\Omega)$ has an asymptotic normal distribution.

Estimation

Approach I readily suggests estimators of c, d, l_p, l_q. Let $\hat{C}_{qq} = \hat{B}_{qp}\hat{B}_{pp}^{-1}\hat{B}_{pq}\hat{B}_{qq}^{-1}$, and similarly define $\hat{C}_{pp}$ – see (2.2). Clearly, $\hat{C}_{rr}$ is consistent for $C_{rr}(r=p,q)$, and has eigen roots $\hat{g}_1, \ldots, \hat{g}_m$ which are distinct w.p. 1 by Assumption 1. The estimators $(\hat{\lambda}_q^i, \hat{\lambda}_p^i)$ of $(\lambda_q^i, \lambda_p^i)$ are given by — see (2.5) —

$$\hat{C}_{qq}\hat{\lambda}_q^i = \hat{g}_i\,\hat{\lambda}_q^i, \quad \hat{C}_{pp}\hat{\lambda}_p^i = \hat{g}_i\,\hat{\lambda}_p^i \qquad (i=1,\ldots,m) \qquad \ldots(3.1)$$

duly normalised by $\hat{\lambda}_r^{i'}\hat{\Omega}_{rr}\hat{\lambda}_r^i = 1$. And the estimators $(\hat{l}_q, \hat{l}_p)$ of the optimal weight vectors (l_q, l_p) are given by — see (2.7) —

$$\hat{C}_{qq}\hat{l}_q = \hat{g}_*\hat{l}_q, \quad \hat{C}_{pp}\hat{l}_p = \hat{g}_*\hat{l}_p, \qquad \text{...(3.2a)}$$

$$\hat{l}_q'\hat{\Omega}_{qq}\hat{l}_q = 1, \quad \hat{l}_p'\hat{\Omega}_{pp}\hat{l}_p = 1, \qquad \text{...(3.2b)}$$

where $\hat{g}_*$ is $\hat{g}_i$ for some $i \in [l,...m]$ for which the squared correlation, $(\hat{\lambda}_q^{i\,\prime}\hat{\Omega}_{qp}\hat{\lambda}_p^i)^2$, is the maximum. The price-quantity indexes (reported in section 4) are therefore computed as

$$P_c = \underline{p}'\hat{l}_p, Q_c = \underline{q}'\hat{l}_q. \qquad \text{...(3.3)}$$

Also, following (2.9), we estimate c, d as

$$\hat{c} = \hat{l}_p'\hat{\Omega}_{pp}\hat{B}_{pq}\hat{B}_{qq}^{-1}\hat{l}_q, \quad \hat{d} = \hat{l}_q'\hat{\Omega}_{qq}\hat{B}_{qp}\hat{B}_{pp}^{-1}\hat{l}_p. \qquad \text{...(3.4)}$$

Asymptotics

We first note that $(\hat{B},\hat{\Omega})$ is consistent for (B,Ω). Consequently, and because the eigen vectors and roots are continuous functions of the elements of the matrix, it follows by the Slutsky theorem that $\hat{l}_p, \hat{l}_q, \hat{c}, \hat{d}, \hat{g}_*$ are all consistent for the respective population entities. The following distributional results are also useful in the development below. First, it is known that

$$\sqrt{n}\,\mathrm{vec}(\hat{B} - B) \xrightarrow{a} N(0, \Sigma_b), \qquad \text{...(3.5a)}$$

where '$\xrightarrow{a}$' stands for 'asymptotically distributed as', and the expression for Σ_b is familiar; the rows and corresponding columns of Σ_b associated with the known elements of vec B consist of only zeros. Second, for the m.l.e. $\hat{\Omega}$ of the (2m x 2m) matrix Ω we have

$$\sqrt{n}\,\mathrm{vec}(\hat{\Omega} - \Omega) \xrightarrow{a} N(0, \Sigma_\omega). \qquad \text{...(3.5b)}$$

The $(4m^2 \times 4m^2)$ matrix Σ_ω is given by

$$\Sigma_\omega = (I + K)(\Omega \otimes \Omega), \quad K = \sum_{i.j=1}^{2m} (H_{ij} \otimes H_{ij}'),$$

$$H_{ij} = e_i e_j',$$

e_j being the 2mxl vector whose elements are zero except the jth which is unity — see Muirhead (1982, p.90) or Magnus and Neudecker

(1979). Finally, $\hat{B}$ and $\hat{\Omega}$ are asymptotically uncorrelated.[6] This uncorrelation property continues to hold with respect to $\hat{B}$ and the counterpart of $\hat{\Omega}$ based on the restricted reduced form residuals.[7]

(i) Asymptotic Distribution of $\hat{l}_q$

From (3.2a) we have (using the Δ-method),

$$0 = \hat{C}_{qq}\hat{l}_q - \hat{g}_*\hat{l}_q = \hat{C}_{qq}\Delta\hat{l}_q + \Delta\hat{C}_{qq}l_q + C_{qq}l_q - [\hat{g}_*\Delta\hat{l}_q + \Delta\hat{g}_*.l_q + g_*l_q], \qquad \text{...(3.6a)}$$

and from (3.2b) we have

$$1 = \hat{l}'_q\hat{\Omega}_{qq}\hat{l}_q = (\Delta\hat{l}'_q)\hat{\Omega}_{qq}\hat{l}_q + l'_q\Delta\hat{\Omega}_{qq}\hat{l}_q + l'_q\Omega_{qq}\Delta\hat{l}_q + l'_q\Omega_{qq}l_q \qquad \text{...(3.6b)}$$

where we have written $\Delta\hat{f} = \hat{f} - f$ when plim $\hat{f}$ is f. We recall that $C_{qq}l_q = g_*l_q$ and $l'_q\Omega_{qq}l_q = 1$. Hence, taking plims of $\sqrt{n}$ times the terms in (3.6a) we find that

$$(C_{qq} - g_*I)\sqrt{n}\Delta\hat{l}_q \xrightarrow{a} \sqrt{n}\Delta\hat{g}_*.l_q - \sqrt{n}\Delta\hat{C}_{qq}l_q. \qquad \text{...(3.7)}$$

It is convenient to remove $\Delta\hat{g}_*$ from (3.7), which is achieved by premultiplying (3.7) by $(I - l_q l'_q\Omega_{qq})$:

$$[(I - l_q l'_q\Omega_{qq})(C_{qq} - g_*I)]\sqrt{n}\Delta\hat{l}_q \xrightarrow{a} -(I - l_q l'_q\Omega_{qq})\sqrt{n}\Delta\hat{C}_{qq}l_q. \qquad \text{...(3.8a)}$$

Also, a similar plim operation on (3.6b) shows that

$$2l'_q\Omega_{qq}.\sqrt{n}\Delta\hat{l}_q \xrightarrow{a} -l'_q\sqrt{n}\Delta\hat{\Omega}_{qq}l_q \qquad \text{...(3.8b)}$$

---

6. This uncorrelation property may be verified in view of the following: (i) The instrument set used by the 3SLS in (1.2) is X; (ii) $\sqrt{n}(\hat{B} - B)$ entails $X'(U_q, U_p)/\sqrt{n}$ where the rows of (U_q, U_p) are the independent realisations on (u'_q, u'_p); (iii) the unconstrained reduced form residuals are $\hat{V}_r = [I - X(X'X)^{-1}X']V_r$, the rows of $V = (V_q, V_p)$ being the independent realisations on (V'_q, V'_p); and (iv) $X'[I - X(X'X)^{-1}X'] = 0$.

7. Let $\hat{V}^0_q(\hat{V}^0_p)$ denote the residuals from the restricted reduced form for the quantity (price) vector. The uncorrelation result derives from the fact that plim $(\hat{V}_r - \hat{V}^0_r) = 0$, r=p,q.

It is worth noting that the additional linear combination of $\Delta\hat{l}_q$ in (3.8b) arises only because the normalisation on $\hat{l}_q$ entails a stochastic matrix $(\hat{\Omega}_{qq})$; this would not occur if the matrix were non-stochastic.

One of the 'm' linear combinations of $\Delta\hat{l}_q$ in (3.8a) is redundant, as the mxm matrix on the left of (3.8a) has rank m-1. Also, the columns of this matrix are orthogonal to the vector $\Omega_{qq}l_q$ on the left of (3.8b), which shows that replacement of any row of this matrix — say the first — by $l'_q\Omega_{qq}$ results in an (mxm) matrix which is necessarily non-singular. In view of this, we work with the result:

$$\left[\frac{2l'_q\Omega_{qq}}{S_1(I-l_ql'_q\Omega_{qq})(C_{qq}-g_*I)}\right]\sqrt{n}\Delta\hat{l}_q \xrightarrow{a} \left[\frac{-l'_q\sqrt{n}\Delta\hat{\Omega}_{qq}l_q \equiv -\sqrt{n}e_{1q}}{-S_1(I-l_ql'_q\Omega_{qq})\sqrt{n}\Delta\hat{C}_{qq}l_q \equiv -\sqrt{n}e_{2q}}\right] \quad \ldots(3.9a)$$

where S_1 is the selector matrix such that S_1A is A without its first row. Or,

$$J_q\sqrt{n}\Delta\hat{l}_q \xrightarrow{a} -\sqrt{n}e_q(\text{say}) \Rightarrow \quad \sqrt{n}\Delta\hat{l}_q \xrightarrow{a} -J_q^{-1}\sqrt{n}e_q. \quad \ldots(3.9b)$$

Clearly, we need to determine the asymptotic distribution of $e_q = (e_{1q}, e'_{2q})'$. First, $e_{1q} = l'_q\Delta\hat{\Omega}_{qq}l_q = (l'_q \otimes l'_q)$ vec $\hat{\Omega}_{qq}$ is asymptotically a zero mean normal variable by (3.5b), and the asymptotic variance $V(\sqrt{n}e_{1q})$ is 2 by Proposition 1, Appendix B. Second, e_{2q} is also asymptotically normal with mean zero: It is linear in $\Delta\hat{C}_{qq}l_q$, which in turn is asymptotically linear in

$$\eta = \left[(\Delta\text{vec}\hat{B}_{qq})', (\Delta\text{vec}\hat{B}_{pq})', (\Delta\text{vec}\hat{B}_{qp})', (\Delta\text{vec}\hat{B}_{pp})'\right]' \quad \ldots(3.10a)$$

which latter is $\xrightarrow{a} N(0,*)$ by virtue of (3.5a). More fully, by Proposition 2 (Appendix B),

$$\sqrt{n}\Delta\hat{C}_{qq}l_q \xrightarrow{a} \sqrt{n}M\eta, \quad M = [M_{qq}, M_{pq}, M_{qp}, M_{pp}] \quad \ldots(3.10b)$$

where the m^2xm^2 matrices M_{rs} are given by

$$M_{qq} = -(B_{qq}^{-1}l_q)' \otimes C_{qq}, M_{pq} = (B_{qq}^{-1}l_q)' \otimes B_{qp}B_{pp}^{-1},$$

$$M_{qp} = (B_{pp}^{-1}B_{pq}B_{qq}^{-1}l_q)' \otimes I_m, M_{pp} = -(B_{pp}^{-1}B_{pq}B_{qq}^{-1}l_q)' \otimes B_{qp}B_{pp}^{-1};$$

consequently,

$$\sqrt{n}\Delta\hat{C}_{qq}l_q \xrightarrow{a} N(0, MV(\sqrt{n}\eta)M') \qquad ...(3.10c)$$

where the expression for $V(\sqrt{n}\eta)$ is familiar in the 3SLS context. Finally, e_{1q} and e_{2q} are asymptotically uncorrelated in as much as $\hat{\Omega}$ and $\hat{B}$ are.

We thus deduce:

Theorem 7

Let J_q and M be as defined in (3.9) and (3.10b), respectively, and η be the random vector defined in (3.10a). Then, $\sqrt{n}\Delta\hat{l}_q$ is asymptotically normally distributed with zero mean and variance,

$$V(\sqrt{n}\Delta\hat{l}_q) = J_q^{-1}V\begin{pmatrix}\sqrt{n}e_{1q} \\ \text{------} \\ \sqrt{n}e_{2q}\end{pmatrix} J_q'^{-1}$$

$$= J_q^{-1}\left[\begin{array}{cc} 2, & 0 \\ \hline 0, & S_1(I - l_q l_q' \Omega_{qq})V(\sqrt{n}\Delta\hat{C}_{qq}l_q) \\ & x(I - \Omega_{qq}l_q l_q')S_1' \end{array}\right] J_q'^{-1},$$

where

$$V(\sqrt{n}\Delta\hat{C}_{qq}l_q) = MV(\sqrt{n}\eta)M'.$$

Remark 2

Some comments are in order on the asymptotic distribution of $\hat{l}_q$ in a few special cases. (a) Suppose Ω_{qq} is known. Then the linear combination in (3.8b) disappears, which in fact originated with our use of a random matrix ($\hat{\Omega}_{qq}$) in formulating the normalisation on $\hat{l}_q$. The distribution of $\hat{l}_q$ is now governed by (3.8a), which is a system of m equations in $\hat{l}_q$ of which one is redundant, indicating that the distribution now is necessarily degenerate. Rather than dropping one equation, however, one may also use a g-inverse of the matrix on the left of (3.8a) to solve for $\Delta\hat{l}_q$. To see details, suppose (without loss of generality) $g_* = g_m$, and write

$C_{qq} - g_* I = C_{qq} - g_m I = \Lambda_q.\text{diag}(f_1, f_2, ... f_{m-1}, 0).\ \Lambda_q^{-1}$ where $f_i = g_i - g_m$, and $\Lambda_q = (\lambda_q^i)$ is the matrix of the eigen vectors. Then, continuing to write l_q for λ_q^m, a g-inverse to use is $R_q = (I - l_q l_q' \Omega_{qq}) x \Lambda_q.\text{diag}(1/f_1, ..., 1/f_{m-1}, 0).\Lambda_q^{-1}$[8] whereupon we have

$$\sqrt{n}\Delta\hat{l}_q \xrightarrow{a} R_q(I - l_q l_q' \Omega_{qq})\sqrt{n}\Delta\hat{C}_{qq} l_q \qquad ...(3.11)$$

$$\xrightarrow{a} R_q \sqrt{n}\Delta\hat{C}_{qq} l_q; \qquad (\because R_q l_q = 0)$$

hence

$$\sqrt{n}\Delta\hat{l}_q \xrightarrow{a} N(0, R_q V(\sqrt{n}\Delta\hat{C}_{qq} l_q) R_q').$$

Needless to say, the distribution of $\hat{l}_q$ is given by (3.11) whenever the matrix in the normalisation $l_q'(.)l_q = 1$ is non-stochastic. (b) Consider the standard case treated in the statistical literature with focus on the distribution of eigen vectors and roots in which: Ω_{qq} is an identity matrix; $\hat{C}_{qq}$ is Wishart distributed according to $W_m(C_{qq}, n-1)$; and Λ, the matrix of eigen vectors of C_{qq}, is orthogonal $(\Lambda' = \Lambda^{-1})$ — e.g. Anderson (1984, Ch.13). The asymptotic distribution of $\hat{l}_q$ is again given by (3.11) where, now,

$$R_q = (I - l_q l_q')\Lambda D_f \Lambda', \quad D_f = (1/f_1, 1/f_2, ..., 1/f_{m-1}, 0)$$
$$= \Lambda D_f \Lambda';$$

whence,

$$V(\sqrt{n}\Delta\hat{l}_q) = \Lambda D_f \Lambda' V(\sqrt{n}\Delta\hat{C}_{qq} l_q)\Lambda D_f \Lambda',$$

which is, by Proposition 3 (Appendix B),

$$= g_m(\equiv g_*)\sum_{j\neq m} \frac{g_j}{(g_j - g_m)^2} \lambda_q^j \lambda_q^{j\prime},$$

as in Anderson (1984, Theorem 13.5.1).

---

8. The matrix on the left of (3.8a) is $T_q = (I - l_q l_q' \Omega_{qq})\Lambda_q.\text{diag}(f_1, ... f_{m-1}, 0).\Lambda_q^{-1}$; that $T_q R_q T_q = T_q$ is verified by noting that $\Lambda_q^{-1} l_q = (0, 0, ... 0, 1)'$.

(ii) Asymptotic Joint Distribution of $\hat{l}_q, \hat{l}_p$.

The asymptotic distribution of $\hat{l}_p$ is deduced by simply interchanging the roles of the subscripts p and q in theorem 7. Let (J_p, e_p) be so obtained from (J_q, e_q) of the theorem. Then we have:

Theorem 8

Let $\hat{l} = (\hat{l}'_q, \hat{l}'_p)'$. Then $\sqrt{n}\Delta\hat{l}$ is asymptotically normally distributed with mean zero and variance,

$$V\begin{bmatrix}\sqrt{n}\Delta\hat{l}_q \\ \sqrt{n}\Delta\hat{l}_p\end{bmatrix} \begin{bmatrix} J_q^{-1}V(\sqrt{n}e_q)J_q'^{-1} & , & J_q^{-1}\mathrm{Cov}(\sqrt{n}e_q, \sqrt{n}e_p)J_p'^{-1} \\ & , & J_p^{-1}V(\sqrt{n}e_p)J_p'^{-1} \end{bmatrix}$$

We already know the analytic form of the diagonal blocks of the variance matrix in Theorem 8. The form of the off-diagonal block is also easily determined by noting that the asymptotic covariance involved therein has the form — see Proposition 4 (Appendix B) and the discussion just prior to it —

$$\mathrm{Cov}\left(\begin{bmatrix}\sqrt{n}e_{1q} \\ \sqrt{n}e_{2q}\end{bmatrix}, \begin{bmatrix}\sqrt{n}e_{1p} \\ \sqrt{n}e_{2p}\end{bmatrix}\right) = \begin{bmatrix} 2\mu_*^2 & , & 0 \\ 0 & , & \mathrm{Cov}(\sqrt{n}e_{2q}, \sqrt{n}e_{2p}) \end{bmatrix};$$

the covariance of e_{2q}, e_{2p} is easily calculated since they are particular linear transforms of the vector η in (3.10a).

(iii) Asymptotic Distribution of $\hat{c}$ *and* $\hat{d}$.

Consider first $\hat{c}$ (3.4). Some tedious but straightforward calculations show that

$$\begin{aligned}\sqrt{n}\Delta\hat{c} \xrightarrow{a} & l'_p\Omega_{pp}B_{pq}B_{qq}^{-1}\sqrt{n}\Delta\hat{l}_q \\ & + l'_qB_{qq}'^{-1}B'_{pq}\Omega_{pp}\sqrt{n}\Delta\hat{l}_p \\ & + \left[(B_{qq}^{-1}l_q)\otimes l'_p\,\Omega_{pp}\right]\sqrt{n}\Delta \mathrm{vec}\hat{B}_{pq} \\ & - \left[(B_{qq}^{-1}l_q)'\otimes l'_p\Omega_{pp}B_{pq}B_{qq}^{-1}\right]\sqrt{n}\Delta \mathrm{vec}\hat{B}_{qq} \\ & + \left[(B_{pq}B_{qq}^{-1}l_q)'\otimes l'_p\right]\sqrt{n}\Delta \mathrm{vec}\hat{\Omega}_{pp}.\end{aligned} \qquad \text{...(3.12)}$$

In view of (3.5a)-(3.5b) and Theorem 8 we conclude that $\hat{c}$ is asymptotically normally distributed with mean 0 and variance σ_c^2. Using Theorem 8 and the asymptotic properties of $\hat{B}, \hat{\Omega}$, it is possible to obtain σ_c^2; the exercise, however, is not particularly illuminating, so we abandon the effort. Of course, one also finds that $\sqrt{n}\Delta\hat{d} \xrightarrow{a} N(0, \sigma_d^2)$ where σ_d^2 is obtained from σ_c^2 by simply interchanging the roles of the subscripts p and q. Working out the joint asymptotic distribution of $\hat{c}$ and $\hat{d}$ is also straightforward, and is not pursued here.

4. AN APPLICATION

Here we empirically implement the preceding analysis in the context of the U.S. red meat market. As in Waugh (1942), we confine attention to two major constituent items, namely beef and pork; we also utilise annual data for the period: 1965-1990. As a first step, we formulate and estimate a conventional structural equation system that interlinks the markets for the two items. Though the intent here is primarily to demonstrate implementability of our analysis, some effort is expended to ensure that the model we work with is 'realistic', in that the coefficient estimates — especially the $\hat{B}$ — are significant with expected signs.

The Model

The model we estimate is obvious from Table 3.1, and hence is not separately spelled out here. The endogenous variables are

$l_n q^{(bf)}$ = logarithmic quantity of beef
$l_n q^{(pk)}$ = logarithmic quantity of pork
$l_n p^{(bf)}$ = logarithmic price of beef
$l_n p^{(pk)}$ = logarithmic price of pork;

and the predetermined variables are

$q_{-1}^{(bf)}$ = quantity of beef lagged one period,
$q_{-1}^{(pk)}$ = quantity of pork lagged one period,
$p_{-1}^{(pk)}$ = price of pork lagged one period
DPI = per capita disposable income
PC = price of corn
PRIME = prime rate of interest.

Table 3.1

3SLS Estimate of the Model

DEMAND			SUPPLY		
Dependent Variable =>	(Beef) $l_n\ q^{(bf)}$	(Pork) $l_n\ q^{(pk)}$	Dependent Variable =>	(Beef) $l_n\ p^{(bf)}$	(Pork) $l_n\ p^{(pk)}$
$l_n\ p^{(bf)}$	-0.5535	0.6332	$l_n\ q^{(bf)}$	0.6006	
	(5.319)	(3.964)		(15.276)	
$l_n\ p^{(pk)}$	0.5899	-0.7747	$l_n\ q^{(pk)}$		0.2962
	(6.312)	(5.028)			(3.604)
$l_n\ q^{(bf)}$		0.8442	PC	0.0024	0.0018
		(6.677)		(2.458)	(2.503)
$l_n\ q^{(pk)}$	0.693		PRIME	0.0511	
	(8.410)			(2.641)	
$q^{(bf)}_{-1}$	0.3765		$p^{(pk)}_{-1}$		0.5446
	(4.517)				(4.408)
$q^{(pk)}_{-1}$		0.1218			
		(1.050)			
DPI	0.0119	0.0404			
	(0.245)	(0.534)			

Note: Figures in parentheses are the |t| values.

Data and Source

All quantity variables are on a per capita basis and are measured in pounds. The prices of beef and pork are in dollars per 100 pounds. These four variables are taken from the Agricultural Statistics, US Department of Agriculture. The latter is also the source for the prime rate. The price of corn is in cents per bushel, and the data on it are taken from The Statistical Abstract of the United States. The per capita disposable income figures are taken from the Economic Report of the President.

Empirical Findings

Table 3.1 presents the 3SLS results for the model employed here. The results are mostly sensible, and provide us with:

$$\hat{B}_{qq} = \begin{bmatrix} 1 & , & -0.8442 \\ -0.6930 & , & 1 \end{bmatrix}, \qquad \hat{B}_{pq} = \begin{bmatrix} 0.5535 & , & -0.6632 \\ -0.5899 & , & 0.7747 \end{bmatrix},$$

$$\hat{B}_{qp} = \begin{bmatrix} -0.6006 & , & 0 \\ 0 & , & -0.2962 \end{bmatrix}, \qquad \hat{B}_{pp} = \begin{bmatrix} 1 & , & 0 \\ 0 & , & 1 \end{bmatrix};$$

$$\hat{C}_{qq} = \begin{bmatrix} -0.1660 & , & 0.2402 \\ 0.0379 & , & -0.1975 \end{bmatrix}, \qquad \hat{C}_{pp} = \begin{bmatrix} -0.1660 & , & 0.1185 \\ 0.0767 & , & -0.1975 \end{bmatrix}.$$

Table 3.2 presents the eigen roots $(\hat{g})$ and vectors $(\hat{l}_q, \hat{l}_p)$, as also the squared correlations $\hat{\mu}^2 \,(= \hat{l}_q' \hat{\Omega}_{qp} \hat{l}_p)^2$, corresponding to the roots; the SE's for the elements of $\hat{l}_q, \hat{l}_p$ were computed following Theorem 8.

It is comforting that the estimates in Table 3.2 are all significantly different from zero. There is, however, something disappointing about the weight vectors associated with the larger $\hat{\mu}^2$: The weights on quantities, as also the weights on prices, are of opposite signs, thus rendering the resulting P_c and Q_c unacceptable. As Waugh would have it, we reluctantly opt for "rejecting the weights associated with maximum correlation coefficient",[9] and settle for the lower $\hat{\mu}^2$. Fortunately, in this 'next best' situation, the weight vectors have the desirable property that their elements are all positive. Accordingly, the weight vectors corresponding to the root $\hat{g} = \hat{g}_2$ in Table 3.2 are our choice in computing the indexes proposed here.

Next, the estimates of the coefficients c and d, computed according to (3.4) using the weight vectors corresponding to the root $\hat{g}_2$ turn out to be

$$\underset{(2.1545)}{\hat{c} = 0.5171}, \qquad \underset{(2.7439)}{\hat{d} = -0.1646} \qquad \text{...(4.1)}$$

where the figures in parenthesis are the | t | values. These coefficient estimates have expected signs and are significantly different from zero. Also interesting is the fact that, though $\hat{c}$, $\hat{d}$, $\hat{g}_2$ were computed in isolation, it is indeed true that $\hat{c}.\hat{d} = -0.0851 \equiv \hat{g}_2$; recall that c.d = g. The standard error of $\hat{c}$ was computed following the asymptotic

9. Waugh (1942, p.296). He also mentions that he had to abandon the criterion of maximum correlation in a number of applications he happened to investigate.

normal distribution of $\hat{c}$ noted in (3.12), and that of $\hat{d}$ was obtained analogously.

Table 3.2

Eigen Roots, Eigen Vectors and Squared Correlations

$\hat{g}$	$\hat{l}_q$	$\hat{l}_p$	$\hat{\mu}^2$
	Beef : -22.5106	Beef : -7.3472	
$\hat{g}_1$ = -0.2784	(3.8237)	(4.5660)	0.7391
	Pork : 10.5362	Pork : 6.9726	
	(4.1407)	(6.9427)	
	Beef : 33.3276	Beef : 9.2357	
$\hat{g}_2$ = -0.0851	(6.1040)	(3.2628)	0.4359
	Pork : 11.2220	Pork : 6.2369	
	(3.1000)	(3.0573)	

Note: Figures in parentheses are the |t| values.

As a point of curiosity, we also estimated c and d by 3SLS from the group demand and supply equations taken in the form — see (1.5):

$$Q_c + x'\hat{\Gamma}_q\hat{a}_q = -cP_c + \text{error} \quad \text{(Group demand)}$$

$$P_c + x'\hat{\Gamma}_p\hat{a}_p = -dQ_c + \text{error} \quad \text{(Group supply)}$$

where the aggregator vectors are estimated as $\hat{a}_r = \hat{B}_{rr}^{-1}\hat{l}_r$ — see (1.6), the $\hat{l}_r$ being eigen vectors corresponding to $\hat{g}_2$ in Table 3.2. The 3SLS produced the estimates $\tilde{c} = 0.5171$ ($|t| = 106.9206$) and $\tilde{d} = -0.1647$ ($|t| = 55.7246$) which are virtually identical to those given in (4.1); the |t| values are of course considerably higher than those in (4.1), and for obvious reasons.

We do not undertake to compute demand-supply elasticities: $\beta = \dfrac{P_c}{Q_c}\cdot\dfrac{\partial Q_c}{\partial P_c}$, using the estimates $\hat{c}$ and $\hat{d}$.

Finally, Table 3.3 permits a comparative view of the indexes (P_c, Q_c) proposed here, and those of the type suggested by Waugh (1942) and Theil (1960); a better visual perspective is accessible in Figure 3.1

and Figure 3.2. The Waugh indexes (P_{uc}, Q_{uc}) were computed using the weight (eigen) vectors corresponding to the *lower* root (squared correlation) in the sample counterpart of (2.15); the vectors corresponding to the maximum root had again the sign problem we noted in connection with our indexes. The Theil indexes (P_T, Q_T) did not suffer from the sign problem: they in fact use the weight (eigen) vectors corresponding to the maximum root in the sample version of (2.17a). The table initialises the indexes to 100 for 1965.

Table 3.3

The Constrained, Unconstrained (Waugh) and Theil Indexes (*)

Year	Q_c	Q_T	Q_{uc}	P_c	P_T	P_{uc}
1965	100.0	100.0	100.0	100.0	100.0	100.0
1966	100.6	100.3	100.6	101.9	102.0	101.8
1967	101.5	101.5	101.5	98.7	98.5	98.9
1968	102.1	102.1	102.1	100.1	99.7	100.5
1969	102.2	102.0	102.1	104.5	104.5	104.5
1970	102.7	102.5	102.6	103.4	103.2	103.6
1971	103.1	103.3	103.1	102.6	101.7	103.4
1972	102.9	102.5	102.8	110.1	109.9	110.3
1973	101.4	100.6	101.2	119.4	119.6	119.2
1974	102.9	102.2	102.7	116.4	116.4	116.3
1975	102.0	100.2	101.5	121.8	122.4	121.3
1976	103.5	101.7	103.0	117.7	118.3	117.1
1977	103.1	101.6	102.7	117.5	118.0	117.1
1978	102.3	101.0	102.0	124.5	124.8	124.2
1979	101.2	101.1	101.2	127.8	127.2	128.3
1980	101.2	101.5	101.3	129.5	129.3	129.7
1981	101.1	101.1	101.1	127.3	126.9	127.5
1982	100.4	99.9	100.3	130.2	130.3	130.0
1983	101.0	100.6	100.9	127.8	127.7	128.0
1984	100.9	100.5	100.8	128.9	128.8	129.1
1985	101.1	100.7	101.0	125.7	125.6	125.8
1986	101.0	100.2	100.8	127.3	127.5	127.2
1987	100.3	99.8	100.2	129.5	129.4	129.5
1988	100.5	100.3	100.4	128.6	128.0	129.1
1989	99.8	99.9	99.8	129.7	129.1	130.3
1990	99.2	99.1	99.2	133.6	133.4	133.8

(*) Q_c (P_c) = Constrained quantity (price) index
Q_{uc} (P_{uc}) = Unconstrained (Waugh) quantity (price) index
Q_T (P_T) = Theil's quantity (price) index.

Surprisingly, the differences among the price indexes are almost non-existent, which is brought out dramatically in Figure 3.1. As to the quantity indexes, however, it is invariably the case that Theil's index is smaller than the other two; our index is persistently higher than Waugh's though, again surprisingly, the discrepancies are small.

5. CONCLUSION

The paper is addressed to the price-quantity indexes deduced concurrently through linear aggregation of all the demand equations, as also all the supply equations, for 'm' interrelated commodity markets in equilibrium. The price index is $P = \underline{p}'\lambda_p$ and the quantity index is $Q = \underline{q}'\lambda_q$ where $\underline{p}$, $\underline{q}$ are m-vectors of prices and quantities, respectively. The 'm' pairs of demand-supply equations constitute a conventional 2m-equation structural system, which makes for a broader framework than employed in previous model-based analyses. To the extent a structural system depicts some economic theory, the indexes formulated here are immune to the criticism that the indexes amount to "measurement without theory". The present indexes, unlike most available to date, also permit measurement of the effect on them of a change in the level of a predetermined variable — most likely, a policy variable — appearing in the equations for any constituent market.

Aside from performing their traditional role of measuring general movements in prices and quantities, the indexes also take on a non-traditional role of being serviceable in the measurement of price slopes and/or elasticities of group demand and/or supply equations, a role first demanded of them by Bergstrom. To enable the indexes to perform this non-traditional role, we have insisted that the group demand and supply equations, which are linear aggregates of individual demand and supply equations, constitute a conventional two-equation structural system in which P and Q are the only two endogenous variables. This calls for what we have called a 'consistent aggregation condition (CAC)' to be imposed on the weight vectors λ_p and λ_q, under which the vectors emerge as eigen vectors of certain matrices involving the structural parameters of the multimarket system. Following the standard practice in the statistical literature, we resolve the issue of the optimal choice of λ_p, λ_q using the criterion of

Price Indexes

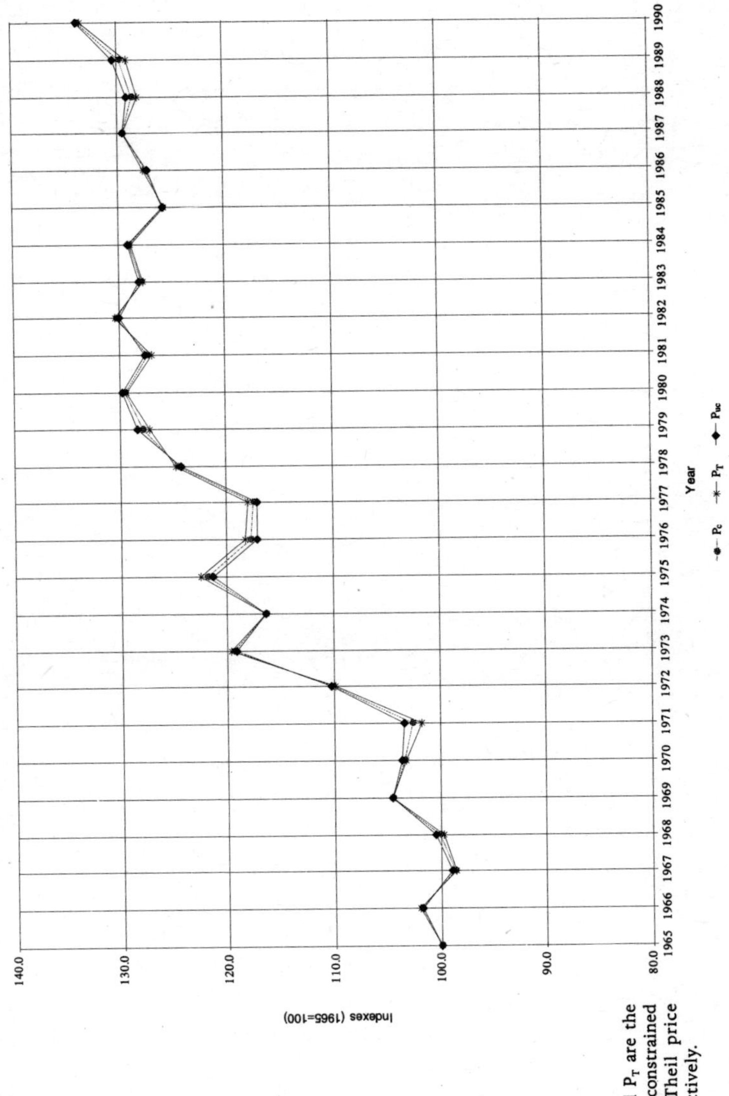

Note: The P_c, P_{uc}, and P_T are the constrained, unconstrained (Waugh) and Theil price indexes, respectively.

Figure 3.2

Quantity Indexes

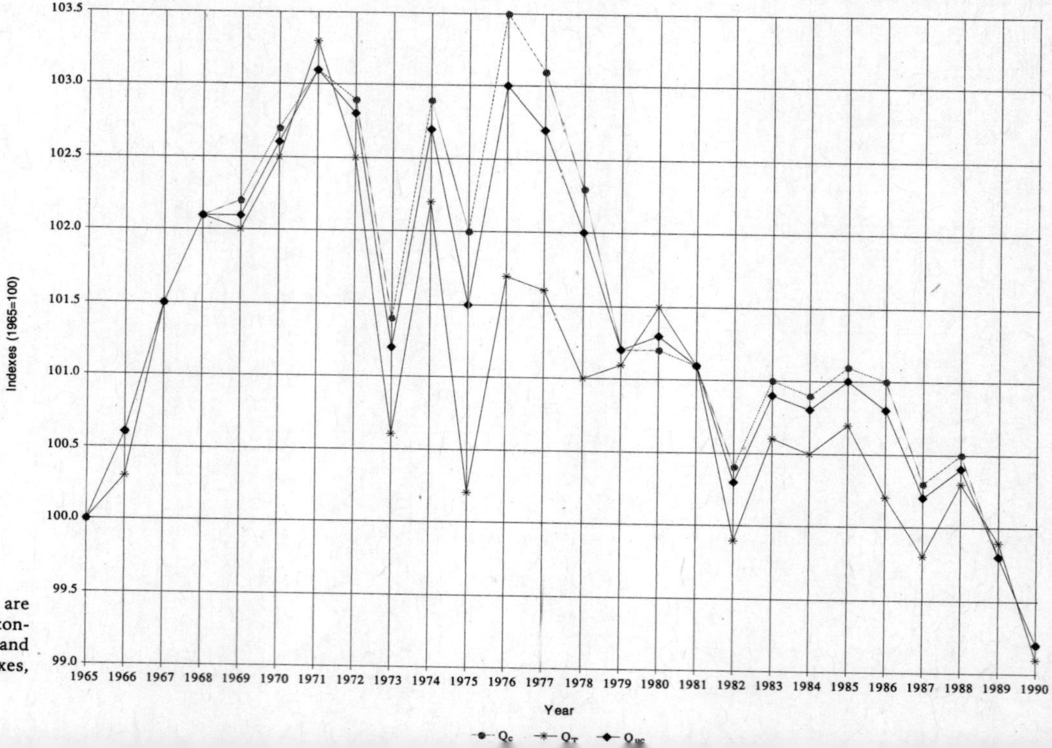

Note: The Q_c, Q_{uc}, and Q_T are the constrained, unconstrained (Waugh) and Theil quantity indexes, respectively.

maximum correlation between the indexes. The choice problem is recognised as a constrained canonical correlation problem — an extension of the Hotelling-Hooper theme where the choice vectors are subject to the CAC constraint.

We also implemented our analysis in the context of the U.S. red meat market, singling out two major constituent items, namely beef and pork. Apparently, the maximum correlation criterion does not always lead to sensible weight vectors, which forced us to settle for the vectors corresponding to the second highest squared correlation. We also offer a comparative view of our indexes *vis-à-vis* the Waugh and Theil indexes.

Finally, on the methodological front, the asymptotic distribution theory worked out for the eigen vectors is of independent interest, in as much as the stochastic matrices involved are asymmetric, unlike in the mainstream multivariate analysis. Of course, we confine attention to the less troublesome case where the matrices have distinct, non-zero and real roots. While the assumption of real roots is eminently realistic in our context, it should be desirable to extend the present analysis to situations where the matrices involved in the CAC are possibly singular.

• This paper is based, in part, on the doctoral dissertation of the second author—Salih (1993).

APPENDIX A

Proofs of Theorems

Proof of Theorem 1

Let

$$\underline{q}^0 = K_q \underline{q}, \quad \underline{p}^0 = K_p \underline{p}$$

be the quantity and the price vectors under new units of measurement; the diagonal K_q and K_p are the scaling matrices. The multimarket system in terms of $\underline{q}^0, \underline{p}^0$ differs from the old system (1.2) only in respect of the coefficients for these vectors; the coefficients are the counterparts of B_{rs} given by

$$B^0_{rs} = K_r B_{rs}, \quad (r, s = p,q).$$

The new indexes are

$$Q^0 = \underline{q}^{0\prime} \lambda^0_q, \quad P^0 = \underline{p}^{0\prime} \lambda^0_p \qquad \text{...(A.1)}$$

where the weight vectors satisfy the CAC (2.2) in terms of B^0_{rs}. We need to show that

$$Q^0 = Q = \underline{q}' \lambda_q, \quad P^0 = P = \underline{p}' \lambda_p. \qquad \text{...(A.2)}$$

The coefficients c and d — hence also g = c.d — remain invariant under new units of measurement. Thus from the CAC restrictions we have

$$(B^0_{qp} B^{0-1}_{pp} B^0_{pq} B^{0-1}_{qq} - gI)\lambda^0_q = 0$$

$$\Rightarrow (K_q C_{qq} K_q^{-1} - gI)\lambda^0_q = 0$$

$$\Rightarrow (C_{qq} - gI) K_q^{-1} \lambda^0_q = 0$$

$$\Rightarrow K_q^{-1} \lambda^0_q = \lambda_q; \qquad \text{(by (2.2)}$$

similarly, $K_p^{-1} \lambda^0_p = \lambda_p$. This confirms (A.2), and hence the theorem.

Proof of Theorem 5

We have — see (2.6) and (2.8)— $\mu^2_* = [\text{Corr}(P_c, Q_c)]^2 = \max(\mu^2)$ where it is convenient to take μ^2 as a root of $\overline{S}_{qq}$ for any given root g of C_{qq}/C_{pp}. Also, $\bar{\mu}_*^2 = [\text{Corr}(P_{uc}, Q_{uc})]^2$ is the maximum root of $|\Omega_{pq}\Omega_{qq}^{-1}\Omega_{qp} - \bar{\mu}^2\Omega_{pp}| = 0$, the detrimental equation associated with the eigen value problem in (2.15b). The theorem is proved by showing that the root μ^2 of $\bar{S}_{qq}$ for any root g is less than or equal to $\bar{\mu}_*^2$.

For any root g of C_{qq}/C_{pp}, from (2.20) we have

$$\mu^2 = \lambda_q^{*'}[H_{qp}\lambda_p^*.\lambda_p^{*'}H_{pq}]\lambda_q^*$$

$$\leq \lambda_q^{*'}\lambda_q^*.\max(\alpha^2) = \max(\alpha^2)$$

where α^2 is an eigen root of $H_{qp}\lambda_p^*.\lambda_p^{*'}H_{pq}$ of unit rank; whence

$$\max(\alpha^2) = \text{tr}(H_{qp}\lambda_p^*.\lambda_p^{*'}H_{pq})$$

$$= \lambda_p^{*'}H_{pq}H_{qp}\lambda_p^*$$

$$\leq \lambda_p^{*'}\lambda_p^*.\max(\bar{\mu}^2) = \max(\bar{\mu}^2)$$

where $\bar{\mu}^2$ is an eigen root of $H_{pq}H_{qp}$, i.e., a root

$$|H_{pq}H_{qp} - \bar{\mu}^2 I| = 0, \text{i.e.,} |\Omega_{pq}\Omega_{qq}^{-1}\Omega_{qp} - \bar{\mu}^2\Omega_{pp}| = 0.$$

Hence $\mu^2 \leq \max(\bar{\mu}^2) = \bar{\mu}_*^2$, which proves the theorem.

APPENDIX B

Some Asymptotic Variance-Covariance Results

Refer to (3.9). We first establish

Proposition 1

The asymptotic variance of $\sqrt{n}e_{1q}$ is 2.

Proof

We have, from (3.9),

$$e_{1q} = l'_q \Delta\hat{\Omega}_{qq} l_q = (l'_q \otimes l'_q)\Delta \text{vec } \hat{\Omega}_{qq}.$$

Since $\hat{\Omega}_{qq}$ is the m.l.e. of Ω_{qq}, a suitable adaptation of the result in (3.5b) shows that the asymptotic variance of $\sqrt{n}e_{1q}$ is

$$V(\sqrt{n}e_{1q}) = (l'_q \otimes l'_q)[I + \sum_{ij=1}^{m}(e_i e'_j \otimes e_j e'_i)] \text{ x } (\Omega_{qq} \otimes \Omega_{qq})(l_q \otimes l_q)$$

$$= l'_q \Omega_{qq} l_q . l'_q \Omega_{qq} l_q + h = 1 + h,$$

where e_j is the mx1 vector whose only non-vanishing element is the jth, which is unity. The scalar 'h' in (B.1) is

$$h = (l'_q \otimes l'_q).\sum_{ij}(e_i e'_j \otimes e_j e'_i).\Omega_{qq} \otimes \Omega_{qq}.(l_q \otimes l_q)$$

$$= \text{tr}\left[\sum_{ij}(e_i e'_j \otimes e_j e'_i).(F \otimes F)\right], \quad F = \Omega_{qq} l_q l'_q$$

$$= \sum_{ij} \text{tr}(e_i e'_j F \otimes e_j e'_i F)$$

$$= \text{tr}(F^2) = \text{tr}\Omega_{qq} l_q l'_q . \Omega_{qq} l_q l'_q$$

$$= \text{tr}\Omega_{qq} l_q l'_q = 1. \text{ Hence the proposition.}$$

With reference to the stochastic vector in e_{2q} (3.9a) we find that,

Proposition 2

$\sqrt{n}\hat{C}_{qq} l_q \xrightarrow{a} M\eta$ where M is defined in (3.10b) and the random vector η is defined in (3.10a).

Proof

Write $\hat{C}_{qq} = \hat{R}.\hat{T}; \quad \hat{R} = \hat{B}_{qp}\hat{B}_{pp}^{-1}, \quad \hat{T} = \hat{B}_{pq}\hat{B}_{qq}^{-1}$.

Evidently,

$$\sqrt{n}\Delta\hat{C}_{qq} \xrightarrow{a} (\sqrt{n}\Delta\hat{R})T + R\sqrt{n}\Delta\hat{T} \qquad \text{...(B.2)}$$

where plim $\hat{R} = R = B_{qp}B_{pp}^{-1}$ and plim $\hat{T} = T = B_{pq}B_{qq}^{-1}$; $\hat{R}\hat{B}_{pp} = \hat{B}_{qp} \Rightarrow$

$$(\sqrt{n}\Delta\hat{R})B_{pp} + R\sqrt{n}\Delta\hat{B}_{pp} \xrightarrow{a} \sqrt{n}\Delta\hat{B}_{qp}; \text{ and } \hat{T}\hat{B}_{qq} = \hat{B}_{pq} \Rightarrow \qquad \text{...(B.3)}$$

$$(\sqrt{n}\Delta\hat{T})B_{qq} + T\sqrt{n}\Delta\hat{B}_{qq} \xrightarrow{a} \sqrt{n}\Delta\hat{B}_{pq}. \qquad \text{...(B.4)}$$

Substituting for $\sqrt{n}\Delta\hat{R}$ in (B.2) from (B.3), and likewise for $\sqrt{n}\Delta\hat{T}$ from (B.4), one finds that,

$$\sqrt{n}\Delta\hat{C}_{qq}l_q \xrightarrow{a} -C_{qq}\sqrt{n}(\Delta\hat{B}_{qq})B_{qq}^{-1}l_q + B_{qp}B_{pp}^{-1}(\sqrt{n}\Delta\hat{B}_{pq})B_{qq}^{-1}l_q$$

$$+ (\sqrt{n}\Delta\hat{B}_{qp}).B_{pp}^{-1}B_{pq}B_{qq}^{-1}l_q$$

$$- B_{qp}B_{pp}^{-1}(\sqrt{n}\Delta\hat{B}_{pp})B_{pp}^{-1}B_{pq}B_{qq}^{-1}l_q. \qquad \text{...(B.5)}$$

The proposition follows from using the fact that $\Delta\hat{C}_{qq}l_q = \text{vec}(\Delta\hat{C}_{qq}l_q)$ and that $\text{vec}ABC = (C' \otimes A)\text{vec}B$.

Proposition 3

Let $\hat{C}_{qq}$ be Wishart distributed as $W_m(C_{qq}, n-1)$, $\Lambda_q C_{qq} \Lambda'_q =$ $\text{diag}(g_1, g_2, ..., g_m)$ where $\Lambda_q = (\lambda_q^i)$ consists of the eigen vectors of C_{qq}, and $F_q = \Lambda_q.\text{diag}(1/f_1, 1/f_2, ... 1/f_{m-1}, 0).\Lambda'_q$ where $f_i = g_i - g_m$, $i = 1, ..., m-1$. Then the asymptotic variance of $F_q\sqrt{n}\Delta\hat{C}_{qq}\lambda_q^m$ is

$$F_q V\left(\sqrt{n}\hat{C}_{qq}\lambda_q^m\right)F_q' = g_m \sum_{j \neq m} \frac{g_j}{f_j^2}\lambda_q^j \lambda_q^{j'}.$$

Proof

First, by virtue of (3.5b),

$$V(\sqrt{n}\hat{C}_{qq}\lambda_q^m) = (\lambda_q^{m'} \otimes I)\left[I + \sum_{i,j=1}^{m} e_i e_j' \otimes e_j e_i'\right](C_{qq} \otimes C_{qq})x(\lambda_q^m \otimes I)$$

$$=A_1 + A_2 \text{ (say)}.$$

We have

$$A_1 = \lambda_q^{m'} C_{qq}\lambda_q^m . C_{qq} = g_m \cdot \sum_{j=i}^{m} g_j \lambda_q^j \lambda_q^{j'} ; \text{ and}$$

$$A_2 = \sum_{ij} \lambda_q^{m'} e_i . e_j' C_{qq} \lambda_q^m . e_j e_i' . C_{qq} = C_{qq}\lambda_q^m \lambda_q^{m'} C_{qq} = g^2{}_m \lambda_q^m \lambda_q^{m'} .$$

Hence,

$$F_q(A_1 + A_2)F_q' = \left(\sum_{i \neq m} \frac{1}{f_i} \lambda_q^i \lambda_q^{i'} \right)\left(g_m \sum_{j=1}^{m} g_j \lambda_q^j \lambda_q^{j'} + g^2{}_m \lambda_q^m \lambda_q^{m'} \right)\left(\sum_{i \neq m} \frac{1}{f_i} \lambda_q^i \lambda_q^{i'} \right)$$

$$= g_m \sum_{j \neq m} \frac{g_j}{f_j^2} \lambda_q^j \lambda_q^{j'} ,$$

as was to be shown.

Finally, in Theorem 8, the off-diagonal block of the variance entails $\mathrm{Cov}(\sqrt{n}e_{1q}, \sqrt{n}e_{1p})$, $\mathrm{Cov}(\sqrt{n}e_{1q}, \sqrt{n}e_{2p})$, $\mathrm{Cov}(\sqrt{n}e_{2q}, \sqrt{n}e_{1p})$ and $\mathrm{Cov}(\sqrt{n}e_{2q}, \sqrt{n}e_{2p})$. The middle two covariances vanish because e_{1q}, e_{1p} are linear in $\Delta\mathrm{vec}\hat{\Omega}$ while e_{2q}, e_{2p} are linear in $\Delta\mathrm{vec}\hat{B}$, and the last covariance is easily determined because e_{2q}, e_{2p} are specific linear transforms of the random vector $\eta = (\Delta\mathrm{vec}\hat{B}_{rs})$ — see (3.9a), (3.10a) and (3.10b). Proposition 4 evaluates the first covariance.

Proposition 4

The asymptotic covariance of $\sqrt{n}e_{1q}$ and $\sqrt{n}e_{1p}$ is $2\mu_*^2$, where $\mu_* = l_q'\Omega_{qp}l_p$.

Proof

We write: $e_{1q} = l_q'\Delta\hat{\Omega}_{qq}l_q = (l_q', 0)\Delta\hat{\Omega}\binom{l_q}{0}$

$\equiv m_q'\Delta\hat{\Omega}m_q$, say; similarly, $e_{1p} = l_p'\Delta\hat{\Omega}_{pp}l_p = (0, l_p')\Delta\hat{\Omega}\binom{0}{l_p}$

$\equiv m_p'\Delta\hat{\Omega}m_p$, say. Then

$$\mathrm{Cov}(\sqrt{n}e_{1q}, \sqrt{n}e_{1p}) = \mathrm{Cov}[(m_q' \otimes m_q')\sqrt{n}\Delta\mathrm{vec}\hat{\Omega}, (m_p' \otimes m_p')(\sqrt{n}\Delta\mathrm{vec}\hat{\Omega})]$$

$$= (m_q' \otimes m_q')\left[I + \sum_{ij}^{2m} (e_i e_j' \otimes e_j e_i')(\Omega \otimes \Omega) \right](m_p \otimes m_p) \quad \text{[using (3.5b)]}$$

$$= (m_q' \Omega m_p)^2 + h = \mu_*^2 + h$$

where the scalar 'h' is

$$= \sum_{ij} m_q' e_i . e_j' \Omega m_p \otimes m_q' e_j . e_i' \Omega m_p$$

$$= \sum_{ij} e_i' m_q m_p' \Omega e_j . e_j' m_q m_p' \Omega e_i$$

$$= tr(m_q m_p' \Omega)^2 = (m_q' \Omega m_p)^2 = \mu_*^2 .$$

Hence the proposition.

References

Anderson, R.G., B.E. Jones and T.D. Nesmith, (1997). "Monetary Aggregation Theory and Statistical Index Numbers", *Federal Reserve Bank of St. Louis Review* 79 January/ February, 31-51.

Anderson, T.W., (1984). *An Introduction to Multivariate Statistical Analysis*. New York: John Wiley & Sons, Inc.

Auerbach, A.J., (1982). "The Index of Leading Indicators: Measurement Without Theory, Thirty Years Later", *Review of Economics and Statistics* 64, 589-595.

Barnett, W.A., M.J., Hinich and P. Yue, (2000). "The Exact Theoretical Rational Expectations Monetary Aggregate", *Macroeconomic Dynamics*, 4, 197-221.

Bergstrom, A.R., (1956). "The Use of Index Numbers in Demand Analysis", *Review of Economic Studies*, 23, 17-26.

Clements, K.W. and H.Y. Izan, (1981). "A Note on Estimating Divisia Index Numbers", *International Economic Review*, 22, 745-747.

————. (1987). "The Measurement of Inflation: A Stochastic Approach", *Journal of Business and Economics Statistics*, 5, 339-350.

Dhrymes, P.J., (1970). *Econometrics: Statistical Foundations and Applications*, New York: Harper and Row.

Diewert, W.E., (1995). "Axiomatic and Economic Approaches to Elementary Price Indexes", *NBER Working Paper #5104*.

Diewert, W.E. and A.O. Nakamura, (1993). *Essays in Index Number Theory*, Volume 1. Amsterdam: North-Holland.

Hooper, J.W., (1959). "Simultaneous Equations and Canonical Correlation Theory", *Econometrica* 27, 245-256.

Hotelling, H., (1936). "Relations Between Two Sets of Variates", *Biometrika* 28, 321-377.

Kloeck, T. and G.M. De Wit, (1961). "Best Linear Unbiased Index Numbers", *Econometrica* 29, 602-616.

Koopmans, T., (1947). "Measurement Without Theory", *Review of Economics and Statistics* 29, 161-172.

Magnus, J.R. and H. Neudecker, (1979). "The Commutation Matrix: Some Properties and Applications", *Annals of Statistics* 7, 381-394.

Muirhead, R.J., (1982). *Aspects of Multivariate Statistical Theory*, New York: John Wiley & Sons, Inc.

Rao, C.R., (1973). *Linear Statistical Inference and Its Applications*. New York: John Wiley & Sons.

Rao, D.S.P. and E.A. Selvanathan, (1992). "Uniformly Minimum Variance Unbiased Estimators of Theil-Tornqvist Index Numbers", *Economics Letters*, 39 , 123-127.

Salih, M., (1993). "Optimal Linear Aggregation of Markets and the Construction of Price and Quantity Indexes", Ph. D Dissertation, State University of New York at Buffalo.

Samuelson, P.A. and S. Swamy, (1974). "Invariant Economic Index Numbers and Canonical Duality: Survey and Synthesis", *American Economic Review* 64, 566-593.

Selvanathan, E.A. and D.S.P. Rao, (1992). "A Econometric Approach to the Construction of Generalized Theil-Tornqvist Indices for Multilateral Comparisons", *Journal of Econometrics* 54, 335-346.

Selvanathan, E.A., (1991). "Further Results on Aggregation of Differential Demand Equations", *The Review of Economic Studies* 58, 799-805.

————. (1989). "A Note on the Stochastic Approach to Index Numbers", *Journal of Business and Economic Statistics* 7, 471-474.

Selvanathan, E.A., (1991). "Standard Errors for Laspeyres and Paasche Index Numbers", *Economics Letters* 35, 35-38.

Theil, H., (1960). "Best Linear Index Numbers of Prices and Quantities", *Econometrica* 28, 464-480.

Waugh, F.V., (1942). "Regressions Between Sets of Variables", *Econometrica* 10, 290-310.

4

Patterns and Determinants of Economic Growth in Indian States

K.L. KRISHNA

1. INTRODUCTION

While economists have been interested in the issues of economic growth for more than two hundred years, there has been an explosion of research on the empirics of economic growth during the last fifteen years or so. There is now a better understanding of growth fundamentals. Some stylised facts about growth based on recent research have been documented. The patterns of growth of the group of developed countries and the group of developing countries have been found to be quite different. The growth of most developing countries is found to be characterised by instability and volatility.

The literature on the sources of growth of nations has grown since mid-1950s, and the issue of determinants of growth has occupied the attention of economists for the last decade and a half. However, our understanding of the determinants of growth is very incomplete. There is growing scepticism about the methodology of cross-country regressions employed in the analysis of determinants. Although high frequency panel data used in recent growth research provides many more observations and permits experimentation with better specifications and estimation methods, it cannot be claimed that the resulting parameter estimates are necessarily better estimates or closer to the true values of the parameters.

This paper deals with the literature on the patterns and determinants of economic growth in major Indian states during the past four decades, 1960-2000. To place the issues in a proper perspective, we attempt, in Section 2, a very synoptic overview of major recent developments in empirical research on growth. In the next section, while reviewing the literature on the inter-state differentials in levels and growth of per capita state domestic product (SDP), we present the evidence on the patterns of growth in 14 major states during the four decades of 1960s, 1970s, 1980s and 1990s. We pay particular attention to the issues of instability and volatility of growth at the state level, and comment on the relative position of each state at the end of 1990s in regard to level and growth of per capita SDP. Section 4 reviews the available studies on determinants of growth of Indian states, after referring to two major recent contributions on sources of growth in the Indian economy. We offer some concluding remarks in Section 5.

Researchers on economic growth in Indian states have to depend on the available data compiled by official agencies. While the quality of official data has improved over time, there is considerable scope for further improvement. SDP data for different states may not be strictly comparable, on account of differences in coverage, methodology and quality of basic data. Lack of suitable price deflators for arriving at comparable SDP data in constant prices is a major problem faced by researchers. It is high time that the official agencies at the Centre and states pay more attention to the issue of generating estimates of SDP comparable between states and over time. A continuous data series for all the major states for the post-Independence period will be of immense value. The importance of the quality of SDP data cannot be over emphasised at the present juncture. Attempts should be made to build continuous and comparable data series on growth correlates. A beginning should be made with the compilation of data series on labour and capital stock at the state level.

2. EMPIRICS OF GROWTH RESEARCH

Since the time of Adam Smith's classic Inquiry into the Nature and Causes of the Wealth of Nations in 1776, economists have paid considerable attention to the issue of understanding economic growth. The empirics of growth has been an important area of research since mid-1950s when Abramovitz (1956) and Solow (1957) highlighted the large contribution of total factor productivity (TFP) to output growth. The large body of literature on sources of growth in different countries using the Aggregate Growth Accounting

Framework has enhanced our understanding of the relative roles of factor accumulation and TFP growth in economic growth. Very recently the Global Research Project (GRP) "Explaining Growth" supported by the Global Development Network (GDN) has attempted a comprehensive assessment of growth experiences of 70 developing and transition economies belonging to six geographical regions of the world. The first phase of GRP, already completed, consisted of thematic reviews on Sources of Growth, Markets and Growth, Microeconomics of Growth and Political Economy of Growth, undertaken at the regional level. [See Squire and McMohan (2002)]. The second phase of GRP, now in progress, consists of nearly 70 individual country studies on economic growth during the period 1950-2000. The first theme of GRP Phase I dealing with sources and determinants of aggregate growth is of particular interest in the context of the study of growth in Indian states. Soludo and Kim (2002) attempt a critical overview of research on sources and determinants of growth both by reference to the existing literature on the subject and by drawing upon the results of the just completed six regional papers on this theme. Ahluwalia and Williamson (2003) have put together the thematic papers for the South Asian region.

The key issue of growth accounting is the role of TFP growth in economic growth. TFP growth being obtained as a residual, its estimate crucially depends on the assumptions of the growth accounting framework and the quality of the data on output and inputs. It is well known that quality of data on capital input is not very satisfactory in the case of developing countries, in general.

In the regional studies of GRP and the other literature, both, factor accumulation and TFP growth have been found to be important. However, their relative importance depends on the weights of capital and labour in growth accounting and many growth "puzzles" still remain.

Easterly and Levine (2001) document five stylised facts of economic growth research during the past decade. These are:

1) TFP, rather than factor accumulation accounts for most of the cross-country differences in the level or growth rate of GDP per capita.

2) GDP per capita shows divergence across countries over the long run.

3) Factor accumulation is persistent while growth is not, and the growth paths of countries exhibit remarkable variation. The correlation between per capita growth rates in 1960-76 and 1977-92 across 135 countries is only 0.08.

4) Economic activity is highly concentrated, with all factors of production flowing to the richest areas. The role of economic geography in economic growth needs greater attention.

5) National policies are closely associated with long-run economic growth rates. However, there is no consensus as to which policies are most important for economic growth. The policies examined refer to openness to trade, fiscal policy, financial development and macroeconomic policy.

These facts do not support models with diminishing returns, constant returns to scale, some fixed factor of production, or an emphasis on factor accumulation. However, empirical work does not yet decisively distinguish among the different theoretical conceptions of TFP growth. Easterly and Levine suggest that economists should devote more effort toward modelling and quantifying TFP. More research is needed on determinants of growth, such as technology and externalities.

The literature on the major determinants of per capita growth rates, based on the general framework of cross-country regressions, is also quite voluminous. The theoretical foundations of this approach can be traced to the neo-classical Solow-Swan-Ramsey model of growth as extended to incorporate government policies, human capital, fertility decisions and the diffusion of technology. According to the model, economies converge to the steady state where the growth rates of the economies are determined only by TFP growth. If all the economies in a group have the same steady state, poorer economies in the group should grow faster, which is called ***absolute convergence***. Baumol (1986) found evidence in support of absolute convergence among developed economies. For economies which differ in their steady states, Barro (1991) suggested the possibility of conditional convergence, which means that the farther away the economy is from its steady state, the faster it should grow. The typical equation for a cross-country growth regression is of the following form:

$$\frac{1}{T}\ln(y_{Ti}/y_{Oi}) = \alpha + \beta \ln(y_{oi}) + \gamma x_i + \varepsilon_i$$

The dependent variable is the annual growth rate of per capita income (y) over the period (o, T) for country i, and the explanatory variables are log y_{Oi}, y_{Oi} being initial level of per capita income, and x_i, where x_i is a set of variables that are supposed to determine country i's steady state level of per capita income and ε_i the disturbance term for country i. For conditional convergence to hold, the estimate of β should be significantly negative.

Empirical studies on the determinants of cross-country differences in growth performance have encountered various fundamental difficulties (See Soludo and Kim, 2002). These include the lack of clear guidance from economic theory on the vector of variables to be included in '*x*', specification uncertainty and lack of robustness of the parameter estimates and estimation methods.

The variables included in '*x*' in regional studies of GRP are of four broad categories: initial conditions, exogenous shocks, policy and institutions, and human resources.

One major conclusion of Soludo and Kim after a careful review of the literature is that "we know as much as we don't in terms of what determines the differences in cross-national growth performances". It is not clear from the accumulated evidence as to which factor is the most dominant and how the various factors affect economic growth. Another important conclusion is that the methodology of cross-national growth regression needs careful scrutiny. Detailed country case studies need much more attention in future for a better understanding of the factors behind growth.

Growth variability and volatility is one of the central issues. This aspect was somewhat ignored so far. Pritchett (2000) provides evidence to show that "a single time trend does not adequately characterise the evolution of GDP per capita in most developing countries". Instability in growth rates over time for a single country and volatility of growth are the general features of growth in developing countries. These stylised facts about the instability and volatility of growth rates have implications for the use of high-frequency (yearly) panel data in cross-country growth research. The use of such data particularly with fixed effects for countries, to investigate long-run growth correlates appears to be fraught with problems. Use of annual data in conjunction with country-specific fixed effects eliminates long-period variation and confounds dynamics, specification, endogeneity and statistical power.

Pritchett (2000) classifies potential growth correlates according to three features: time series persistence, exogeneity and model rationale. Variables with high persistence are usually exogenous, with little feedback from growth. Volatile variables can be either exogenous (terms-of-trade shocks) or endogenous (foreign investment). Model rationale refers to the information relevant to the extent of exogeneity and the component of growth affected and the expected time scale of the impact.

Pritchett draws attention to four problems with growth regressions using higher frequency data, particulary those with country specific effects. These problems are lower statistical power, greater measurement error, endogeneity and dynamic misspecification. In view of these four problems, it cannot be asserted that the higher frequency data regressions give better results than time-averaged cross section regressions. The nature of the difference between the two coefficent estimates for any growth correlate cannot be predicted *a priori*. For this reason panel data regression results may not be of much help in undestanding long-term growth.

Pritchett (2000) makes the important point that growth regressions, as a tool for analysing long-term growth determinants, has reached the point of diminishing returns. He is sceptical of the use of even the dynamic generalised method of moments (GMM) estimators as a fruitful approach for analysing the determinants of economic growth. He offers some suggestions on approaches for future research on the determinants of growth:

1. Analysis of the episodes of growth acceleration or the onset of growth deceleration. It will be worthwhile to examine the economic, political, institutional and policy conditions that accompany such break points.

2. Analysis of discrete episodes in the evolution of potential growth determinants.

3. Cross-sectional analysis of *changes* in growth rates over time. This approach has been explored by Rodrik (2000), for the first time.

To summarise this section, the literature on the sources and determinants of economic growth is indeed vast. A great deal has been learnt from this literature. But our understanding of the economic growth of countries is still very incomplete. There is considerable scope for the exploration of new approaches suggested by Pritchett (2000).

Much of what has been stated above about economic growth of countries applies to economic growth of states in India.

3. PATTERNS OF ECONOMIC GROWTH IN INDIAN STATES: 1960-2000

There is a vast amount of literature dealing with economic growth in Indian states. The study by Nair (1983) alone covers the decade of 1950s. Almost all other studies cover the later decades. There is considerable overlap in regard to the time periods covered in these studies. We shall review these studies and present in the process the patterns of growth in the major states of India over the period 1960-2000. Our discussion of most of the studies will be brief.

Nair's (1983) pioneering analysis covered 14 major states. He had put together data on SDP for the years 1950-51, 1955-56, 1960-61 to 1975-76 from different official and unofficial sources. The study showed that inter-state disparities in per capita NSDP, as measured by the coefficient of variation (CV), had declined over the period 1950-51 to 1964-65, but increased between 1964-65 and 1976-77. The CV was about 24 per cent in 1950-51, 18 per cent in 1964-65 and 28 per cent in 1976-77. Punjab (including Haryana), Gujarat and West Bengal were the high income states in 1950-51, 1960-65 and 1971-76. Bihar, Orissa and Uttar Pradesh were at the bottom of the income scale.

Roychoudhury (1993) reported that the CV of per capita NSDP in current prices had increased between 1967-68 and 1977-78, but declined between 1977-78 and 1985-86. However, the CV in terms of constant price data showed a persistent increase during the entire period 1967-68 to 1985-86.

Das and Barua (1996) examined several dimensions of regional economic disparities among 23 states/union territories during the period 1970–92. Theil's entropy measure of inequality was computed for economy wide NSDP and NSDP in different sectors for each of the years 1970 to 1992. It was found that inter-state inequality increased in almost all sectors.

Mathur (2001) in continuation of his earlier work, analysed several facets of national and regional economic growth since 1950s, but with a specific focus on the 1980s and 1990s. The study reported a steep acceleration in the coefficient of variation of per capita incomes in the post-reform period of 1991-96. A tendency towards convergence was noticed within the group of middle-income states, while divergence was evident within the groups of high and low-income states.

Kurian (2000) attempted a comparative analysis of 15 major states in respect of a variety of indicators bearing on social and economic development. He classified the states into two groups: "Forward" group consisting of Andhra Pradesh, Gujarat, Haryana, Karnataka, Kerala, Maharashtra, Punjab and Tamil Nadu, while the "backward" group consisted of Assam, Bihar, Madhya Pradesh, Orissa, Rajasthan, Uttar Pradesh and West Bengal. In some parts of his analysis he compared the indicators for the two groups of states.

Kurian, taking a holistic view of development, drew attention to inter-state disparities by presenting recent data for states on demographic characteristics, social characteristics, magnitude and structure of SDP, poverty ratio, developmental and non-developmental revenue expenditures, Eighth Plan outlay and its sectoral distribution, disbursal of financial assistance for investment, indicators of physical infrastructure development and indicators of financial infrastructure. The paper pointed out that a sharp dichotomy between the forward and backward groups of states had emerged.

Kurian inferred that governmental efforts during 1950-80 achieved only partial success in mitigating regional disparities. The enhanced role of the private sector since the early 1980s seemed to have aggravated the disparities. It was argued that focussed investments in social and infrastructural sectors and purposeful decentralisation of decision-making and financial powers combined with accountability would facilitate faster socio-economic development of the backward regions.

A single time trend may not adequately characterise the evolution of SDP per capita over time in most of the Indian states. Instability in growth rates over time is often a reality. Pritchett (2000) found considerable evidence of instability in growth rates in his analysis of patterns of economic growth in developing countries over the period 1960-92. Dholakia (1994) in his analysis of inter-state disparities in growth rates of 20 Indian states over the 30-year period 1960-61 to 1989-90 identified empirically the optimal year of shift in growth trend separately for each state, through the estimation of kinked exponential trend curve model. The results of this exercise are presented in Table 4.1. Earlier, Ganesh Kumar (1992) found through a similar exercise that over the period 1950-51 to 1989-90 the growth rate at the all-India level recorded a shift of 1.6 percentage points in the year 1981-82. These results for all-India are shown in the last row of Table 4.1.

In only five out of 20 states shown in Table 4.1 the growth rate remained stable over the 30-year period. These states were Haryana, Punjab, Rajasthan, Tamil Nadu and Arunachal Pradesh. In four states it decelerated at different time points; in Orissa as early as in 1967-68 and in Kerala in 1972-73. The implausibly high growth rate for Orissa during 1960-61 to 1967-68 could be due to data inaccuracy.

In the remaining 11 states, the growth rate accelerated from different years: for example, in Bihar the growth rate accelerated from 1967-68 by 3.6 percentage points and in West Bengal from 1982-83 by 2.6 percentage points.

The results in Table 4.1 convey the impression that the patterns of SDP growth in Indian states over the 30-year period 1960-90 were indeed very diverse. Majority of the states experienced shift in the growth rate either in later 1960s or in early 1970s, many years ahead of the shift in the growth rate at the national level in 1981-82. Only three states, Himachal Pradesh, Karnataka and West Bengal registered improvement in growth rates after 1981-82. Allowance for a second shift in the growth rate in the methodology might have uncovered another shift for some of the states in the second half of the 30-year period.

It must be stated at this point that the growth rates for the different states calculated by Dholakia and reported in Table 4.1 are

Table 4.1

SDP Growth Acceleration/Deceleration in Indian States during 1960-61 to 1989-90

State	*Year of Shift*	*Growth Rate (%) in the First Sub Period*	*Increase/ Decrease in Growth Rate*	*R^2 of the Kinked Trend Curve*
(1)	(2)	(3)	(4)	(5)
Cases of Acceleration				
Andhra Pradesh	1968/69	1.6	2.1	0.970
Assam	1979/80	3.2	2.8	0.985
Bihar	1967/68	0.2	3.6	0.980
Gujarat	1973/74	3.0	1.8	0.954
Himachal Pradesh	1985/86	2.9	2.5	0.981
Karnataka	1985/86	3.7	2.6	0.987
Madhya Pradesh	1979/80	2.5	3.4	0.944
Maharashtra	1972/73	2.9	2.0	0.992
Tripura	1972/73	2.4	2.4	0.986
Uttar Pradesh	1974/75	2.1	2.3	0.976
West Bengal	1982/83	2.5	2.6	0.985
Cases of Deceleration				
Jammu and Kashmir	1985/86	4.2	-3.0	0.987
Kerala	1972/73	3.9	-2.0	0.990
Manipur	1977/78	5.6	-1.5	0.986
Orissa	1967/68	10.1	-7.2	0.969
Cases of Unchanged Growth				
Arunachal Pradesh	—	7.1	—	0.990
Haryana	—	5.4	—	0.976
Punjab	—	5.1	—	0.995
Rajasthan	—	3.5	—	0.914
Tamil Nadu	—	2.8	—	0.963
All India	**1981/82**	**3.5**	**1.6**	**0.997**

Notes: (i) The period begins with 1970-71 for Assam and Arunachal Pradesh, with 1965-66 for Haryana and Punjab, with 1967-68 for Himachal Pradesh.

(ii) For Andhra Pradesh the period ends with 1988-89, and for Manipur the period ends with 1990-91.

(iii) For All India, the period extends from 1950-51 to 1989-90.

Source: Dholakia (1994), Tables 1 and 3.

not consistent with the growth rates presented later in Table 4.3. The price deflators used by Dholakia for obtaining constant price series appears to be different from the ones used by Chaudhuri (2000) and others. The absence of appropriate state-specific price deflators is a serious problem faced by users of SDP data series for Indian states.

Chaudhuri in a comprehensive and insightful study (2000) traces the overall economic growth experience of 19 Indian states over the four decades: 1960s, 1970s, 1980s and 1990s. The analysis makes use of three data series, Central Statistical Organisation (CSO) being the data source in each case. The first series for the years 1960-61 to 1979-80 relates to net SDP. The second series, for the period 1980-81 to 1997-98, incorporated improvements in methodology and extension of coverage. The third series with base 1993-94 with significant extensions/changes in the coverage of economic activities was available at the time of the study for the years 1993-94 to 1997-98. The second and third series relate to gross SDP and GDP. As noted by Chaudhuri, the data for the different states and all-India may not be entirely comparable and this fact has to be kept in mind in any analysis using these data bases.

Income Level Differentials

For the analysis of income level differentials, SDP per capita of each state for each year is expressed as a percentage of all-India GDP per capita. These relatives are calculated separately for data in current and constant prices. For each state, Chaudhuri presents three-year averages of the income relatives centred on the years 1961-62, 1965-66, 1970-71, 1975-76, 1981-82, 1985-86, 1990-91 and 1997-98 in Table 4.2 of his paper (data in current prices) and Table 4.3 of the paper (data in constant prices). The index of per capita SDP for the states for the years 1961-62, 1970-71, 1981-82, 1990-91 and 1997-98 with all-India = 100 is presented in Table 4.2.[1]

In 1961-62, the leading states in terms of per capita income level in descending order were Maharashtra (with income relative of 125), West Bengal (118), Gujarat (116) and Punjab (115); states in the vicinity of the national average were Tamil Nadu (102), Haryana

1. Chaudhuri's analysis included two small states, Goa and Delhi. These states had the highest per capita income levels throughout the period 1960-98.

(101), Assam (99) and Karnataka (96); states substantially below the national average were Rajasthan (90), Andhra Pradesh (88), Jammu and Kashmir (83), Kerala (80), Himachal Pradesh (79), Uttar Pradesh (77), Madhya Pradesh (75), Orissa (75) and Bihar (68).

Table 4.2

Index of Per Capita State Domestic Product at Constant Prices (All-India = 100): Selected Years (Three year average centred on)

State	1961-62		1970-71		1981-82		1990-91		1997-98	
Andhra Pradesh	88	(11)	89	(12)	89	(12)	80	(10)	91	(10)
Assam	99	(8)	90	(11)	80	(14)	68	(15)	63	(14)
Bihar	68	(16)	63	(16)	58	(18)	53	(16)	48	(17)
Gujarat	116	(4)	126	(4)	123	(6)	118	(5)	147	(5)
Haryana	101	(7)	135	(3)	146	(4)	152	(4)	137	(6)
Himachal Pradesh	79	(14)	104	(7)	102	(8)	99	(6)	91	(10)
Jammu & Kashmir	83	(12)	86	(13)	106	(7)	79	(11)	72	(13)
Karnataka	96	(9)	102	(8)	94	(10)	95	(7)	110	(8)
Kerala	80	(13)	92	(10)	91	(11)	83	(8)	100	(9)
Madhya Pradesh	75	(15)	75	(14)	82	(13)	74	(12)	77	(12)
Maharashtra	125	(2)	124	(5)	145	(5)	152	(4)	169	(3)
Orissa	75	(15)	89	(12)	73	(17)	69	(14)	59	(16)
Punjab	115	(5)	162	(2)	170	(3)	169	(3)	150	(4)
Rajasthan	90	(10)	89	(12)	76	(16)	81	(9)	84	(11)
Tamil Nadu	102	(6)	95	(9)	94	(10)	99	(6)	123	(7)
Uttar Pradesh	77	(14)	74	(15)	78	(15)	73	(13)	62	(15)
West Bengal	118	(3)	115	(6)	101	(9)	95	(7)	84	(11)
Delhi	211	(1)	200	(1)	249	(1)	248	(1)	197	(2)
Goa	N.A		162	(2)	211	(2)	224	(2)	209	(1)
Coefficient of variation	18.2%		24.1%		28.7%		33.1%		35.4%	

Correlation Matrix for the Index Series

Year					
1961-1962	1.00	0.89	0.90	0.89	0.81
1970-1971	—	1.00	0.96	0.96	0.89
1981-1982	—	—	1.00	0.98	0.91
1990-1991	—	—	—	1.00	0.94

Source: Chaudhuri (2000), Table 3.

Note: Figures in parantheses are ranks.

In 1990-91, on the eve of the introduction of the major economic reforms in the country, Punjab (169), Haryana (152), Maharashtra (152) and Gujarat (118), in descending order, enjoyed the highest levels of per capita income, Tamil Nadu (99), Himachal Pradesh (99), West Bengal (95) and Karnataka (95) were quite close to the national average. The rest of the states were appreciably below the national average.

By 1997-98, six years or so after the introduction of reforms, Tamil Nadu (123) and Karnataka (110) substantially improved their relative status in per capita income terms and joined the ranks of the group of four advanced states — Maharashtra, Gujarat, Punjab and Haryana; Kerala reached the national average. Andhra Pradesh, Himachal Pradesh, West Bengal and Rajasthan too improved their relative status and moved closer to the national average. Assam, Uttar Pradesh, Orissa and Bihar suffered a further decline in relative status. The relative status of Madhya Pradesh, improved marginally, although it lagged far behind the national average throughout the period.

The coefficient of variation given in the last row of the table shows that inter-state disparities widened steadily over time and this was inspite of the policy of balanced regional development pursued right from 1950-51.

The correlations between the index series for different years are given beneath Table 4.2. All the correlations are quite high. Most of them are equal to or greater than 0.89. The implication of high positive correlations is that relative positions of the states did not undergo too many changes.

Growth Differentials

We shall now analyse the inter-state growth differentials in the four successive decades, namely, 1960s, 1970s, 1980s and 1990s, for the group of 14 major states listed in Table 4.3. For the first decade, the NSDP figures are in 1960-61 prices, for the second decade in 1970-71 prices and for the subsequent periods in 1993-94 prices. The state-wise annual rates of growth of SDP per capita for the different periods are given in Table 4.3. In the last row of the table the rates of growth of per capita GDP for all-India are given.

Table 4.3

Annual Growth Rates (%) of SDP Per Capita for 14 Major States: 1960s, 1970s, 1980s and 1990s

State/ All India	1960-61 to 1969-70	1970-71 to 1979-80	1981-82 to 1989-90	1990-91 to 1999-2000	1991-92 to 1995-96	1996-97 to 1999-2000
(1)	(2)	(3)	(4)	(5)	(6)	(7)
Andhra Pradesh	-0.4	1.1	4.4	3.8	4.0	4.0
Bihar	-1.3	0.6	2.2	0.8	-2.9	4.0
Gujarat	0.1	2.0	4.3	4.6	6.5	3.2
Haryana	2.6	2.2	3.8	2.7	0.9	3.8
Karnataka	1.2	1.8	3.6	5.2	5.1	6.7
Kerala	1.4	-0.2	2.0	4.7	5.3	4.2
Madhya Pradesh	-1.1	-1.0	1.9	3.2	1.9	2.9
Maharashtra	0.4	3.3	3.9	4.6	5.7	3.8
Orissa	7.3	0.3	3.4	1.0	3.9	1.6
Punjab	3.5	3.2	3.8	2.5	2.4	3.5
Rajasthan	-1.1	0.2	4.6	3.4	1.8	3.0
Tamil Nadu	0.1	1.6	4.0	5.4	5.6	5.1
Uttar Pradesh	-0.2	0.4	2.6	2.1	0.9	3.4
West Bengal	0.0	0.7	2.0	5.0	4.8	5.7
Coeff. of Var. (%)	258	94	29	44	79	32
All India	**0.8**	**1.2**	**3.4**	**3.9**	**3.5**	**4.4**

Correlation Matrix for Growth Rate Series

Period						
1960-1970	1.00	0.17	0.12	-0.36	0.17	-0.34
1970-1980	—	1.00	0.54	0.35	0.26	0.19
1981-1990	—	—	1.00	0.32	0.30	0.10
1990-2000	—	—	—	1.00	0.72	0.64
1991-1996	—	—	—	—	1.00	0.26

Sources : (i) Growth rates for 1960s and 1970s are trend growth rates taken from Chaudhuri (2000).

(ii) Growth rates for 1980s and 1990s are annual averages based on SDP data in 1993-94 prices.

The all-India per capita GDP growth rate for the 1960s was 0.8 per cent per annum. The inter-state variation in per capita SDP growth rate was very pronounced with the coefficient of variation taking the value 258 per cent. Some of the initially high-income states like Maharashtra and Gujarat registered very low growth rates, the low-income state of Orissa registered the highest growth rate of 7.3, and this high figure may partly be a reflection of the poor quality of the data. Five large states showed negative growth. Two northern states, namely Punjab and Haryana achieved impressive growth rates. Kerala and Karnataka had growth rates above the national growth rate.

During 1970s, the all-India growth rate improved to 1.2 per cent (from 0.8 per cent). Maharashtra and Punjab and to a lesser extent Haryana and Gujarat achieved high growth rates. Karnataka and Tamil Nadu too achieved growth rates higher than the all-India average. The growth rate for Andhra Pradesh, which showed negative growth in the previous decade, was slightly below average. Madhya Pradesh persisted in showing a negative growth rate of the order of 1.0 per cent. Kerala too showed a negative growth rate, albeit of a small magnitude. Growth rate for Orissa plummeted to 0.3 per cent. The coefficient of variation of the growth rates was much less (94 per cent) compared to 1960s.

During the period 1980-81 to 1990-91, the all-India growth rate accelerated steeply to 3.4 per cent from 1.2 per cent in the previous decade. All 14 states achieved growth rates above 1.9 per cent and improved their performance compared to the previous decade. The performance of Rajasthan (4.6 per cent), Andhra Pradesh (4.4 per cent), Gujarat (4.3 per cent) and Tamil Nadu (4.0 per cent) was impressive. Haryana (3.8 per cent), Maharashtra (3.9 per cent), Punjab (3.8 per cent) and Karnataka (3.6 per cent) too surpassed the all-India average. Bihar, Kerala, Madhya Pradesh, Uttar Pradesh and West Bengal registered growth rates far below the all-India average. The coefficient of variation of growth rates was the least (29 per cent) in this decade.

During the 1990s, when the all-India growth rate accelerated further to 3.9 per cent, Tamil Nadu (5.4 per cent), Karnataka (5.2 per cent), West Bengal (5.0 per cent) and Kerala (4.7 per cent) fared exceedingly well. Gujarat (4.6 per cent) and Maharashtra (4.6 per cent) further improved their performance. However, Haryana and Punjab suffered marked deceleration. Other states which decelerated in 1990s relative to 1980s were Andhra Pradesh (from 4.4 to 3.8 per cent), Bihar (from 2.2 to –0.8 per cent), Orissa (from 3.4 to 1.0 per cent), Rajasthan (from 4.6 to 3.4 per cent) and Uttar Pradesh (from 2.6 to 2.1 per cent). The inter-state variability of growth rates in this period increased. The cross-state correlation of growth rates between 1980s and 1990s is rather small (+0.32), indicating instability of growth rates.

While in the 1980s all states improved their growth performance relative to the previous two decades, the performance in the 1990s was quite uneven.

States that took advantage of the reforms of the 1990s and allowed much latitude in policymaking at the state level seemed to have performed better at the expense of the other states. In columns (6) and (7) of Table 4.3, growth rates for 1991-92 to 1995-96 and 1996-97 to 1999-2000 are compared. The differences between these two subperiods are quite considerable. At the all-India level, the second subperiod marked an improvement of 0.9 percentage points. Karnataka and West Bengal which had achieved high growth rates of 5.1 per cent and 4.7 per cent in the first subperiod further improved to 6.7 per cent and 5.7 per cent, respectively. Gujarat and Maharashtra decelerated considerably, from 6.5 per cent to 3.2 per cent and 5.7 per cent to 3.8 per cent, respectively. Six other states, namely, Bihar, Haryana, Madhya Pradesh, Punjab, Rajasthan, and Uttar Pradesh improved their performance in the second subperiod relative to the first subperiod. There was steep deceleration in the case of Orissa from 3.9 per cent to 1.6 per cent and in the case of Kerala from 5.3 per cent to 4.2 per cent. Andhra Pradesh maintained a moderate growth rate of 4.0 per cent, in the two subperiods and in relative terms the state's growth rate showed deterioration. The correlation of the growth rates for the two subperiods, though positive, is rather low (0.26), again pointing to instability of growth rates.

The growth patterns of the 14 major states are quite diverse. Growth was characterised by considerable instability. All the states improved their growth performance considerably in the 1980s. During the first five years of the reform period i.e., during 1991-92 to 1995-96, only Gujarat, Karnataka, Kerala, Maharashtra, Orissa, Tamil Nadu and West Bengal further improved their growth record. Of these seven states, Gujarat, Maharashtra, Kerala, Orissa and Tamil Nadu received a setback in the second half of the 1990s, while Karnataka and West Bengal forged ahead with better growth performance. Bihar, Haryana, Madhya Pradesh, Punjab, Rajasthan and Uttar Pradesh fared much better in the second half of the 1990s. At the end of the 1990s, the fourteen major states could be classified as follows:

Category		*States*
High income and high growth	:	Maharashtra, Gujarat, Tamil Nadu and Karnataka
High income and low growth	:	Punjab and Haryana
Low income and high growth	:	West Bengal and Kerala
Low income and low growth	:	Andhra Pradesh, Madhya Pradesh, Rajasthan, Orissa, Bihar, and Uttar Pradesh

Volatility of Growth

Apart from instability, volatility appears to be a dominant characteristic of the economic growth of Indian states. In this paper the coefficient of variation of year-to-year growth rates for a state is taken as the measure of volatility. Dasgupta *et al.* (2000) computed this measure for the period 1970-71 to 1995-96. We have computed this measure for 1980s, 1990s and the two subperiods of 1990s. The figures are presented in Table 4.4.

Over the long period of 1970-71 to 1995-96, the four most volatile states were Orissa (631 per cent), Rajasthan (625 per cent), Gujarat (424 per cent) and Uttar Pradesh (413 per cent). The three least volatile states were Punjab (84 per cent), Maharashtra (158 per cent) and Kerala (178 per cent).

The volatility of growth at the national level was lower in the 1990s (49 per cent) than in the 1980s (68 per cent). During 1980s, Gujarat (297 per cent), Rajasthan (291 per cent), Madhya Pradesh (276 per cent) and Orissa were the most volatile states. Punjab (64 per cent), Karnataka (100 per cent), Maharashtra (113 per cent) and Uttar Pradesh (119 per cent) were the least volatile states.

During 1990s, while volatility at the national level declined, states like Orissa (856 per cent) and Bihar (706 per cent) experienced extreme volatility. Economic growth in West Bengal (30 per cent), Kerala (47 per cent), Tamil Nadu (52 per cent) and Karnataka (69 per cent) was least volatile.

Table 4.4

Volatility Measures of SDP Per Capita Growth for 14 Major States: 1970-95, 1980s and 1990s

State/All India	*Coefficient of Variation of year-to-year Growth Rates (%)*				
	1970-71 to 1995-96	*1981-82 to 1989-90*	*1990-91 to 1999-2000*	*1991-92 to 1995-96*	*1996-97 to 1999-2000*
(1)	(2)	(3)	(4)	(5)	(6)
Andhra Pradesh	358	150	113	109	135
Bihar	327	221	706	197	80
Gujarat	424	297	227	216	198
Haryana	261	205	134	290	107
Karnataka	277	100	69	65	44
Kerala	178	204	47	51	49
Madhya Pradesh	N.A.	276	154	317	66
Maharashtra	158	113	99	104	82
Orissa	631	272	856	114	463
Punjab	84	64	74	39	59
Rajasthan	625	291	256	580	218
Tamil Nadu	255	126	52	72	26
Uttar Pradesh	413	119	141	210	124
West Bengal	194	167	30	39	11
All India	**N.A.**	**68**	**49**	**72**	**29**

Sources: (i) The figures for 1970-71 to 1995-96 are from Dasgupta *et al* (2000).
(ii) The figures for 1980s and 1990s are based on SDP data in 1993-94 prices.

Most of the 14 states were characterised by instability and volatility of growth rates during the period 1970-2000. Only a few states recorded almost steady improvement in growth performance during the last two decades. Several states continued to lag behind others. Raising the growth rates in such states is the major policy imperative in the coming decades.

4. DETERMINANTS OF GROWTH IN INDIAN STATES

At the outset, we shall briefly comment on the sources of growth at the national level. We have two sets of estimates, one by

Sivasubramonian and the other by Dholakia. Sivasubramonian (2002) recently undertook a very careful analysis of the sources of growth in the Indian economy during the period 1950-2000, and showed that TFP accounted for 32 per cent of GDP growth. The relative importance of TFP varied over time; TFP's contribution was highest (43 per cent) during 1950-64 and least (13 per cent) during 1965-80 and relatively moderate (35 per cent) during 1980-2000. Dholakia (2002), a veteran in productivity analysis, showed that TFP accounted for about 22 per cent of GDP growth during the pre-liberalisation period 1960-85, and for about 48 per cent during the liberalisation period 1985-2000. The two sets of estimates, which of course need to be reconciled, highlight the importance of TFP in Indian economic growth.

Qualitative Assessment of Determinants

Sachs *et al.* (2002) attempt a detailed qualitative assessment of the factors behind inter-state growth differentials. The authors argue that the manufacturing sector rather than the agriculture sector is a more consistent engine of growth and it is likely to play a growing role in a liberalised economy. The most suitable sites for sustained manufacturing growth in India as in China are along the coast, especially at the four large port cities of Mumbai (Maharashtra), Kolkata (West Bengal), Chennai (Tamil Nadu) and Kandla (Gujarat). High-tech services or financial services are much less dependent on coastal locations. The most important state for service sector activities is Maharashtra. Other key states include Tamil Nadu, Karnataka, Delhi and Andhra Pradesh.

Urbanisation is likely to be a key determinant of growth. A 10-percentage-point higher rate of urbanisation is associated with 1.3 percentage points a year higher annual growth.

Sachs *et al.* (2002) note that there are major differences across Indian states in the area of policy reform. Maharashtra, Tamil Nadu, Gujarat, Karnataka and Andhra Pradesh have been more reform-oriented; Haryana, Kerala, Orissa, Madhya Pradesh, Punjab, Rajasthan, and West Bengal are somewhat behind in undertaking policy reform. Bihar and Uttar Pradesh are far behind. With the exception of Andhra Pradesh, the reform oriented states are also the fastest growing states in the post-reform period.

Sachs *et al.* list several possible hypotheses for the lack of unconditional convergence among Indian states:

(1) The geographical differences in India are larger than in the US, Europe and Japan.

(2) Population movements in India do respond very slowly to income differentials.

(3) Policies of the national or state governments do not facilitate convergence and

(4) Economic convergence is slower at lower levels of economic development as in India (or China).

Coastal access and climate are also factors in convergence.

The Indian states vary considerably in social indicators such as infant mortality rate and adult literacy. The simple correlation between growth and literacy is positive, but disappears once we control for urbanisation which is correlated both with growth and with the degree of literacy.

Sachs *et al* observe that there is much more growth potential in India than has been achieved to date. While in India, per capita growth rates of states have ranged between two and eight per cent per annum, China's provinces have achieved between eight and thirteen per cent a year growth during 1992-98.

Many coastal cities (Thiruvananthapuram, Kochi, Bhubaneshwar, and Visakhapatnam) have not so far attracted FDI. Continuing control of the Central Government over regional infrastructure has frustrated the efforts of the reform-oriented state governments. A careful balance will have to be struck between two kinds of investments in the rural hinterland: physical infrastructure and human capital — mainly education and health, to raise the productivity of the rural population.

Quantitative Assessment of Determinants

Several recent studies attempted a quantitative assessment of determinants of growth in the states of India. Some studies have attempted to test the hypothesis of β-convergence. Both types of studies will be reviewed in this section.

A very perceptive and influential paper by Ahluwalia (2000) analysed the growth performance of 14 major Indian states in the post-reform period 1991-92 to 1998-99 and compared it with the performance in the previous decade. The paper attempted to analyse the causes of the growth disparities and to identify the policy measures needed for the acceleration of future growth in the slow growing states.

The paper noted that the dispersion of growth rates of states increased considerably in the post-reform period: the coefficient of variation of growth rates increased from 15 per cent in the 1980s to 27 per cent in the 1990s. Growth accelerated in the richest states of Gujarat and Maharashtra, while it decelerated in the poorest states of Bihar, Uttar Pradesh and Orissa.

In regard to determinants of growth in the post-reform period, private investment rate, literacy rate, tele density, proportion of villages electrified and per capita energy consumption were found to be individually positively correlated with SDP growth.

Shand and Bhide (2000) analyse the sources of economic growth in 15 major states over the period 1970-71 to 1995-96. The paper presents useful data for each state on sectoral distribution of NSDP for triennia ending in 1972, 1982, 1990 and 1995, on average annual growth rates of aggregate NSDP and on sectoral NSDP in constant (1980-81) prices for the periods 1971-80, 1981-90, 1991-95 and 1992-95.

By way of analysing the determinants of growth, the authors present rank correlation coefficients between NSDP growth rate and (i) alternative measures of size of state (ii) relative sizes of sectors, (iii) life expectancy and literacy, and (iv) banking infrastructure and social expenditures.

Panel data regressions from data for 15 states over three time periods, 1972-82, 1982-90, and 1992-95, suggest agricultural growth has positive impacts on industrial growth and service sector growth. Agricultural growth is affected positively by land productivity in agriculture and negatively by the share of agriculture. The regression results are useful in understanding growth. However, careful attention to issues of specification and estimation of the relationships may yield more convincing results. The study suggests that reform in the agriculture sector will yield very beneficial results as growth in this sector is found to have a positive and significant impact on overall growth. The importance of infrastructure and human development has also been brought out.

In a related study, Bhide and Shand (2000) bring out the stark differences between "progressive" and "backward" states. In the 1990s, the four fastest growing states, Maharashtra, Gujarat, Tamil Nadu and West Bengal together accounted for 56 per cent of the growth in real NSDP, the share of Maharashtra alone being 28 per cent. Good performers such as Maharashtra achieved high growth in all three sectors of agriculture, industry and services. Poor performers such as Orissa and Assam fared badly in all the three sectors. Infrastructure appears to have a facilitating role. Growth appears to be negatively related to the size of public administration.

Karnik *et al.* (2000) examined the role of institutional and political factors in the economic performance of Indian states. A Gallup organisation's opinion poll of CEOs of about 100 companies, some Indian and rest transnational, covering the years 1995, 1997 and 1999 constituted the data base for the analysis. This data set is similar to that employed by Knack and Keefer (1996) in their cross-country study on institutions and economic performance. The poll asked respondents to rank 27 Indian states on the basis of their perceptions regarding infrastructural, institutional and political conditions in the states in order to explain the attractiveness of these states as investment destinations.

A two equation model consisting of an investment equation and social infrastructure equation was estimated from cross-sectional data for each year (1995, 1997, 1999) and from pooled data for 21 states. The results suggest that rather than physical infrastructure, social infrastructure as determined by institutional and political factors is an important determinant of the attractiveness of a state as an investment destination.

Ghosh, Marjit and Neogi (1998) used the data for 26 states for 35 years, 1960-61 to 1994-95 to test the hypothesis of absolute convergence and found strong evidence for divergence. The coefficient of variation of per capita SDP declined mildly between 1961-62 and 1981-82 from 33.9 per cent to 31.8 per cent. The CV increased steadily after 1981-82 reaching the value of 43.4 per cent in 1993-94. The study used the consumer price index number for agricultural labourers available for 15 states for deflating the nominal net SDP figures to obtain the real SDP figures. This was an improvement over studies which used some all-India level deflator.

In an important contribution, Rao *et al.* (1999) analysed the determinants of growth of per capita SDP with data for the 14 major states. Growth rates of per capita SDP were estimated from semi log trend equations for six different periods all ending in 1994-95: 1965-94, 1970-94, 1975-94, 1980-94, 1985-94 and 1990-94. The growth rate so estimated was the dependent variable in the regressions for the different periods. The explanatory variables were (a) initial level of per capita GDP ($\ln y_o$), (b) literacy rate in the initial year as a proxy for human capital stock (ln literacy), (c) ratio of state government expenditure to SDP (G/Y) averaged for the period, (d) private industry investment in the state proxied by the ratio of loans given by all-India fiancial institutions to SDP (ln AIFI) and (e) adoption of technological change in the agriculture sector proxied by the consumption of fertilisers per hectare of sown area (ln FERT).

The coefficient on the initial income variable was significantly positive in the regressions for longer periods 1965-94, 1970-94 and 1975-94, indicating β-divergence. The coefficient was negative for the shorter periods 1980-94, 1985-94 and 1990-94. However, it was significant only in the case of the growth regression for the 15 year period 1980-94. Thus the evidence in support of convergence hypothesis was quite weak and the evidence for divergence was strong.

The variable proxying private investment was found to be the most important determinant of growth. Next in importance was the literacy variable. However, its coefficient had a perverse sign in some regressions. Other variables were not significant.

It is not very clear why growth over six different periods, the lengths of the period varying between 5 and 30 years, were considered for the analysis.

The authors went into the possible reasons for divergence and found that the skewed distribution of public expenditures attracted larger flows of investments to more affluent regions of the country. Affirmative measures to correct imbalances in the spread of infrastructure were needed. The authors argued that the impact of explicit centre-state transfers on regional inequalities was moderate and these effects were outweighed by implicit transfers through subsidised lending and through tax-exportation.

Subrahmanyam and Rao (2000) used per capita NSDP data for 17 major states for the years 1965-66 to 1996-97. The study distinguished between the "Green Revolution" period of 1965-84 and the "Liberalisation" period of 1985-97 and tested the hypothesis of absolute convergence. No evidence of convergence was found in either period. The tendency for divergence was strong in the liberalisation period, while it was mild in the green revolution period. The performance of the manufacturing sector was found to be highly divergent in the liberalisation period.

Dasgupta *et al.* (2000) used per capita NSDP data in 1980-81 prices over the period 1960-61 to 1995-96 for 21 states to analyse inter-state disparities in growth. However, much of the analysis related to the period 1970-71 to 1995-96. One interesting feature of this study was that it highlighted the inter-state diversity in volatility of year-to-year growth rates, with the coefficient of variation ranging between 84 per cent for Punjab and 630 per cent for Orissa. In addition to Orissa, Rajasthan, Gujarat, UP and Delhi displayed high volatility of growth rates.

The study compared for each state four estimates of the growth rate over the period 1970-71 to 1995-96: the arithmetic mean, the geometric mean, the median of year-to-year growth rates and the trend exponential growth rate. There were considerable differences among the four estimates, though the ranking of the states in terms of the alternative estimates was similar. The arithmetic mean of year-to-year growth rate and the trend exponential growth rate were found to be close to each other.

σ-convergence was analysed with respect to aggregate SDP, SDP in agriculture, manufacturing, service sector and infrastructure sector. Convergence was found only in the service and in the infrastructure sectors. There was evidence of absolute divergence. No test of conditional convergence was reported.

The analysis of Nagaraj *et al.* (2000) used panel data for 17 states including Assam, Himachal Pradesh, and Jammu and Kashmir, for the years 1960-94. The growth regression included, apart from lagged per capita SDP, the share of agriculture, the relative price of agricultural and manufactured goods, several infrastructure indicators and fixed effects for states as explanatory variables. Evidence for conditional convergence was found. The results of the study suggested that focusing investment efforts on physical infrastructure (electricity irrigation and railways) and social infrastructure (human development) would raise the overall effectiveness of public investment and raise growth. The paper drew attention to the issue of fiscal federalism in implementing public investment programmes.

In the light of Pritchett's (2000) strictures against the use of high frequency data for growth regressions, the econometric results of the study have to be interpreted with due caution.

In a recent study, Aiyar (2001) followed the panel data regression approach with data for a sample of 19 states over the period 1971-96 and used the Least Squares with Dummy Variable (LSDV) method of estimation. He maintained a clear distinction between absolute and conditional convergence and estimated the corresponding models. The dependent variable in each model was the growth rate over a five year period. Literacy rate (LIT) and private capital investment (PVK), the latter proxied by the amount of bank credit per capita, were the explanatory variables. The assumption was that these variables had a bearing on the state's steady state growth rate.

Two regressions were computed. For regression 1, which assumed a common steady state, the estimated convergence rate was *minus* 0.013, implying absolute divergence at the rate of 1.3 per cent over a five year period. For regression 2 which included LIT and PVK and fixed effects for the 19 states, the estimated convergence coefficient was very high at 0.199. Thus, the results of the study provide strong evidence for absolute divergence and conditional convergence. The estimated partial elasticities with respect to LIT and PVK were statistically significant with values equal to 0.76 and 0.15 implying strong effects of the conditioning variables on growth of per capita SDP. The results are interesting. But they are subject to the serious limitations of the use of high-frequency panel data in the context of analysis of growth determinants highlighted by Pritchett (2000).

Singh and Srinivasan's (2002) study refers to 1990s. It attempted to analyse inter-state differences in the growth of per capita SDP in 1998-99 over that in 1990-91. Fourteen major states were in the sample. The major focus of this part of the paper was to examine the role of capital flows in explaining inter-state differences in growth rate. Three financial variables were explored: FDI approvals per capita during the decade 1991-2000, per capita bank credit (as a proxy for private investment) in 1990 and credit-deposit ratio for 1990. The evidence for convergence or divergence was found to be inconclusive. The results suggested complementarity between domestic and foreign capital flows. The study made an important point that the SDP measure excluded remittances by internal and external migrants, and to this extent, it was not a suitable measure of income accruing to residents of the state. The paper considered possible reforms in inter-governmental relations. In this regard its approach is similar to that of Rao *et al.* (1999).

Mathur (2001) analyses some facets of national and regional economic growth since 1950s, but with a specific focus on the eighties and nineties. During 1991-96 a steep acceleration in the rise of the coefficient of variation of per capita incomes is noticed. Within the group of middle-income states a tendency towards convergence is noticed; there is evidence of divergence within the groups of high and low-income states.

The studies reviewed above have differed in regard to the sample of states covered, period(s) of analysis, and the explanatory variables used to represent the steady state in the growth regressions. While most of the studies have achieved some success in accounting for the differences in growth rates across states (and over time in the case of panel regressions), they have not helped in reaching a consensus on convergence or divergence or in identifying the growth determinants. The Nagaraj *et al.* (2000) study brought out the importance of physical and social infrastructure in addition to that of terms-of-trade (between industry and agriculture) and the share of the agriculture sector in SDP. But this result cannot be accepted at its face value in the light of the limitations of the panel data approach highlighted by Pritchett (2000).

The finding of Rao *et al* (1999) that private investment and literacy are significant determinants of growth appears plausible. The finding of conditional divergence also appears credible.

In conclusion of this section, it must be added that there is need for exploring other approaches to explaining growth, as suggested by Pritchett (2000).

5. CONCLUDING REMARKS

This paper has attempted a somewhat preliminary account of the patterns and determinants of growth in Indian states during the period 1960-2000. Much of the paper has covered 14 major states which together account for a little over 90 per cent each of the population and the GDP of the country.

It has been found that growth in the different states during 1960-2000 was characterised by instability and volatility. The degree of volatility was very high in some states. It would be instructive to extend the analysis to sectoral growth rates and identify the sectors contributing to volatility and instability.

Inter-state disparities in income levels and growth rates as measured by the coefficient of variation increased over time. However, the relative positions of many states remained unchanged.

Although the evidence was not conclusive, several of the studies pointed to conditional divergence, implying that long term growth rate and initial income level displayed negative association when allowance was made for differences in steady state levels.

The growth regressions based on cross-section data or panel data left much to be desired, as is true of growth regressions in general. Detailed case studies of the growth experiences of individual states need to be explored in future on the lines suggested by Pritchett (2000).

This paper has had a narrow scope in the context of studying economic performance of Indian states. It is worthwhile to extend it in various directions. Some illustrative areas are: (a) Sectoral aspects of SDP growth – agriculture industry and service sectors. (This has been attempted by Bhide, Shand and Mathur); (b) Human Development; (c) Infrastructure Development; (d) Poverty Reduction; and (e) Fiscal Viability.

• The paper was written when the author was at the Indian Council for International Economic Relations (ICRIER). The author wishes to thank Dr. Isher Ahluwalia, Dr. Rakesh Mohan and Dr. Arvind Virmani for their support and encourgement and Messers Rajeev Ranjan Sharan and Sovanbrata Talukdar for competent research assistance and Mr. Jai Mansukhani for skilful and expeditious type setting of this paper.

References

Abramovitz, M., (1956). "Resource and Output Trends in the United States since 1870", *American Economic Review*, Vol. 46, 5-23.

Ahluwalia, I.J. and J. Wiliamson, (eds) (2003). *The South Asian Experience With Growth*, Oxford University Press, New Delhi.

Ahluwalia, M.S., (2000). "Economic Performance of States in Post Reforms Period", *Economic and Political Weekly*, May 6, 1637-1648.

Aiyar, S., (2001). "Growth Theory and Convergence Across Indian States: A Panel Study" in Callen, T. *et al*, (eds.), *India at the Cross Roads: Sustaining Growth and Reducing Poverty*.

Bajpai, N. and J.D. Sachs, (1999). "The Progress of Policy Reform and Variations in Performance at the Sub-National Level in India", *Development Discussion Paper No. 730*, Harvard Institute for International Development.

Banerjee, A., P. Bardhan, K. Basu, M. Datta Chaudhuri, M. Ghatak, A.S. Guha, M. Majumdar, D. Mookherjee and D. Ray, (2000). "Strategy for Economic Reform in West Bengal", *Economic and Political Weekly*, October 12-18, 4203-4218.

Barro, R.J., (1991). "Economic Growth in a Cross Section of Countries", *Quarterly Journal of Economics*, Vol. 106, 407-443.

Barro, R.J. and X. Sala-i-Martin, (1995). *Economic Growth*, Mc Graw-Hill, New York.

Baumol, W. (1986). "Productivity Growth, Convergence and Welfare", *American Economic Review*, Vol. 76, 1072-1085.

Bhalla, S.S. and R. Chawdry, (2001). "Economy of Indian States: 1960-1997", Annexure III.

Bhide, S. and R. Shand, (2000). "Inequalities in Income Growth in India Before and After Reforms", *South Asia Economic Journal*, Vol. 1, No.1, March, 19-51.

Cashin, P. and R. Sahay, (1996). "Internal Migration, Centre-State Grants and Economic Growth in the States of India" *IMF Staff Papers*, Vol. 43, No.1, 123-171.

Chaudhuri, S., (2000). Economic Growth in the State – Four Decades – I", *Money and Finance*, October-December, 45-69.

Das, S.K. and A. Barua, (1996). "Regional Inequalities, Economic Growth and Liberalisation: A Study of the Indian Economy", *Journal of Development Studies*, Vol. 32, No. 3, 364-390.

Dasgupta, D., P. Maiti, R. Mukherjee, S. Sarkar and S. Chakrabarti, (2000). 'Growth and Interstate Disparities in India", *Economic and Political Weekly*, July 1, 2413-2422.

Dholakia, B.H., (2002). "Sources of India's Accelerated Growth and the Vision of the Indian Economy", *Indian Economic Journal*, Vol. 49, No.4, 27-46.

Dholakia, R.H., (1994). "Spatial Dimension of Acceleration of Economic Growth in India", *Economic and Political Weekly*, August 27, 2303-2309.

Easterly, W. and R. Levine, (2001). "What Have We Learned from a Decade of Empirical Research on Growth?, It's Not Factor Accumulation: Stylised Facts and Growth Models", *World Bank Economic Review*, Vol. 15, No. 2, 177-220.

Ganesh Kumar, N., (1992). "Some Comments on the Debate on India's Economic Growth in the 1980s", *The Indian Economic Journal*, 39 (4), 102-111.

Ghosh, B., S. Marjit and C. Neogi, (1998). "Economic Growth and Regional Divergence in India, 1960 to 1995", *Economic and Political Weekly*, June 27, 1623-1630.

Karnik, A., A. Samant and N. Asher, (2000). "Economic Performance of Indian States: Institutional and Political Determinants", Department of Economics, University of Bombay, *mimeo*.

Knack, S. and P. Keefer, (1996). "Institutions and Economic Performance: Cross Country Tests Using Alternative Institutional Measure", *Economics and Politics*, 207-228.

Kurian, J., (2000). "Widening Regional Disparities", *Economic and Political Weekly*.

Marjit, S and S. Mitra, (1996). "Convergence in Regional Growth Rates: Indian Research Agenda", *Economic Political Weekly,* August 17, 2239-242.

Mathur, A., (2001). "National and Regional Growth Performance in the Indian Economy: A Sectoral Analysis", paper presented at *National Seminar on Economic Reforms and Employment in Indian Economy,* IAMR.

Nagaraj, R., A. Varoudakis and M.A. Veganzones, (2000). "Long-Run Growth Trends and Convergence Across Indian States", *Journal of International Development,* Vol. 12.

Nair, K.R.G., (1983). *Regional Experience in a Developing Economy,* Wiley Eastern, New Delhi.

Pritchett, L., (2000). "Understanding Patterns of Economic Growth: Searching for Hills among Plateaus, Mountains, and Plains", *World Bank Economic Review,* Vol. 14, No.2, 221-250.

Rao, M. Govinda, R.T. Shand and K.P. Kalirajan, (1999). "Convergence of Incomes Across Indian States: A Divergent View", *Economic and Political Weekly,* March 27, 769-778.

Rodrik, D., (2000). "Where did all the Growth Go?: External Shocks, Social Conflict and Growth Collapses", *mimeo.*

Roy Choudhury, U.D., (1993). *Inter-state Variations in Economic Development and Standard of Living,* NIPFP, New Delhi.

Sachs, J.D., N. Bajpai and A. Ramiah, (2002). "Geography and Regional Growth" *The Hindu,* February 25 and 26.

Sala-I-martin, (1997). "I Just Ran Two Million Regressions", *American Economic Review,* Vol. 87, 178-183.

Sarker, P.C., (1994). "Regional Imbalances in Indian Economy Over Plan Periods", *Economic and Political Weekly,* March 12, 621-623.

Shand, R. and S. Bhide, (2000). "Sources of Economic Growth: Regional Dimensions of Reforms", *Economic and Political Weekly,* October 24, 3747-3757.

Singh, L. and S. Singh, (2002). "Deceleration of Economic Growth in Punjab: Evidence, Explanation and a Way-out", *Economic and Political Weekly,* February 9, 579-586.

Singh, N. and T.N. Srinaivasan, (2002). "Indian Federalism, Economic Reform and Globalisation", *mimeo.*

Sivasubramonian, S., (2004). *The Sources of Economic Growth in India: 1950-51 to 1999-2000,* Oxford University Press, New Delhi.

Solow, R.M., (1957). "Technical Change and the Aggregate Production Function", *Review of Economics and Statistics,* Vol. 39, 312-320.

Soludo, C.C. and J. Kim, (2002). "Sources of Aggregate Growth in Developing Regions: Still More Questions Than Answers?", in L. Squire and G. Mc Mohan (eds.), *Explaining Growth: A Global Research Project,* Global Development Network, Washington D.C. processed.

Squire, L. and G. McMohan, (eds.) (2002). *Explaining Growth: A Global Research Project,* Global Development Network, Washington, D.C., processed.

Subrahmanyam, S. and R. Rao, (2000). Convergence of Income Across States, CESS Discussion Paper.

5

Measurement and Analysis of Agricultural Growth in India

A Critical Appraisal

A. VAIDYANATHAN

1. INTRODUCTION

In a predominantly agrarian economy, marked by relatively low levels of living standard and high dependence on agriculture as a source of employment and income, the growth of agricultural production and productivity has a crucial bearing on the rate of growth in other sectors which can be sustained without inflation. It will also affect the pace at which employment can be diversified, real wage rates improved and poverty incidence and nutritional deficiencies reduced. It is natural therefore that the following questions have attracted and continue to attract widespread attention: How fast is agricultural output growing overall by crop and region? Is the rate of growth constant, increasing or decreasing over time? How unstable is output? Is the degree of instability increasing or decreasing? What are the sources of growth? Is output growth commensurate with the increased use of inputs? Is total factor productivity increasing and if so, what are the contributory factors?

These and related questions have figured prominently in academic literature and policy debates on agricultural performance and policy. Techniques of quantitative analysis—ranging from simple regressions through sophisticated multivariate analysis to optimisation models for complex systems — have been extensively used in the process. The purpose of this paper is to review the experience in applying these techniques, point out their potentials and pitfalls, and comment on the robustness of the inferences and insights they have to offer on the above-mentioned questions.

2. GROWTH AND INSTABILITY

Trend Fitting

Statistical trend fitting to estimate growth rate of output, area and yield has a long history. The methodological issues involved have been discussed in a systematic way on at least two occasions. One such discussion is presented by B.S. Minhas in his rapporteur's review of papers on "Measurement of agricultural growth", presented at the 1966 annual conference of the Indian Society of Agricultural Economics. He highlighted the uncritical and mechanical application of econometric techniques and cautioned against wrong interpretation of results. He gave a number of suggestions on the use of linear regression functions to estimate growth rates and for proper interpretation of the results.

Through the 1970s the extent to which the 'Green Revolution' had resulted in a significant acceleration in growth of output and yields became the subject of debate. Systematic testing of the alternate functional forms to time series data showed that the trends in output, area and yield both overall, and across crops and regions, are dissimilar (Srinivasan 1979, Sawant 1997).

There have also been some attempts to test for break in trends using different techniques: kinked experimental trend (Boyce, 1987); estimating separate regressions for the period before and after the time point when the break is believed to have occurred, and introducing dummy variable in a constant growth rate function to check whether the intercept or the slope has changed significantly at specified points (Sen and Sengupta, 1995). However, official publications such as the economic survey and the five year plans as well as researchers[1] continue to use the constant growth rate function to measure growth and compare performance of crops and regions.

For the most part these exercises deal with national and state level trends. A number of studies of district level variations in

---

1. Refer papers presented at annual conference of ISAE in 1997.

agricultural performance are available: Bhalla and Alagh (1979), Bhalla and Tyagi (1989) and Bhalla and Singh (1998) being the most detailed and best known. They are mostly based on changes in averages of output area and yield at different points of time. Point to point comparisons, even when based on three or five year average however can be misleading because of particular conjuncture of good and bad years. This risk is high in areas with low and erratic rainfall pattern as in Rajasthan (Vidyasagar, 1980). The use of time series can avoid this, but runs into other problems arising from the fact that district estimates are subject to much larger errors and because the proportion of area (and hence production) for which estimates are available varies systematically over time (Vaidyanathan, *et al.* 1994).

Methodological issues in trend fitting were again discussed in detail at a seminar held in 1980[2]. Dandekar, summarising the proceedings, emphasised the distinction between the use of estimated trend as a summary measure of growth during a given period and as a basis for projections. Discussing the basis for positing different functional forms, choosing the "best fit" and interpreting the results, he underlined the fact that each form implies a certain hypothesis as to whether output (or area or yield) is expected to grow at constant or variable rates and what the expected nature of variability is. The choice of the best fitting function should not however be decided only (as is often done) on the basis of R^2 or the significance of the coefficients.

Influence of Weather

Further, when we describe the movement of agricultural output over time by means of a function of time, we do not imply that observed movements of output have occurred as a result of sheer passage of time, but because of many active factors and circumstances including variations in inputs, technology and weather. While inputs and technology may reasonably be posited as an increasing function of time, weather is not. If weather variables have no time trend and year to year variations are in a statistical sense random and if they do not affect the time profile of inputs and technology or their impact on output, the effects of weather fluctuations can be taken as

2. Papers presented at the Seminar are published in IJAE, April-June, 1980.

subsumed in the residual "error" term of the estimated regressions. The time trends could then be taken as reflecting the impact of systematic changes in the level of inputs and the efficacy of their use over time.

Both assumptions are open to question. There are indications of systematic patterns of variation in weather variables (especially rainfall) even over a span of a decade. Moreover, since rainfall is a significant determinant of soil moisture available for crops, it could have a sizeable influence on cropped area, crop patterns, input levels and yields in rainfed areas and, in so far as supply to irrigation systems depends on rainfall in their catchment, in irrigated areas as well.

This aspect came into prominence in early debates on the impact of HYV on output growth and induced efforts to estimate output trends net of the weather effect. These attempts showed that weather corrected trends differ significantly from uncorrected time trends in most states though not uniformly (Cummings and Ray, 1969; Mukherjee and Vaidyanathan 1988, Vaidyanathan, 1979). These exercises, however, suffer from limitations arising from difficulties of constructing a meaningful composite weather index including factors other than total or seasonal rainfall and inadequate knowledge of the relation between weather, on the one hand and area cropped and yields, on the other. The possibilities of extending and refining the measurement and estimation of weather effects have not evoked much interest among researchers.

Assessment of Instability

Another issue, and one whose resolution is related to trend fitting, concerns verification of the hypothesis that faster growth goes with greater instability of output. This hypothesis, originally advanced by Sen (1967), attracted wide attention after the advent of HYV and other elements of the so-called "Green Revolution" technology. For a proper testing of this hypothesis it is necessary to measure deviations of actual output in the relevant time series from the trend line fitted to the series rather than the deviations from the mean of series. The estimates of deviations from the trend being sensitive to the functional form chosen, it is important to use the best fitting function for the purpose.

Usually, the best fitting function for estimating trends differs between crops, regions and periods. Nevertheless, practically all studies of instability (e.g. Mehra, 1981; Hazell, 1982; Dhawan, 1988; Ray 1983, 1987) use a single functional form (usually of the constant growth rate variety) to de-trend the series for all crops, periods and regions. This procedure clearly gives an erroneous and misleading basis for assessing relative instability (Vaidyanathan 1979, Krishnaji, 1980). Moreover, as Hazell (1982) has shown, inferences on growth instability relations based on aggregate data can be quite misleading. A part, perhaps a large part, of the apparent increase in variability at the national level was found to be due to synchronous movement of area and yield across regions and over time.

3. SOURCES OF GROWTH

Decomposition Analysis

Prior to 1960, much of the analysis of changes in crop output focussed on the relative contributions of changes in area and in yield per unit area. In 1959, a decomposition scheme was suggested to measure the relative contributions of area changes (keeping crop patterns and yield constant), pure yield effects (reflecting impact of changes in yields keeping cropped area and patterns invariant) and the contribution of crop pattern changes (with area and yield of individual crops kept constant). The difference between the sum of these three effects and actual change in output reflect the interactions among the above three elements. (Minhas and Vaidyanathan, 1965). This prompted revision in the official index of agricultural production giving indices of area sown, along with indices of output reflecting crop pattern shifts (with constant yield) and per hectare yields (with constant crop patterns). Minhas (1966) also outlined a multiplicative scheme for estimating the contribution of changes in pure yield and crop pattern effects and the interactions between the two to changes in value of output per hectare.

This scheme was further extended and refined by Dharam Narain (1977) to capture effects of change in the spatial distribution of area under different crops. Dharam Narain's analysis showed that the spatial shifts make a significant difference to the estimated contribution of yields to overall output growth and that the effect differed from period to period. In his exercise, which covered the period 1962-73, crop pattern and locational shifts accounted for a significant part of productivity increases in the fifties, while pure yield effect contributed the major part of the increase in the 1960s. (For a critique and suggested refinement see Vidyasagar, 1980).

These schemes have been used by several others (Bhalla and Alagh 1979; Dayal, 1966; Vidyasagar, 1980) to estimate the contribution of different elements to observed growth. Some (e.g. Minhas and Vaidyanathan 1965; Vidyasagar, 1977) used the additive scheme or its modified form to account for changes in output between different points of time. Others (Minhas, 1966 and Dharam Narain, 1977 at the all-India level and Parikh, 1966 at the state level) have estimated the multiplicative model on the basis of time series data. Neither is free of problems.

On the one hand, given wide fluctuations in output due to vagaries of weather, measuring growth based on point-to-point comparisons of three or five year surveys can give a misleading picture of the underlying trend. On the other hand, the application of the multiplicative scheme to time series which rests on the assumption that each of the component elements conforms to the constant growth rate hypothesis is open to question. We know as a fact that this is not so. Abandoning the assumption and deriving expected outputs as the product of the trend values of each component estimated from best fitting function for it, runs into serious econometric problems. If corrections for weather are to be made, as they need to be, the task becomes even more difficult. These issues seem to be so daunting as to discourage further empirical research using these schema. Perhaps, more could be done if time series indices for areas, crop pattern and yields are available at the state level.

Factors Underlying Growth

Decomposition of change in output into its main constituent elements was seen as a convenient starting point for deeper analysis of growth. It facilitates analysis of changes/variations in each of the elements in terms of distinct sets of factors influencing them. Thus, the area actually cultivated at a given time for instance depends on the extent of cultivatable land, weather factors, irrigation and prevailing costs and prices. Crop patterns are determined by climate, extent and quality of irrigation and relative returns to competing crops, which in turn depends on relative prices and yields of different crops. Per hectare yields are essentially a function of the level, seasonal pattern and reliability of rainfall, level and composition of nutrients applied to crop, the seed varieties used, and the prices of inputs relative to output. The investigation can be further enriched by deeper analysis of the factors (some natural, some to do with technology, some to do with public policy) influencing each of the key factors.

A number of empirical studies of the determinants of cropping intensity, cropping patterns and crop yields are available. Some use cross-section data, some time series. Some focus on state level analysis. Several have attempted disaggregated analysis at the sub-state level, agro-climatic regions, districts, and districts grouped by rainfall and irrigation development. They provide some useful insights: for example on the role of irrigation and rainfall characteristics in determining cropping intensity (Ray, 1985, Mahendra Dev *et al*, 1989); the relation between irrigation and the type of irrigation on the one hand and the extent of crop diversification on the other (Vaidyanathan *et al*, 1994); the importance of irrigation and fertiliser use in determining land productivity (Ranade, 1980; Parikh, 1966; Dhawan, 1988); the existence of synergy between irrigation and yield response to fertilisers, the differences in these respects between regions and the progressive decline in the yield response to fertiliser use (Vaidyanathan *et al.* 1994). Factors affecting the spread of fertilisers, (including the effect of relative prices), yield response to fertilisers and optimum allocation of nutrients have also been extensively explored. (Desai and Singh, 1973; Desai and Vaidyanathan 1994; Nagaraj, 1980; Parikh, 1978; Parikh and Srinivasan, 1974).

There has been some work to assess the impact of relative prices on the area allocated to particular crops (see Askari and Cummings, 1976), but hardly any on the impact of prices on efficiency of input use, or the effect of relative price of input-output on yield levels of individual crops much less of all crops. The role of agrarian structure, institutional arrangements for input supply and marketing and, more generally, agricultural infrastructure and government pricing policies have not received as much systematic attention. The complexity of input-output relations in agriculture and data limitations (due to non-availability or lack of reliability) have constrained and impeded sustained work on these lines.

Most of these studies focus on one or other element of the output decomposition scheme. There have however been a couple of attempts (see Parikh, 1966 and Mukherjee and Vaidyanathan, 1988) to apply it to account for the trend rate of output growth at the state level. Parikh (1966) applied the multiplicative decomposition scheme to estimate the contribution of changes in area (taking into account the possibility that the quality of land entering into or going out of cultivation may affect yield independently of other factors), crop pattern shifts and pure yield effects on the trend growth in total output. Overall per hectare yield is estimated as a function of irrigation ratio, fertiliser intensity and time; the last element reflecting the composite effects of crop pattern changes, technical progress and other omitted variables.

Mukherjee and Vaidyanathan (1980) estimated crop area as a function of time and weather (rainfall) and the expected value of per hectare yield (including the effect of crop pattern change) as a function of irrigation and fertilisers. The product of the expected values of area and yield are then compared with the observed output. The time pattern of residues is then screened: a rising trend can be interpreted as indicative of improved efficiency of input use (due to a number of factors including seed variety, irrigation quality, improved cultivation practices etc.).

Production Functions

Econometric estimation of "production functions" has been widely used for analysis of spatial and temporal variations in output and yields. During the sixties and seventies, when questions relating to efficiency of resource allocation and existence of scale economies in Indian agriculture attracted much attention, there was a veritable spate of papers which estimated production functions based on cross section data from farm level surveys. A detailed review (Venkat Reddy Kata, 1990) of some 70 studies in this genre reveals the following features:

1) A variety of functional forms - linear, quadratic, Cobb Douglas, CES, transcendental, etc. — were fitted, Cobb Douglas being the most frequent.

2) A large majority of the studies estimated the relation between total output and selected inputs.

3) A small proportion focussed on variation in per hectare output. The number of input variables included in the estimation ranged from two to eight, five being the most frequent number.

4) Estimates were made for different combination of inputs. Land, human labour, animal labour and fertilisers figured in most exercises.

5) Irrigation, total recurring costs and seeds were used in some. Land was variously specified in terms of "standard acres", net sown area and gross cropped area. However, in a majority of cases it is not clear which concept is used.

6) About one-third of the regressions covered by the review related to specific crops (mainly rice and wheat), about one-half to crop production as a whole and the rest covered both. Multi-collinearity is widespread. The proportion of variance in output explained was relatively high.

7) Coefficients for various inputs had the expected (positive) sign in a majority of the cases. They turned out to be negative in about a sixth of the regressions results analysed.

8) Positive coefficients were not significant at a five per cent level in large number of cases: nearly 80 per cent in the case of animal labour; 60 per cent in irrigation; over 40 per cent for human labour and fertilisers/manures. Coefficients estimated from different regressions were not stable.

Commenting on the empirical estimates of agricultural production functions, Rudra (1982) noted that variables included are different; common variables are defined or measured differently. Even when they are comparable in this respect, differences between estimates for different times are large. 'One does not improve fits by introducing a large number of variables. Lumping of all material inputs may give as good a fit; dropping of material inputs other than land and labour does not seem to reduce fits.' Aggregation and measurement of heterogeneous inputs poses problems. Aggregation by value means departure from the concept of the production function, which relates basically to technological relations between inputs and outputs. 'If one is using the blunt weapon of an arbitrary functional form for the sake of convenience of fitting, one may not at the same time gain anything in sharpness by carefully and separately measuring different individual items'. The nature and quality of fits (judged by R^2, coefficient values, and 't' values) are so different from each other that no generalisation is possible for the country as a whole on the basis of fits for different regions or for any region from fits for different time periods.

Attempts to explain spatial and temporal variations in output (yields) also used multiple regression techniques and the Cobb Douglas functional form in specifying the input-output relation. But there is considerable variation in the specification of input variables: some (e.g., Radhakrishna, 1964), which based their analysis on farm survey data, included area, human and bullock labour and other selected inputs individually or in combination. Mukhopadhyay (1976), who used pooled cross-section and time series of district level macro data, included irrigated areas, fertilisers, tractors, literate and illiterate labour as input variables.

Studies which sought to estimate total factor productivity in an attempt to assess the contribution of technical progress (and research) as distinct from increased input use to growth of output/yields (e.g., Evenson and Jha 1973; Bisaliah 1977; Karam Singh 1977; Bal and Kahlon, 1977; Kumar and Rosegrant, 1994) also included a similar wide range of inputs. Most of these studies found that technical progress accounted for a significant part of the realised increase in output in the areas and periods covered by them. For reasons which we will cite presently, both the specification of the 'production function' and the inferences drawn from these estimates is open to serious question. Kaliarajan and Shand (1997) proposed a way of circumventing this by directly estimating the contribution of progress in technology and more effective use of available technology and inputs. Whether and how this is empirically feasible is a question on which the present author has serious doubts.

Be that as it may, it is relevant to note Mukhopadhyay's summing up of the results of his attempts to explain variations in agricultural productivity in the wheat regions using production functions:

"The empirical findings of the study (based on time series) are different from conventional cross-sectional production studies. The coefficients for inputs of land, irrigation, fertilisers, tractors, educated labour are rather small and only the first three have statistically significant 't' values. The sum of the coefficients indicates a low elasticity of aggregate output with respect to these inputs. The major reason for such small coefficients seem to be that there are a large number of relevant factors specific to regions, but omitted from analysis and the inputs are considered in a highly aggregated form". He goes on to point out that inter regional differences in response are very large 'perhaps due to large differences in quality of inputs, as well as their climate, management efficiency, tenure systems, cultural practices... and cumulative effects of past technology and investments'. (Mukhopadhyay, 1976: 60-61).

Partly due to lack of reliable data and partly from a skepticism of the production function approach, several studies (e.g., Sapre and Deshpande, 1964; Parikh, 1966, 1970; Parikh and Trivedi, 1982) confined themselves to examine the extent to which differences in levels of (changes in) key bio-physical factors (namely, rainfall, irrigation, fertilisers and, in one case, soil fertility) could account for inter regional variations in per hectare yields (and differences in their growth). Mukherjee and Vaidyanathan (1988) used, besides rainfall, a composite input index comprising irrigation and fertilisers and introduced time as a variable to capture technical progress. Mukherjee and Vaidyanathan (1988) used a formulation with irrigation and fertiliser as separate variables.

More recently Vaidyanathan *et al.* (1994) used district level data to estimate the relation between yields on the one hand and rainfall, irrigation and fertilisers on the other. For this purpose districts were grouped into homogenous rainfall-irrigation categories and the relation (using a linear, additive function) estimated across districts in each category at different points of time. There were significant differences in the coefficients for the explanatory variables between groups at a point in time as well as their behaviour over time; fertiliser coefficients varied systematically across rainfall and irrigation categories, and showed a generally declining trend over time. The results of these exercises are suggestive but hardly definitive or strong.

There are several reasons for this. One, and an obvious one, has to do with coverage and quality of data. The country has no doubt a nationwide system to compile data on land use, rainfall, irrigation, fertiliser use, crop areas and yields. Even so there are gaps, problems of quality and comparability across states and over time. Estimates of crop and irrigated areas are in many states compiled by different agencies; concepts vary; they are prone to biased reporting. The quality of reporting system has deteriorated because village officials are expected to do many more and varied tasks, supervision and verification by higher officials has progressively weakened; and in some states the system of appointing local persons as *patwaris* has been given up.

Though yield estimates of all major crops are based on sample crop cutting surveys, the responsibility for selection of plots and conduct of experiments is distributed between different agencies. There is reason to believe that the supervision and independent checks to ensure adherence to prescribed design and procedures have slackened. A number of minor but high value crops are not based on proper surveys and estimates of different agencies vary widely. The output of fruits and vegetables for instance are believed to have grown rapidly but there is no reliable basis to assess their magnitude accurately. Sample surveys are designed to give state level estimates with a reasonable margin of error.

District level estimates are not based on sample crop cuts alone; a considerable amount of 'judgement' goes into them. They are therefore subject to much larger, but unknown and variable, margins of error. Moreover, district level estimates of output do not cover all crops. For several reasons, they are based on state level average yields. Even so the proportion of total cropped area for which output estimates are available varies across districts and over time. In a majority of district the coverage of the estimates shows a significant rising or falling trend (see Vaidyanathan *et al.* 1994). Outputs are generally valued on the basis of national average prices thus ignoring regional differences in quality and prices. Statistics of fertiliser use relate to quantities distributed and not quantities actually consumed. Disaggregated analysis has to contend with the problem of high and probably increasing noise in the data.

There are however deeper conceptual and estimation problems. 'Production function' defines the relation between output and inputs. This requires a clear concept of the production process as well as a proper specification of the form of the relationship between inputs and output. Conventionally, economic theory has viewed output (measured as value added) as a function of primary factors, namely, labour and capital. Alternative functional forms capture differences in respect of returns to scale and the degree of substitutability between inputs. The basic model has been refined to take into account the fact that output is a function not only of the quantity of the input, but also of changes in the productivity per unit of input due to changes in the quality of particular inputs and more importantly, changes in productivity per unit of all factors reflecting economies of scale, technological changes, learning etc. Much of the work on production functions in industry, and for the economy as a whole, is based on this concept. Though there are problems about data and interpretation, these analyses being conceptually well grounded, their results provide useful insights stimulating further refinements.

Applying this framework to agriculture has been problematic. For one thing, besides capital and labour, a third primary factor, namely land, is involved in crop production. We have fairly good time series data on the extent of cultivated area overall and crop-wise. But 'area' is not a satisfactory measure of land input in as much as its quality is highly variable. Land quality is also difficult to measure. In so far as it is a function of investments in irrigation and land improvement they may be taken as being captured by capital. But innate differences due to differences in depth, texture, composition and nutrient status also affect productivity. These are too complex to be reduced to a single index, though some attempts to do this have been made. One way to circumvent these problems is to focus on the relation between per hectare yields and per hectare inputs of capital and labour.

This also runs into problems because part of the capital stock (irrigation and land improvement) is yield augmenting while another part (animals and tractors, harvesters) affects the intensity of human labour input rather than per hectare yields. There is also the problem arising from the lack of comprehensive and comparable data on capital and labour inputs. Attempts to construct such a series

(Dasgupta, 1984) are dated and unsatisfactory because of large data gaps. Capital stock created by public investments can be, and have been, estimated from budget and plan data. Data on wells, irrigation equipment, animals, farm machinery owned by farmers are compiled periodically: once in five years by the livestock census and once in 10 years by the National Sample Survey. The latter also gives values of these assets. Being infrequent, construction of a time series involves arbitrary interpolation. The alternative, used in some studies, of using annual charges of availing services provided by capital stock derived from farm surveys is vitiated because often the rates imputed or actually paid bear no relation to the costs incurred in providing them.

Similar problems arise in constructing time series of labour inputs. The population census gives estimates, at decennial intervals, of the number of workers in agriculture but not of the number of days for which they worked in agriculture. The NSS employment surveys provide estimates of the latter but only at five year intervals. Interpolation to get a time series again involves arbitrary assumptions. Sample surveys of farms (especially the cost of cultivation surveys) do provide time series with details, by crop and operation, of labour inputs. But they are not of much use in estimating conventional production functions in the absence of series on capital.

Because of these limitations, researchers have tended to use the proportion of area irrigated, fertilisers, pesticides, area under HYV, human, animal and machine labour in estimating the equations. Data on the total quantum of natural inputs (irrigated area, fertilisers, pesticides, and HYV of some crops) seed for crop production are available up to the district level, but not for others. Time series of these variables for a representative sample of farm can be constructed for individual crops and for all crops from the cost of cultivation surveys. Regrettably, these data remain largely unused for study of input-output relations. Both sets of data are also incomplete in key respects especially in respect of the quality of irrigation and the nutrient content of farmyard manures.

There are also serious difficulties in specifying the functional relation between production and these inputs. Linear, Cobb Douglas, CES and similar functions are meaningful when input variables relate to primary factors. But they are not meaningful when a motley array of variables, seed, fertilisers, irrigation, labour, machinery etc. are included among inputs without a clear concept of the production process, the role of different kinds of inputs and the precise nature of their relation to output.

Thus, the linear form implies that the yield increment per unit of each incremental output is constant and quite independent of its level and the level of others. The level of particular inputs and their impact on output response are, in many instances, dependent on the level and quality of other inputs. Thus, the level of fertiliser use as well as the yield response to it is very much a function of the soil moisture regime, the genetic potential of the seed varieties used and to some degree the level of inputs for control of weed, pests and diseases. The incidence of pests and disease (and the cost of controlling them) is a function of, among other things, seed varieties, crop and soil moisture conditions. In view of this, none of the usual forms of production functions are appropriate.

On the other hand, Cobb Douglas or other similar forms implicitly assume that all inputs are substitutable over the entire range of application when in fact we know that several of them (especially water and fertilisers) are complementary over some ranges and substitutable in other ranges. Moreover, the yield response to fertiliser is marked by a strong synergy with the extent and quality of irrigation and the seed variety used. In view of the complex patterns of complementarity and substitution between the various inputs which figure in much of the econometric estimation of input-output relations in agriculture, modelling these relations as being linear and additive or capable of mutual substitution without limit is clearly inappropriate. It is therefore hardly surprising that the estimated coefficients in many of the production function estimates are often not significant, their values unstable and sensitive to the number and type of inputs included in the estimating function. In some cases, the coefficients even show the wrong signs! Faced with the pervasive problem of multicollinearity, analysts tend to drop variables with non-significant coefficients and report results for those variants which give statistically significant and 'plausible' values. Under these circumstances, it is difficult to make coherent sense of the estimated regressions, either as tests of hypotheses regarding the factors determining output and the relation between inputs and output, or as a basis for judging the impact of specific inputs on productivity. It is even more difficult to see how the unexplained residual between expected values estimated from incomplete and mis-specified functions and observed outputs can be attributed to productivity of inputs and used as a measure of total factor productivity.

An Alternative Approach

In order to avoid these pitfalls, it is arguable that in the absence of reliable data on the level of primary factor inputs, the conceptualisation and estimation of input-output relations would gain by rethinking the nature of the production process, keeping in view the pecularities of the production process in agriculture. This calls for making a clear distinction between the conventional, primary factors centred, concept of the production process and one which views it as a biochemical process. The two are of course inter-related and the inter-relations need to be explored. But this is best done as a separate exercise. Confounding the two concepts in specifying the production function does not add much to our understanding of the factors underlying spatial or temporal variations in productivity; the mere fact that the parameters are or are not significant does not get rid of this basic problem.

Crop production involves a biological process, which is influenced by several bio-physical factors including soil characteristics, moisture availability (from rainfall, irrigation) the genetic potential of seed, quantum of plant nutrients applied, and plant protection chemical inputs. Capital investment in the form of land improvement and irrigation augments production potential by providing more abundant, timely and assured soil moisture; capital invested in draught animals, machinery and equipment together with human labour essentially enable various operations involved in cultivation necessary for the biological process to work.

Some part of this human-animal-machine labour is applied to the preparation of land and seedbed and for sowing; some parts are needed and used to apply nutrients, weeding the field and protecting plants from pests and disease. The intensity and quality of the energy input in these operations does not affect yield directly but via the quantum of biochemical inputs and their management. It is sometimes argued that mechanisation directly increases productivity by facilitating timely land preparation and sowing, thus enabling more intensive cropping and shortening the time taken for harvesting one crop and preparing the land for the next. But so far available evidence in support of this view is scanty and weak. Energy input in harvesting, threshing and post-harvest operations do not determine yields, rather they are determined by the level of yields.

For all practical purposes the impact of human, animal and machine labour inputs on output/yields can be considered separately from, though related to, the biochemical input application. The relations of, and interactions between, biochemical inputs on the one hand and capital and labour inputs on the other, the determinants of the composition of capital and labour inputs and those of bio chemical inputs of course need to be examined. But their relation to output can be analysed separately. This will help substantially reduce the confusion which confounds much of the current analysis of input-output relations.

Viewing yield as a function of soil moisture regime and local composition of nutrients provides a clearer, better defined and more meaningful concept of production function than the ones currently in use.[3] Of the various biochemical inputs, soil moisture and nutrients play a crucial and central role. The soil moisture regime (which is a function of soil conservation, irrigation and management of irrigation) affects potential yield response curve of a given variety to increased nutrients. The spread of irrigation (or higher retention of local rainfall) shifts the yield response curve for fertilisers upward and to the right. All other factors, better varieties, more effective plant protection improved cultural practices, the quality of water management and learning from experience, can be visualised as affecting yield by shifting the position of the fertiliser response curve.

On this reasoning, the information required to estimate the biochemical production function can also be greatly economised. Once the expected yield, given quantum of soil moisture, nutrient levels and composition, are estimated, deviations of observed yield from the expected yield based on quantum of the two inputs alone,

3. It does not preclude the use of conventional forms where output is related to the primary factors if and when the necessary data are available.

gives a measure of the impact of the rest of the variables. In the context of a progressive improvement in quality and management of these other inputs — and this seems a reasonable characterisation of the experience of the past 4-5 decades, one would expect the residual to give a better and more meaningful measure of the efficiency of use of water and nutrients than the current model of TFP change.

This approach has been tried with some success. Crop production is defined as function of basic biochemical inputs, namely, land, rainfall, irrigation and plant nutrients. Seed varieties and plant protection inputs are seen as determining the position of the fertiliser response function under a given rainfall-irrigation regime. Output is the product of area and yield, each being determined by a different set of factors. Besides weather, the quantum of nutrients per unit area and irrigation, the genetic potential of seed determines attainable yield per unit of area. More and better irrigation and better varieties shift the nutrient response curve upward and outward. The actual response curve will depend on how effectively pests and disease are controlled; the more effective the control the higher will be the response curve. Realised response curve could also be affected by better management of inputs through a process of learning over time. Accordingly, yield function of the following type has been proposed and tried:

$$y = f\ (\text{rainfall, irrigation ratio, nutrients, time})$$

The expectation being that the effects of seed improvement, better techniques of weeding, and pest/disease control, and learning will be increasing function of time. Because of the high correlation between irrigation and fertiliser use, a composite index of irrigation and fertiliser use based on their productivity increment due to irrigation prior to advent of fertiliser and the yardstick of yield response to fertiliser with traditional varieties have been used (Vaidyanathan and Mukherjee, 1980).

The results are suggestive but neither definitive nor strong. There are several problems: inadequacy of irrigation ratio as a measure of quantum and quality of water availability; the lack of data on quantum of manures and their nutrients composition being the most obvious. The availability of detailed farm level data, combined with improvement in measure of soil moisture conditions, and perhaps in the functional forms, opens possibilities for further refinement by stratifying regions to permit analysis by homogeneous soil, climate and irrigation regimes, and estimating the relations for different, relatively homogenous strata.

There are of course difficulties in getting a proper measure of soil moisture regimes; handling multicollinearity between soil moisture and fertiliser use; getting estimates of total nutrient application and its composition covering both chemical fertilisers and farm yard manures and taking into account possible adverse effects of land degradation, changing chemical composition of water (due to pollution from agro chemicals and industrial/urban effluents).

The available data on soil moisture regimes are limited to rainfall, area irrigated and the proportion of area irrigated by different sources. Rainfall and the proportion of area irrigated, the only data currently available to capture soil moisture conditions, are inadequate. The density of rain gauging stations is too thin and the reportage of irrigated area is unsatisfactory. What we need ideally is a composite index of the volume of soil moisture available from rainfall and irrigation preferably along with its seasonal distribution. This would call for more systematic compilation of metereological data, volume of water released from reservoirs and pumping from ground water. The first two can be obtained by streamlining existing arrangements but estimating groundwater extraction would require surveys of water extraction from representative sample at the regional level on a regular basis.

Statistics of fertiliser distribution by nutrient are available up to the district level. Though not identical with consumption (due to border trade and stock changes), they can be taken as a reasonable indicator of relative levels of, and changes in, fertiliser use. The major problem however is that no data on nutrient from manures are available even at the state level. Detailed data on levels of fertilsers and manure application collected in the cost of cultivation surveys for a representative sample of farms can be used to get state level estimates. Incidentally, they also provide a basis for estimating source wise area actually irrigated. However, the problem of evaluating nutrient content of farm yard manures of highly variable types and qualities will remain.

The third problem arises from multicollinearity between irrigation and fertilisers: one way would be to construct a composite index of the two inputs. Another would be (a) to estimate the difference between average yields of irrigated and rainfed areas (and where possible between different types of irrigation) before the advent of fertilisers; (b) using it to estimate the increase in average overall yields due to spread of irrigation (without any or very small amount of fertiliser); (c) difference between estimate (b) and actual yields. The estimated relation between (c) and the level and composition of fertilisers and the pattern of the residuals could then be examined to see if there are systematic patterns and how they relate to the spread of improved varieties, education, cultivation practices and other factors which operate via shifting of the fertiliser response function.

Reliability of data will remain a problem. While every effort needs to be made to improve their quality and ensure comparability across space and time, it is not possible in the nature of thing to ensure absolute accuracy. All data are subject to errors and noise of various kinds. This is not a crippling limitation for studying variations and factors underlying them. Much can be gained by careful and discriminating use of available data. The more so when as in the case in India — we have the relevant data at the district and state level from official statistics as well as from more detailed farm level data based on continuing sample surveys.

References

Askari and Cummings, (1976). *Estimating Agricultural Supply Response: A Survey of Econometric Evidence*, Prayer, New York.

Bal H.K. and A.S. Kahlon, (1977). "Methodological Issues in Measurement of Returns to Investment in Agricultural Research", *Indian Journal of Agricultural Economics*, Vol 32, No.3, July-Sept.

Bhalla G.S. and D.S. Tyagi, (1989). *Patterns of Indian Agricultural Development: A District Level Study*, Institute for Studies in Industrial Development, New Delhi.

Bhalla G.S. and Y.K. Alagh, (1979). *Performance of Indian Agriculture: A Districtwise Study*, Sterling, New Delhi.

Bhalla, G.S. and Gunvant Singh, (1998). "Recent Developments in Indian Agriculture", Centre for Study of Regional Development, School of Social Sciences, Jawaharlal Nehru University, *mimeo*.

Bisaliah, S. (1977). "Decomposition Analysis of Output Change under New Production Technology", *Indian Journal of Agricultural Economics*, Vol 32, No.3, July-Sept.

Boyce, James K., (1987). *Agrarian Impasse in Bengal: Institutional Constraints to Technical Changes*, Oxford University Press, New Delhi.

Cummings, Ralph W. and S.K. Ray, (1969). "Food Grains Production: Relative Contribution of Weather and New Technology", *Economic and Political Weekly*, September.

Das, Gupta A.K. (1984). *Growth and Composition of Agricultural Capital Stock in Indian States 1961-1977*, Hindustan Publishing Corporation, New Delhi.

Dayal, (1966). "Agricultural Growth Rates and their Components", *Indian Journal of Agricultural Economics*, Oct-Dec.

Desai, Bhupati M. and N.V. Namboodiri, (1997). "Determinants of Total Factor Productivity in Indian Agriculture", *Economic and Political Weekly*, Dec.

Desai, Gunvant and A. Vaidyanathan, eds., (1994). *Strategic Issues in Future Growth of Fertilisers in India*, IFPRI, Washington, DC.

Desai, Gunvant and Surinder Singh (1973). "Growth of Fertiliser Use in the districts of India: Performance and Policy Implications", IIAM, Anand, *mimeo*.

Desai, Gunwant (1982). *Sustaining Rapid Growth in India's Fertiliser Consumption*, IFPRI, Washington DC.

Dharam, Narain (1977). "Growth of Productivity in Indian Agriculture", *Indian Journal of Agricultural Economics*, January-March.

Dhawan, B.D., (1988). *Irrigation in India's Agricultural Development: Productivity, Stability and Equity*, Commonwealth Publishers, New Delhi.

Evenson, Robert E. and Dayanath Jha, (1973). "Contribution of Agricultural Research System to Agricultural Production in India", *Indian Journal of Agricultural Economics*, Oct-Dec.

Hazell, Peter (1982). *Instability in Indian Foodgrain Production*, IFPRI Research Report 30, Washington DC.

Kalirajan, K.P. and R.T. Shand (1997). "Souces of Output Growth in Indian Agriculture", *Indian Journal of Agricultural Economics*, Vol 52, No.4, Oct-Dec.

Karam, Singh (1977). "Returns to Investment in Agricultural Research in Punjab", *Indian Journal of Agricultural Economics*, Vol. 32, No.3, July-Sept.

Krishnaji, N. (1980). "Measuring Agricultural Growth", Indian Society of Agricultural Economics, Seminar on Data Base and Methodology for study of Growth Rate in Agriculture, *Indian Journal of Agricultural Economics*, January–March.

Kumar, Praduman and Mark Rosegrant (1994). "Productivity and Sources of Growth for Rice in India", *Economic and Political Weekly*, Dec.

Mahendra, Dev, S., S.M. Deshpande and E. Kamaiah, (1989). "Estimation of Yield Functions with Binary Choice Models, Analysis by Agroclimatic Regions in India", *mimeo*.

Mehra, Shakunthala (1981). "Instability in Indian Aagriculture in the Context of the New Technology", *IFPRI Research Report 25*, Washingon DC.

Minhas, B.S. and A.Vaidyanathan (1965). "Growth of Crop Output in India 1951-54 to 1958-61", *Journal of the Indian Society of Agricultural Statistics*.

Minhas, (1966). "Rapporteurs Report on Measurement of Agricultural Growth", *Indian Journal of Agricultural Economics*, October-December.

Mitra, Ashok K., (1990). "Agricultural Production in Maharashtra: Growth and Instability in the Context of New Technology", *Economic and Political Weekly*, Dec.

Mukherjee, Chandan and A.Vaidyanathan, (1980). "Growth and Fluctuations of Foodgrains Yields: A Statewise Analysis", *Indian Journal of Agricultural Economics*, Apr-Jun.

————. (1988). "State-wise Analysis of Agricultural Growth in Recent Advances", in *Agricultural Statistics Research*, (eds). Prem Narain *et al.*, John Wiley, New Delhi.

Mukhopadhyay, Sudhin (1976). *Sources of Growth in Agricultural Productivity: A Cross Section-Time Series Study in India*, Macmillan, New Delhi.

Nagraj, R. (1980). "Determinants of Fertiliser Use and Its Growth", unpublished M. Phil thesis, Center for Development Studies, Trivandrum.

Narain, Dharam (1977). "Growth of Productivity in Indian Agriculture", *Indian Journal of Agricultural Economics*, Jan-Mar.

Narayana, N.S.S. and Ganesh Kumar, (1993). "On Analysing Growth and Instability of Agricultural Performance: A Case Study of Cereal Crop Yields in India and Andhra Pradesh", *mimeo*, Indian Statistical Institute Economic Analysis Unit.

Narayana, Reddy M., J.C. Katyal, Y.V.R. Reddy and C.A. Ram, (1998). "Estimating Agricultural Growth: A Piecewise Regression Approach", *Indian Journal of Agricultural Economics*, Apr-Jun.

Parikh, A. and P. Trivedi, (1982). "Impact of Irrigation and Fertilisers on the Growth of Output in Andhra Pradesh", *Indian Journal of Agricultural Economics*, Apr-Jun.

Parikh, K.S., (1978). "HYV and Fertilisers: Synergy or Substitution : Implications for Policy and Prospects for Agricultural Development", *Economic and Political Weekly*, Review of Agriculture, March.

Parikh, K.S. and T.N. Srinivasan, (1974). *Optimum Requirements of Fertilisers for the Fifth Plan Period*, Indian Statistical Institute and Fertiliser Association of India.

Parikh, Ashok (1966). "State-wise Growth Rate in Agricultural Output: An Econometric Analysis", *Artha Vignana*, March.

————. (1970). "Cropwise, Districtwise Production Functions", *Indian Journal of Agricultural Economics*, Jan-Mar.

Radhakrishna, D. (1964). "A Study of Marginal Productivity of Agricultural Inputs", *Indian Journal of Agricultural Economics, Vol 19, No.1, Jan-March.*

Ranade, C.G., (1980). "Impact of Crop Pattern on Agricultural Production", *Indian Journal of Agricultural Economics*, Apr-Jun.

Rawal, Vikas and M. Swaminathan, (1998). "Changing Trajectories: Agricultural Growth in West Bengal", *Economic and Political Weekly*, Oct.

Ray, S.K., (1983). "Growth and Instability in Indian Agriculture", Institute of Economic Growth, Delhi, *mimeo*.

————. (1987). *Intensification of Agriculture: A Study of Plans of East Uttar Pradesh*, Hindustan Publishing Corp, New Delhi.

Rudra, Ashok, (1982). *Indian Agricultural Economics: Myths and Reality*, Allied Publishers, New Delhi.

Sapre S.G. and V.D. Deshpande, (1964). "Inter District Variations in Agricultural Efficiency in Maharashtra", *Indian Journal of Agricultural Economics*, Vol 19, No.1, Jan-Mar.

Sawant, S.D., (1983). "Investigation of the Hypothesis of Deceleration in Indian Agriculture", *Indian Journal of Agricultural Economics*, Oct-Dec.

————. (1997). "Regional Variations in Agricultural Performance During the Last Two Decades", *Indian Journal of Agricultural Economics*, Conference Issue.

Sen, S.R., (1967). "Growth and Instability in Indian Agriculture", *Journal of the Indian Society of Agricultural Statistics.*

Srinivasan, T.N., (1979). "Trends in Agriculture in India, 1949-50 to 1977-78", *Economic and Political Weekly*, August.

Vaidyanathan A., (1978). "HYV and Fertilsers: Synergy or Substitution: A Comment", *Economic and Political Weekly*, June.

————. (1979). "On Analysing Agricultural Growth", *Journal of the Indian Society of Agricultural Statistics.*

————. (1994). "Second India Series Revisited: Food, Agriculture and Water", Madras Institute of Development Studies, *mimeo.*

Vani B.P. and Vinod Vyasulu, (1996). "Growth, Variability and Instability of three Major Cereal Crops in Karnataka", *Economic and Political Weekly*, June.

Vaidyanathan A, Asha Krishnakumar, A. Rajagopal and D. Varatharajan, (1994). "Impact of Irrigation on Productivity of Land", *Journal of the Indian School of Political Economy*, Oct-Dec.

Venkat Reddy Kata, (1990). *Agricultural Production Functions: An Appraisal*, Ajanta Publishers, Delhi.

Vidya Sagar, (1977). "A Component Analysis of Food Grain Economy in Rajasthan, 1956-61 to 1969-74", *Indian Journal of Agricultural Economics*, January-March.

————. (1980). "Decomposition of Growth Trend and Selected Issues", *Indian Journal of Agricultural Economics*, April-June.

6

Estimation of Decline in Marginal Productivity of Land Using Stochastic Production Function

G. MYTHILI

1. INTRODUCTION

Specification of state dependent factors is very crucial in the estimation of input-output relation. This is particularly important in the case of agriculture as farming in less developed and developing economies often become vulnerable to factors such as amount of rainfall, distribution of rainfall over seasons, variation in temperature, occurrence of pests and diseases and other natural factors. It is a known fact that farmers have to make many decisions before knowing many of these factors, and therefore they operate in an uncertain environment. Though some of the practices and input levels could be adjusted as and when the conditions change, it remains largely true, that the adjustments are difficult once the decisions are taken. Hence, specification of random factor in input-output relation is a major issue to be resolved before attempting to estimate parameters of production function and changes in the parameters over time. Most of the existing empirical work rely on simple neoclassical framework where random terms are introduced in an *ad hoc* manner. In this backdrop, this paper will employ a more general stochastic production function and estimate decadal changes in the marginal productivities of factors.

2. MOTIVATION FOR THE STUDY

It is a known fact that for rapid increase in food production there is an environmental price to be paid. It is reflected in the loss of natural vegetation and biological diversity, soil erosion and surface and ground water depletion. Of this, land degradation is a serious threat to the sustainable use of resource. Land degradation is caused mainly due to loss of topsoil due to wind and water erosion. Topsoil exposure in view of exploitative cropping pattern is a major problem. Decline in soil productivity is due to frequent use of land and practice of monoculture, salination of soil etc. More often soil erosion is caused by lack of proper knowledge to undertake protective measures. There is necessity for ever-increasing use of modern inputs like chemical fertiliser due to fall in the productivity of land for a given input level. This leads not only to increasing cost of cultivation but also unsustainable use of natural resource which imposes cost on the future generation. The hypothesis that there is a gradual decline in the marginal productivity of land must be substantiated and quantified with the use of proper methodology and functional specification. It also requires appropriate data set spread over different types of natural and climatic conditions.

The objective of the study is to identify the correct functional form for specifying stochastic production function and to estimate marginal productivities of factors. The assumption maintained in our study is that the state dependent random factors need not be neutral with respect to different inputs and hence with respect to marginal productivities. Our aim is to highlight decadal changes in marginal productivities of land. We would like to provide empirical evidence to the conjecture that there has been a decline in land productivity in the long run because of massive use of modern inputs and lack of proper protection measures for land, and secondly to quantify the extent of marginal decline.

The plan of the paper is as follows. After reviewing the relevant literature and the gaps in the literature in the third section, we give the methodology and data source in the fourth section. The fifth section gives specification of production function. Sixth section presents preliminary investigation of the data and inputs and output distribution. This section also provides estimation technique and results. The final section concludes.

3. A NOTE ON LITERATURE

The conventional deterministic model has been criticised mainly for the fact that the random term has been introduced in the input-output relation in a multiplicative form.

$$Q = f(x).v$$

Where 'x' is a vector of inputs and other shift variables and 'v' is a random term. This means random term is neutral with respect to marginal productivities, and marginal rate of substitution is independent of random term. Moreover, if we assume variance in output reflects riskiness of the prospect, then it means risk always increases with the increase in input levels. To overcome this particular drawback, Just and Pope (1978) proposed a modification of the relation where mean and variance effects in the input-output relation have been separated.

$$Q = f(x) + g(x).\ v$$

In this specification f(x) captures mean effect and g(x) captures variance effect. If $E(v) = 0$, $E(v^2) = \sigma^2$ then $E(Q) = f(x)$ and $var(Q) = g^2\sigma^2$. The importance of this specification lies in the distinction between protective inputs (like irrigation and pesticides) and non-protective inputs (like fertiliser). An input is a protective input if its increase results in reduction in variance. Whereas increase in non-protective inputs leads to higher variance, giving positive marginal risk effect. Even in this specification the inputs responses are not allowed to interact with the random effects. Just and Pope (1978, 1979) proposed maximum likelihood and a three step feasible generalised least squares (FGLS) procedures for estimating the function. Buccola and Mc Carl (1986) examined the properties of Just and Pope's three stage method for small samples using Monte Carlo experiments. This procedure was utilised by Saha (2001) to study risk in HYV in the Indian context.

As regards functional form, most of the studies use Cobb Douglas but this does not accommodate zero inputs. Translog also has a problem in handling zero values for inputs. Bliss and Stern (1982) used linear form to accommodate zero inputs but this has a stringent assumption of constant marginal productivities. Rudra (1982) proposed a modified version of Cobb Douglas in which those variables which take zero values for some observations appear in exponential form. But this implies that marginal returns to factors have always increasing returns to scale. In the Cobb Douglas specification, the elasticity coefficients are neutral with respect to state of nature. Saha's study adopted Rudra's formulation while distinguishing between essential and less essential inputs with a flexibility to accommodate positive output with zero inputs for less essential. Saha's production function takes the form,

$$y = f(x) + \varepsilon h^{1/2} x, \quad E(\varepsilon) = 0 \qquad V(\varepsilon) = \sigma^2$$

$$f(x) = (a_0 + \Sigma a_{1i} Z_i + \Sigma a_{2i} Z_i^2) \Pi M_k^{a_3^k}$$

where Z_i and M_k are less essential and essential inputs respectively.

$$h(x) = \exp(\beta_0 + \Sigma \beta_{1i} Z_i + \Sigma \beta_{2k} M_k)$$

and the marginal productivity is given as

$$MP_i = \left(a_{1i} + 2a_{2i} Z_i\right) \prod_k M_k^{a_3^k}.$$

This is, in fact, expected marginal productivity, because the marginal productivity in this functional form is stochastic. Moreover, interpreting the coefficients in f(x) poses a problem because f(x) itself is a product of two functions of different forms.

A different school of thought started with the proposition of simultaneity problem in the estimation of production function, which could be overcome by specifying factor share functions. This was first proposed by Klein (1953) and later applied by Wolfson (1958). Mundlak (1961) and Hoch (1962) were trying to overcome simultaneity problem through covariance analysis. Mundlak found that the elasticity estimates are different in this model as compared to OLS model. Mundlak attributed the difference between sum of elasticities and unity to the managerial capacity of the factors. Firm specific decision parameter has been explicitly introduced in the production function which was assumed to be unknown to the researcher.

$$Q = CX^{\beta} e^{m+u}$$

Where, 'm' is the firm specific management effect and 'u' is the usual stochastic term.

However, the present study assumes that any firm specific managerial decision not known to the researcher could be indirectly captured by assuming that the farmers are rational decision makers.

All the cross-section studies assume that technology is given. In a couple of interesting studies Mundlak (1988, 1993) assumed heterogenous technology and introduced it endogenously in the production decisions. He made a distinction between unconstrained and constrained inputs. The specific feature is that the implemented technology is determined jointly with the level of the unconstrained inputs conditional on state of nature. The specified function should allow for a change in implemented technology and in the use of inputs due to change in state variables.

$$\mathrm{Ln}\ (y) = T\ (s) + \beta\ (s,x) \ln\ (x) + u$$

Where 'y' is output, 'x' is input vector and 's' is a state variable. T is an intercept indicating implemented technology. Variations in 's' affect slope and intercept.

$$\frac{\partial \ln y}{\partial s} = \frac{\partial T}{\partial s} + \ln x \frac{\partial \beta}{\partial s} + \beta \frac{\partial \ln x}{\partial s}$$

The last term gives output response to change in inputs under constant technology whereas the first two terms reflect response of implemented technology to the state variables. This type of specification is more relevant for cross-country studies when the technology is expected to vary across countries. Only constraint in this specification is that the function may not guarantee concavity properties. Apart from natural factors the state variable may also include political environment, incentives etc.

Saha *et al.* (1994) developed a model where production technology and risk preference structure are jointly estimated. This study found that the joint estimates of utility function and production function parameters were found to be superior than separate estimation. They used expo-power utility function which facilitate flexible risk preference structure in contrast with many standard functions where risk preference is imposed. The expo-power utility function is of the form:

$U(y) = \phi - \exp(-\beta W^{\alpha})$. Where W is wealth, ϕ, α and β are parameters. This facilitates all types of risk preferences.

Love and Buccla (1991) proposed joint estimation of firm's decision and production technology in an uncertain environment. The specific feature of this model is simultaneous estimation of input demand and production. Negative exponential utility function was used to specify risk preference structure and fertiliser is the only input considered in the model. The utility function is

$$U(\Pi) = -\exp(-\lambda\,\Pi) \text{ where } \Pi \text{ indicates absolute risk aversion.}$$

Nelson and Preckel (1989) used conditional Beta distribution to specify stochastic production function. The study focussed on yield response to N, P and K fertilisers.

The unconditional Beta distribution is of the form:

$$P(Y) = \frac{\Gamma(\alpha+\beta)}{\Gamma(\alpha)\Gamma(\beta)} * \frac{Y^{\alpha-1}(y^{u}-Y)^{\beta-1}}{Y^{u(\alpha+\beta-1)}} \qquad 0 \le Y \le Y^{u}$$

This distribution is transformed into a conditional distribution by expressing α and β as functions of 'x', the vector of inputs.

The more recent literature by Ruben and Ruijven (2001) discuss about bioeconomic models which are used to analyse the impact of different types of economic incentives (i.e., price policies, market development and public investment) on farmers' resource allocation decisions, as well as their implication for the natural resource base in terms of changes in nutrients and organic matter balance. Sustainability measure may be indicated by factors such as frequency of leaving the land fallow for soil recovery and use of soil conservation measures. The objective of the planner is to identify economic incentives to farmers that permit them to improve the application of inputs into more efficient production system that satisfy both welfare and sustainability criteria. Farmers' decision-making regarding the adoption of new technologies has been analysed with bio economic farm household models by Kuyvenhoven *et al.* (1998) where production decisions are linked with options that favour sustainable production.

The present study highlights the importance of non-neutral shifts in the elasticity parameters with respect to state dependent factors. It adopts the specification used by Sankar and Mythili (1991) who introduced a modified version of quadratic form which incorporated explicit state dependent input response coefficients. It has taken into account the fact that the effects of state dependent shifts on the production function need not be neutral with respect to all the inputs (Feder, 1980).

4. SOURCE OF DATA

Farmers' adjustment and response to state dependent factors is crucial and a one-period cross-section data does not capture the effect in a proper way. Therefore, the appropriate data set is panel data. Moreover, to study the decline in marginal productivities from the perspective of sustainable use, it is necessary to allow for a longer time gap. The present study uses the farm level panel data covering three years period each in two different decades; earlier period covers 81-82, 82-83 and 83-84 and the data used were compiled by Farm Management Study Centre of Ministry of Agriculture, Government of India. For the latter period, 90-91 to 92-93, we have utilised data from Cost of Cultivation of Principle Crop (CCPC) Scheme implemented by Directorate of Economics and Statistics, Government of India. The data give detailed components of cost and output in physical and monetary terms, plotwise for each farmer. We have chosen groundnut (peanut) crop cultivated in the irrigated tract for the present study. This is a very important cash crop for the state of Tamil Nadu. From the state we have selected a region of North and South Arcot districts, as this region is the most significant one for groundnut cultivation. Also, the study by Farm Management Study Centre on which we rely for the earlier periods' data and results, focussed on groundnut crop for their study. The total samples were 465 for the selected region for the earlier period 1981-82 to 83-84; 212 for the selected region and 554 for the state of Tamil Nadu for the latter period 1990-91 to 92-93.

The risk and uncertainty involved in groundnut is very high as compared to other crops in the State. The risk is more because, the initial investment for this crop is quite huge in comparison with other crops. Seed cost alone forms 40 per cent of the total cost. If weather factors are adverse then the loss would be high, whereas for the competing crop like paddy, with seed cost accounting for only a marginal 7 per cent to 8 per cent, the initial investment is low and hence crop failure at a later stage does not cost them much. Groundnut yields higher returns if it happened to be a average normal season. The reason for this is that the commodity is scarce and prices keep soaring. Higher returns with higher risk means there is a trade off between mean return and variance indicating risk.

5. ANALYTICAL FRAMEWORK

Having said that the weather induced random factor affects different inputs differently, it is necessary to specify a relevant functional form which captures these effects. As mentioned earlier, this study adopts the functional form used by Sankar and Mythili (1991). The functional form is quadratic in nature. It also incorporates interaction terms which reflects weather induced variability. It is specified as:

$$Q = \beta' X + \frac{1}{2} X' \gamma X + \omega' X$$

In the above specification, β and γ are fixed parameters and ω is a vector of random variables with E (ω) = 0 and Var (ω) = E(ω'ω)

$$E(Q) = \beta' X + \frac{1}{2} X' \gamma X$$

$$\text{Var }(Q) = X' E(\omega' \omega) X$$

This type of function also allows zero inputs and is easy for estimation. It does not impose constant returns to scale. Translog functional form can also be attempted on a similar argument but that does not allow zero inputs which results in considerable loss of degrees of freedom as the observation with zero values for some variables, for instance fertiliser, will have to be dropped.

The marginal productivities are estimated as follows:

$$Q = \alpha_0 + \alpha_1 D_1 + \alpha_2 D_2 + \Sigma_i \beta_i X_i + \Sigma_i \gamma_{ii} X_i^2 + \sum_{i \neq j} \sum \gamma_{ij} X_i X_j + \Sigma_i \omega_{i1} X_i D_1 + \Sigma_i \omega_{i2} X_i D_2 + \varepsilon$$

$$MP_i = \beta_i + 2\gamma_{ii} X_i + \Sigma_j \gamma_{ij} X_j \quad \text{for the reference year}$$
$$= \beta_i + 2\gamma_{ii} X_i + \Sigma_j \gamma_{ij} X_j + \omega_{i1} \quad \text{for the second year}$$
$$= \beta_i + 2\gamma_{ii} X_i + \Sigma_j \gamma_{ij} X_j + \omega_{i2} \quad \text{for the third year}$$

6. EMPIRICAL ANALYSIS

The empirical analysis consists of 1) finding average input use and output distribution 2) estimation of stochastic production function and 3) computation of the marginal productivities at constant prices to facilitate comparisons.

Average Input Use and Output Distribution

Preliminary analysis with average input utilisation are shown in Tables 6.1 to 6.3. For this we have utilised farm level data pertaining to earlier and latter periods. It is obvious from the pattern of input utilisation that the major changes have occurred between 80s and 90s mainly in the utilisation of chemical fertilisers and pesticides. There is a significant substitution of machine labour for bullock labour. As we do not have data at the disaggregated level for machine labour, we provide information only on chemical fertilisers to see the changes in utilisation. It is clear from the following tables that significant increase has been reported over the decade; particularly in nitrogenous fertiliser. Phosphate has also shown increase while potash has shown moderate increase.

Table 6.1

Average N, P, K Use per hectare for the Selected Region
(Earlier Period)

Fertiliser (Kgs. per Hectare)	*1981-82*	*1982-83*	*1983-84*
N	8.3	11.0	16.5
P	8.6	12.5	19.5
K	8.1	14.1	28.0

Table 6.2

Average N, P, K Use per hectare for the Selected Region
(Later Period)

Fertiliser (Kgs. per Hectare)	*1990-91*	*1991-92*	*1992-93*
N	23.7	13.9	13.2
P	47.5	29.9	25.2
K	48.0	38.0	35.8

Table 6.3

Average N, P, K Use per hectare for the State of Tamil Nadu
(Later Period)

Fertiliser (Kgs. per Hectare)	*1990-91*	*1991-92*	*1992-93*
N	19.1	17.8	15.5
P	34.3	25.3	23.4
K	43.0	31.8	29.2

Distribution of holdings by yield per hectare and average yield levels are reported in Tables 6.4 to 6.6.

Table 6.4

Percentage Distribution of Holdings according to Yield per hectare for the Selected Region (Earlier Period)

Yield per hectare (in quintals)	*1981-82*	*1982-83*	*1983-84*
1-10	19.6	55.4	32.4
10-12	29.7	14.9	32.4
12-15	29.4	13.5	17.3
15 and more	21.3	16.1	10.0
Mean	**13.7**	**11.8**	**11.0**

Table 6.5

Percentage Distribution of Holdings according to Yield per hectare for the Selected Region (Later Period)

Yield per hectare (in quintals)	*1990-91*	*1991-92*	*1992-93*
1-10	24.6	22.1	28.2
10-12	21.1	18.2	9.0
12-15	19.3	10.4	16.7
15-20	15.8	37.7	14.1
20-25	12.3	9.1	10.3
25 and more	7.0	2.6	21.8
Mean	**14.5**	**14.5**	**17.5**

Table 6.6

Percentage Distribution of Holdings according to Yield per hectare for the State Tamilnadu (Later Period)

Yield per hectare (in quintals)	*90-91*	*91-92*	*92-93*
1 - 10	27.0	16.8	23.8
10-12	11.7	10.9	10.6
12-15	14.1	18.3	19.0
15-20	18.4	33.7	23.8
20-25	11.7	10.4	9.5
25 and more	17.2	9.9	13.2
Mean	**16.1**	**16.4**	**17.4**

There has been an increase in the mean yield level to the tune of 35 per cent over the decade. It is evident that, the year 90-91 is not a good year and 91-92 a good year and 92-93 a normal year. In the year 90-91 there were more concentration of holdings under the lowest decile of 1-10 quintals per hectare. During 91-92, more number of holdings were reported in the range of 15-20 quintals per hectare. During 92-93, in the selected region, even though 28 per cent were reported in the lowest yield group, about 22 per cent reported in the highest yield group.

Production Function and Marginal Productivity Estimates

The model defined in the section on analytical framework has been utilised to estimate production function and marginal productivity estimates.

It is important to note that 'ω' is a random variable in the theoretical model. In the empirical model, ω's are turned out to be parameters when the year effect is specified for each year. So 'ω' is really ωD in the empirical function. The empirical estimation could also be carried out with 2 different random terms using the model of Just and Pope (1978). But based on the meaningfulness of estimated coefficients , the present study decided to use single type of random term. In the estimated model, 'ω' takes only three values namely $\omega 1$, $\omega 2$ and $\omega 3$ one for each year. It is assumed that the weather-specific random term is captured in the year effect. The empirical model is given below:

$$Q = \alpha_0 + \alpha_1 D_1 + \alpha_2 D_2 + \Sigma_i \beta_i X_i + \Sigma_i \gamma_{ii} X_i^2 + \sum_{i \neq j}\sum \gamma_{ij} X_i X_j + \Sigma_i \omega_{i1} X_i D_1 + \Sigma_i \omega_{i2} X_i D_2 + \varepsilon$$

Definition of variables:

Q = Main product in quintals

X_1 = Area planted in hectare

X_2 = Human labour hours

X_3 = Animal and machine cost

X_4 = Cost on fertiliser and pesticides

D_1 = Year dummy for the second year

D_2 = Year dummy for the third year

The analyses for the period 81-82 to 83-84 have also included few more dummy variables, *viz.* a dummy variable representing farmers who use pumpsets, two dummy variables for size groups, and a dummy variable representing zonal distinction. These variables were found to be insignificant in the latter periods. Hence, they have been dropped from the analysis.

The parameters of year X input terms indicate the interaction effect of weather and inputs on the output level. The year dummy is assumed to incorporate weather-specific factors. The advantage with this framework is marginal productivities are also influenced by the nature of interaction of weather-specific factors on the input levels.

It is pertinent to mention about measurement of input variables. To compute human labour hours, male, female and child labour are aggregated using farm management norms of aggregation. The weights are one, two-third and half respectively, though for some operations like transplanting or harvesting female labour is equally productive. Hired and family labour are simply added assuming that they are perfectly substitutable.

Table 6.7

Production Function Estimates for Irrigated Groundnut 81-82 to 83-84

Variables	*Selected Region*	
	Coefficient	*t value*
Constant	-1.0098	
X_1	9.7061	6.52818
X_2	0.0652	4.12658
X_3	-0.0136	-2.89362
X_4	0.0013	0.52000
X_1^2	-2.0403	-2.13242
X_2^2	-0.00038	-6.33333
X_3^2	0.00003	3.00000
X_4^2	0.00001	1.00000
Year1X_1	-6.828	-3.83746
Year1X_2	0.0113	0.62778
Year1X_3	0.009	1.80000
Year1X_4	0.0024	1.00000
Year2X_1	4.8245	2.56595
Year2X_2	-0.0441	-2.02294
Year2X_3	-0.0104	-1.31646
Year2X_4	-0.0049	-1.68966
X_1X_2	0.0703	39.05556
X_1X_3	-0.0273	-5.93478
X_1X_4	0.0033	1.13793
X_2X_3	0.00014	2.80000
X_2X_4	-0.00008	-2.66667
X_3X_4	0.00002	2.00000
Z	-1.0395	-2.45513
S1	-0.0838	-0.14320
S2	-0.2629	-0.41983
P	1.3289	3.55321
$\bar{R}^2$	0.9011	

Source: Sankar and Mythili (1991).

Note: It is to be noted that the variables X_2 and X_3 are different from the ones that have been considered for the latter period which are defined in the text under the head definition of variables. In the above table, the variable X_2 is measured as human labour days of eight hours each and X_3 as bullock labour hours. Machine input is not included.

Table 6.8

Production Function Estimates for Irrigated Groundnut 1990-91 to 1992-93

Variables	*Selected Region*		*Tamil Nadu*	
	Coefficients	*t value*	*Coefficients*	*t value*
Constant	1.365743	1.250	–0.434295	–0.489
X_1	4.772023	1.201	18.222338	6.235
X_2	–0.003462	–0.911	–0.004162	–1.494
X_3	0.003655	3.051	–0.000122	–0.129
X_4	0.009912	3.423	0.008035	3.401
X_1^2	–0.555521	–0.146	–0.794568	–0.584
X_2^2	0.0000023	1.213	–0.0000012	–0.813
X_3^2	0.00000012	0.278	0.00000064	3.853
X_4^2	0.00000038	0.450	0.0000022	2.837
Year1X_1	17.7626	4.579	-7.671219	-2.823
Year1X_2	–0.006242	–1.626	0.011052	3.872
Year1X_3	–0.004803	-3.518	–0.002954	–2.828
Year1X_4	0.001379	0.450	–0.0002702	–0.112
Year2X_1	8.519718	2.285	-5.987584	–2.157
Year2X_2	0.0002214	0.060	0.005907	2.087
Year2X_3	–0.003845	-3.041	–0.0008142	–0.899
Year2X_4	0.006891	2.503	0.001395	0.617
X_1X_2	0.000490	0.100	0.0002086	0.087
X_1X_3	–0.002290	–1.172	–0.0009817	–0.952
X_1X_4	–0.008214	-3.993	–0.005158	–2.744
X_2X_3	0.00000113	0.892	0.00000172	2.421
X_2X_4	0.0000005	0.325	0.00000142	0.990
X_3X_4	0.00000134	1.857	–0.00000135	–2.580
Year 1 dummy	–1.861135	–1.351	0.136012	0.129
Year 2 dummy	-2.723502	–1.835	–0.891767	–0.773
$\bar{R}^2$	0.94048		0.83056	

If we look at earlier period production function estimates, it is evident that for land, human labour and bullock labour inputs, the coefficients are significant. Diminishing returns are noted in these two inputs. Of the four square terms, three are significant. Zonal effect is also significant.

It is interesting to note that for the later period, in the selected region, animal and machine labour and chemical inputs are significant at 5 per cent level. It is also to be noted that, out of eight weather-specific factor and input interaction terms, five are significant which justifies the inclusion of these terms in the model. We have also conducted an F test for inclusion of these interaction terms and the contribution of these to the total explained variation is quite significant. Of the terms that capture inter-input interaction, only land-chemicals term is significant. Comparison with Tamil Nadu reveals that, diminishing returns is noticed for both land and human labour variables. Adjusted R^2 is higher for the region which is 0.9404.

In the following Tables we provide value of marginal productivities for the earlier and later periods.

Table 6.9

Value of Marginal Productivity for the Selected Region (For the Earlier Period)

(in Rupees)

Inputs	*81-82*	*82-83*	*83-84*	*Expected value*
Land in hectare	2564	998	5754	3105
Human labour hours	2.18	3.08	0.61	1.96
Fertiliser and pesticide cost	1.43	2.56	–0.12	1.29

Note: The variable 'animal and machine labour cost' has been dropped because the definition and measurement of this variable in this analysis is different from what we have done for the later period. Hence it is not useful for comparison.

Table 6.10

Value of Marginal Productivity for the Selected Region (For the Later Period)

(in Rupees)

Inputs	*1990-91*	*1991-92*	*1992-93*	*Expected Value*	*Expected Value at 81-84 Average Price*
Land in hectare	–2360.78	10829.75	2673.62	3714.20	2018
Human labour hours	1.96	-2.53	1.673	0.37	0.20
Animal and machine cost	2.63	-0.6653	0.035	0.67	0.36
Fertiliser and pesticide cost	3.95	5.515	6.818	5.43	2.95

Table 6.11

Value of Marginal Productivity for the State Tamil Nadu (For the Later Period)

(in Rupees)

Inputs	*90-91*	*91-92*	*92-93*	*Expected value*	*Expected value at 81-84 average price*
Land in hectare	9215	4592	4125	5977	3249
Human labour hours	–2.252	5.852	1.364	1.655	0.90
Animal and machine cost	0.9438	–1.1776	0.3152	0.03	0.02
Fertiliser and pesticide cost	3.92	4.23	3.86	4.00	2.17

If we index the expected value at the average of 81-82 to 83-84 price, it is very obvious that the land productivity has declined from Rs. 3105 to Rs. 2018 per hectare for irrigated groundnut, which works out to about 35 per cent decline in productivity. Similar decline has also been noticed in human labour productivity. These results substantiate the fact that farmers are continuously increasing their chemical input application as it enjoys higher returns over time. In the process, what they ignore is the damage done to the soil and land productivity, which will substantially affect productivity in the long run. Sustainable use of inputs has been overlooked.

It is very interesting to note that, the selected region which happened to be the best region for cultivating the crop traditionally in terms of soil and weather pattern, experienced more decline, which is inferred from the land returns value at 80s prices for the entire state. For the entire state, value of marginal productivity of land is higher than that of the region. It is very clear that over the period, the advantage of cultivating the favourable crop has been eroded due to continuous decline in land productivity. Animal and machine labour and chemical inputs obtain greater returns in the selected region as compared to the state Tamil Nadu.

7. CONCLUDING REMARKS

The point that proper specification of random effects is important in the estimation of input-output relation has been emphasised in this paper. The specification which incorporates non-neutral random weather effects with respect to various inputs has been utilised. There has been only a single study using this framework in the literature for estimating production function in agriculture using farm level data during early part of 80s. This study has utilised a single crop, groundnut, for the selected region of the state Tamil Nadu. But the earlier study pertained to a panel data of a single decade and hence long-term decline in productivity could not be ascertained. This has been attempted in this paper. We have found empirical evidence to the conjecture that 'increasing application of modern inputs cause problems of unsustainable use of land'. We quantified the magnitude of decadal decline in land productivity after adjusting for variation in all the other factors. This worked out to 35 per cent. More empirical results are needed to advice on the future direction towards which the farm research and the policies must be heading. The results indicate the importance of developing biofriendly inputs and taking it to the farm level. More research is needed on the cost comparisons and long run benefits of modern versus bioinputs to make definite conclusions.

The Directorate of Economics and Statistics, Government of India, and Tamil Nadu Agricultural University, Coimbatore, are gratefully acknowledged for the data relating to the period 1990-91 to 1992-93. The author learnt the basic concepts when working in the project 'Farm Management Study Centre' under the guidance of Prof. U. Sankar. The information extracted from the project and the guidance is duly acknowledged. The exposure gained during the period when the author spent her time as a Ford Foundation Post Doctoral Fellow in the Department of Agricultural and Resource Economics, University of California at Berkeley was very helpful.

References

Bliss, C.J. and Stern, N.H., (1982). *Palanpur: The Economy of an Indian Village*, Oxford University Press.

Buccola, S.T. and B.A. McCarl, (1986). "Small Sample Evaluation of Mean-Variance Production Function Estimators", *American Journal of Agricultural Economics*, 68: 732-738.

Feder, G., (1980). "Farm Size, Risk Aversion and the Adoption of New Technology Under Uncertainty", *Oxford Economic Papers*, Vol. 32, No. 2.

Hoch, Irving, (1962). "Estimation of Production Function Parameters Combining Time-Series and Cross-Section Data", *Econometrica*, 30(1): 34-53.

Just, R.E. and Pope, R.D., (1978). "Stochastic Specification of Production Functions and Economic Implications", *Journal of Econometrics*, Vol. 7.

————. (1979). "Production Function Estimation and Related Risk Consideration", *American Journal of Agricultural Economics*, Vol. 69.

Klein, Lawrence R., (1953). *A Textbook of Econometrics*. Evanston, IL: Row, Peterson and Co.

Kuyvenhoven, A. Ruben R and G. Kruseman, (1998). "Technology, Market Policies and Institutional Reform for Sustainable Land Use and Food Security", *Agricultural Economics*, 19.

Love, H.A. and S.T. Buccola, (1991). "Joint Risk Preference-technology Estimation With A Primal System", *American Journal of Agricultural Economics* 73, 765-74.

Mundlak, Yair, (1961). "Empirical Production Function Free of Management Bias", *Journal of Farm Economics*, 43(1): 44-56.

————. (1988). "Endogenous Technology and the Measurement of Productivity", 316-331 in *Agricultural Productivity: Measurement and Explanation*, ed. by Susan M. Capalbo and John M. Antle. Washington, D.C.: Resources for the Future.

————. (1993). "On the Empirical Aspects of Economic Growth Theory", *American Economic Review*, 83(2): 415-420.

Nelson, C.H. and P.V. Preckel, (1989). "The Conditional Beta Distribution As A Stochastic Production Function", *American Journal of Agricultural Economics* 71, 370-78.

Ruben, R. and A.V. Ruijven, (2001). "Technical Coefficients for Bio-economic Farm Household Models: A Meta Modelling Approach with Applications for Southern Mali", *Ecological Economics*, Vol. 36, No.3.

Rudra, Ashok, (1982). *Indian Agricultural Economics: Myths and Realities*, Allied Publishers.

Saha, A., (2001). "Risk in HYV and Traditional Rice Cultivation: An Enquiry in West Bengal Agriculture", *Indian Journal of Agricultural Economics*, Vol. 56, No.1, Jan-March.

Saha, A., C.R. Shumway and H. Talpaz, (1994). "Joint Estimation of Risk Preference Structure and Technology Using Expo-power Utility", *American Journal of Agricultural Economics* 76, 173-84.

Sankar, U. and Mythili, G., (1991). *Uncertainty and Farm Production Decisions*, Himalaya Publishing House.

Wolfson, Robert J., (1958). "An Econometric Investigation of Regional Differentials in American Agricultural Wages", *Econometrica*, 26(2): 225-257.

7

Valuing Community Labour: Why Not?

GOPAL K. KADEKODI
MAN MOHAN AGARWAL

1. INTRODUCTION

There is very little written on community labour in economic literature. Generally, it is treated as part of leisure or priced at a zero wage rate, with an inelastic supply emerging at times of natural calamities, fight for national freedom and honour, or as social work, and sometimes as a *prestige good*. With the growth of concern on preserving the commons, particularly after having recognised the complementarity between private property resources and common property resources, the status of community and voluntary labour has been elevated as *participatory labour* or community contribution (Ostrom, 1990; Bromley, 1991; Okley, 1991).

This paper makes an attempt to rationalise the need for recognising the contribution of such voluntary labour, either participatory at a notional 'recognition value' or, at wage rates below the market wage rates. There are three arguments by which community labour can be brought under recognition on the lines of market labour earning wages in productive activities. The first one is the complementarity between private property resources (PPR) and common property resources (CPR) because of which the productivity of PPR shifts up and becomes higher. Second, CPRs are better managed with community labour than by any other property rights system (Chopra and Kadekodi, 1993). But when it comes to recognition, generally it is only that part of the labour, which is engaged on private property resources, that gets the usual recognition (e.g., minimum wage regulations, cost and inflation linked wage rate fixation and so on). The efficiency and equity consideration in the management of CPRs calls for recognising voluntary labour. Finally, the need to analyse the contribution by community and voluntary labour arises to bridge the disequilibrium in the labour market, with labour force wanting to move to normal goods production, thereby ignoring the management of CPRs. Such moves can lead to unsustainable use and management of common property resources.

One may like to identify some of the major components of contributions by community labour in the management of common property resources. A list of activities and contributions involved in the management of wastelands and forest development, likely to emerge from local communities participating in a development programme, is provided in Box 7.1 as an illustration

Box 7.1

What do the Local Communities Contribute?

1. Partners in decision-making on choice of species selections (e.g., in grass and plantations);
2. Participation in actual regeneration and protection;
3. Participation in developing eco-tourism;
4. Cultivation of Non-timber forest products (e.g., mix of fruits, fuel wood and medicinal plants, lac, leaf and bark collections);
5. Assistance in reducing the damages from, and to wildlife;
6. Providing knowledge base on types of investments (e.g., water harvesting structures such as *Ahar,* soil and moisture conservation measures, fire alarm and protection systems);
7. Providing indigenous knowledge on value of herbs, medicinal plants, market linkages etc.;
8. Providing timely labour and capital for regeneration and protection (e.g., social fencing).

One may not ignore the values of these, though the difficulty in deriving and estimating them, both analytically and empirically, may remain.

It is the irony of social development everywhere that, except for actual payments as wages in land regeneration programmes, most of the other contributions by the locals are not fully compensated for.

In order to value these contributions, a number of methodological questions need to be addressed (which are not dealt in this paper).[1]

In Section 2, the complementarity between PPR and CPR is elaborated. Some evidence at the macro level is provided from India. It is followed in Section 3 with a model to identify the contribution by voluntary labour. In the process of goods production, the nature and role of PPR and CPR are analysed. This in turn allows bringing about equilibrium value of community or voluntary labour *vis-à-vis* the usual production labour in direct production activities. Section 4 provides a case study at the village level, of linking CPR with PPR and the extent of contributions by community labour. The last Section draws the attention of the reader to institutionalise the system of recognising participatory labour and also initiate methods of rewarding it.

2. COMPLEMENTARITY BETWEEN CPR AND PPR

The natural dependency between common and private property resources is quite well known among the users of those resources; but is also getting more and more attention and recognition from ecologists, environmentalists, social-scientists and policy-makers (Hardin, 1968; Dasgupta, 1982). Traditional economic thinking at best treats them as substitutes. Known examples are substitution of good topsoil and nutrient contents (a CPR) by chemical fertiliser (a PPR), fuel wood by LPG or electricity and so on. On the contrary, in the context of sustainable development, it is the complementarity between CPR and PPR that needs to be understood in theory and strengthened in practice (Ciriacy-Wantrup and Bishop, 1975; Jodha, 1991; Chopra and Kadekodi, 1991). Economic theory has dealt with complementarity problems very marginally, with the exception of Hicks (1939), who devoted one entire chapter to it.

In a rural economic setting, the households own private property resources such as cultivable land, livestock, agricultural equipments (i.e., capital), private wells, seeds, fertilisers and so on. The

1. For a detailed account of contributions by community labour, its measurement and valuation *see* Kadekodi (1998).

productivity of these private resources depends not only on the quality and quantity of such resources but also upon access to a number of common property resources such as forest or village grass land, leaf biomass from forests, water harvesting and retaining structures, non-timber forest products and the most important source of energy namely, fuel wood. In other words, there is a very high level of complementarity between these two types of resources.

Table 7.1 bears this out at the Indian state level. It is clear from the Table and Figure 7.1 that there is considerable degree of complementarity between CPR, PPR and wastelands. The estimated correlation coefficient between CPR and PPR is 0.8. States having large private operational holdings (i.e., PPRs) are also endowed with large common grazing and other lands. However, there are one or two exceptions, such as Himachal Pradesh having low operational holdings but relatively large CPRs, or Kerala state with large operational holdings but with very little CPRs. As against the total CPRs of 74 million hectares among the major states in India, the wastelands and PPRs are about 70 and 178 million hectares, respectively.

3. A MODEL OF VALUING COMMUNITY LABOUR

Labour plays two different roles when it comes to productive activities. One component of it acts as a substitute factor of production with private resources such as private land or capital. Another component acts as an input in the management of CPRs.[2] It is the CPR, which in turn acts as a complementary input to PPR in the production processes. A model is developed here to capture these structural characteristics. Ultimately, the purpose of this model is to

2. Under the situation described in Section 2, CPR here does not include all the possible public goods and CPRs. They are restricted only to such commons which have a direct bearing or strong complementarity on the use of private resources. However, it is still possible to extend the approach to include all the public goods having weak complementarity with private resources, to which labour allocation on community basis can be worked out. In that case, labour allocation will be based on three different roles they play in the economy. As an example, watershed management is a direct complementary activity to private agricultural activity. However, managing good air quality is important as a public good, but has a weak compelmenarity to crop agriculture.

evaluate the value of voluntary labour devoted to the management of common property resources (CPR).

Table 7.1

Private and Common Property Resources at State Level (In 1990-92 Period, '000 hectares)

State	*Operational Holding*	*Current Fallow*	*PPR*	*CPR*	*Wasteland*
Andhra Pradesh	14460	2485	16945	6286	5949
Assam	3160	88	3248	1984	1592
Bihar	10900	1765	12665	5348	2582
Gujarat	10290	1039	11329	3386	4580
Haryana	3710	169	3879	187	374
Himachal Pradesh	1020	45	1065	5019	3060
Jammu & Kashmir	1010	97	1107	525	7061
Karnataka	12320	1290	13610	3661	2712
Kerala	1800	44	1844	124	165
Madhya Pradesh	22110	762	22872	14109	9186
Maharashtra	20930	869	21799	7196	7931
Meghalaya	300	59	359	732	973
Nagaland	970	118	1088	871	1032
Orissa	5300	119	5419	4547	2072
Punjab	4030	82	4112	359	378
Rajashtan	20970	1814	22784	14196	11017
Tamil Nadu	7470	1264	8734	2399	2298
Tripura	310	1	311	311	236
Uttar Pradesh	17990	1084	19074	2687	6557
West Bengal	5660	395	6055	646	505
Total	**164710**	**13589**	**178299**	**74573**	**70260**

Sources: CMIE, Statistical Abstract, 1993 NRSA, Hyderabad, Kadekodi (1997).

Note: PPR: Private Property Resources (Operational Holding + Current Fallow), CPR: Common Property Resources = private lands having some access to the commons+permanent pastures and grazing lands+culturable waste lands+fallow other than current+protected and unclassed forest lands.

Figure 7.1

CPR - PPR Linkages ('000 Hectares)

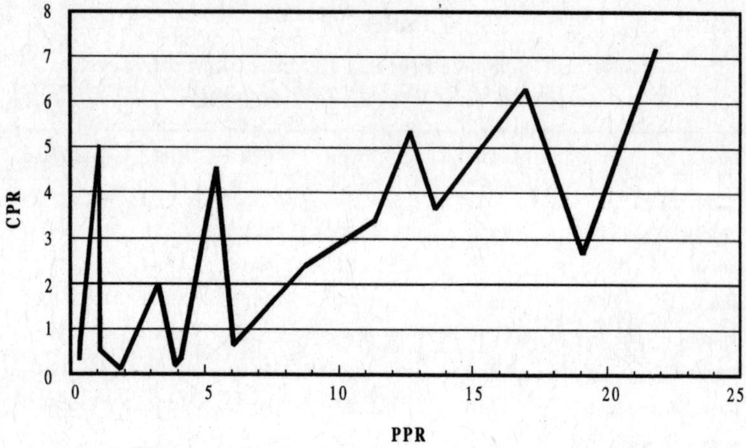

The starting point for this evaluation is the recognition that there can be complementarity or substitution between private property resources (PPR) and CPRs.[3]

Let Lp = labour employed in goods production. If the total labour force is denoted as L, then, Lm=(L- Lp) will be available either for leisure or for voluntary labour for the management of CPRs, or both[4]. A generalised production function is specified as:

Y=F(P, R, Lp), where Y= output of goods and services, P= private resources, R= common property resource. The production function is assumed to be a linear homogeneous function. The production of normal goods and services Y requires inputs of private resources P, common property resources R, and labour Lp.

Let, y=Y/L = per capita output; p= P/L = per capita private resources; r= R/L = per capita common property resources; and

3. The examples given in the previous section are mainly on complementarity between CPR and PPRs. Examples of substitution are fodder purchased from the market as against collecting from the common grazing grounds, or fertilizer in place of natural soils.

4. One can still disaggregate labour deployment additionally for leisure. Just to keep the model simplistic, it is assumed away (say as a fraction of L_m).

u= Lp/L = share of labour deployed on private resources, and m=(1-u) is the share of labour available as voluntary for CPR management. The production function is then rewritten as:

$$y = u.\ f(p/u,\ r/u) \qquad ...(1)$$

In the economy, let the labour force be growing at the rate $\dot{L}./L = n$. The common property resource R is assumed to get augmented mainly due to the contribution of the voluntary labour, attributable to better preservation and regeneration.[5] Specifically, the rate of change in R is assumed to be an increasing function of the share of voluntary labour time 'm', in the preservation of CPR.

$$\dot{R}/R = g(m), \text{ with } g' > 0 \text{ and, } g'' < 0 \qquad ...(2)$$

We now specify the use of output in the economy for consumption and investment. Let the rate of savings in the economy be 's', and all the savings are assumed to be invested for augmenting the private property resources, P. This will help in designing investment strategies as well as in deducing optimal consumption paths.

$$\dot{P} = s\,Y \qquad ...(3)$$

$$\text{or, } \dot{P}/P = s.(Y/P) = s.(y/p)$$

The rates of changes in per capita private property resources and per capita common property reosurces, 'p' and 'r' respectively, can therefore be written as:

$$\dot{p}/p = \dot{P}/P - \dot{L}/L = s.y/p - n \qquad ...(4)$$

$$\dot{r}/r = \dot{R}/R - \dot{L}/L = g(m) - n, \qquad ...(5)$$

Let x be defined as P/R = p/r. It stands as a proxi of carrying capacity of the CPR. It is an indicator of support that a unit of common property resource can provide to complement the private resources.[6] It can also be interpreted as a relative measure of factor intensities. The rate of change in this carrying capacity indicator is given by:

---

5. For sake of simplicity, capital inputs in augmenting R are ignored here.
6. Examples are, amount of livestock that can be sustained per unit of grazing land; or agricultural land per unit of forest land that can sustain the crop yield rate.

$$\dot{x}/x = \dot{p}/p - \dot{r}/r = s.y/p - g(m) \qquad ...(6)$$

With equations 1-6, the basic economic model of managing CPR and PPR for production activities is complete. We now state the objective of this economic model. The ultimate objective of the economic model is specified to be to maximise the rate of consumption. Stated mathematically,

$$\text{Maximise } \int_0^\infty (1-s).y.e^{-\lambda t}\,dt \qquad ...(7)$$

$$\text{subject to } \dot{p}/p = sy/p - n \quad \text{and}$$

$$\dot{r}/r = g(m) - n$$

where, λ is the rate of discount; m= (1-u); p(0) and r(0) are given.

This inter-temporal optimisation problem has two choices, namely a choice of 'u' as labour allocation between private resource management and the management of common property resources (m=1-u), and 's' the rate of savings. The problem can be solved by setting up its current value Hamiltonian as:

$$H = (1\text{-}s).y + q\ (s.y - n.p) + v\ [g(m) - n]r \qquad ...(8)$$

$$= (1\text{-}s+q.s).y - n.p.q + v\ [g - n]\ r$$

Here, 'q' and 'v' are the shadow prices (co-state variables) of per capita private property resources 'p', and common property resources 'r', respectively. Let the relative shadow price of PPR and CPR be defined as w = q/v.

Maximising Hamiltonian with respect to 'u' yields the following condition:

$$\partial H/\partial u = h[\partial y/\partial u] - v.r.g' = 0; \quad \text{or} \qquad ...(9)$$

$$\partial y/\partial u = (v/h).r.\ g', \text{ where } h = (1\text{-}s+sq) = [1\text{-}(1\text{-}q)s]. \qquad ...(9a)$$

Here 'h' stands for value of net consumption benefit. It has two components: (1-s) is the direct consumption benefit with a saving rate of 's' (valued at its numerere unity). The shadow price of private resources being 'q', sq stands for the long run consumption benefit from investment at the rate 's'. Therefore, (1-s+sq) represents the present value consumption benefit from this inter-temporal optimisation. The left hand side of equation (9a) therefore stands for the consumption benefit from using labour in production at the margin. The right hand side, on the other hand, represents the value of contribution by marginal voluntary labour in managing the CPRs.

From equation (5), we have $\dot{r} = [g - n].r$. Therefore, $\partial \dot{r} / \partial(m) = r.g' > 0$. Therefore, equation (9a) can be re-written as:

$$h[\partial y / \partial u] = v[\partial \dot{r} / \partial(m)]. \qquad ...(9b)$$

Here, $v[\partial \dot{r} / \partial(m)]$ can be interpreted as the shadow price of voluntary labour in CPR management, and $h[\partial y/\partial u]$ as the shadow price of labour in the production of 'y' goods. Optimum allocation of labour between the production of normal goods 'y' and management of common property resources, as voluntary labour, requires that the shadow prices of these two labour allocations be equal. Shadow price of voluntary labour depends upon the shadow prices of CPR and that of labour in PPR use; and on its present value consumption benefit $h = (1-s+qs)$. Therefore, the value of voluntary labour can be deduced from this optimal labour allocation model. The amount of voluntary labour required and its recognition value are given by equation (9b).

Following the usual law of diminishing returns, note that $\partial y/\partial u$ is a decreasing function of 'u', and g' is non-negative as 'g' is an increasing function of (m). What follows from equation (9) is that the optimum level of $u=u^*$ is determined by the intersection of $\partial y/\partial u$ and $(v/h).r.\ g'$ functions as shown in Figure 2.

The optimum choice of the savings rate 's' can be optimally made from the definition of the Hamiltonian H given in equation (8). Note that maximising H with respect to 's' is the same as maximising $h = (1-s+sq)$. Since $0 \leq s \leq 1$, three possible solutions for 's' exist. They are:

If $q < 1$ then $s = 0$, and hence $h=1$: Phase I ...(10a)

If $q > 1$, then $s = 1$, and $h = q > 1$: Phase II ...(10b)

If $q = 1$, then $s \in [0,1]$ and hence $h = 1$: Phase III ...(10c)

The third phase is the stationary state situation. Depending upon the initial endowments of PPR and CPR, either of the other two phases will be observed first, before entering the stationary state and satisfying condition 10c.[7]

Figure 7.2

Optimal Labour Allocation

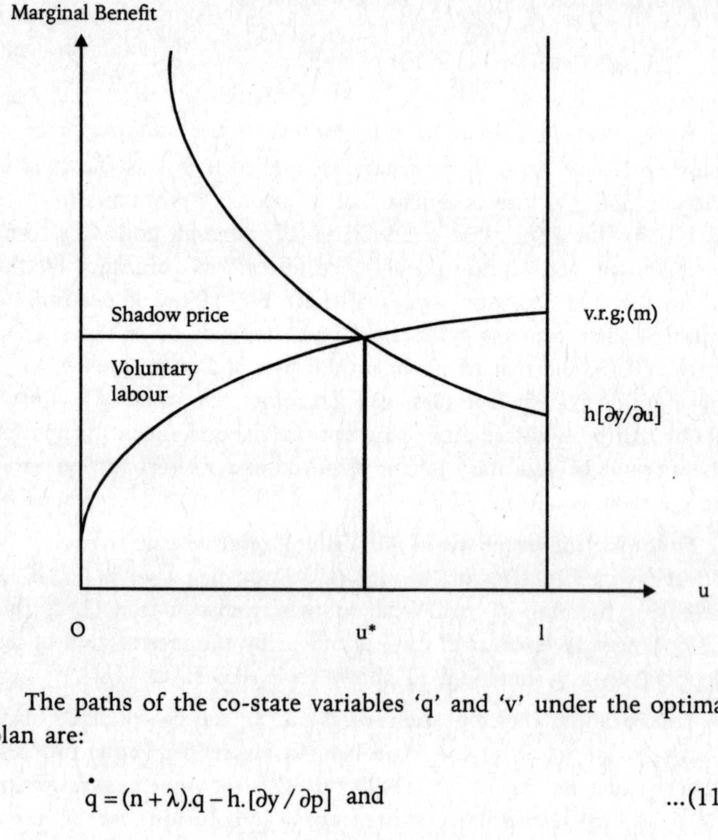

The paths of the co-state variables 'q' and 'v' under the optimal plan are:

$$\dot{q} = (n+\lambda).q - h.[\partial y / \partial p] \text{ and} \quad \text{...(11)}$$

$$\dot{v} = v.[n+\lambda-g] - h.[\partial y / \partial r] \quad \text{...(12)}$$

Furthermore the relative shadow price ratio w=q/v will have the following path condition:

7. The phases I and II referred here are to be interpreted as trajectories towards a steady state, depending upon the initial endowments of the two resources 'p' and 'r'.

$$\dot{w}/w = g + h/v\,(\partial y/\partial r) - h/q(\partial y/\partial p) \qquad \text{...(12.a)}$$

Let us examine the steady state conditions first, namely Phase III. Setting $\dot{q} = 0$, $\dot{v} = 0$, $\dot{x} = 0$, (in equation 11, 12 and 6) we have the following optimum outcomes in this phase:

$q=1$ and hence $h=1$; and $\dot{q} = 0$, implying $[\partial y/\partial p]=[n+\lambda]$; ...(13)

$\dot{v} = 0$, implying, $[\partial y/\partial r]= v\,(n + \lambda - g)$. Note from equation (12) that, for $\dot{v} = 0$, and v to be positive, one should have $(n+\lambda-g)>0$; and

$\dot{x} = 0$, implying $s.y/p = g(m)$, or $s= g(m)/(y/p)$

Under the steady state conditions, the marginal productivity of private property resource should equal the natural rate of population growth plus the discount rate, and that of common property resource should be equal to rate of population growth plus the discount rate minus the growth rate of CPR. The optimum saving rate equals the ratio of the rate of growth of CPR and output per unit of PPR. Since s (y/p) is equal to the rate of growth of private property resources $(\dot{p}/p)$, and g(m) is the rate of growth of common property resources, it then follows from these steady state conditions that both the resources grow at the same rate, leaving constant the carrying capacity of the economy. It also follows that their relative shadow price 'w' does not change in this phase.

Either of the two trajectories will appear depending on the initial endowments p(o) and r(o) of the two resources. Therefore, these two phases are analysed separately.

Phase 1: When $q < 1$; then $s = 0$, and $h = 1$; it then follows from (2), (3) and (6) that:

$$\dot{P}/P = 0 \text{ and } \dot{R}/R = g(m), \text{ and} \qquad \text{...(14)}$$

$$\dot{x}/x = -g(m) < 0. \qquad \text{...(15)}$$

This is the situation when PPR are initially quite high. In this phase, common property resource alone increases continuously at the rate g(m). Private property resources being already too high, there is no need to mobilise any more savings for investing on PPRs. The entire produce 'y' is to be consumed. The ratio of PPR and CPR (which is the carrying capacity 'x') therefore continuously decreases at the same rate as the increase in CPR. The corresponding shadow price paths of 'q' and 'v' are:

$$\dot{q} = q[n+\lambda] - [\partial y/\partial p] \quad ...(16)$$

$$\dot{v} = v(n+\lambda-g) - [\partial y/\partial r] \quad ...(17)$$

With too high PPR and too low CPR initially, it implies that (∂y/∂p) is too small and (∂y/∂r) too high as compared to the steady state situation. It then follows from equation (12a) that the relative shadow price w=q/v increases in this phase. With no augmentation of PPR, q(t) will be rising towards 1 and the shadow price of CPR, v(t) decreases.

The results of this phase 1 can be analysed now. The private property resources do not grow any further in this phase. This situation can arise when the initial private property resource endowment p(o) are too high relative to the common property resources r(o).[8] Then, under the optimal plan, there is no need to enhance PPRs at the cost of reduced consumption benefits. Therefore, savings out of normal goods production for augmenting private property resources is zero, so that private resources do not increase. Common property resources however, will have to increase till the optimum carrying capacity is reached. With such an allocation plan, relative scarcity of CPR decreases and that of PPR increases (as reflected in their shadow price paths (16) and (17)). Moreover, the marginal productivity of PPR, (∂y/∂p) is likely to be small but is increasing for two reasons. The decline in the per capita private resources raises its own productivity directly. Also, because of complementarity, the increase in CPR raises the productivity of PPR indirectly. The common property resource, however, will be increasing and its marginal productivity declining.

Labour is required both in normal goods production and for augmenting the CPR as community labour. Labour's marginal productivity in the production of normal goods, (∂y/∂u) will be increasing, and will be shifting due to increasing productivity of PPR. Thus, as compared to the initial labour allocation u*, h (∂y/∂u) curve

8. As an example, the average livestock population per hectare of common grazing land in Kumaon hills in India is ranging from 1.6 to 3.3 in 1992-93, as against a sustainable carrying capacity level of 0.16 livestock.

will shift upwards. The behaviour of the curve of shadow price of voluntary labour (v.r.g') is complicated. Note that r(t) is increasing, but v(t) is decreasing. Therefore, v.r.g' can be going up or down. Since (∂y/∂u) increases unambiguously, whereas there are two opposite forces acting on v.r.g'(m), shift in former is likely to be larger and the result is likely to be an increase in the allocation of labour to normal goods production, and an increase in the shadow price of labour. So in this phase, with increasing CPR, there is a tendency for labour to shift out of producing CPRs, as the role of voluntary or community labour is decreasing. Such a decrease is an optimal response and does not mean a decline in the spirit of community feeling or an increase in individualism of the capitalist ethic.

Next is the alternative scenario when the initial private resources p(o) are scarce and CPRs r(o) are in plenty. In other words, the initial carrying capacity x(o) is too small. This shall be called Phase II.

Phase II: q>1, then s = 1, and h = q >1. Once again from equation (2), (3) and (6), we have:

$$\dot{x}/x = y/p - g(m); \qquad \text{...(18)}$$

$$\dot{p}/p = y/p - n: \text{ highest possible growth rate} \qquad \text{...(19)}$$

$$\dot{r}/r = g(m) - n \qquad \text{...(20)}$$

In this phase, the stock of PPR is quite low. With s =1, the entire produce is to be invested on PPR development, making it grow at the highest possible rate. The optimum strategy will be to invest all the income on private property resource augmentation (i.e., $\dot{p} = Y$). With all the produce going for investment, as against consumption, consumption and investment will have the same highest shadow value of unity (i..e., q = h >1). It can then be seen that while the CPR continues to grow at the rate g(m) determined by the level of voluntary labour, the carrying capacity, 'x' will be rising.

The paths of shadow prices of the two factors are

$$\dot{q} = q\,[n+\lambda - \partial y/\partial p] \qquad \text{...(21)}$$

$$\dot{v} = v\,(n+\lambda - g) - q[\partial y/\partial r] \qquad \text{...(22)}$$

Being a situation of very low initial PPR, in the optimal plan it is allowed to grow at the highest possible rate. With this, the marginal productivity of PPR, which was initially high, declines rapidly to reach $(n + \lambda)$ at the steady state level. Accordingly, it follows from equation (21) that the shadow price of per capita PPR decreases towards unity, as a consequence of increasing PPR in this phase. CPR continues to increase in this phase. The path of shadow price of per capita CPR however, depends upon both the rate of growth of per capita CPR (i.e., $\dot{r}/r = g(m) - n$) and the marginal productivity of per capita CPR. Once again, with too low PPR and very high CPR the marginal productivity of per capita PPR $(\partial y/\partial p)$ is quite high and $(\partial y/\partial r)$ is too low. Therefore, it follows from equation (12a) that the relative shadow price q/v decreases in this phase.

The shadow wage rate of CPR labour (equal to h $(\partial y/\partial u)$ will be shifting up in phase II when PPR is growing at its highest rate. In other words, in the situation when PPR resource augmentation is to be carried out, there is every reason for recognising the contribution of the community labour.

4. A CASE STUDY OF GAINS FROM CPR LABOUR

We now present a much talked about case study of selected villages in Shivalik range of Himalayan foothills (Kadekodi, 1995). Three village scenarios are presented in a tabular form in Tables 7.2 to 7.4. Unless specifically mentioned, all the data and information are at the village levels only.

It can be viewed from Table 7.2 that the common property resources (namely forest lands around the villages providing fuelwood and fodder, water tanks built in the forest slopes to arrest rain water irrigating the agricultural lands) are equally important as the private resources (such as cultivable land, livestock, and human labour defined in Table 7.2 as workforce). Table 7.3 shows that CPR-PPR linkages and the incomes generated attributable to the linkages. Fodder for livestock and irrigation water for agriculture provide the major linkages. The income flows on a per capita basis from PPR related activities as well as from CPR management are also shown. Table 7.4 shows the average income per worker only from the village level PPR and CPR management activities mentioned in Tables 7.2 and 7.3. While the income from agriculture, dairying etc., are directly measured as PPR incomes, that of CPR are deduced. Implicit in these

Table 7.2

CPR-PPR Resource Dimensions in Three Villages

Sl. No.	*Particulars*	*Units*	*Sukhomajri*	*Jattanmajri*	*Dhamala*
	Private Property Resources				
1.	Total cultivated land	Acres	109.8	66.4	100.6
2.	HHs owning land	%	90.4	62.3	41.2
3.	Buffaloes				
		1977	136	82	111
		1986	182	116	161
4.	Cows				
		1977	28	2	21
		1986	6	2	12
5.	Goats				
		1977	89	2	NA
		1986	10	2	5
6.	Draught Animals				
		1986	89	37	44
7.	Av. No. of Milch Animals	Number/hh	2.32	2.95	2.16
8.	HHs owning Milch Cattle	%	94	90	74
9.	Workforce working outside the village	%	32	19	25
10.	Total workforce	Number	321	200	305
	Common Property Resources				
11.	Forest Land	Acres	1219	597	517
12.	Storage Capacity of Irr. Tanks	Ha. Mt.	9.16	3.96	6.67
13.	Command Area	Acres	92.7	59.3	131.0

NA=not available; HH=household; Irr.=irrigation; Av.=average

computations is an assumption that the elders in the villages provide the CPR labour, whereas the younger people work either in dairying, agriculture or outside the village as wage earners. Clearly, the income dimensions of CPR labour are no less important. Interestingly, they are almost 33 per cent to 60 per cent of any other wage income that the villagers are earning.

5. CONCLUSIONS ON RECOGNISING AND REWARDING LABOUR

Village common lands, forests and water bodies have been found to be integral parts of village resources, providing complementary inputs to private property resources in the management of various

Table 7.3

Resource Linkages and Livelihood Conditions

Sl. No.	*Particulars*	*Units*	*Sukhomajri*	*Jattanmajri*	*Dhamala*
	CPR-PPR Linkages				
1.	Operational Holdings Irrigated by CPR Tanks	%	23.6 (129)	2.5 (275)	12.1 (191)
2.	HHs Receiving Irr. from CPR Tanks	%	49	8	22
3.	Fodder from CPR Forests	Kg./animal/day	29.7 (66)	20.0 (41)	13.4 (67)
	Average Income Flows Attributable to CPR-PPR Linkages				
4.	Income from Operational Holdings	Rs. /Acre	2604	2050	1205
5.	Dairy Income	Rs./ animal	961 (73)	762 (144)	968 (114)
6.	HH. Income Per cap.	Rs.	2522	3532	2496
7.	Fuelwood Consumption	Rs./hh	1247 (164)	1451 (43)	1036 (53)

HH=household;cap.=capita;Bracketed numbers are coefficient of variation.

Table 7.4

Implications for Sustainable CPR-PPR Incomes

Particulars	*Units*	*Sukhomajri*	*Jattanmajri*	*Dhamala*
PPR returns per workforce	Rs.	926	515	566
CPR income per elder (=participating labour)	Rs.	685	916	507
Wage income per work-force working on PPR (60 days@Rs.25 per day).	Rs.	1500	1500	1500

PPR returns = crop income + income from dairying-wage income of 50 per cent of within village workforce.

CPR income = savings in fodder value from market purchase+value of organic manure attribted to stall feeding+value of incremental fuelwood availability.

Participating labour = village total at the rate of one member per household.

productive activities. However, asymmetric attention is given in providing social security and protection to labour deployed in the management of private and common property resources. The Minimum Wage Acts, insurance schemes to wage earners, power of unionisation of labour are instances of various methods of giving recognition to labour employed in managing PPR. On the other hand, the efforts village women, elderly people and even enlightened youth who spend lots of their productive (labour) time in protecting and promoting common property resources, is at best understood as 'social service', and nothing more. This, in a way, is an asymmetric situation in the labour market, bringing some kind of artificial inequity and status in the labour market.

The fact that under the optimal plan, the CPR continues to grow in all the phases is mainly attributable to the complementarity of PPR and CPR. It is the growth of CPR that makes the shadow price of voluntary labour $v[\partial r/\partial (m)]$ also grow. The shadow price of PPR on the other hand, declines following the diminishing marginal productivity of labour deployed for it. It is this dichotomy in the value of labour that needs to be recognised. In order to promote better CPR management, therefore, it is essential that community labour should be increasingly recognised and rewarded. Only then can the complementarity between CPR and PPR be internalised for optimal resource use and sustainable development.

In real life situations of degraded and neglected common property resources, but high growth of private resources, it follows from the model developed in this paper that, along the growth path of the economy, it is logical to have increasing value or recognition for community labour. Going back to the Indian example, in situations such as in Rajasthan, Madhya Pradesh, Maharashtra or Andhra Pradesh, specific efforts need to be made to bring a value system for recognising, rewarding and promoting community contribution to the preservation of common property resources. Case studies from these states and the village scenario from Shivalik foothills do indicate the role and relevance of such voluntary labour. It is also time to develop a system to reward them. One approach will be to create special Village Level Funds for the benefit of the village communities to develop village production system in a sustainable way. Such funds can be treated as rewards and recognition for the contribution of voluntary labour. Under the Constitution of India, *Panchayats* can assume such a role.

• The authors are thankful to Charles Perrings for his comments on an earlier version of the paper. They alone are responsible for all errors and omissions

References

Bromley, D.W., (1991). "The Commons, Common Property and Environment Policy", *Environmental and Resource Economics,* Vol.2(1), 1-17.

Chopra, K. and Kadekodi, G.K., (1991). "Participatory Institutions: The Context of Common and Private Property Resources", *Environmental and Resource Economics, 1, 353-*372.

————. (1993). "Watershed Development : A Contrast With NREP/JRY", *Economic and Political Weekly,* June 26, 1993, A-61-A-67.

Ciriacy-Wantrup, S. V. and Bishop, R. C. (1975). "Common Property as a Concept in Natural Resource Policy", *Natural Resources Journal,* (15), 713-727.

Dasgupta, P., (1982). *The Control of Resources,* Basil Blackwell Publications, Oxford.

Hardin, Garett, (1968). *The Tragedy of Commons, Science,* Vol. 162, Dec. 13.

Hicks, J.R., (1939). *Value and Capital,* London, Oxford University Press.

Jodha, N.S., (1991). "Environmental Concerns and Common Property Resources – Missing Dimensions", International Centre for Intergrated Mountain Development, *mimeo.*

Kadekodi, Gopal K., (1995). "Resource and Livelihood Linkages: The Context of Operationalising Sustainable Development" in Skutsch, M.M. and Hans Opdam (eds.): *Towards Sustainable Development,* University of Twente, Enschede.

————. (1998). "Valuation of Voluntary Contribution by Communities in the Management of Common Property Resources", *IEG Working Paper No. E/191/98.*

Okley, P., (1991). *Projects with People : The Practice of Participation in Rural Development,* International Labour Office, Geneva.

Ostrom, Elinor, (1990). *Governing the Commons: The Evolution of Institutions for Collective Action,* Cambridge University Press, Cambridge.

8

A Relative View of Absolute Poverty

Some Implications for Identification, Aggregation and Policy Intervention

S. SUBRAMANIAN
TARADAS BANDYOPADHYAY

1. INTRODUCTION

It is customary to view the problem of poverty-measurement as being constituted by two exercises. First, the *identification* exercise deals with the specification of a distinguishing criterion in terms of which the poor members of a population can be separated from the non-poor. Second, once the set of poor individuals has been identified by reference to the distinguishing criterion, the *aggregation* exercise is concerned with putting together information on the incomes of the poor with a view to deriving a real-valued index of poverty. The predominant convention in the poverty-measurement literature has been to solve the identification problem by specifying a *unique* level of income, called the poverty line, designed to classify the population into its poor and non-poor members.

Should the poverty norm be founded on 'absolutist' or 'relativist' principles? The poverty literature reflects many differences of opinion on this question; and many of the differences, it appears, can be traced to the confusion occasioned by the fact that the term 'relative' has been employed by different practitioners in different senses. Section 2 offers a very quick recapitulation of some elements of this controversy. Section 3 points to the plausibility of Sen's (1983) suggestion that a useful approach to the conceptualisation of poverty is to view it as an absolute notion in the space of capabilities to function and a relative notion in the space of resources. The implication of this for the identification exercise, in terms of the entailment of using interpersonally variable poverty lines, is spelt out in Section 4. Section 5 deals with the aggregation problem, and presents a family of poverty indices, when the poverty norm is interpersonally variable. In Section 6, some implications of our alternative approach to poverty measurement for optimal budgetary policy in the context of direct income transfer schemes are explored. Concluding observations are offered in Section 7. So as not to clutter the text with an excess of formalism, the bulk of the technical discussion has been relegated to two Appendices at the end of the paper.

2. MOTIVATION

A considerable amount of debate has been generated on the respective merits of the so-called 'absolutist' and 'relativist' approaches to the conceptualisation of poverty. A particularly clear statement of contending positions on the controversy is available from a perusal of the exchanges between Sen (1983, 1985) and Townsend (1985). As it happens, and as Sen clarifies in his reply to Townsend, the controversy is perhaps more apparent than real, as the following very brief review will indicate.

One approach to the 'identification' problem is the basic needs approach. In terms of this approach the poverty line is required to be defined with reference to a commodity bundle that may be regarded as constituting a bundle of basic necessities. Given a corresponding conformable price vector, this reference bundle can be converted into an equivalent income requirement. What Townsend (1979, 1985) would regard as a 'relativist' approach to the conceptualisation of poverty would seem to consist in acknowledging the possibility of variations in the notion of 'basic necessities' across individuals, regions and time periods. As he puts it (Townsend, 1979; pp 17-18): "Any rigorous conceptualisation of the social determination of need dissolves the idea of 'absolute' need. And a thoroughgoing relativity applies to time as well as place. The necessities of life are not fixed. They are continously being adapted and augmented as changes take place in society."

Although Townsend speaks here of a 'thoroughgoing relativity', his case appears, in the main, amount to a demand for some flexibility in an absolute norm of poverty. Indeed, Sen would appear to be on the same side as Townsend on this question (vide the Sen (1985) – Townsend (1985) exchange), as is evident from Sen's (1983) endorsement of Adam Smith's view that people should be able to 'live without shame' — a concession to the reasonableness of allowing the poverty norm to vary with extant perceptions of needs. Sen's objection to a wholly 'relativistic' conception of poverty seems to reside in resisting the identification of the poverty line with some measure of central tendency of the income distribution, in which case poverty would tend to be conflated with some "imperfect representation of inequality as such" (Sen, 1983; p.156). A lucid disentanglement of the 'absolutist-relativist' confusion is available in Sen's distinction of the 'domains' or 'spaces' over which these notions are invoked. As this distinction serves as a basic motivation for this paper's concern, we quote Sen (1983; pp.160, 161, 163) at some length to underline the crucial issues involved:

> If [the] thesis of the capability focus of the standard of living is accepted (and I believe the case for it is quite strong), then several other things follow. One of these happens to be some sorting out of the absolute-relative disputation in the conceptualisation of poverty. At the risk of oversimplification, I would like to say that poverty is an absolute notion in the space of capabilities but very often it will take a relative form in the space of commodities or characteristics. ... If we view the problem of conceptualising poverty in this light, then there is no conflict between the irreducible absolutist element in the notion of poverty (related to capabilities and the standard of living) and the 'thoroughgoing relativity' to which Peter Townsend refers, if the latter is interpreted as applying to commodities and resources. ... The varying commodity requirements of meeting the same absolute need applies not merely to avoiding the shame from failing to meet conventional requirements, and to being able to participate in the activities of the community, but also to a number of other needs. ... The capability to live without shame emphasised by Adam Smith, that of being able to participate in the activities of the community discussed by John Rawls, are examples of capabilities with extremely variable resource requirements.

3. 'ABSOLUTIST' CAPABILITIES AND 'RELATIVISTIC' RESOURCES: SOME ILLUSTRATIVE EXAMPLE

The lengthy quotation terminating the preceding section highlights the following principle: that it makes sense to invoke 'relativism' in the context of the space of incomes/resources that are required to achieve a given level of needs identified 'absolutistically' in the space of capabilities to achieve certain functionings — a functioning being what Sen calls a state of being or doing. A number of applications of this principle are available. By way of illustration, three such applications are briefly discussed in what follows:

(a) Consider, for example, the opposition that has frequently been expressed to the stipulation of a unique calorific norm intended to facilitate identification of the undernourished. While the 'need to avoid undernourishment' can be postulated as an 'absolute' requirement in the space of capabilities, the calorific resources needed to achieve this 'functioning' (of freedom from undernourishment) may well be interpersonally variable (on which see, in particular, the work of Sukhatme, e.g., Sukhatme (1978, 1981, 1982) and Sukhatme and Margen (1980)). These calorific requirements may vary across individuals depending, *inter alia,* on body weight, build, work-status, gender and age.

(b) For another example, consider the problem of federal finance in a country like India where the Central Government has the responsibility of seeing to the devolution of grants amongst its constituent states. One of the criteria according to which allocations are made is that of poverty; and a recurrent quarrel between the states and the Centre has revolved around the States' demand to employ 'state-specific' poverty lines to take account of regional variations in needs, tastes and availabilities in order to arrive at a set of realistic poverty norms, rather than let a single poverty line do justice for all the states. That this is a potentially non-trival issue has been underlined clearly in what amounts to a note of dissent written by a member of the 1993 Expert Group on Estimation of Proportion and Number of Poor constituted by the Indian Planning Commission. Reproduced below[1] are extracts from a 'Supplementary Note' submitted by S. Guhan, one of the members of the Expert Group:

The [Expert] Group has recommended that the all-India calorie norms and the relevant consumption baskets at the all-India level may both be uniformly adopted for all States. Standardisation of calorie norms and the consumption basket have been found to be necessary to enable aggregation of State-wise estimates and comparison across states at each point of estimation.

While I recognise that the devices adopted by the Group are necessary for the stated purposes, I feel that the estimates recommended do not

1. See the Report of the Expert Group on Estimation of Proportion and Number of Poor, Planning Commission, Government of India, New Delhi, July 1993; the extracts quoted in the text are from PP.50-51 of the Report.

give a full and true picture of poverty at state levels because the standardisation procedure necessarily ignores State-wise differences in normative calorie requirements and in consumption baskets. In a country as large and diverse as India, these parameters vary considerably across states because of differences in climate and terrain, levels of urbanisation, average incomes, income distribution, local availabilities of cereals and other food items, consumer preferences, cultural patterns and so on. These variations have been discussed by the report itself while dealing with the calorie intake criterion and with variations in the consumption pattern across states and over time.

In view of these state-wise differences, I feel that the Group could have recommended a separate set of state-level estimates in addition to the series recommended by it in order to approximate more closely to poverty at the state level. This will involve taking account of state-level normative calorie requirements and state-level differences in consumption baskets. The former cannot be done at present for want of technically-determined normative calorie requirements at the state level. State-level consumption baskets are however available and it is possible to adopt them for deriving state-level poverty estimates. On this basis, the separate set of state-level estimates could be based on all-India calorie norms (for want of anything better), state-level consumption baskets in the base year, and state-level price indices and deflators relatable to the respective base year consumption baskets at the state level. There is no reason not to provide such estimates.

The separate set of state-level estimates I recommend will give better insight into two important dimensions of poverty in India. First, they will enable state governments and their citizens to follow the levels and trends of poverty in their states as closely as the available data will permit. This is, or ought to be, a matter of concern and interest since in India's dual polity, politically and administratively, each state has a separate identity. Second, it is also a matter of interest to consider how state X stands in relation to state Y in terms of their respective poverty profiles defined on the basis of standards appropriate to each.

For reasons that I have not been able to fully understand or appreciate, the Group could not be persuaded to accept my suggestion for providing a set of State-level estimates on the basis indicated by me in addition to the series which we have all recommended. Perhaps, the rest of the Group too did not fully understand or appreciate the value and validity of my arguments. I have reiterated my suggestion in this supplemental note in the hope that it will at least find favour with the Planning Commission and the State governments. In that case, the federal dimension of poverty will also get duly recognised and those interested in this topic need not rest content with abstractions such as an 'all-India' consumption pattern....

(c) For a third example[2], consider the conventional practice adopted by the governments of several countries when reporting intertemporal poverty trends : the time series is

2. This part of the paper draws heavily on Subramanian (1990).

> presented on the basis of single poverty line (corrected only for secular price changes), which makes no allowance for changing perceptions, expectations and other objective factors that would argue a case for inter-temporally varying poverty lines. Such statistics effectively hide the fact that, figuratively speaking, the economy would have had to run faster and faster in order to stay at the same ('needs-adjusted') level of poverty. A case in point is that of time-series poverty estimates for the Indian economy.

Using a rural (respectively, urban) poverty line of Rs. 15 (respectively, Rs. 20) of consumption expenditure per person per month at 1960-61 prices, and employing the Consumer Price Index of Agricultural Labourers (respectively, the Consumer Price Index of Industrial Workers) for the rural (respectively, urban) areas for the purpose of expressing the base year poverty lines at current prices, National Sample Survey data on the distribution of consumption expenditure can be exploited in order to yield a time–profile of the headcount ratio of poverty for the country as a whole (obtained as a population-share weighted average of the rural and urban headcount ratios). Table 8.1 reports the country-wide headcount ratio of poverty for selected years between 1960-61 and 1983-84. It can be seen from Table 8.1 that there has been a rising trend in poverty from 1960-61 to 1966-67, followed by a declining trend from 1967-68 to 1983-84. But taking the period as a whole, there is no discernible trend of either increase or decline: the estimated slope coefficient of a linear regression of the headcount ratio (HCR) on time (T) fails to be significantly different from zero at even a 10 per cent level:

$$\underset{(49.49)}{}\text{HCR} = 48.09 - 0.31T;\ R^2 = 0.12$$

$$(49.49)\,(-1.31)$$

The estimates of the headcount ratio presented in Table 8.1 have been based on a poverty line that has been assumed to remain constant (in real terms) over time. This could be an exceedingly conservative way of viewing poverty in a dynamic context. Townsend's view (cited earlier) of a non-fixity of needs over time can be captured by allowing for a secular upward revision of the absolute poverty line. In the present context of discussion, given that per capita income in India has been growing at a compound

Table 8.1

The Time-Profile of the Headcount Ratio of Poverty (HCR) in India when the Poverty Line (in Real Terms) is Intertemporally Unvarying*

Year	*HCR* (per cent)*
1960-61	39.14
1961-62	39.38
1963-64	45.85
1964-65	46.88
1965-66	50.12
1966-67	55.02
1967-68	52.44
1968-69	49.62
1969-70	48.09
1970-71	45.52
1972-73	43.94
1973-74	44.91
1977-78	40.92
1983-84	34.94

Source: Calculated from data on the distribution of consumption expenditure in various Rounds of the Central Statistical Organisation's National Sample Survey: Tables with Notes on Consumer Expenditure.

rate of over 1 per cent per annum from the 1960s, one could give expression to the legitimacy of the 'rising expectations' of the poor by allowing the (real) poverty line to be revised upward at a compound rate of 1 per cent per annum. At this rate, 'minimum needs' will double every once in seventy years; and it appears not unreasonable, given the tremendous modernity and material progress that has been witnessed by the world in the last seventy years, that an average Indian's necessities of life in 1998 should be estimated at twice the level that might have been appropriate for 1928. Employing the norms of poverty measurement alluded to earlier — but with the difference that the rural and the urban poverty lines of monthly per capita consumer expenditure levels of Rs. 15 and Rs. 20 respectively at 1960-61 prices are allowed to be augmented at a compound rate of 1 per cent per annum — the headcount ratio of poverty can be recomputed for the earlier reference period, and the results are presented in Table 8.2. The estimated slope coefficient of a linear regression of the headcount ratio (HCR^*) on time (T) is now positive, and significant at the 10 per cent level :

$$HCR^* = \underset{(29.29)}{48.20} + \underset{(1.83)}{0.44T}; \quad R^2 = 0.22$$

Allowing for non-stationary of needs makes for a situation — and this is hardly surprising in which the time-trend of poverty is a good deal less flattering than it otherwise might have been.

Table 8.2

The Time-Profile of the Headcount Ratio of Poverty (HCR) in India when the Poverty Line (in Real Terms) is augmented at the Compound Rate of 1 per cent per annum

Year	*HCR (per cent)*
1960-61	39.14
1961-62	40.09
1963-64	48.15
1964-65	50.04
1965-66	54.05
1966-67	59.46
1967-68	57.80
1968-69	55.75
1969-70	55.06
1970-71	53.24
1972-73	52.92
1973-74	54.65
1977-78	54.82
1983-84	51.60

Source: Same as for Table 8.1.

4. IDENTIFICATION

If the arguments of the preceding sections are taken seriously, then the almost universally employed convention of using a single level of income 'z' to serve as the dividing line between the poor and the non-poor must be regarded as doing considerable injustice to these arguments, except in the special and improbable case where all individuals have the same ability to transform incomes into functionings. The logical fallout of our discussion, if we wish to assess poverty in income space, must be the specification of an individual-specific poverty line z_i for every individual 'i' in the set $N = \{1, 2, \ldots, n\}$ of individuals constituting society. So, first, the usual practice of letting a unique poverty line 'z' do service for distinguishing the poor from the non-poor must yield place to an identification exercise entailing the stipulation of an entire n-tuple $\{z_1, \ldots, z_i, \ldots, z_n\}$ of poverty lines — one poverty line for each individual.

Let $\{x_1, \ldots, x_i, \ldots, x_n\}$ be an n-vector of incomes. The set of poor individuals, under the 'conventional' approach to the identification exercise, would be given by

$$Q_c = \{i \in N \mid x_i < z\}$$

The set of poor individuals, under our 'alternative' approach to the identification exercise, would be given by:

$$Q_a = \{i \in N \mid x_i < z_i\}.$$

Notice that, unlike in the case of identification through a unique poverty line, it is no longer true that if individual 'j' is non-poor and individual k has a higher income than 'j', then it must follow that 'k' is also non-poor. So the following possibility (*) cannot be ruled out:

(*) $\exists$ j, k$\in$N: $x_k > x_j$, $x_k < z_k$ and $x_j > z_j$ — whence $k \in Q_a$ but $j \notin Q_a$.

A situation such as (*) may arise in the following way: you may have more income than I, but you may be counted among the poor and not I, if the income you need to avoid poverty exceeds the income you actually have, while the income I need to avoid poverty can be met sufficiently out of the income I happen to have. For example, if we both share the same basic need of achieving the functioning of mobility, you, by virtue of being handicapped may require resources, say money for a wheelchair, which you cannot afford even though your income may be higher than mine, and my income suffices to enable me to achieve the functioning of mobility. The point reflected in (*) is simple enough, but it serves to underline the fact that the use of an ordered income vector is of no particular analytical significance for the identification exercise under our alternative approach to the conceptualisation of poverty.

5. AGGREGATION

Recall from Section 4 that under the conventional approach to the identification problem, the set of poor individuals is given by

$Q_c = \{i \in N \mid x_i < z_i\}$.

For every $i \in Q_c$, let g_i be the income-gap, or the income shortfall from the poverty line z, of the ith person:

$g_i = z - x_i, \ \forall i \in Q_c$

For all $i \in Q_c$, the income-shortfall ratio s_i measures the income – gap of person i as a proportion of the identified poverty line:

$s_i = g_i / z, \ \forall i \in Q_c$

Now, the extent of poverty in a society could be expressed as a normalised, weighted sum of the income-shortfall ratios of the poor. When the weights are the income-shortfall ratios raised to the power (α-1), where $\alpha \geq 0$ is a measure of 'poverty aversion', then under suitable normalisation, Foster, Greer and Thorbecke (hereafter FGT; 1984) obtain a family of poverty indices given by:

$P_\alpha = (1/n) \sum_{i \in Qc} S_i^\alpha$, for all $\alpha \geq 0$

We have focused attention on this family of indices because these indices are familiar ones widely employed in both the conceptual and applied literature, and they also satisfy a number of desirable properties.

In the alternative approach involving the use of an entire n-tuple of individual-specific poverty lines $\{z_i\}$, the set of poor persons is given (as we have seen) by

$Q_a = \{i \in N \mid x_i < z_i\}$.

For every $i \in Q_a$; we shall let γ_i stand for the income-gap of person i:

$\gamma_i = z_i - x_i, \ i \in Q_a$

and σ_i will stand for the income-shortfall ratio of person i:

$\sigma_i = \gamma_i / z_i, \ i \in Q_a$

It is important to note that the ranking according to the σ_i could, in principle, actually completely invert the ranking according to the x_i : in general, there is no prior reason, in strict logic, to expect any systematic relationship to exist between the ranking according to incomes and the ranking according to proportionate shortfall ratios.

In strict analogy with aggregation under the conventional approach, consider the following family of poverty indices :

$P^{*}_{\alpha} = (1/n) \Sigma_{i \in Q_a} \sigma_i^{\alpha}$, for all $\alpha \geq 0$

Let us now consider certain distinguished values of α[3].

For $\alpha = 0$, $P^{*}_{\alpha} = q_a / n$, where q_a is the number of poor persons in Q_a, *viz.* P^{*}_{0} is the proportion of the population in poverty, represented by the headcount ratio H^{*}.

For $\alpha = 1$, $P^{*}_{\alpha} = (q_a / n)\ [(1/q_a)\ \Sigma_{i \in Q_a} \sigma_i\ ] = H^{*} I^{*}$,

Where I^{*} is the mean of the proportionate income-shortfall ratios of the poor:

$I^{*} = (1/q_a)\ \Sigma_{i \in Q_a} \sigma_I$.

For $\alpha = 2$, $P^{*}_{\alpha} = H^{*} I^{*} (1 + C^2_{\sigma})$,

Where C^2_{σ} is the square of the coefficient of variation in the distribution of shortfall ratios among the poor[4].

For $\alpha \to \infty$, the poverty measure ranks income distributions solely according to the magnitude of the proportionate income-shortfall ratio of the poorest individual, i.e., according to the value of $\max_i \{\sigma_i\}_{\Sigma\, i \in Qa}$. We have here an echo of the 'Rawlsian' rule (in a 'maximax' sense).

A number of axioms – *prima facie* desirable properties – for poverty measures have been suggested in the literature (see, among others, Sen (1976), Donaldson and Weymark (1986), Foster (1984), Foster, Greer and Thorbecke (1984), and Kakwani (1980)). Some

---

3. The corresponding poverty measures, under the conventional approach, would be given by the following (see FGT, 1984). For $\alpha = 0$, $P_o = q_c/n$, viz. P_o is the proportion of the population in poverty, or headcount ratio. For $\alpha = 1$, $P_1 = (q_c/n) [(z-\mu^P)/z]$. where μ^P is the average income of the poor. If I denotes $(z - \mu^P)/z$, the proportionate shortfall of the average income of the poor, then $P_1 = HI$. For $\alpha = 2$, the poverty measure turns out to be a function of the incidence of poverty (captured by H), the depth of poverty (captured by I), and the extent of inequality in the distribution of poor incomes (captured by the square of the coefficient of variation C^2_p in the distribution of the income of the poor). It can be verified that $P_2 = H[I^2 + (1-I)^2 C^2 p]$. For $\alpha \to \infty$, the poverty measure P_{α} becomes a sort of Rawlsian maximun measure in the sense that income distribution are ranked solely according to the poverty of the poorest individual. For values of α greater than unity, the poverty measure becomes increasingly sensitive to distributional considerations.
4. To see that this is indeed the case, note that

$$P^{*}_2 = (1/n)\Sigma_{i \in Q_a} \sigma_i^2 = (q_a/n)[(1/q_a)\Sigma_{i \in Q_a}\{(\sigma_i - I^{*}) + I^{*}\}^2]$$
$$= (q_a/n)[(1/q_a)\Sigma_{i \in Q_a}\{(\sigma_i - I^{*})^2 + I^{*2}\}]$$
$$= (q_a/n)[I^{*2}(1/q_a)\Sigma_{i \in Q_a}\{(\sigma_i - I^{*})/I^{*}\}^2 + I^{*2}] = H^{*}[I^{*2} C^2_s + I^{*2}].$$

very well-known axioms are the monotonicity, the transfer, the transfer-sensitivity and the decomposability axioms. Corresponding to the transfer and transfer-sensitivity axioms in the 'conventional' framework, we present in this paper reformulations – which we christen respectively the 'equity' and the 'equity-sensitivity' axioms – appropriate for the 'alternative' framework (of interpersonally variable poverty lines). Appendix 1 carries a brief discussion of the definition and meaning of the various axioms. For the present, we take note of a result in FGT (1984) which asserts that the poverty measure P_α satisfies the decomposability axiom for all $\alpha \geq 0$, the monotonocity axiom for all $\alpha > 0$, the transfer axiom for all $\alpha > 1$ and the transfer sensitivity axiom for all $\alpha > 2$. Precisely analogously, and employing the same stratagem of proof adopted in FGT (1984), the following result can be proved.[5]

Proposition: P^*_α satisfies the decomposability axiom for all $\alpha \geq 0$, the monotonicity axiom for all $\alpha > 0$, the equity axiom for all $\alpha > 1$, and the equity-sensitivity axiom for all $\alpha > 2$.

Finally, notice the straightforward fact that P^*_α is a generalisation of P_α : the FGT family P_α drops out of the family of indices P^*_α as a special case under the assumption that all individuals have exactly the same capacity for transforming incomes into functionings, i.e., $z_i = z$ for all $i \in Q_a$.

6. OPTIMAL BUDGETARY POLICY: THE CASE OF DIRECT INCOME TRANSFERS

There are various kinds of public intervention schemes for the alleviation of poverty that one can think of. These would include such programmes as direct income transfers, wage employment schemes, commodity subsides and credit disbursement. Typically, the quantum of funds available for these exercises — call it a budget of fixed size B — would not suffice to extricate the entire poor population from poverty. Therefore, it becomes important to determine what part of the budgetary resource (if any) should go to which contenders for it from among the population of the poor. The object, presumably, would be to achieve that allocational

5. The proof is omitted, but is available on request from the authors.

pattern which will minimise poverty. This, in turn, would require an unambigous specification of the index in terms of which poverty is measured. The FGT family of poverty indices, in this context, presents itself as a ready candidate for the measurement of poverty: for parametric variation in α, which will reflect the policy maker's concern for the welfare of the poor, one can identify the corresponding optimal budgetary rule.[6]

In Appendix 2, we present a taxonomy of budgetary rules for the case of direct income transfers ('doles'), under the assumption that every person's income is an item of public knowledge. This is done for each of the two approaches to poverty conceptualisation we have discussed – the 'conventional' and the 'alternative' one: this is intended to highlight the fact that the alternative approach we have reviewed is not just an abstract conceptual refinement of the conventional approach, but a departure that has rather concrete implications for possible misdirection of limited resources for the alleviation of poverty.

A concrete arithmetical example may help to illustrate the point. Consider a 10-person (non-descendingly ordered) income vector (x_1, ..., x_{10}). For specificity, let us imagine that $x_1 = 1$, $x_2 = 2$, $x_3 = 2.7125$, $x_4 = 4.4375$, and $x_5 = 8$. Suppose also that $Q_a = \{1,2,3,4\}$, *viz.* $z_i \geq x_i$ for all $i \in \{1,2,3,4\}$ and $z_i < x_i$ for all $i \in \{5,6,7,8,9,10\}$. Specifically, let it be the case that $z_1 = 5$, $z_2 = 6.5$, $z_3 = 8$, and $z_4 = 9.9375$. Under the specifications of the example, it is easy to see that $x_1 = 1 < x_2 = 2 < x_3 = 2.7125 < x_4 = 4.4375$; $z_1 = 5 < z_2 = 6.5 < z_3 = 8 < z_4 = 9.9375$; $\gamma_1 = 4 < \gamma_2 = 4.5 < \gamma_3 = 5.2875 < \gamma_4 = 5.5$; $\sigma_1 = 0.8 > \sigma_2 = 0.692 > \sigma_3 = 0.661 > \sigma_4 = 0.5534$.

Suppose the budget B is of size 8.50. From our analysis of optimal budgetary rules in Appendix 2, it should be immediate that the ordering according to the γ_i, the z_i and the σ_i will dictate that the optimal transfer schedule will be the same whether we minimise poverty according to the index P^*_0, the index P^*_1, or the index $P^*_{\alpha>1}$: in each case, the optimal transfer schedule will be given by:

$$t_1^* (= \gamma_1) = 4;\ t^*_2 (=\gamma_2) = 4.5;\ t^*_3 = t^*_4 = 0$$

6. For two treatments of the problems, see Bourguignon and Fields (1991) and Gangopadhyay and Subramanian (1992); the latter is drawn on for the presentation in a part of Appendix 2.

Now, let us look at the same problem from the perspective of the conventional approach to the conceptusaliation of poverty. To do this, we need to make some rather specific assumption about how the unique poverty line 'z' is determined. Let us imagine that the policy maker sets z at 7.75. This figure may have been arrived at on the basis of some such procedure as the following. Suppose the planner employs a nutritional norm of K kilocalories per person per day as a 'minimal satisfactory', level of calorific intake, and decides to peg the monetary poverty line 'z' in terms of the level of income at which, given the income distribution (x_1 .... x_{10}) and the income-related pattern of consumer expenditure, the consumption of the norm of K kilocalories per day is realised. (This, substantially, is the procedure that has been employed by the Indian Planning Commission in the Seventh Plan to arrive at a country-wide poverty line). Suppose, then, that the 'z' which is compatible with this procedure is 7.75. Then, in line with our analysis in Appendix 2, the optimal income transfers, for parametric variation of α in the FGT family of poverty indices P_α, will look as follows.

For $\alpha = 0$, t^*_4 (= g_4) = 3.3125; t^*_3 (= g_3) = 5.0375; t^*_2 = 0.15; t^*_1 = 0. (Notice that, after bridging the poverty gaps of individuals 4 and 3, we are left behind with 0.15 of the budget, which has been allocated to individual 2, although, strictly speaking, it would make no difference to the value of the poverty index if this last amount were simply wasted: this follows from the fact that the headcount ratio violates the monotonicity axiom).

For $\alpha = 1$, since any feasible allocation which exhausts the budget is an optimal solution, a transfer schedule which is identical to that in the $\alpha = 0$ case, must also be optimal in the $\alpha = 1$ case: t^*_4 = 3.3125; t^*_3 = 5.0375; t^*_2 = 0.15; t^*_1 = 0. For $\alpha > 1$, it can be readily verified that the maximum level to which the poorest person's income can be raised, in accordance with the formula reviewed in Appendix 2, is given by x^* = 4.6625. Then, the optimal transfer schedule is given by: $t^*_1 = (x^* - x_i)$ for all i = 1,2,3,4, viz. t^*_1 = 3.6625; t^*_2 = 2.6625; t^*_3 = 1.95; t^*_4 = 0.225.

The fact that, in principle, optimal budgetary policy under the 'conventional approach' could result in a more or less severe misdirection of resources in relation to budgetary policy that would be dictated under the 'alternative' approach, is thus clearly brought out.

7. CONCLUDING OBSERVATIONS

We have explored, in this paper, a general framework for a conceptualisation of poverty that regards the phenomenon as an absolute notion in the domain of functionings and a relative notion in the domain of resources. Using this as a point of departure, we have attempted to examine some implications of this approach for the identification and aggregation exercises in the context of the measurement of poverty, and for optimal budgetary stances in the context of policy aimed at the alleviation of poverty. To this end we have considered some simple formalities associated with an analysis of the problem, which we hope may offer some insights into issues that require deeper investigation.

For analytical purposes we have worked within a framework that allows for the postulation of an entire n-tuple of individual-specific poverty lines. From purely pragmatic considerations, however, this constitutes a virtually impossible task for any policy-making machinery to handle. At an immediate level of practical applicability, there would certainly appear to be a case for at least a tractable number of well-defined, group–specific poverty lines. More concretely, even rough heuristics should enable the policy maker to identify a plurality of poverty lines based on a categorisation of a country's population according to different criteria. Such categorisation could be, for example, along demographic lines (sex, age, etc.); according to occupational structure (manual work, non-manual work, etc.); according to climatic variations (temperate regions, extreme regions, etc.); according to regional variations in availabilities, food habits, tastes, community practices/expectations, and the like; and so on. The point, briefly, is that instead of making the infeasible best the enemy of the feasible good, there is an informationally manageable case for at least a rough-and-ready specification of a set of population-specific poverty lines. The specification may lack absolute quantitative precision. But even a measure of 'directional sensitivity' displayed by such a specification may be an improvement on the monist tradition of insistence on a unique poverty line across the board.

APPENDIX 1

Some Properties of Poverty Measures

Presented below are the decomposability, monotonicity, equity and equity-sensitivity axioms alluded to in Section 5 of the text. We begin with a statement of the decomposability axiom. It is always a useful property in a poverty measure if the extent of poverty in a society can be decomposed into the poverty levels of its various constituent subgroups. More formally, we have:

Decomposability Axiom: The decomposability axiom requires that if P^j is the poverty index for the jth subgroup when there are say, 'm' subgroups in the population, then it should be possible to express the overall poverty index P as the weighted sum of the subgroup poverty indices., the weights being the respective subgroup population shares, viz. $P = \Sigma_j (n_j/n)P^j$, where n_j is the population of the jth subgroup, $j = 1, ...m$.

In stating the remaining three axioms, we shall have to reformulate these in relation to their canonical forms, to take account of the fact that we are now working in a framework that allows for interpersonally variable poverty lines. We begin with the monotonicity axiom which essentially requires that the poverty measure should be positively responsive to a worsening in the poverty status of any poor person. More precisely, we have:

Monotonicity Axiom: Other things equal, an increase in the income shortfall ratio of a poor person should raise the value of the poverty measure.

Analogous to the transfer and the transfer-sensitivity axioms in the conventional framework, we shall here define a pair of axioms which we shall call, respectively, the 'equity' and the 'equity-sensitivity' axioms. These axioms, as their names suggest, essentially impart a degree of 'equality-consciousness' to the poverty measure. The equity axiom requires that an increase in the income shortfall ratio of a poor person which is matched by an identical decline in the income shortfall ratio of a poorer person should cause the poverty measure to register a decline in value. The equity-sensitivity axiom requires the poverty measure to be relatively more sensitive to this sort of 'compensating change', the poorer is the pair of persons subjected to changes in their respective income shortfall ratios.

A *permissible pairwise change in the income shortfall ratio*, λ, for individuals 'k' and 'j', when k's proportionate shortfall σ_k is not greater than that of 'j', σ_j, is such that λ satisfies $(\sigma_j - \lambda) \geq (\sigma_k + \lambda)$, or, equivalently,

$$\lambda \leq (\sigma_j - \sigma_k)/2. \qquad \text{...(A1.1)}$$

Notice that the upper limit on λ dictated by (A1.1) guarantees that the relative ranks of 'k' and 'j' in the vector σ of income shortfall ratios remains unchanged. (Notice that if $z_j = z_k$ ($= z$, say), then (A1.1) would read as $\lambda_z \leq (x_k - x_j) / 2$ — which, precisely, is the requirement in the canonical framework for ensuring that the transfer t ($: = \lambda_z$) from 'k' to 'j' is a rank-preserving transfer in the ordered income vector). We can now state the axioms:

Equity Axiom: Other things equal, a permissible pairwise change in the income shortfall ratios for two poor individuals should reduce the value of the poverty measure.

Equity-Sensitivity Axiom: Other things equal, a permissible pairwise change in the income shortfall ratios for two individuals who are a fixed proportionate income shortfall apart should have a greater downward impact on the value of the poverty measure, the poorer are the pair of persons subjected to the pairwise change. Formally, $\Delta P(k, j) < \Delta P(n, m) < 0$, whenever $\Delta P(k, j)$ [respectively, $\Delta P(n, m)$] is the change in the value of the poverty index P due to a permissible pairwise change λ as in (A1.1) for 'k' and 'j' [respectively, for n and m], and $j, k, m, n \in Q_a$, $(\sigma_m - \sigma_n) = (\sigma_j - \sigma_k)$, > 0, $\sigma_j > \sigma_m$ and $\sigma_k > \sigma_n$.

APPENDIX 2

Optimal Budgetary Rules for Income Transfers

Budgetary Rules under the Conventional Approach

Given an ordered income vector $(x_1, \ldots\ldots x_n)$, and a budget of size B, let t_i be the income transferred to the ith poorest person. Then, the allocational problem confronting the planner can be set up in terms of the following programming exercise:

Minimise $P_\alpha (\{t_i\}_{i \in Qc}) = (1/n)\ \Sigma_{i \in Qc} (s_i - t_i / z)^\alpha\ \{t_i\}_{i \in Qc}$ ...(A2.1)

Subject to $\Sigma_{\,i \in Qc}\ t_i \leq B;\ \ t_i \leq z - x_i\ \ \forall_{\,i \in Qc;}\ \ t_i \geq 0\ \ \forall\ i \in Q_c$

We shall present the optimal solution to this problem for some distinguished values of α in the FGT family of indices.

For $\alpha = 0$, we simply minimise the headcount ratio H. Clearly, the strategy required is one of 'skimming off the surface'. That is, we start with the least poor individual and, through a sequence of progressive and income-equalising transfers we raise as many people as possible to the poverty line 'z', till the budget is exhausted. Formally, let Q_c" be a set of richest individuals in the set Q_c such that

$\Sigma_{\,i \in Qc''} (z - x_i) = B.$

Then, the optimal schedule is given by: $t^*_i = 0\ \ \forall i \in (Q_c \backslash Q_{c''})$ and $t^*_i = z - x_i\ \ \forall i \in Qc''$.

For $\alpha = 1$, it is easy to check that

$P_1 (\{t_i\}_{\,i \in Qc}) = (1/n)\ \Sigma_{\,i \in Qc} s_i - (1/n)\ \Sigma_{\,i \in Qc} t_i / z.$

This can alternatively be written as

$P_1 (\{t_i\}_{\,i \in Qc}) = P_1' - (1/n) \Sigma_{\,i \in Qc}\ ti / z$

Where, P'_1 is the value of the poverty index prior to the implementation of the transfer scheme. Clearly, minimisation of P_1 would require making the second term on the right hand side of the preceding equation as large as possible. This, in turn, would entail setting $\Sigma_i t_i = B$, which yields

$P_1(\{t_i\})_{\,i \in Qc}) = P_1' - B/nz.$

Since this expression is independent of the t_i, therefore, for $\alpha = 1$, any feasible transfer schedule which exhausts the budget is also an optimal one.

For $\alpha > 1$, one can verify that the optimal budgetary rule is a sort of 'lexicographic maximin rule'. It requires that we start with the poorest person and raise his income to that of the next poorest person. If the budget is exhausted by this transfer, we stop the exercise here; otherwise, the incomes of the two poorest individuals are raised to the level of the third poorest individual's income. The process continues until we reach that marginal unit at which the budget is exhausted. This solution, therefore, is a sort of inversion of the one dictated for $\alpha = 0$. This brings out the way in which optimal budgetary policy varies with the distribution-sensitivity of the underlying poverty measure. Thus, as we proceed from $\alpha = 0$ to $\alpha \rightarrow \infty$, the focus of targeting attention moves from the 'able' to the 'needy'. Formally, the optimal solution for $\alpha > 1$ assumes the following form.

Let Q^*_c be the set of poorest individuals in the set Q_c such that

$\Sigma_{i \in Q^*_c} (x_{q_c}{}^* - x_i) = B,$

where $x_{q_c}{}^*$ is the income of the richest individual in the set Q_c^*.

Then, the optimal transfer schedule would be:

$t_i^* = x_{q_c}{}^* - x_i \;\forall i \in Q^*_c$ and $t_i^* = 0 \;\forall i \in (Q_c \setminus Q^*_c)$. (This budgetary rule is what Anand (1983) calls the redressal of poverty rule)

Budgetary Rules under the Alternative Approach

The programming problem, under the alternative approach to poverty-conceptualisation, can be set up as follows:

$$\underset{\{t_i\}_{i \in Qa}}{\text{Minimise}}\; P^*_\alpha (\{t_i\}_{i \in Qa}) = (1/n)\Sigma_{i \in Qa} (\sigma_i - t_i/z)^\alpha \qquad \text{...(A2.2)}$$

subject to $\Sigma_{i \in Qa} t_i \leq B;\; t_i \leq z_i - x_i \;\forall i \in Q_a;\; t_i \geq 0 \;\forall i \in Q_a$

Once more, we consider the set of optimal budgetary rules that would correspond to different values of α in the family of indices P^*_α.

For $\alpha = 0$, it is not hard to see that minimisation of the headcount index H^* would require us to begin by raising to his/her poverty line the person with the lowest income-gap γ_i, and continuing this process by moving on to the person with the next lowest income-gap, and bridging his/her poverty gap, and so on until the budget is exhausted. To describe the solution formally, we first need to re-index the elements of the set Q_a in a new ordering such that $\widetilde{\gamma}_1 \geq \widetilde{\gamma}_2 \geq \ldots \geq \widetilde{\gamma}_{q_a}$. Now, let Q_a'' be a set of richest individuals, in terms of income gaps, in the set Q_a such that

$$\Sigma_{i \in Q_a''}(z_i - x_i) = B.$$

Then, the optimal schedule is given by

$$t_i^* = 0 \forall i \in (Q_a \setminus Q_a'') \text{ and } t_i^* = z_i - x_i \forall i \in Q_a''.$$

Thus what is of crucial importance in determining optimal budgetary policy in the $\alpha = 0$, case is *the ordering according to income gaps.*

For $\alpha = 1$, the minimand in (A2.2) is given by the following expression:

$$P_1^*(\{t_i\}_{i \in Q_a} = (1/n)\Sigma_{i \in Q_a}\sigma_i - (1/n)\Sigma_{i \in Q_a}(t_i / z_i).$$

This, alternatively, can be written as:

$$P_1^*(\{t_i\}_{i \in Q_a}) = P_1'^* - (1/n)\Sigma_{i \in Q_a} t_i / z_i,$$

Where P'^*_1 is the value of the poverty index prior to the implementation of the transfer scheme. Clearly, minimisation of P_1^* would require making the second term on the right hand side of the preceding equation – call it T – as large as possible. To this end, we shall first find it convenient to re-index the elements of the set Q_a in a new ordering such that $\widetilde{z}_1 \leq \widetilde{z}_2 \leq \ldots \leq \widetilde{z}_{q_a}$.

Then the term T can be written as

$$T = (1/n)[(t_1 / \widetilde{z}_1) + \ldots + (t_{q_a} / \widetilde{z}_{q_a})].$$

Equivalently,

$$T = (1/n\pi_{i \in Q_a}\widetilde{z}_i)\ (t_1 y_1 + t_2 y_2 + \ldots + t_{q_a} y_{q_a}),$$ where, $\forall i \in Q_a : y_i = \Pi_{j \neq i}\widetilde{z}_j$. Now notice that since $\widetilde{z}_1 \leq \widetilde{z}_2 \leq \ldots \leq \widetilde{z}_{q_a}$, $y_1 \geq y_2 \geq \ldots \geq y_{q_a}$. Therefore, to make T as large as possible, we should start out by making t_1, as large as possible, then t_2 as large as possible, and follow the sequence until the budget is exhausted. Let Q'_a be an ordered set of individuals, indexed in non-decreasing order of their respective individual-specific poverty norms, in the set Q_a, such that $\Sigma_{i \in Q_a}{}'(z - x_i) = B$.

Then, the optimal transfer schedule will be given by

$t_i^* = 0 \forall i \in (Q_a \setminus Q_a')$ and $t_i^* = z_i - x_i \forall i \in Q_a'$.

Briefly, the crucial point to note is that optimal budgetary policy for $\alpha = 1$ is determined by the ordering according to the *poverty lines*. Note also, by way of contrast, that under the conventional approach any feasible transfer schedule is also an optimal one.

For $\alpha > 1$, we obtain an optimal budgetary rule which is once again similar to the Rawlsian 'lexicographic maximin rule'. It requires that we start with the person with the highest income-gap ratio and equalise his income-gap ratio with that of the person with the second highest such ratio. If the budget is exhausted by the transfer needed to achieve this, we stop the exercise here; otherwise, the income-gap ratios of the two individuals with the highest such ratios, are lowered to the income-gap ratio of the individual with the third highest such ratio. The process continues until we reach that marginal unit at which the budget is exhausted. This solution, therefore, is again a sort of inversion of the one dictated for $\alpha = 0$. This, once more, brings out the way in which optimal budgetary policy varies with the distribution-sensitivity of the underlying poverty measure. Formally, the optimal solution for $\alpha > 1$ assumes the following form.

We first re-index the elements of the set Q_a in a new ordering such that $\tilde{\sigma}_1 \geq \tilde{\sigma}_2 \geq \ldots \geq \tilde{\sigma}_{q_a}$. Let Q_a^* be an ordered subset of individuals, with the highest income-gap ratios, of the set Q_a, such that

$\Sigma_{i \in Q_a^*} (z_i - x_i) = B$.

Then, the optimal transfer schedule will be given by

$t_i^* = z_i - x_i \forall i \in Q_a^*$ and $t_i^* = 0 \forall i \in (Q_a \setminus Q_a^*)$.

It is only with such a schedule that the poorest individual's proportionate income-gap ratio can be made as small as possible — which is precisely the content of the Rawlsian rule. Importantly, we have to take note of the fact that the optimal budgetary policy in the $\alpha > 1$ case is determined by the ordering according to the *proportionate income-gap ratios.*

References

Anand, S., (1983). *Inequality and Poverty in Malaysia: Measurement and Decomposition*, New York : Oxford University Press.

Bourguignon, F. and G.S. Fields, (1990). "Poverty Measures and Anti-poverty Policy", Recherches Economiques de Louvain, 56.

Donaldson, D. and J.A. Weymark, (1986). "Properties of Fixed-Population Poverty Indices", *International Economic Review*, 27.

Foster, J., (1984). "On Economic Poverty: A Survey of Aggregate Measures", Advances in *Econometrics*, 3.

Foster, J., J. Greer and E. Thorbecke, (1984). "A Class of Decomposable Poverty Measures", *Econometrica*, 52.

Gangopadhyay, S. and S. Subramanian, (1992). "Optimal Budgetary Intervention in Poverty Alleviation Schemes", in S.Subramanian (ed.): *Themes in Development Economics: Essays in Honour of Malcolm Adiseshiah*, Delhi: Oxford University Press.

Kakwani, N., (1980). "On a Class of Poverty Measures", *Econometrica*, 48.

Sen, A.K., (1976). "Poverty: An Ordinal Approach to Measurement", *Econometrica*, 44.

————. (1983). "Poor, Relatively Speaking", *Oxford Economic Papers*, 35.

————. (1985). "A Sociological Reply to the Measurement of Poverty – A Reply to Professor Peter Townsend", *Oxford Economic Papers*, 37.

Subramanian, S., (1990). "Unemployment, Poverty and Inequality", (Section II of Chapter 12), in Malcolm S. Adiseshiah (ed.): *Eighth Plan Perspectives*, New Delhi : Lancer International.

Sukhatme, P.V., (1978). "Assessment of Adequacy of Diets at Different Income Levels", *Economic and Political Weekly*, 13.

————. (1981). "On Measurement of Poverty", *Economic and Political Weekly*, 16.

————. (1982). "Measurement of Undernutrition", *Economic and Political Weekly*, 17.

Sukhatme, P.V., and S.Margen (1980). "Relationship Between Undernutrition and Poverty", *Indian Economic Review*, 16.

Townsend, P., (1979). "The Development of Research on Poverty", in *Social Security Research: The Definition and Measurement of Poverty*, London: Department of Health and Social Security.

————. (1985). "A Sociological Approach to the Measurement of Poverty – A Rejoinder to Professor Amartya Sen", *Oxford Economic Papers*, 37.

• The authors thank, without implicating, Professor Prasanta Pattanaik for very useful discussions on the subject of this paper. R. Dharumaperumal helped out with word-processing of the paper. Subramanian Acknowledges the hospitality of the University of California, Riverside, where a preliminary version of this paper was written in the course of a Visiting Professorship.

9

A Review of India's Recent Trade Policy Reforms

KALIAPPA KALIRAJAN

1. INTRODUCTION

What motivated the policy makers in 1991 to initiate the economic reforms in India that have been long overdue? Two major reasons can be suggested: one relating to the international arena and the other concerning the national arena. In the international arena, the rapidly changing 'global economy' is the compelling reason for the economic reforms. Liberalisation in China and other communist countries such as Vietnam has dramatised the urgent need for liberalising the economy. The collapse of the bilateral relation with the USSR and the Gulf War probably accelerated the process. On the national front, the fiscal problems that began in the mid 1980s and the debt crisis that surfaced in 1990s precipitated the urgent need for macroeconomic reforms. The fiscal crisis was no sudden accident. The gross fiscal deficit grew from 4 per cent of the GDP in the mid-1970 to 6.3 per cent during the first half of the 1980s and to 8.2 per cent during the second half of the 1980s. As a result, the internal debt of the Government accumulated rapidly, rising from 35 per cent of GDP at the end of 1980-81 to 53 per cent at the end of 1990-91 (Ministry of Finance).

How did it happen? The Government has intervened in economic activities at all stages: production, consumption, marketing and pricing of inputs and outputs. Domestic markets have become distorted through a number of physical constraints on the free movement of goods, particularly agricultural commodities and through regulatory and other interventions. For example, in the case of wheat, informal restrictions on movement are often imposed on the surplus states of

Punjab, Haryana and Uttar Pradesh. Private trade has not been encouraged in primary grain markets. The low output prices and subsidised inputs have created massive inefficiencies in production through depressed productivity coupled with excessive use of inputs, and in macroeconomic terms, increasingly serious fiscal imbalance in government budgets (Joshi and Little, 1996).

Why have the policymakers been carrying on with such inefficient intervention policies? Government intervention has produced some positive effects on economic growth too. On the positive side, it is often argued that the achievement of food security through self-sufficiency in cereal grains has been the most important accomplishment of the agricultural sector and would not have occurred without government intervention. It is also argued that, government intervention in agriculture was needed to minimise the impact of uneven income distribution on the incidence of poverty in different regions of the country resulting from weather fluctuations and fluctuating market forces. Further, being a democracy with a pluralist society has made it necessary for India to obtain a reasonable consensus across different interest groups before policy changes could be implemented and this has been a major cause for the slow pace of reforms.

Nevertheless, the balance of payments situation worsened beyond tolerable limits in 1991. The current account deficit doubled from an annual average of 1.3 per cent of GDP in the first half of 1980s to 2.2 per cent during the second half (Reserve Bank of India). These deficits forced the Government to borrow overseas. Consequently, the debt service burden rose from 10 per cent of current account receipts in 1980-81 to 22 per cent in 1990-91 (Ministry of Finance). Thus, both the internal and external debts and the associated macroeconomic problems such as inflation signalled a warning to policymakers that macroeconomic reforms could not be delayed any longer.

In pursuit of solving the above serious problems, reform measures were introduced in fiscal, monetary, industry, exchange rate and trade policies to stimulate the economy. A simple model of economic reforms is presented in the next section. The impact of reforms on India's international trade is empirically examined in the following section. The next section discusses the specific policy reforms that were implemented from July 1991 to June 2001 to improve India's international trade and a final section brings out the overall conclusions of this paper.

2. A SIMPLE MODEL OF ECONOMIC REFORMS

In Figure 9.1, points *B* and *B'* show the maximum possible or potential output that can be produced with given input levels and technology in a static sense. In other words, these levels of outputs could not have been obtained with fewer inputs with the existing technology. However, the economy is producing at point *A*, where the output is less than the country's potential output, given its frontier production possibility set. The country is producing at point *A* due to various non-price and organisational factors, which are the consequences of government policies, that exert influence on production. Now, there are two basic options for the Government, which are not mutually exclusive. The Government may choose to cut and to intensify the use of inputs to produce at *B'* to move on further to *B*. Alternatively, the government may choose to maintain the same input level and to effectively use the inputs to produce at *B*. However, policy emphasis needs to be different depending on which path the Government would like to choose. Suppose, the Government chooses the path from *A* to *B'*, then policy emphasis needs to be more on reducing the levels by encouraging substitution and intensive use of inputs. Relatively major emphasis then would be on fiscal policy reforms aimed at pruning government expenditure.

On the other hand, if the Government chooses the path from *A* to *B*, then the emphasis needs to be on improving the competitive structure to achieve efficient use of inputs. Accordingly, those policies that exert influence on competitive structure, such as trade policy, exchange rate policy and investment policy play a dominant role in the reform process[1]. Developing countries with serious supply

1. The reform path is not as simple as it is discussed here. Generally, a combination of both paths A to B and A to B′ will constitute a reform process. For example, ".. until the 1960s in Japan and until the 1980s in Korea and Taiwan, export-promotion policies were superimposed on the import-substitution policies rather than replacing them." (Hayami, 1998, p.18). However, within a reform process, a particular path may be given higher priority from time to time. In most of the IMF structural adjustment programs, higher priority is given first to choose the reform path A to B′, which may increase unemployment and reduce imports at least in the short run.

bottlenecks and unemployment problems tend to go more for the choice of the path from *A* to *B* relative to the path from *A* to *B'* to *B*. As discussed earlier, data reveal that since mid-1970s and until recently, the Government has not been able to reduce the fiscal deficit consistently. On the other hand, economic growth has risen on average to 6.5 per cent per annum since reforms compared to the average annual growth rate of 3.5 per cent of the pre-reform period. This indicates that India has been relying more on the reform path of moving from *A* to *B* by initiating trade policy, investment policy and exchange rate policy reforms aimed at improving the competitive structure of the economy.

Figure 9.1

Production Possibility and Potential and Actual Production Points

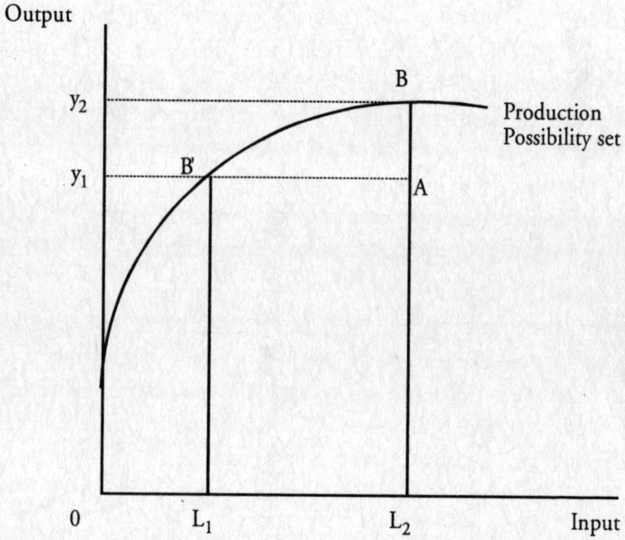

In this paper analysis is restricted to examine the types of trade policy reforms that have been implemented in India since 1991 and their impact on export promotion and import liberalisation. The empirical evidence from a number of studies points to a strong and significant effect of openness to trade on growth performance (Srinivasan, 1998: 202-8). An important empirical question that is investigated in this paper is: how open has India's trade been after a decade of economic reforms?

Reforms, India's GDP and Trade

Literature shows that dramatic policy changes in some countries have not always led to significant improvements in actual performance. The end results in terms of the actual performance of the economy provide a measure not only to show how effectively the policy reforms were carried out, but also to gauge the appropriateness of such reform measures towards the stated objectives. Based on the above modelling of India's reform process, and with the assumption that India has been effectively implementing appropriate reform measures, it is rational to expect significant growth in GDP and trade consistently.

Figure 9.2 shows India's total exports, total imports and GDP at current market prices in US dollars. Consistently, the ratio of imports to GDP has been higher than the ratio of exports to GDP in the 1990s and the gap has been widening. Figure 9.3 shows India's merchandise exports, merchandise imports, and GDP at current market prices in US dollars. The ratio of merchandise exports to GDP steadily increased from 4 per cent in 1970-71 to 11 per cent in 2000-01, which indicates the rising importance of exports to the Indian economy. During 2000-01, exceeding the target of 18 per cent, the merchandise exports at US$ 44 billion have grown by 19.8 per cent over 1999-2000 (RBI, 2001).

India has been always enjoying trade surplus with respect to services trade even before reforms, though it used to be less than a billion US dollar until recently. After the reforms only in 1995-96, due to the world recession, India had negative balance in services trade. However from 1996-97, surplus in services trade has been surging steadily. Export of services touched the level of US$ 15 billion during 1999-2000 from US$ 13 billion in 1998-99, which translates into a growth rate of 15 per cent. This success is mainly attributable to 'miscellaneous services' component, mainly software services, which touched US$ 9 billion in 2000-01 from US$ 6.5 billion in 1999-2000 registering a growth rate of about 35 per cent

(RBI, 2001)[2]. Thus, services trade has been recently helping the economy to narrow the current account balance.

Figure 9.2

Total Exports, Imports as percentage of GDP (US$ Million at Factor Cost and Current Prices)

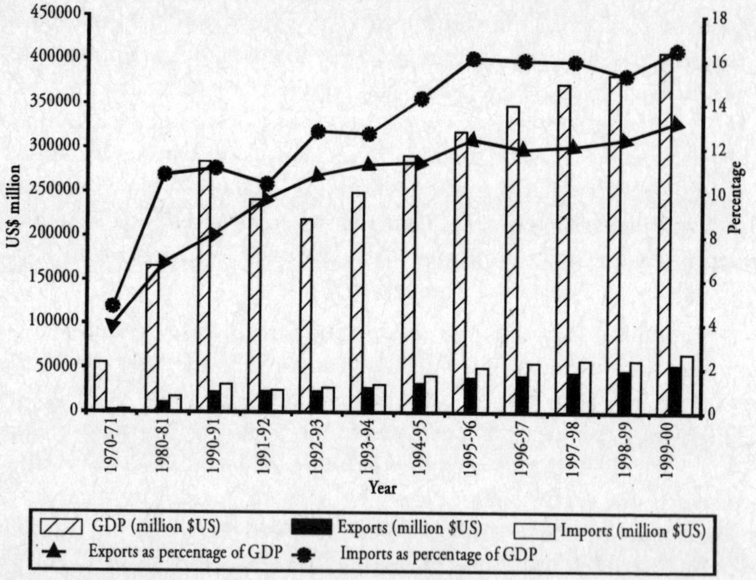

Source: RBI (2001)

Is Rupee Trade still alive? Before the collapse of communist planned economies in Eastern Europe and the break-up of the Soviet Union, India had "Rupee trade" agreements with the Soviet Union, Czechoslovakia, Romania, GDR (East Germany) and Poland. Conventional import-export licensing rules, tariffs and export incentives were not applied to this trade. Before the mid-1980s, the total Rupee trade accounted for about 20 per cent to 25 per cent of India's exports and about 10 per cent to 12 per cent of its imports

2. Software exports in physical form are captured under the item "merchandise exports" in the data on India's Balance of Payment (BoP), while software exports through on-site and off-site routes are recorded under computer services in "miscellaneous receipts" which form part of "non-factor services" under invisibles.

Figure 9.3

Merchandise Exports, Imports and GDP (in US$ million)

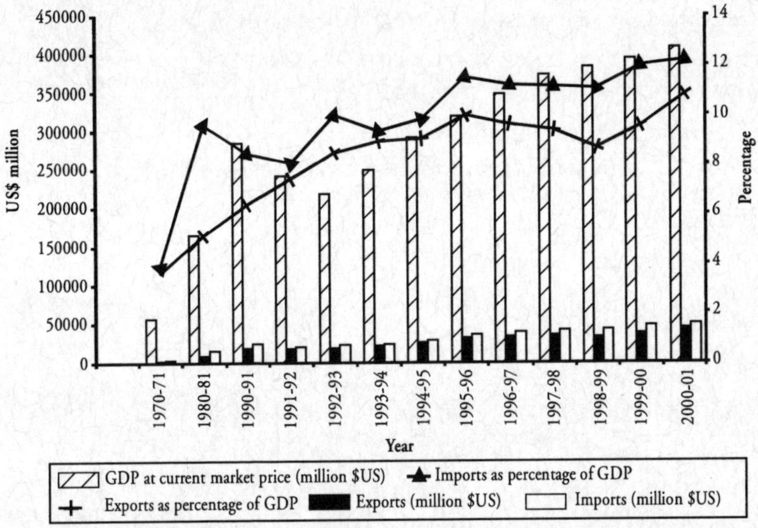

Source: RBI (2001)

(Figure 9.4). The resulting trade surplus, most of which was with the Soviet Union, was used to pay for services and to repay loans in connection with Soviet projects in India and military assistance. Between 1990 and 1993, the Rupee payment agreements with the Soviet Union and the four east European countries were replaced with a series of separate agreements with the Soviet successor States and the eastern European countries. The agreements affirmed the principle in each case that trade would take place in convertible currencies on MFN principles without new special trade arrangements (Pursell, 1996). Indian industries which supplied generally low quality large scale bulk exports that include tea, tobacco, garments, fertilisers, newsprint, drugs and pharmaceuticals to the Soviet Union and eastern Europe, initially faced difficulties in adjusting to the loss of these markets. However, it appears that on the whole they have succeeded in switching their exports to more demanding hard currency markets. There has been a massive redirection of trade since 1990-91, with exports to these countries falling from about 20 per cent of total exports before 1985-86 to 3.5 per cent in 1999-00, and imports declining from 10 per cent to 12 per cent of total imports to only 2.1 per cent in 1999-00. As this trade was conducted in a very non-transparent way with respect to the products and the firms involved, its disappearance since 1991-92 is an important liberalisation of the Indian trade regime.

Figure 9.4

India's Trade with the Former Soviet Union and Eastern Europe (Rupee Trade) as Percentage of the Total Trade

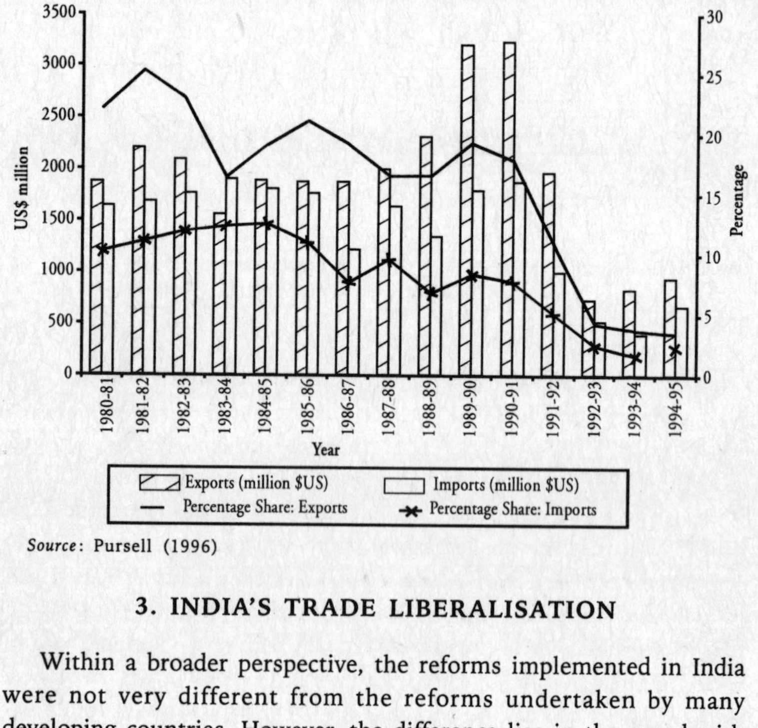

Source: Pursell (1996)

3. INDIA'S TRADE LIBERALISATION

Within a broader perspective, the reforms implemented in India were not very different from the reforms undertaken by many developing countries. However, the difference lies in the speed with which these reforms were implemented. Just like the Chinese case, India's reforms were implemented in a gradual manner. Nevertheless, the reasons for the gradual approach to reforms are different between China and India. Being the largest democracy with a pluralist society in the world has made it necessary for India to obtain a reasonable consensus across different interest groups before policy changes could be implemented and this has been the major cause for the slow pace of reforms. The main thrust of trade policy reforms have been to open up India's trade and hence the policy measures concern with export promotion and import liberalisation. How open is India's trade today after a decade of trade policy reforms?

Export Promotion Measures

EXIM Policy 1992-97

When the Eighth Plan commenced, the three-year Import-Export policy (1990-93), valid until March 1993 was in operation. With a view to reinforcing the trade policy reforms and complementing the fiscal, industrial and investment measures, the new five-year Export-Import Policy (1992-97) was introduced with effect from April 1992. For the first time, the policy was given an export bias. Earlier this policy was known as Import-Export policy; the new policy was titled Export-Import policy (EXIM Policy). Several schemes were introduced or modified to eliminate regulatory measures and discretionary controls impinging on free trade. Major schemes and their impacts on India's exports and imports are discussed in the following pages.

Just before the launching of the EXIM Policy 1992-97, on March 1, 1992, the Liberalised Exchange Rate Management System (LERMS) was introduced. Under the LERMS, exporters were required to surrender 40 per cent of the foreign exchange earning at the official exchange rate. The Government would use the amount to import essential items such as petroleum, fertilisers and life saving drugs. The exporters were allowed to sell the remaining 60 per cent of the foreign exchange or use it to finance their own imports, which facility was not given to exporters in the pre-reform period. This system acted as a self-correcting mechanism to keep trade deficit under control. With effect from June 1992, the 15 per cent Foreign Exchange Conservation (Travel) Tax was abolished. The travel tax had become redundant with the introduction of partial convertibility of rupee and Liberlaised Exchange Rate Management System (LERMS) under which foreign exchange for travel had to be obtained at the market rate. Along with this change in the exchange rate regime, the import licensing system was abolished for capital goods, intermediates and components; these items could be imported on open general licence (OGL) subject to payment of tariffs (Ministry of Commerce).

To promote investment by Non-Resident Indians, a new deposit scheme was introduced in June 1992, under which accounts in Indian rupees could be opened with authorised dealers by remittance of funds in freely convertible foreign exchange from abroad or by transfer of funds from the existing non-resident (external)/FCNR accounts. No penalty was to be levied for premature withdrawal of existing non-resident deposits for the purpose of making investment in the proposed scheme. Full convertibility of rupee on trade account (current account) was introduced and dual or partial exchange rate was abolished. In March 1993, the exchange rate was unified and transactions on trade account were freed from exchange control (CMIE, 2000).

The export promotion capital goods (EPCG) is a scheme to liberalise capital goods imports. This was introduced to boost exports. The EPCG scheme allows exporters to import machinery, both new and second-hand, duty free or at concessional duty, if the importer agrees to achieve a fixed export target within a specified period of time. Under the scheme, the duty on import of capital goods was reduced from 25 per cent to 15 per cent subject to an export obligation of three times the c.i.f. value of imports and the period of achievement was increased from four years to five years. The scheme was very popular when customs duty on capital goods was high. Currently, under the EPCG scheme, import of capital goods carry 10 per cent customs duty though duty free imports are also permitted, subject to a minimum import volume. Exemptions are available for certain sectors like agriculture and garments even if the minimum floor limit is not met. If a computer system is imported under this scheme, supporting manufacturers and service providers are also eligible to import capital goods. Industry uses this scheme for modernisation and upgradation purposes (CMIE, 2000).

As a consequence, capital goods imports increased by 23 per cent in 1993-94 over 1992-93. This facilitated exports to register a growth rate of 30 per cent in 1993-94 over the previous year. Manufacturing exports increased by 29 per cent, which is five-percentage point more than the previous year's growth. Trade deficit drastically declined to US$ 1 billion in 1993-94 from US$ 3 billion in 1992-93. These data clearly indicate that schemes such as the EPCG have really paid off. This situation is analogous to the Chinese reform process. When the

Chinese reform started in 1978 with the introduction of the household responsibility system replacing the commune system, economic growth surged in the following years.

The other major schemes are as follows: Duty Exemption Scheme (DES), Scheme for Gems and Jewellery, and policies enlarging the scope of instruments of export promotion such as export oriented units (EOU)[3] and export processing zones (EPZ), joint ventures and different types of trading houses.[4]

Duty Exemption Scheme: Under this scheme, import of raw materials, intermediates, components, consumables, parts, accessories, packing materials and computer software required for direct use in the export product is permitted duty free for processing and export by the competent authority under the categories of advance licences, advanced intermediate licence, special imprest licence, licences under export production programme, advance customs clearance permit and advance release orders.[5]

Scheme for Gems and Jewellery: Exporters of gems and jewellery are allowed to import inputs by obtaining Replenishment Licences and Diamond/DTC Imprest Licences (DTCIL). The replenishment licences are transferable. Exports effected in fulfilment of export obligation against DTCILs do not qualify for this benefit. The latter licence can be issued in advance for import of rough diamonds and for export of cut and polished diamonds. Though DTCILs are not transferable, imported goods may be transferred but the responsibility to fulfil the export obligation vests in the licencee. These licences carry an export obligation fixed in the inverse ratio of 65 per cent of replenishment. That is, if the licence is issued for a CIF value of $65, the FoB value of export obligation will be $100.

3. EOUs can be started anywhere in the country and mostly they are located in places where there are easy access to raw materials and other inputs such as power and transportation. It can be private, government owned or joint ventures. Government does not fund the EOUs, though they provide some concessions such as duty free imports (Ministry of Commerce).

4. Details on different types of trading houses are given in Appendix I.

5. Advance licences are issued under the Duty Exemption Scheme (DES) for duty free import of inputs and are subject to fulfilment of a time-bound export obligation as well as specified rate of value addition. These licences may be either value-based or quantity-based and are regulated in freely convertible currency, their FOB value of exports and CIF value of imports to be specified accordingly. It is allowed to dispose of raw materials imported against advance licences without prior permission of the concerned authorities (Ministry of Finance).

The export oriented unit (EOU) and export promotion zone (EPZ) schemes were liberalised. 100 per cent foreign equity participation in EOU/EPZ units was allowed (Ministry of Commerce).

The EXIM Policy 1992-97 was modified in March 1993 giving a new thrust to exports of agricultural and allied sectors, and services in which the country has a comparative advantage. Ironically, minimum export price was introduced to discourage the export of non-basmati and low-grade rice, which would affect the domestic market. This was a step backward from marching towards free trade and also not in the interest of the farmers because the border price for rice was lower than the international price during the early nineties. Also, export of high value durum wheat and of non-fair average quality of jowar were allowed only subject to ceiling. These measures, which were discouraging rather than encouraging exports of cereals, were introduced to build buffer stocks of grains for the use of the public distribution system.

The EXIM Policy was modified in 1995 to boost agricultural exports. The highlights were: (a) in the category of agricultural and food exports only beef and tallow were in the negative list during 1995-96; (b) horticulture and floriculture exports were encouraged by providing various supports to farmers such as airfreight subsidy; and (c) quantitative ceiling and minimum export price in respect of rice was abolished: exports of wheat up to 2.5 million tonnes in case of non-durum wheat and 0.5 million tonnes in case of durum wheat was permitted; and in the case of coffee, free sale quota was raised to 70 per cent for large producers and 100 per cent for small producers. As a consequence to these policy changes, fruits, vegetables and flowers emerged as export products. EOUs in floriculture facilitated export of the perishable products. Airfreight subsidy provided a boost to these export items.

EXIM Policy 1997-2002

Some of the major policy changes include (a) bringing down the threshold limit for EPCG zero duty scheme from Rs. 50 million to Rs. 10 million for agricultural and allied sectors and from Rs. 200 million to Rs. 10 million for electricals, textiles, leather, gems and jewellery, sport goods and food processing and to Rs. 1 million in case of the software sector; (b) modifying

DEPB scheme to neutralise not only the basic customs duty but also the special customs duty which was introduced as a temporary measure in 1998; and (c) freeing exports of oilseeds for consumption purpose and vegetables from any quantitative and licensing requirements (Ministry of Commerce).

Several modifications to the earlier schemes were done mainly to boost services trade, particularly IT exports. For example, the export promotion capital goods (EPCG) scheme for services sector was introduced. Under this scheme, capital goods were allowed to be imported for rendering services for which payments are received in a freely convertible currency. The scheme is applicable to professionals and other providers of services such as architects, consultants, economists, charted accountants, engineers and tour operators. Exemption was given to exports under all export promotion schemes from the applicability of the special additional duty of 4 per cent introduced in the 1998-99 budget. Promotional measures and procedural changes that were made in 1998 include facilities such as extension of holiday for EOU/EPZ to 10 years, sub-contracting facility for Domestic Tariff Area and permission to set up private software technology parks.

In order to promote trade among SAARC countries, India unilaterally removed all QRs on imports of 2300 items from SAARC countries with effect from August 1, 1998. On December 28, 1998, a free trade agreement was concluded between India and Sri Lanka which would result in zero import tariff for most commodities on both sides by 2007. Following the third round of negotiations held under SAARC Preferential Tariff Agreement (SAPT), the Revenue Department notified on August 11, 1999 concessional customs duties — ranging from 25 per cent to 60 per cent for least developed countries (Bangladesh, Maldives, Nepal and Bhutan) and 10 per cent to 50 per cent for the other three countries — covering items in 1800 tariff lines which account for 60 per cent of imports (Ministry of Finance).

On 31st March 1999, the following new schemes to boost service exports were introduced. The setting up of special economic zones (SEZs) was announced with a view to providing internationally competitive and hassle-free environment for exports. Together with the Foreign Direct Investment policy initiatives for SEZs, it is expected that these zones will have the potential to act as "magnets" for investments from home and abroad for export production. As a first step, four existing Export Processing Zones (EPZs) — at Kandla, Santa Cruz, Cochin and Surat — were converted into SEZs with effect from 1st November, 2000. Setting up of new SEZs in the following areas has been progressing steadily: Positra (Gujarat), Nangunery (Tamil Nadu), Kakinada-Vizag (Andhra Pradesh), Paradip (Orissa), Kulpi (West Bengal) and Bhadohi (Uttar Pradesh). It is too early to judge their success. However, their success will depend on how effectively domestic regulations and infrastructure bottlenecks are eliminated in these zones. In order to provide an impetus to infrastructure development, deemed export benefits have been extended to infrastructure projects with a minimum investment of Rs. 100 crore.[6]

With a view to making exports a national effort by involving all the state governments, a scheme has been evolved for granting assistance to the states on the basis of their export performance for

---

6. Deemed Exports refer to those transactions in which the goods supplied do not leave the country. The following categories of supply of goods by the main/sub-contractors shall be regarded as Deemed Exports under the Export and Import Policy, provided the goods are manufactured in India:
   (a) Supply of goods against Advance Licence/under the Duty Exemption/Remission Scheme (DERS);
   (b) Supply of goods to Export Oriented Units (EOUs) or units located in Export Processing Zones (EPZs) or Special Economic Zones (SEZs) or Software Technology Parks (STPs) or to Electronic Hardware Technology Parks (EHTPs);
   (c) Supply of capital goods to holders of licences under the Export Promotion Capital Goods (EPCG) scheme;
   (d) Supply of goods to projects financed by multilateral or bilateral agencies/funds as notified by the Department of Economic Affairs, Ministry of Finance under International Competitive Bidding in accordance with the procedures of those agencies/funds, where the legal agreements provide for tender evaluation without including the customs duty;
   (e) Supply of capital goods, including in unassembled/disassembled condition as well as plants, machinery, accessories, tools, dies and such goods which are used for installation purposes till the stage of commercial production and spares to the extent of 10 per cent of the FOR value to fertiliser plants;
   (f) Supply of goods to any project or purpose in respect of which the Ministry of Finance, by a notification, permits the import of such goods at zero customs duty;
   (g) Supply of goods to the power and refineries not covered in (f) above;
   (h) Supply of marine freight containers by 100 per cent EOU (Domestic freight containers–manufacturers) provided the said containers are exported out of India within six months or such further period as permitted by the Customs; and (i) Supply to projects funded by UN agencies.

development of export related infrastructure. To facilitate an equitable allocation of resources, this amount will be distributed on the basis of absolute export performance as well as on the basis of incremental one. To begin with, an allocation of Rs. 2.5 billion is proposed for 2001-02, which would be suitably increased in the subsequent years. There would be subsequent annual allocation for this Fund. The amount would be utilised by the states for complementary export related infrastructure, such as roads connecting the production centres with ports, research and development of state-specific ethnic products, development of cold chains for agro exports, development of minor ports, creation of new export promotion industrial parks, human resource development and for the purpose of developing marketing infrastructure. The units may be allowed to dispose of obsolete or unusable capital goods, spares and other goods in the domestic tariff area (DTA) on payment of applicable customs duty. Such disposal shall, however, be subject to the Import Policy in force.

Under the SEZ scheme, the goods cleared from the Zone will be treated as imported goods. Therefore, in case of DTA clearances, though the duty charged will be central excise duty, this duty will be equal to the aggregate of all duties of customs (WTO). In other words, the SEZ units will have to pay full customs duty (applied duty) on their DTA clearances. The only laws which will operate within the SEZs will be those related to labour and banking.

An SEZ unit shall maintain proper year-wise financial account of all foreign exchange inflow by way of exports and other receipts, all foreign exchange outflows on account of imports, payment of dividend, royalty, fees etc., consumption and utilisation of the materials and sale in the DTA. RBI will permit banks to open branches in the SEZ and permit transactions to be operated in dollars for all units.

Most of the units within SEZ may be employing less than 1000 workers. With the recent change in the labour laws announced in the Union Budget 2001-2002 that a firm employing less than 1000 employees is not required to get the approval from the Government to layoff any employee or to close down the unit, labour laws particularly may not be a constraint. Further, the new law allows outsourcing and employing contract labour, which facilitates reducing employer-employee frictions in work places (Ministry of Finance).

With the view that agriculture is the responsibility of state governments, the Central Government has insisted through the revised EXIM policy of 1997-2002 that the state governments should identify and develop product-specific agricultural export zones (AEZ). It is expected that the states will identify product-specific AEZ for end-to-end development from a geographically contiguous area. They will also have to evolve a comprehensive package of services provided by all state government agencies, agricultural universities, and some Central institutions and agencies for 'intensive delivery' in these zones. The AEZ would have access to the Centre's proposed market access initiative, which will provide market research, warehousing and retail marketing infrastructure in select countries, and direct market promotion activities. Two AEZs exist as of now, one in Tamil Nadu and another in Gujarat.

Imports Liberalisation

India retained import of items under five categories — the prohibited list, the special import licence (SIL) list, the restricted list, the canalised list and the free list. The number of items included in these lists keeps changing. Of these, the restricted list has been freed and SIL abandoned and freed. The canalised list is being retained, but under a new nomenclature (the special list) and a new set of products. Thus, at present, the number of import lists has come down to three — the prohibited list, the special list and the free list. The prohibited list contains only a few products prohibited on grounds of religious and cultural sensitivity and the list includes tallow, fat and oils of animal origin, animal rennet and wild animals including their parts and products and ivory. Bulk agricultural commodities that include grains excluding feed grade maize, edible oils, oilseeds, sugar, and non-agricultural products such as urea, petroleum products are in the special list that was earlier called canalised list. Imports of these items should be done by state agencies.

Apart from the special list of consumer products, gold will continue to be imported through designated banks. Import of all primary products of plant and animal origin will also be subject to import permits to be issued by the ministry of agriculture after an import risk analysis based on sanitary and phyto-sanitary measures and provisions. In addition, conditions have been prescribed for the import of new and second hand cars for ensuring road safety. Import of foreign liquor, processed food products and tea wastes has to be made subject to already existing domestic regulations concerning health and hygiene. Rest of the commodities are in the free list. Imports of these freed items attract high tariffs with bound rates.

EXIM Policy 1992-97

In 1990, prior to economic reforms, India's peak tariff[7] was at 300 per cent. During 1992-93, the peak rate was reduced to 150 per cent (WTO, 1998). The Government also introduced a system of value-based advanced licences to export houses, trading houses and star trading houses which permitted duty free imports of necessary raw materials as components up to a stipulated ratio of the value of anticipated exports. Special Import Licences (SIL), which could be traded in the market, were issued to certain categories of exports like exports to Asian clearing union countries, deemed export, trading houses and manufacturers who have acquired the ISO 9000 or other internationally certified quality. Before the Uruguay Round Agreement (URA), only 5 per cent of India's tariff lines were bound. The Government indicated that after the URA came into force, about 68 per cent of India's tariff lines would be bound. As of December 1st, 1995 more than 3000 tariff lines covering raw materials, intermediates and capital goods were freed from import licensing requirements. Removing these goods from licence requirements is good news for traders. Also, India had to act in accordance with the WTO negotiations. However, by replacing licences with high tariffs, India indicates that its promotion of free trade is not without restraint.

In 1995-96, on industrial raw materials, components and capital goods, India had bound tariffs at 40 per cent (where they were above 40 per cent in 1993-94) and at 25 per cent in other cases. Countervailing duties at the rate of 30 per cent to 40 per cent were imposed as additional tariff above this 25 per cent for goods other than raw materials, components and capital goods. Nevertheless, QRs

---

7. Peak tariff rate is the general guide for setting the tariff rates. Higher tariff rates are exceptions. However, higher tariffs should be equal to or lower than the WTO approved bound rates.

were present as the rest of the goods were classified into either negative list or special licence list during that period. India indicated ceiling bindings of 100 per cent on primary products, 150 per cent on processed products and 300 per cent on edible oils. With an improvement in India's BoP, the country was under pressure to eliminate the QRs. India had entered into bilateral agreement with the EU, New Zealand and Australia, to remove QRs on 1,429 items from April 1st, 2003. Such an understanding was not reached with the USA.

EXIM Policy 1997-02

During 1997-98, the peak rate of import duty was reduced to 40 per cent *ad valorem* except for passenger luggage, alcoholic beverages, dried grapes and a few other products. The peak rates for imports of raw materials and capital goods for projects were reduced to 30 per cent and 20 per cent, respectively. However, the special additional customs duty was raised from 2 per cent to 5 per cent on all imported goods except petroleum products and certain project imports[8]. A surcharge of 10 per cent on basic duty was introduced in 1998-99 mainly to control imports of consumer goods.

From 1 April 2001, removal of QRs became necessary, in the face of India losing the case against the USA. By replacing QRs with high tariffs, India indicates that its promotion of free trade is not without restraint. In fact, high tariffs have been imposed on goods removed from QRs to protect the domestic industry from overseas competition. WTO permits tariff setting, so far as the applied rates do not surpass bound rates. India's applied rates are mostly lower than the bound tariffs. India is now imposing tariffs up to the allowable maximum for imported agricultural and consumer goods to protect domestic production. The recently announced peak tariff rate is 35 per cent plus a 3.5 per cent surcharge on tariffs and a 4 per cent special duty on items from which QRs have been removed. In addition, countervailing duties ranging from 16 per cent to 32 per cent are imposed on certain goods. Basic tariffs have been increased on vegetable oils from 25 per cent to 45 per cent, on tea, coffee,

8. The argument for imposing the additional duty was to provide some relief to domestic producers from internal sales tax.

copra and coconut from 35 per cent to 70 per cent. Uniform rates of 75 per cent and 85 per cent are imposed on crude edible oils and refined oils, respectively. Maximum tariffs on imports of rice are 80 per cent. Without doubt, these tariffs substantially raise the import prices of several agricultural products. The duty on used cars has been put at 105 per cent, which translates into 180 per cent including countervailing and special additional duties.

The total numbers of customs duty rates during 2001-02 are 35 per cent, 25 per cent, 15 per cent and 5 per cent. The Special Additional Duty imposed in 1998-99 (for all products except for petroleum products) is still applicable. However, the surcharge of 10 per cent on basic duty that was introduced in 1998-99 is now removed. At present, most consumer goods, which have been in the free list of imports effective from 1st April, 2000, are being placed at the peak rate 35 per cent plus the surcharge. A number of agricultural and horticultural products placed on the free list of import in earlier years are being brought to the peak rate to ensure adequate protection to Indian farmers (Table 9.1).

For sensitive agricultural products such as wheat, rice, sugar and edible oils in which the Indian experience with supply management has underlined the importance of occasional tariff adjustments, the Finance Minister would make suitable enabling provisions to fix the statutory tariff rates at approximately high levels.

What is this experience, and why does it result in upward tariff adjustments? The main approach of the Government policy has been to regulate international trade in a manner to ensure adequate availability of essential food items to consumers at reasonable prices and to protect farmers from foreign competition. Concerning exports, the objective is to maximise agricultural exports in order to earn foreign exchange and provide remunerative prices to the farmers keeping in view the prime consideration of ensuring adequate availability of essential commodities to the domestic consumers at reasonable prices. Concerning agricultural imports, the policy aims to regulate imports keeping in view the domestic demand and supply situation, the interests of the farmers and consideration of out-flow of foreign exchange.

Table 9.1

Items on which Import Duties have been raised in April 2001

(Per cent)

Items	*Previous Tariff*	*Revised Tariff*
Skimmed Milk Powder	0	60
Wheat	0	50
Rice in the husk (paddy or rough)	0	80
Husked (brown) rice	0	80
Semi-milled or wholly milled rice,	0	70
Broken rice	0	80
Maize (corn) seeds	0	50
Grain sorghum	0	50
Millet (Jowar)	0	50
Arecanut	35	100
Apples	35	50
Tea	15	35
Coffee	15	35
Sugar (+a countervailing duty of Rs. 850 per tonne)	40	60

Source: Ministry of Commerce.

Whenever supply appears to be meeting the demand, then import of that concerned commodity will be restricted through high tariffs or canalisation, even when the international price is lower than the domestic price. When supply exceeds demand, then export is encouraged only after building up buffer stock for the public distribution system. Imposing minimum export price and/or ceilings has regulated exports of rice and wheat.

In the case where there is excess demand, and particularly the international price is lower, the Government has encouraged imports by imposing lower tariffs. A recent example is edible oils imports. Some of the main reasons have been an increase in edible oil consumption, stagnating oil seeds production and falling international prices. In addition to this, the differential duty structure in favour of refined oil led to an upsurge in edible oil imports. When in 1992-93 the Golden revolution to achieve self-sufficiency in oil production was launched, many oil solvent extractors set up the extraction units as they saw huge potential in the market. But with oil seeds production not catching up with the demand plus lower per hectare yield of just 850 Kgs, compared to the world average of 1600 Kgs of oil seeds, the country had to resort to external sources.

At present, India has more than 15,000 oilseeds crushing units, more than 600 solvent extractors, more than 400 vegetable oil refiners and more than 190 Vanaspati oil units. All these are working at below 40 per cent capacity utilisation. With such a low capacity utilisation the solvent extraction industry is in doldrums, many of these units have already been shut down. The Government is keen to protect the domestic oilseeds industry. Recently, in Budget 2002, it increased the basic duty on RBD (Refined, Bleached and Deodorized) Palmolein to 85 per cent from 65 per cent and maintained the special additional duty at 4 per cent. It even increased the basic duty on Crude Palm imports by 50 per cent to 75 per cent. This decision is likely to impact already sulking solvent extraction industry. For refined soybean, however, the Government maintained the *status quo* with 45 per cent basic customs duty.

What are the implications of this government agricultural tariff policy? The implication is that such a provision may lead to the misuse of bound rates. For the uninitiated, bound tariff rates are the highest tariff rates that a country agrees, under the WTO regime, to apply to a particular import or class of imports. The general peak tariff rate is 35 per cent, also too high in relation to almost any other country.

The need for applied rates to be close to, or the same as, bound ones is not good. Because, the very logic of bound rates is to keep them at the highest level possible, so that such duties may be applied in crisis times. It does not mean that they should in fact be applied all the time. However, the possibility of the producer lobby putting pressure on the Government to raise tariffs even for some minor temporary setbacks in production is very high. The question to ask is if India really wants to revert to its severely protectionist past or to further lower its still-high tariffs.

Has anything else happened that could generally be classified as import liberalisation?

In the case of Customs duty the Government withdrew the surcharge of 10 per cent and with this the peak tariff rate will decline to 35 per cent from 38.5 per cent. Basic Customs duty on specified textile machinery declined to 5 per cent from 15 per cent. Customs duty on silk waste, cotton waste and flax fibre reduced to 15 per cent from a range of 25 to 35 per cent. Customs duty on soda ash was reduced to 20 per cent. Customs duty on polyester chips and nylon chips for manufacture of fibre and yarns was reduced to 25 per cent, and on cut and polished coloured gem stones to 15 per cent from 35 per cent. Duty on rough diamond was reduced to 5 per cent. Customs duty on cement and clinkers was reduced to 25 per cent from 35 per cent. Duty on gold was reduced to Rs. 50 per 10 gm from Rs. 400.

India joined the Information Technology Agreement on 25.3.1997, which aims to expand world trade in information technology products. According to the agreement, customs tariff on IT items need to be brought down to zero (WTO). India has committed to bring down the tariff on 217-bound items. Out of which 95 lines were reduced to zero in 2000, and India has committed to reduce tariff to zero for another 4 lines in 2003, 2 lines in 2004 and 116 lines in 2005.

According to the IT Agreement, customs duty on some components was reduced to zero in the budget 2000-01. And also customs duty on parts of capacitors, resistors and semi-conductors falling under Tariff subheadings 8532.90, 8533.90, 8541.90 and 8542.90 was reduced to zero.

Import of agricultural products like wheat, rice, maize, other coarse cereals, copra and coconut oil has been placed in the category of State Trading though on commercial lines. This is a kind of non-tariff barrier to free trade.

Is it necessary? "License Raj", heavy government interventions, has been a major feature of the Indian economy in the pre-reform period and no market could be free from government intervention. This has generated institutional complementarity in the Indian context in the pre-reform period and it appears that this characteristic of the economy has not changed completely yet. This procedure of State Trading in the agricultural products in the post-reform period has the potential to slow down the process of liberalisation. This State Trading restriction appears to be due to mainly political reasons. Though wheat, rice, maize, coarse cereals, copra, coconut oil and urea are no longer on the QRs list, the

Government has kept an eye on the rural vote bank by restricting their trade by putting them in the special list. Import of all these products continues to remain canalised through state trading enterprises.

This is despite the fact that the Government has armed itself with weapons such as high bound rates under WTO for wheat, rice and maize; sanitary and phyto-sanitary restrictions; safeguard measures to prevent dumping; a "war cell" to monitor imports of 300 sensitive items; besides a new enabling law to impose temporary QRs. Clearly, it is not confident that these will suffice to curb excessive imports of wheat, rice and maize, should the need arise.

What the Government has overlooked here is that even if all these commodities were placed on the free list, no imports would actually take place until it was commercially viable to do so. For instance, no flour miller in north India imports wheat because it is cheaper to procure locally. On the other hand, the milling industry in Tamil Nadu has been importing wheat as the landed cost is lower than transporting domestically from Punjab. Moreover, given the end-user conditions in most of these commodities, it is most unlikely that any speculative trading would take place to harm domestic farmers and bring down prices. Thus, there is no valid reason to have a special list at all which constrains free trade. Domestic supply conditions should be tackled by appropriate domestic policies aimed at improving productive efficiency.

4. CONCLUSIONS

India's import substitution and inward-looking policy regime resulted in high tariffs on many products and creation of non-tariff barriers (NTBs). Hence, reduction and rationalisation of tariffs and removal of NTBs has been an integral part of India's trade policy since 1991. India has taken major steps towards trade liberalisation since 1991, partly on its own initiative and partly from its commitments to WTO. During the WTO Second Trade Policy Review of India, the members complimented India for reduction in the tariffs (WTO, 1998). However, some members raised question about the complex structure of the tariff system, particularly high tariff rates on the import of consumer goods. The average tariff on consumer goods in 1997-98 was reduced to 25 per cent as against 153 percent in 1990-91. The 2000-2001 budget reduced the peak rate to 38.5 per cent. However, the additional special duty and countervailing duties add up and increase the tariff. Thus, simply comparing the peak rates will not give a real picture of trade restrictions. Though the peak rate is used as a guide for imposing tariff, applied tariff can be much higher but below the bound rates. India's applied rates on several items are still very high compared to the ASEAN countries. Though policymakers have mentioned on several occasions inside and outside the Parliament that India's tariff will be similar to ASEAN very soon, with the present tariff structure, it is very difficult to expect that it would happen that soon.

India has bound 68 per cent of its tariff lines compared to 6 per cent prior to the URA. All agricultural tariff lines and 62 per cent of the tariff lines of industrial goods are bound. Though at present, the applied rates are below the bound levels, producer lobby may put pressure at any time on the Government to impose tariff very close to the bound rate. If that happens, this would be equivalent to the previous 'licence raj' system.

What would be the impact of removal of QRs on Indian industries? One reason for the continuation of QRs was that the Indian producers could not compete with the best in the world. The industries that have been reaping the benefits of QRs now want the Government to provide a level playing field. There are also pressures to provide them protection through high tariff walls (Mehta, 2000). It is also contended that Indian exporters still face many obstacles which affect their export prospects, for example, reservation of items for the small scale sector, labour laws which restrict flexibility in hiring and firing, and complicated port procedures. It is time that the Government takes necessary steps in a time bound manner to remove the obstacles facing the exporters. Even when India borrows the Chinese model of SEZs, it still applies the existing labour laws to units in the SEZs. Similarly, reservation for small scale sector in sectors such as toys constrain India's export prospects. The Government must also look at trade policy issues from the interests of consumers and the economy as a whole.

India appears to be using the conventional 'domestic failure argument' against free trade. India's negotiations for upward revision of tariff bindings under Article XXVIII of GATT 1994 in respect of certain agricultural products which were bound during the previous rounds of GATT negotiations at zero or low levels of tariffs warrant attention (WTO, 1998). Upward revision on these tariff bindings for such agro products under Article XXVIII was done with a view to giving the necessary protection to domestic agriculture and agro-industry. This will affect the Indian economy in various ways as long as institutional complementarity is re-established. The existing productive inefficiency in agriculture, public sector industry and small-scale industries are the consequences of heavy protection so far given to the industrial sector. Such domestic failures should be corrected through proper domestic policy measures such as the removal of all subsidies to farmers and industries; and effective removal of internal and international restrictions on agricultural products, particularly cereals. This implies that India's trade liberalising reforms might be forced to slow down or might become counter-productive if highly regulated spheres of other markets remain untouched. It has been acknowledged that India can lift and sustain the growth rate from the low 3.5 per cent per annum to 6.5 per cent per annum through economic reforms. Based on the ratio of total trade to GNP as a proxy of to what extent the economy is involved in world economy, it can be safely asserted that India's trade has been open now compared to that of the pre-reform period, as the ratio increased from 14.1 per cent in 1980 to 20 per cent in 1999. However, when it comes to an international comparison, India still has to open her doors wider. For example, the ratio of total trade to GNP in China increased from 12.6 per cent in 1980 to 37 per cent in 1999. This only indicates that the Indian economy can move forward with further reforms and not with restrictions.

• The author is grateful to participants at the FASID Research Seminar, Professors Hayami, Otsuka and Ohno for their valuable comments and suggestions on an earlier version of this paper. Financial assistance provided by FASID is acknowledged with thanks.

APPENDIX I

Trading Houses

The criterion for recognition as a trading house or a star trading house is either on the basis of the FoB (Free on Board) value or Net Foreign Exchange (NFE) earned on physical exports and export of services during the last three licensing years or preceding licensing year, whichever is opted for by the exporter. However, for the purpose of grant of Super Star Trading House, exports at least in minimum three product groups are required to be essential. The FoB and the NFE criteria are as follows:

Category	*Average FoB value of eligible exports made during the preceding 3 licensing years (in Rupees)*	*FoB value of eligible exports made during the preceding licensing year (in Rupees)*
FoB Criteria		
Trading houses	500 million	750 million
Star trading houses	2.5 billion	3 billion
NFE Criteria Trading houses	300 million	600 million
Star trading houses	1.25 billion	1.5 billion

Source: EXIM Policy 1997-2002.

References

Centre for Monitoring the Indian Economy, (2000). *Trade*, Mumbai: CMIE July.

Hayami, Y., (1998). "Toward an East Asian Model of Economic Development" in Y. Hayami and M. Aoki (eds.) *The Institutional Foundations of East Asian Economic Development*, London: Macmillan, 3-35.

Joshi, V. and I.M.D. Little, (1996). *India's Economic Reforms: 1991-2001*, Delhi: Oxford University Press.

Mehta, R., (2000). "QR Removal and India's Import", Research and Information System for the Non-Aligned and Other Developing Countries, New Delhi, *Monograph*.

Ministry of Commerce, *Export-Import Policy Statements*, Ministry of Commerce, Government of India, New Delhi, (various years).

Ministry of Finance, *Economic Survey*, Economic Division, Ministry of Finance, Government of India, New Delhi, (various years).

————. *Budget Speech of the Finance Minister*, Ministry of Finance, Government of India, New Delhi, (various years).

————. (1991, 1992, 1993). *Tax Reforms Committee Reports, 3 Parts*, Ministry of Finance, Government of India, New Delhi.

Pursell, G., (1996). "Indian Trade Policies Since the 1991/92 Reforms", *mimeo*, World Bank.

Reserve Bank of India, (2001). *Handbook of Statistics on Indian Economy 2000*, Mumbai: RBI.

Srinivasan, T.N., (1998). "India's Economic Performance: A Comparative Analysis", paper in I.J. Ahluwalia and I.M.D. Little (eds.) *India's Economic Reforms and Development: Essays in honour of Manmohan Singh*, New Delhi: Oxford University Press.

World Trade Organisation, *Annual Reports*, WTO, Geneva, (various years).

————. (1999). *Trade Policy Review: India 1998*, WTO, Geneva.

10

Investors' Decision Behaviour and Post-Issue Performance of Firms Under Alternative Regulatory Regimes

SREEJATA BANERJEE

Introduction

The securities markets provide the mechanism of capital allocation into productive channels. Specifically, the primary market facilitates the transfer of resources from surplus spending units — the investors, to the deficit spending units — the entrepreneurs. The secondary market enables the trading of firms' ownership claims that are the outstanding securities. Enabling conditions for the existence of a securities market are existence of supply of securities with an assured maturity value or a security with life up to perpetuity, and existence of demand for such securities that permit holders to liquidate their assets due to adequate demand for the same. Enabling conditions are necessary but the sufficient conditions are: a) participants posses confidence in the issuer of the security, b) participants posses information regarding quality of the security, c) transactions possible at lowest possible cost due to the existence of free transferability of assets and assumption of contract completion. When both enabling conditions are present the market evolves and flourishes. But market fails to achieve an optimum outcome when any one of the sufficient conditions is absent. Consequently, entire market procedure is disrupted. Loss of confidence results in higher transaction costs, when participants incur additional costs of search for information to ensure completion of contracts. If transaction costs are too high, participants may withdraw and the market fails to function. Markets can function if institutional infrastructure, regulatory infrastructure and legal infrastructure are in place (Pardy, 1992). The securities markets are characterised by information imperfections causing incomplete contracts and high transaction costs. From this inherent feature stems the rationale for regulation. The securities markets are prone to information asymmetry and adverse selection that lead to market failure. The regulator has to step-in to prevent market failures. A reflection of this situation is visible in the primary market in India today.

The primary capital market in India has undergone major changes in the late nineties, when financial sector reforms were initiated. The emphasis of the regulatory policy shifted from over-regulation by the Controller of Capital Issues (CCI) to market-oriented dimension of the Securities Exchange Board of India (SEBI). However, the new policy has had a mixed response from the different players in the market. The overwhelming enthusiasm for issuing equity capital by the business sector and investing in new issues by the households observed during the nineties has declined gradually. This study examines the impact of the 'big bang' change of free-pricing of public issues that took place in India, and contrasts it with the earlier regime. We examine here the effect of change from the CCI regime to the SEBI regime on the primary capital market.

The last two decades of the twentieth century witnessed financial regulatory reforms with increasing reliance on prudential norms to promote fairness and transparency, and a larger role of the Government in macroeconomic and allocative regulation for greater stability (Vittas, 1992). A more active role for the regulator became imperative from the realisation that asymmetric information is ubiquitous in capital markets since it suffers from moral hazard, adverse selection and free rider problems. Consequently, the role of the regulator is essential, at least to ensure allocative efficiency. In the present day world, cross-border capital flows and greater integration with the global economy pose serious challenges to the regulator especially in the emerging markets. The question that needs to be examined is 'how far the regulatory authorities entrusted with the function of ensuring transparency, as well as smooth and efficient working of the system have attained their objectives'. It is reasonable that a capital market may be considered allocatively efficient, if investors are sufficiently conscious and aware of investment opportunities and reflect their confidence in the capital market by diverting their investible funds away from other avenues to the capital market.

Interest in the emerging markets has grown since the nineties as regulatory reforms and liberalisation of some developing countries permitted larger cross-border capital flows. Ross (1995) and others studied the growth of the stock market in emerging markets and their risk return ratios (potential) *vis-à-vis* those of developed countries. In order to earn higher returns many institutional investors and pension fund managers invested in emerging markets. This stimulated greater interest in these markets. What needs to be emphasised is that in spite of greater flow of capital (especially in portfolio funds) into these markets, information levels are not up to the standards of the developed economies. The questions that bother the investor in these markets are: (i) What restrictions exist on capital movement? (ii) Is the information available reliable? (iii) Do companies publish comprehensive information? (iv) Are accounting standards adequate? (v) What is the state of investor protection? (vi) Does a regulatory commission for issue and exchange of securities exist in that country?

The argument for regulation is that the regulator steps in to take corrective measures to rectify anomalies, distortions and adverse outcomes that prevail in an unregulated market. Regulators tackle most of the problems of information asymmetry by advising and implementing "disclosure norms" so that investors make informed decisions and avoid the occurrence of adverse selection. But the underlying principle beneath "disclosure norms" is that the investors are adequately equipped to comprehend the intricacies of the information available, and are able to sift, glean and weigh the alternatives before making an investment decision. But are the investors really capable of making such an informed decision? No matter how well intentioned a policy of investor protection may be, it's impact can be evaluated only in the light of the investor's potential capability to assess and judge alternative situations and exercise his choice. Secondly, given the level of information available to a prospective investor, was his expectation from the firm, based on which the decision to invest was made, matched by the firm's performance? In other words, did the investor make a relatively correct decision by investing in a firm with good return potential and avoid investing in a firm that performed poorly. Post-issue decline in operating performance of firms is an area that needs more extensive study.

Initial Public Offerings in the Primary Market

Sizeable literature exists on underpricing. Notable among them are Logue (1973), Reilly (1973), Ibbotson (1975), Ritter (1984) and Aggarwal and Rivoli (1990) all relating to the US market. These studies confirm that Initial Public Offering (IPO) are underpriced particularly in the short run. Dawson's (1987) work on Asian IPOs reveal widespread phenomenon of underpricing. But incorporating investor's perception in pricing of capital issues remains unexplored. The relevance of this literature in the Indian context is doubtful, all the more so because the Indian regulatory authorities until 1992 did not permit firms to freely price their equity capital. Secondly, the pre-issue announcement of profitability and return on investment remain largely unfulfilled. So, despite the investor protection measures adopted by the regulatory authorities, the firms fail to deliver on their promise in their post-issue performance This paper examines these two aspects empirically in the context of the Indian capital market.

The Controller of Capital Issues influenced the capital market in determining the level of premium, if any, that could be charged, in a public issue. This factor significantly contributed to underpricing of the issue. Also a highly conservative view of a firm's future profit earning potential led to issues being made at par and issues at a premium being an exception rather than a rule during the CCI era. Consequently the underpricing influenced public investors to clamour for allotment which led to over-subscription of issues. CCI used the parameters of fair value which was determined by the net asset value (NAV), the profit earning capacity value (PECV), and the market value (MV). The NAV was calculated by taking the true 'net worth' (NW) of a company after deducting all possible liabilities like contingency liability.[1]

In April 1996 and August 1997 SEBI issued guidelines for shares permitting free-pricing to those firms complying with track record of profitability and dividend payment in the previous three years. New

1. The Profit Earning Capacity Value was calculated by capitalising the average after tax profit : 15 per cent in case of manufacturing, 20 per cent in case of trading companies and 17 per cent in case of intermediate companies having more than 40 per cent trading but less than 60 per cent. The Market Value could be estimated only for listed companies. The average market price would be taken into account from the stock market quotations in the preceding three years. The fair value was based on the MV and PECV.

companies promoted by existing firms with a track record of profitability of previous five years were also allowed to freely price their initial public offer provided the participatory firm contributes not less than 50 per cent of the equity of the new firm. Firms without track record could issue equity capital at par value only. All firms issuing capital had to have their draft prospectus vetted by SEBI to ensure disclosure adequacy.

This study examines the impact of change in regulatory regime in the Indian capital market with reference to firms' public issue activity in the primary market in the two different regimes. In order to observe the investors' decision behaviour, a sample of firms listed in the Madras Stock Exchange (MSE) has been selected for analysis at the micro-level from 1987 to 1993. For the post reform regime, two sets of data are used, one from the MSE and the other from the Bombay Stock Exchange (BSE) so that both the regional and national perception is captured. To study the post-issue operating performance of firms, financial ratios, month-end price data as well as the response to public offer of equity have been used. Secondly, to observe how investors' decisions are made, data on some macroeconomic factors like wholesale price index of consumer goods, price of gold bullion, rate of interest earned on fixed deposits and return on national savings certificate have also been included.

This paper contains two sections: in the first an empirical analysis to study the factors that influence the prospective investor's decision making process is undertaken using multiple regression analysis, and in the second section post-issue operating performance of firms *vis-à-vis* the investor's expectation is examined using chi-square test for independence. These exercises are performed for two periods to examine the effect of the change in regulatory regime from the Controller of Capital Issues (CCI) to the Securities Exchange Board of India (SEBI).

Database Sample and Methodology

A sample of firms listed in the MSE has been selected for analysis at the micro-level. In order to study the post-issue operating performance of firms, financial ratios (computed from balance sheets and profit and loss account), month-end price data (from official quotations) as well as the response to public offer of equity have been collected. Secondly, to observe how investors' decisions are made, data on some macro economic factors like wholesale price index of consumer goods, price of gold bullion, rate of interest earned on fixed deposits, and return on national savings certificate have also been collected. The types of data collected for the empirical analysis were of four types: (a) issue specific data, (b) firm specific data, (c) prices of securities and (d) macroeconomic data. Public response data and issue specific data of firm allotment to promoters' group (indicating interest of original owners) as well as data on allotment to financial institutions and employees and premium, were collected from the MSE and BSE files. Basis of allotment and date of listing, were collected from company specific files maintained by the MSE and their ledgers of minutes of meetings of the Listing Committee.

The period of study covers 12 years from June 1986 to June 1998. As the focus of study is the effect of change in the regulatory regime, the time covered has been divided into two phases. The first is between June 1986 and December 1991 when CCI regulated the capital market pursuing orthodox socialist principles, the second between January 1992 and June 1998 when financial market reforms introduced SEBI as the regulatory authority with market-oriented policies.

To evaluate how investors perceived the stocks offered in the primary market, the subscription ratio (SR) is regressed on the different independent variables using multiple linear regression analysis. This is not dissimilar to a demand function analysis, where SR is the demand for the security that is related to the variables, which indicate the price and the quality of the firm and the issue. Thus we can identify the factors that most significantly influence the investors decision. It will also indicate whether there are any major changes in the investors decision behaviour in the two different regulatory regimes of CCI and SEBI. The supply side of this exercise is the number of shares offered to the public. This is not negotiable or altered once the process of public issue starts and hence it can be assumed as given or constant.

Factors Influencing the Investor's Decision

The investor's perception when he makes an investment decision is indicated by SR which is the ratio of the total number of shares applied for by the public (total public response) to the net public offer made by the firm. It represents the level of expectation an investor has at the time of making an investment decision in favour of a particular firm's stock. After closure of an issue, if it is oversubscribed, the firm concerned publishes the subscription ratio and the basis of allotment in the national dailies. A relatively high SR represents greater enthusiasm for the issue implying the superior image projected by the firm in the minds of the investing public, a low SR indicates otherwise. The first quartile values of SR 1.5 or below are those that have not been favoured by prospective investors. To study factors influencing the prospective buyer of equity shares, and what induces him to choose a particular issue against another, the following assumptions are made:-

(1) All investors are aware of the investment opportunities and have access to the same level of information,

(2) All investors are rational so that they invest only in those firms which in their opinion have substantial potential for future earnings/returns,

(3) All investors make their decisions independently,

(4) All investors want to obtain maximum number of shares allotted in their names, given their resources and investment horizons.

A prospective investor could have three broad sets of data available to him:

(a) Those relevant to the issue which were made available by the firm at the time of entering the market — the issue details,

(b) Those relevant to the firms' capital structure, future projections and past performances, again also made available by the firm through annual reports, prospectus, press releases, etc., — the firms specific details,

(c) Those relevant to the macro-economic factors like inflation rate, price of gold bullion, fiscal incentives implicit in government policy etc., which are available to the prospective investor in newspapers and media publications.

In arriving at a decision on investing in a particular firm's equity, an investor would like to take into account the firm's future profit-earning capacity based on it's scale of operations, age, type of industry, etc., factors which reflect the firm's basic characteristics, and the issue price which incorporates the size of the premium charged that reflects a firm's anticipated future returns, and the size of the firm allotment to promoter's group in the public issue (larger promoter's stake is used as a signalling device by original owners of the firms to demonstrate their interest in the concern). Moreover, he would be interested to know if the issue is an IPO or a seasoned offering and already listed in a stock exchange. Perhaps a more dominant factor which influences the demand for a security is its issue price. A public issue made with premium in the CCI era was an exception which indicated a fundamentally strong company, as only profit-making companies were permitted to make premium offers. The following variables are taken into consideration:

IPBV is ratio of issue price to the post-issue book value per share. PS is promoter's stake, firm allotment to promoter's group.[2] Higher stakes by promoters signal the new shareholders about the promoter's confidence in the project's future profitability. BSENX month-end Bombay Stock Exchange Sensitivity Index (BSE SENSEX) corresponding to the month prior to the month of issue to take into account the market sentiment. NW networth[3] is included as a measure of firm size, CPS– is a (binary) dummy variable taking value 0 for firms whose commercial production had not started at the time of the issue and 1 for others. Firms whose production processes were not in full steam involved a higher level of risk and these firms could suffer from cost escalation or other disruptions. AGE is computed from the year of incorporation to the year of public issue. SEL is a dummy variable taking value 0 for listed companies and 1 for new listings. JVPV indicates whether the firm is in the private sector or in the joint sector with government participation, taking values 0 for joint sector and 1 otherwise. IFD — Interest on bank fixed deposits fixed for 36 months to account for the opportunity cost of investing in an equity share.

Of the nine explanatory variables excepting BSENX and IFD others are firm-specific. BSENX is a barometer of the stock market behaviour and IFD is viewed as the opportunity cost of investing

2. PS is ratio of firm allotment to promoter's group to the total public offer.
3. Networth is paid up capital plus reserves and surplus in Rs. crores at 1986-87 prices.

funds in equity. In the preliminary exercise it was found that a regression equation with BSENX as an explanatory variable along with the seven other variables provided a better fit (in terms of adjusted values of coefficients of determination) than with IFD (or price of gold bullion or wholesale price index). Hence, only the results for the equation which contains BSENX are reported.

Estimates of the multiple linear regression coefficients along with the 't' values and R^2 corrected for degrees of freedom for the first period are given in Table 10.1. During the CCI regulatory regime the coefficients of the explanatory variables IPBV, PS, BSENX and CPS have the right signs and are statistically significant at the 5 per cent level. The sign of the coefficient of IPBV is positive, because the issue price as fixed by the CCI used to be well below the share's market value, hence a higher value for the variable was perceived as a measure of better quality. Considering the kind of restriction on pricing that prevailed during the CCI regime, the positive sign of the IPBV is not surprising. A firm permitted to charge a premium on its public issue was perceived as a firm with superior quality. Extending this logic further an issue with a higher premium was considered by the market as an opportunity for obtaining larger returns on underpricing.

Table 10.1

Determinants of Subscription Ratio 1986-91

Variable	*Regressiòn Coefficient*	*'t' Statistic*
IPBV	6.55791	3.854**
PS	12.59651	1.922**
BSENX	.011146	2.511**
NW	–.043883	–1.220
SEL	.382655	0.107
AGE	–.230425	–1.246
JVPV	–.217982	–0.055
CPS	9.166623	2.466**
(Constant)	–10.697361	–1.365

** Significant at 5 per cent level. F = 4.0198**

For comparison of the SEBI regime (period 1992-98) with the old regime (1986-91) a similar equation for the new regime was estimated (Table 10.2). The sign of the coefficient of IPBV has become negative because in a free market regime, other things being equal, higher price results in lower demand. However, the coefficient is not significantly different from zero at 5 per cent level. The regression coefficients of PS and NW are positive and significantly different from zero. This is not surprising as removal of restrictions on the expansion and size of operations in the liberalised economic regime would be indicative.

Table 10.2

Determinants of Subscription Ratio 1992-98

Variable	*Regression Coefficient*	*'t' Statistic*
IPBV	−1.27792	−.499
PS	7.800235	3.196**
BSENX	.007209	1.895**
NW	.064072	2.205**
SEL	3.877398	1.007
AGE	−.053472	−.529
JVPV	6.778219	1.380
CPS	−1.391766	−.397
(Constant)	−23.966733	−1.927

** Significant at 5 per cent level. F = 2.4259**

For comparing the old regime with the new, it is necessary to retain the same set of variables in both equations and they were re-estimated after dropping the variables whose coefficients were not significant. The results are reported in Tables 10.3 and 10.4.

In the re-estimated equations where only five variables are included, it is found that the coefficients of all the included variables are significantly different from zero at 5 per cent level in the CCI regime (Table 10.3). The issue price variable continues to be positive. The coefficient of the variable 'net worth' takes negative sign indicating the investor preference for smaller firms since industrial policy offered special benefits to smaller units at that time. In the later period, with liberalised regulatory policies the coefficient of issue price is not significant (Table 10.4), whereas the coefficient of promoter's stake and net worth are significant at 5 per cent level in the SEBI regime. The coefficients of the other variables CPS and BSENX are however not significant.

Table 10.3

Some Key Determinants of Subscription Ratio (1986-91)

Variable	*Regression Coefficient*	*'t' Statistic*
IPBV	6.78609	4.032**
PS	14.340188	2.251**
BSENX	.010239	2.374**
NW	-.066715	-2.103**
CPS	8.096619	2.437**
(Constant)	-13.375409	-2.229**

** Significant at 5 per cent level. F = 6.75904 **

Table 10.4

Some Key Determinants of Subscription Ratio (1992-98)

Variable	*Regression Coefficient*	*'t' Statistic*
IPBV	-0.64770	-.256
PS	6.233812	2.712**
BSENX	.006116	1.632
NW	.052016	1.829**
CPS	-3.736410	-1.179
(Constant)	-10.459721	-.975

** Significant at 5 per cent level. F = 3.25564**

We observe that the liberalised policies have influenced the investors' decision making behaviour. In the earlier regime, where free-pricing was not permitted, the investors took the issue price as an important deciding factor indicating the quality of the issue. Hence, a higher price induced greater demand for a particular issue (as is indicative from the positive sign of the coefficient of the issue price). On the contrary, in the later phase when market-oriented issue pricing was introduced, the issue price was no longer a significant factor affecting the investors' decision. However, in both the regimes we find the promoters' stake signalling owners continued interest in the company, as an important influencing factor. This result is consistent with the signalling hypothesis as proposed by Leland and Pyle (1977). We observe that only the regression coefficient of PS and NW are significant in the SEBI phase (Table 10.4).

To observe if the trends in the investor's behaviour is similar across the country, the same exercise was carried out for firms entering the market in the same period but listed in the Bombay Stock Exchange. The regression coefficients of the variables PS, BSENX and NW continue to be significantly different from zero (Table 10.5). The coefficient for IPBV, the price component of the issue, is negative but not significant in this case as seen in the data from MSE. The CPS is however positive but not significant. This result indicates that the investors are influenced by very similar factors irrespective of whether they are investing at a regional stock exchange or a national one. They do not consider the price as an indicator of the issue quality as it was in the earlier regime. The interest of promoters' in the firm is an important signal to the prospective investor about the firm's future earning capability. Interestingly, the BSENX is significant and investors across the country are influenced by the market sentiment of the BSE unlike those in the Southern region.

Banerjee and Narasimhan (1999) had undertaken similar exercise with BSE data for the period 1992-95. Multiple regression analysis and three-group multiple discriminant model were used. The study was based on 144 initial public offerings issued between 1st April, 1992 through 31st March, 1995. The explanatory variables include Debt-Equity Ratio DER, Bombay Stock Exchange Sensitivity Index BSENX, Price Earnings Ratio P/E, Promoters' Contribution PROMCON, Project Cost PROJCOST, Issue Size ISUZ, and Lead Manager LDMNGR. In the multiple linear regression analysis, SR is regressed on the different independent variables DER, BSENX, P/E, PROMCON, PROJCOST, ISUZ, and LDMNGR.

Table 10.5

Some Key Determinants of Subscription Ratio for BSE (1992-98)

Variable	*Regression Coefficient*	*'t' Statistic*
IPBV	–0.2701	–0.0876
PS	0.67004	2.1893**
BSENX	0.08206	4.1216**
NW	0.65014	1.8733**
CPS	0.24996	0.4275
(Constant)	4.0029.	0.17634

In the first equation (Appendix 1), where all the seven variables have been entered, it is observed that the coefficient of the P/E variable is negative and the coefficient is significant. This is consistent with the inverse relationship between the price and public response and hence higher prices do not evince favourable response from potential investors. The regression coefficient of ISUZ is positive. This implies that investors prefer large issues to small ones as they probably perceive larger firms to have superior performance potential and wider institutional interest in the secondary market trading. The coefficient of BSENX is also positive and significantly different from zero. These two variables, i.e., issue size and BSE sensitivity index that reflects the secondary market sentiment are positive indicating their direct relation to investors' decisions. The coefficients of the other variables PROJCOST, PROMCON, DER and LDMNGR are all not significantly different from zero.

In the second equation (Appendix 2) stepwise method for entering variables are used, it is observed that the BSENX, the P/E and ISUZ are the only variables included in the equation. The coefficients of all these variables are significantly different from zero at 1 per cent. This result is indicative of the previous exercise done with the data from the regional stock exchange at Madras. It follows therefore that the principal factors influencing the investor's decisions in a public issue are the market sentiment, the price of the issue, its size and the P/E ratio. The degree of leverage, the promoter's contribution and the cost of the project as well as the lead manager's reputation do not have a bearing on the investor's perception of a public issue. In the next section the post-issue operating performance is analysed to study whether the investor's expectation about their investment decision is realised in their holding period return.

Post-issue Performance of Firms and Investor's Perception

Post-issue operating performance analysis of initial public offerings (IPO) that have been undertaken typically focus on post-issue price performance, the exception being Degeorge and Zeckhauser (1993) who examined the operating performance of reverse leveraged buy-outs, (which are special type of IPOs) using financial ratios. Jain and Kini (1994) used M/B (market value to book value) ratio, P/E (price to earnings) ratio and EPS (earnings per share) to measure post-issue operating performance of IPO firms. Their findings suggest that the potential investors initially have high expectations of future earnings growth, that are not subsequently fulfilled. They cite Ritter (1991) and Loughran and Ritter (1995) who have documented long-run investment performance of IPOs. These studies indicate that the decline in operating performance is not anticipated, and investors are constantly surprised by the poor performance of IPOs.

Evidence of positive relation between managerial ownership and post-issue performance have been documented by Jensen and Meckling (1976) in their agency cost hypothesis. The agency hypothesis indicates that higher ownership retention by managers reduces the incentives to undertake non-value maximising projects. Leland and Pyle (1977) proposed their signalling hypothesis. The signalling hypothesis suggests that by retaining a significant ownership stake in the firms, entrepreneurs signal project quality, since false representations can be costly. Not surprisingly, this phenomenon was exhibited in the previous section. Investors were influenced by the stake held by promoters in the public issues and this influence persisted in both the regulatory regimes.

Jain and Kini (1994) investigated the changes in operating performance of firms that made public issues, transforming themselves from privately held to public limited companies, through median values of cash flow and sales data as well as total assets growth. They observed IPO firms over a period of five years after the public issue taking a sample of 682 firms that made public offerings between

1976 and 1988 in USA. Their findings indicate decline in operating performance with a caveat that sales and capital expenditure grow rapidly. Since we are examining the changes that may have occurred in the primary market as a result of the change in the regulatory regime, and its impact on the behaviour of the market participants, we look at the post-issue operating performance of firms that entered the primary capital market in the two regulatory phases.

Greater market-oriented regulatory policies are also necessarily more transparent implying lower levels of information asymmetry. In this study firms' operating performances are observed over a period of two and three years after they have made public issues, this is done for both the regimes separately. The firms have not been segregated into IPOs and seasoned offerings. Contrary to the conventional approach of using stock prices to measure the performance, financial ratios have been used here. In an efficient market where all prices reflect the information available at that point of time, prices can really indicate an equity's intrinsic values. But studies on the Indian capital market reveal that the markets are inefficient both in the weak and semi-strong forms (Ranganathan and Subramanian 1993a, 1993b, Subramanian 1993), hence alternative method of evaluating a company's stock is used here. Security analysts or followers of the fundamental school evaluate actual performance of firms to estimate the intrinsic value of a security. A firm's performance is assessed on the basis of ratios calculated from balance sheet and profit and loss account instead of stock prices only. However, in order to incorporate the price component, accounting ratios which use price have also been included, *viz.* market value to book value and price earnings ratio. The ratios used in this analysis are also those that are currently mandated to be disclosed by firms in guidelines issued by the SEBI. To study how firms have performed, after issuing equity capital to the public, the following four performance indicators are used:

(a) Earnings per share (EPS),

(b) Market value to Book value ratio (MV/BV),

(c) Price earnings ratio (P/E),

(d) Total sales to total assets ratio.

These ratios have been calculated from the companies' annual audited results at an interval of two years and three years subsequent to a public issue. Changes in these ratios can show whether there has been positive growth in the firms' performance or not.

In order to ascertain if a high degree of asymmetric information persists in the Indian primary market, tests are undertaken for linear association between variables representing the two market participants, *viz.* the investors and the firms. To observe the changes between the two different regimes, the same exercise is done for both the time periods under study. In the event of a high level of information asymmetry investors would make adverse selection, applying for equity shares of firms which do not have good future growth and return potential. Promoters on the other hand, having access to information of the true potential of the firm may project a superior image of the firm withholding negative information, thus misleading the prospective investor at the time of the public issue. Subsequently, after, say, two or three years, the investor realises the true potential of the firm in which he has invested, and the investor's expectations are belied. On the other hand, there may be public offers which were not very enthusiastically received by the public investor (who were inadequately informed) but in the medium-term such a firm may turn out to be a virtual gold mine. These are the visible features of asymmetric information in the market.

Earnings Per Share: If investors' expectations correspond with the firm's performance indicated by the EPS[4] then there should exist some linear association between the two ratios EPS and SR. The EPS for the firms are calculated for two time periods. EPS1, EPS2, DIFEPS and GEPS are the different measures used.[5]

The last column in Tables 10.6 and 10.7 provide simple correlation coefficients between SR and each of the performance ratios. These values are very low and we cannot reject the hypothesis of zero correlation between SR and the performance ratios of EPS. These results indicate high level of information asymmetry persisting in the Indian primary market both before and after SEBI emerged.

---

4. Earnings per share is computed by dividing the net operating profits (which is net profit after tax NPAT) by the total number of equity shares outstanding.

5. EPS1=(Net operating profits for year t+2) / total number of equity shares issued, EPS2=(Net operating profits for year t+3) / total number of equity shares issued. EPS2 - EPS1 = DIFEPS, GEPS = [(EPS2 - EPS1/EPS1)]100.

Table 10.6

Correlation of Performance Ratios and Investor Preferences for 1986-91*

	EPS1	*EPS2*	*DIFEPS*	*GEPS*	*SR*
EPS1	1.000	0.7934**	0.3491**	–0.0315	0.0286
EPS2	—	1.000	0.8474**	0.0145	–0.0202
DIFEPS	—	—	1.000	0.0498	–0.0561
GEPS	—	—	—	1.000	0.0757
SR	—	—	—	—	1.000

*: N=80

**: Significant at 5 per cent level.

Table 10.7

Correlation of Performance Ratios and Investor Preferences for 1992-93

	EPS1	*EPS2*	*DIFEPS*	*GEPS*	*SR*
EPS1	1.000	.6194**	–.3021	–.0752	–.0708
EPS2	—	1.000	.5613**	–.2111	–.0518
DIFEPS	—	—	1.000	–.1771	.0128
GEPS	—	—	—	1.000	.0138
SR	—	—	—	—	1.000

*: N=55

**: Significant at 5 per cent level

For the purpose of examining the extent of asymmetric information the chi-square test for linear association was used. An alternative method to Pearson's chi-square is the likelihood ratio chi-square which is based on the maximum likelihood theory and this is often used in analysis of categorical data. To test the null hypothesis that there is no linear association between SR and the performance measures against the alternative hypothesis that there is, first we crosstabulate SR with each of the performance measures, and then compute Pearson's chi-square value and the likelihood ratio.

Cross-tabulation exercise using different class intervals were carried out for all the EPS ratios (EPS1, EPS2, DIFEPS and GEPS) and the chi-square values are consistently not significant. However, the chi-square value was significant for the SEBI regime only for the GEPS which is the percentage change of the EPS values (Table 10.9) indicating that firms reported better performance in the SEBI regime. Greater market orientation of financial sector reforms should bring down levels of information distortions so investors make informed decisions. Hence, investors' expectations may be realised in terms of the returns by investing in the capital market, notwithstanding the risk that is endemic to the capital market.

Table 10.8

Investor Perception Ratio SR Related with GEPS for 1986-91

SR/GEPS	*< 0*	*0 to 50*	*50 to 100*	*100 <*	*Total*
< 1.5	11	6	1	7	25 (31.3)
1.5 to 5	11	1	4	1	17 (22.4)
5 to 10	6	2	1	2	11 (14.5)
10 <	13	3	2	5	23 (30.3)
Total	**41 (53.9)**	**12 (15.8)**	**8 (10.5)**	**15 (19.7)**	**76(100.0)**

Pearson Chi Square Value = 9.5415 DF = 9 Likelihood Ratio = 9.8840 DF = 9.

Table 10.9

Investor Perception Ratio SR Related with GEPS for 1992-93

SR/GEPS	< -500	- 500 to 0	0 to 50	50 to 100	100 <	Total
< 1.5	0	6	2	2	2	12 (21.8)
1.5 to 3	0	6	5	0	3	14 (25.5)
3 to 5	1	1	2	0	0	4 (7.3)
5 <	0	9	3	3	8	25 (45.5)
Total	**1 (1.9)**	**22 (41.5)**	**12 (22.6)**	**5 (9.4)**	**13 (24.5)**	**55 (100.0)**

Pearson Chi-square Value = 21.2681** DF = 12 Likelihood Ratio = 16.3529** DF = 12
** Significant at 5 per cent level.

Market Value to Book Value Ratio: While EPS ratio includes factors directly relevant to a firm's profit earning capacity, the market value to book value ratio incorporates the firm's market price or market value (MV) as well as its net worth in evaluating it's latent potential. So both the market's view of the stock and its intrinsic strength and potential for returns is incorporated. The MVBV1 and MVBV2[6] are the relevant ratios in the second year (t+2) and the third year (t+3) after the public issue. DIFMVBV = MVBV2 – MVBV1. SR is correlated with both MVBV1 and MVBV2 in the CCI regime and only correlated with MVBV2 and DIFMVBV in the SEBI period (Tables 10.10 and 10.11). Data from both regimes were similarly crosstabulated with SR and the different valuation ratios MV1, MV2, MVBV1, MVBV2, DIFMVBV. While the ratio MVBV1 was significant for the CCI regime it was not so in the later phase. On the contrary the MVBV2 is significant in the later phase (Table 10.15). A possible explanation of this could be that the change in the regulatory regime from CCI to SEBI could have been beneficial so that firms which issued capital in the later phase have actually improved their performance.

Table 10.10

Correlation Coefficients of MVBV Ratios and SR for 1986-91

	SR	*MV1*	*MV2*	*MVBV1*	*MVBV2*	*DIFMVBV*
SR	1.0000	.3763**	.2680	.4141**	.2776**	.1060
MV1		1.0000	.5447**	.6406**	.4533**	–.0829
MV2			1.0000	.4305**	.6333**	.3350
MVBV1				1.0000	.6502**	–.0404
MVBV2					1.0000	.5740**
DIFMVBV						1.0000

No. of observations = 72

** Significant at 5 per cent level.

6. MV1 and MV2 are mean closing price for 24th, 25th and 26th month and 35th, 36th and 37th month after the public issue. MVBV1 and MVBV2 are the ratios of the mean market price to the book value. BV is the total paid up capital + specific reserves excluding revaluation reserves and have been computed from annual audited financial reports two and three years after public issue.

Table 10.11

Correlation Coefficients of MVBV Ratios and SR for 1992-93

	SR	*MV1*	*MV2*	*MVBV1*	*MVBV2*	*DIFMVBV*
SR	1.0000	–.1077	.0552	.0926	.3398**	.3335**
MV1		1.0000	.7465**	.5598**	.2205	–.4728**
MV2			1.0000	.3908**	.4753**	–.1080
MVBV1				1.0000	.5720**	–.6527
MVBV2					1.0000	–.0252
DIFMVBV						1.0000

No. of observations = 56

** Significant at 5 per cent.

Table 10.12

Investor Perception SR Related with MVBV1 for 1986-91

SR/MVBV1	*< 0.5*	*0.5 to 2.5*	*2.5 to 5*	*5 to 10*	*10 <*	*Total*
< 2	1	16	7	2	0	26 (36.1)
2 to 5	0	8	6	2	0	16 (22.2)
5 to 10	1	3	1	1	1	7(9.7)
10 to 20	0	1	8	3	0	12 (16.7)
20 <	0	1	7	2	1	11 (15.3)
Total	**2 (2.8)**	**29(40.3)**	**29 (40.3)**	**10 (13.9)**	**2 (2.8)**	**72 (100.0)**

PearsonChi Square Values = 27.8198 ** DF = 16 Likelihood Ratio = 28.6114** DF = 16

** Significant at 5 per cent.

Table 10.13

Investor Perception SR Related with MVBV2 for 1986-91

SR/MVBV2	< 0.5	0.5 to 2.5	2.5 to 5	5 to 10	>10	Total
< 2	2	13	9	0	2	26 (36.1)
2 to 5	0	5	8	2	1	16 (22.2)
5 to 10	1	3	0	1	2	7 (9.7)
10 to 20	0	3	4	3	2	12 (16.7)
>20	0	3	4	3	1	11 (15.3)
Total	**3 (4.2)**	**27 (37.5)**	**25 (34.7)**	**9 (12.5)**	**8 (11.1)**	**72 (100.0)**

Pearson chi Square Value = 19.3491 DF = 16

Likelihood Ratio = 24.3363 DF = 16

Table 10.14

Investor Perception SR Related with MVBV1 for 1992-93

SR/MVBV1	*< 1*	*1 to 3*	*3 to 5*	*>5*	*Total*
< 2	1	11	3	2	17 (30.4)
2 to 5	3	7	2	2	14 (25.0)
5 to 10	1	6	0	3	10 (17.9
10 to 20	1	7	2	0	10 (17.9)
>20	0	2	1	2	5 (8.9)
Total	**6 (10.7)**	**33 (58.9)**	**8 (14.3)**	**9 (16.1)**	**56 (100.0)**

Pearson chi Square Values = 9.9408 DF = 12

Likelihood Ratio = 12.4779 DF = 12

Table 10.15

Investor Perception SR Related with MVBV2 for 1992-93

SR / MVBV2	*< 1*	*1 to 3*	*3 to 5*	*>5*	*Total*
< 2	9	7	0	1	17 (30.4)
2 to 5	9	4	0	1	14 (25.0)
5 to 10	4	3	2	1	10 (17.9
10 to 20	1	8	1	0	10 (17.9)
>20	0	3	1	1	5 (8.9)
Total	**23 (41.1)**	**25 (44.6)**	**4 (7.1)**	**4 (7.1)**	**56 (100.0)**

Pearson chi Square Values = 19.0511** DF = 12 Likelihood Ratio = 22.8121** DF = 12

** Significant at 5 per cent level.

Price Earnings Ratio: It is the ratio[7] of the market price per share to the earnings per share. It has been calculated after a period of two and three years following the public issue.[8] The relevant

7. The price-earnings ratio is a summary measure which primarily reflects a company's growth prospects, risk characteristics, shareholder orientation, corporate image and degree of liquidity.
8. PE1, PE2, DIFPE (absolute difference between PE1 and PE2) and GPE percentage change of PE1 and PE2 in relation to PE1 are computed from the mean month-end closing share price, and the earnings per share calculated from the balance sheets and profit and loss account statements.

variables of P/E ratio is crosstabulated with the investor's perception indicator SR to test for linear association. The mean P/E ratio for t+3 is found to be negative in both regimes but lower in the SEBI phase three years after a public issue, going by the correlation coefficients between SR and the other variables. However, the crosstabulation exercise to examine the presence of any linear association shows that the null hypothesis may not be rejected since all of the chi-square test values statistic are not significant at 5 per cent level except for the crosstabs of SR with PE2 for 1992-93 (Table 10.19). Repeated crosstabs with different class intervals did not give consistent results

Table 10.16

Correlation Matrix of P/E ratios and SR for 1986-91

	SR	*PE1*	*PE2*	*DIFPE*	*GPE*
SR	1.0000	.0134	–.0375	–.0249	.0417
PE1		1.0000	.0004	–.9451**	–.0107
PE2			1.0000	.3264**	–.0439
DIFPE				1.0000	–.0042
GPE					1.0000

No. of observations = 75

** Significant at 5 per cent level.

Table 10.17

Correlation Matrix of P/E ratios and SR for 1992-93

	SR	*PE1*	*PE2*	*DIFPE*	*GPE*
SR	1.0000	–.2424	–.1098	–.1193	–.0325
PE1		1.0000	.2343	–.1497	.2331
PE2			1.0000	.1888	–.1086
DIFPE				1.0000	.0439
GPE					1.0000

No. of observations = 56

Table 10.18

Association between SR and PE2 for 1986-91

SR/PE2	< - 50	- 50 to 0	0 to 10	10 to 20	>20	Total
< 2.5	3	10	6	2	8	29 (38.7)
2.5 to 5	0	1	4	3	6	14 (18.7)
5 to 7.5	0	0	1	2	2	5 (6.7)
7.5 to 10	0	0	2	0	1	3 (4.0)
10 to 20	0	2	2	5	3	12 (16.0)
>20	0	5	2	2	3	12 (16.0)
Total	**3 (4.0)**	**18 (24.0)**	**17 (22.7)**	**14 (18.7)**	**23 (30.7)**	**75 (100.0)**

Pearson chi-square Value = 23.3015 DF = 20 Likelihood Ratio = 25.5157 DF = 20

Table 10.19

Association between SR and PE2 for 1992-93

SR /PE2	< 0	0 to 5	5 to 10	>10	Total
< 1.5	0	6	2	5	13 (23.2)
1.5 to 3	1	8	4	1	14 (25.0)
3 to 5	1	0	2	1	4 (7.1)
>5	10	1	6	8	25 (44.6)
Total	**12 (21.4)**	**15 (26.8)**	**14 (25.0)**	**15 (26.8)**	**56 (100.0)**

Pearson chi-square Value = 25.2202**DF = 9 Likelihood Ratio = 30.5346** DF = 9

** Significant at 5 per cent level.

Sales Turnover and Total Assets Ratio: To measure growth of firm's cash flow revenue, the annual sales turnover for the financial year two and three years after public issue have been used. To examine the post-issue operating performance of firms, Jain and Kini (1994) studied the growth in sales to asset turnover. They documented percentage change of the ratio relative to the firm's sales turnover in year t+1, year t+2 and year t+3 after the year of the IPO as 37.22, 69.92 and 108.09 per cent respectively. Their findings show positive growth in sales to asset turnover.[9]

The crosstabulations and chi-square values computed revealed that for 23.2 per cent of the firms in the CCI regime the difference

9. ST2 and ST3 are sales turnover of year t+2 and t+3 respectively.

between their sales turnover to total assets (DIFSTA) is negative and this percentage rose to 44.9 per cent in the later phase. However, none of the chi-square values are significant at 5 per cent level. Thus, we do not reject the null hypothesis of independence between the investor perception SR and the firms' performance indicators. Contrary to the findings of Jain and Kini (1994) regarding the positive growth of sales to asset ratio there appears to be no positive growth in the sales to asset ratio in this study.

The empirical exercise undertaken above to examine whether the investors' expectations were fulfilled by the performance of firms indicate that there was no linear association between SR and the EPS, P/E, MV/BV and the ST/TA ratio which represent firm's operating performance. In both the regimes, post-issue performance of firms continue to decline albeit the percentage of firms showing poor performance have come down in the SEBI regime. It may not be amiss to say that high levels of information asymmetry continue to persist causing potential investor to make adverse selection. Notable among the findings is the linear association between SR and MVBV ratio for the year t+3 in the SEBI phase, this is an indication of some positive impact of the new liberal regulatory policies of the SEBI.

An alternative method to examine the performance of firms as against the projections or promises made in their offer document was also undertaken. Data of firms which made public offerings between October 1992 and March 1993 were collected to examine to what extent the firms achieved the targeted net profit projected in their prospectus. The actual performance of these firms in terms of their profit earnings were recorded in 1994-95 and again in 1996-97. Tables 10.20 and 10.21 show how many firms were able to reach the promised level of net profit. The actual achievement as a percentage of the projected level was used. Four broad classifications were made:

i) those which could achieve less than 50 per cent of the target,

ii) those which attained more that 50 per cent but less than 95 per cent,

iii) firms that could earn between 96 per cent and 105 per cent of the target and

iv) those which managed to overshoot the projected level and perform better than their own projections.

Table 10.20

Actual Net Profit as Percentage of Projection in 1994-1995

	Actual < 50% of Proj.	*50% < Actual < 95% of Proj.*	*95% < Actual < 105% of Proj.*	*106% <Actual of Proj.*	*Total*
Oct. 92 – Nov. 92	11	4	2	8	25
Dec. 92 – Jan. 93	9	13	3	10	35
Feb. 93 – Mar. 93	21	11	3	6	41
Total	**41 (40.59)**	**28 (27.72)**	**8 (7.92)**	**24 (23.76)**	**101 (100)**

Figures in brackets are percentage of total. More than 95 per cent of the projected level of profit is treated as 'achieving the projected level'.

Table 10.21

Actual Net Profit as Percentage of Projection 1996-1997

	Actual < 50% of Proj.	*50% < Actual < 95% of Proj.*	*95% < Actual < 105% of Proj*	*106% <Actual of Proj.*	*Total*
Oct.92 – Nov 92	3	5	2	15	25
Dec. 92 – Jan 93	5	18	1	11	35
Feb. 93 – Mar 93	12	11	5	13	41
Total	**20 (19.80)**	**34 (33.66)**	**8 (7.92)**	**39 (38.61)**	**101 (100)**

Figures in brackets are percentage of total.

In 1994-95 two years after the public issue, 68.31 per cent of the firms were not able to achieve their projected level of net profit out of which 40.59 per cent could not even manage to attain 50 per cent of the target. Even in 1996-97, which is three years after the issue, 53.46 per cent of the firms failed to earn the projected level of net profit but the percentage of firms which were able to achieve beyond their own projections actually rose from 23.76 per cent to 38.61 per cent. On the average it appears that almost half of the firms which entered the capital market, at this time to raise funds, were not able to meet their projected earnings thereby disappointing their shareholders. The redeeming feature, however is that a fair number of firms were also able to overshoot their projected levels. While 23.76 per cent of firms earned profits higher than their targets two years after the issue, 38.61 per cent of them did so three years after the issue. This investigation into projections made by companies in their public offers and the subsequent performances do not show any systematic pattern. Under performance is matched by performance superior to projections. Nevertheless from an investor's point of view if more than 50 per cent of the companies are not able to attain their targeted levels of profit it can dissuade potential investors from investing in equity due to the possibility of adverse selection caused by the existence of asymmetric information.

Jain and Kini (1994) concluded that "it is difficult to pinpoint the exact reason for the inferior operating performance of IPO firms". It is their view that several possibilities are there. "One explanation is related to the potential for increased agency costs when a firm makes the transition from private to public ownership." This is similar to the agency problem described by Jensen and Meckling (1976) where as a result of conflict of interest between initial owners and shareholders the performance of the firms could suffer. "A second reason could be managers attempt to window-dress their accounting numbers prior to going public." This is a chronic problem in the Indian primary capital market due to the lack of uniformity in accounting principles pursued in the country. "A third explanation for the decline in operating performance is that entrepreneurs time their issues to coincide with the period of unusually good performance which they know cannot be sustained in the future. The common thread running through these three explanations for the post issue decline in operating performance is the presence of information asymmetry and/or conflict of interest between original owners and the new shareholders." If this be true it must be noted that Jain and Kini's work is based on firms operating in USA where levels of transparency are immensely high and regulators of the capital market are upright stalwarts. It gives little solace to the Indian regulatory authority SEBI that despite SEC's wide ranging powers and experience, such high levels of information distortions persist in USA.

This paper examined the factors that influence a prospective investor and the post-issue operating performance of firms. The exercise was done for a period before 1991, when repressive regulatory policies were in force, and afterwards when the liberalised regime came and when SEBI was given statutory powers. Altogether nine explanatory variables were included initially with the subscription ratio (indicating the investor's demand) as the endogenous variable, but later those variables whose coefficients were not significantly different from zero were excluded. In the multiple regression equation for the older regime, the regression coefficients for the issue price, the promoters' stake and the Bombay Stock Exchange Sensitivity Index are significantly different from zero at 5 per cent level of significance. On the other hand for the regression equation of the later regime the regression coefficients of promoter's stake, the BSENX and the net worth are significantly different from zero at 5 per cent level of significance, implying that investors were influenced by the promoters' signal indicating their interest in the project related to the public issue. This result corroborates with the signalling hypothesis (Leland and Pyle 1977). As for the post-issue operating performance of firms, it is found that prospective investors continue to make adverse selection regarding their investment decisions.

The SEBI initiated changes in pricing policy to bring down mis-pricing and under pricing that drove the firms away from the primary market by introducing book-building process. In this method public offer is made through invitation for subscription essentially through a tender process. Eligible investors (usually the institutional buyers) place bids and declare the number of shares they are willing to invest, with the lead manager who acts as the book builder. Prior to the issue, in consultation with the merchant banker, the issuing firm decides the floor price of the issue. This novel method devised by the regulatory authority has also not been too enthusiastically embraced by investors since the quantum and quality of information available to buyers remain poor.

Conclusion

The investment climate in the new millennium is a reflection of the preceding turbulent decade on which the present study was made. The brief period of revival of the primary market witnessed during the technology stock boom in 1997-98 evaporated in the beginning of the millennium due to the overpriced software firms and global meltdown. Valuation of firms at the time of issue and the quality of information that is crucial for making informed decision continue to elude the members of the investing public. The question of participants possessing confidence in the issuer of the security, and having information regarding quality of the security remain in great doubt as we see the Enron, Worldcom and the Anderson debacle unfolding in the developed markets of the US. The Indian capital market particularly the primary market became moribund after the new issues began to be devolved on the lead managers underwriters in 1996. Barring the renewed interest in information technology during the late-nineties the role of the primary capital market has declined. More and more firms needing capital are shying away from the market towards private placements, as the investors fear to tread the market. To renew confidence in the capital market so that it is able to perform its allocative function, the enabling conditions for the existence of the market needs to be ensured. Market sentiments reflected by the BSE sensex is another indicator of the fall in confidence of the participants in the capital market. New powers to the SEBI for streamlining the primary market could attract more funds and the resources in the economy could be allocated in a more efficient manner.

• The author is grateful to participants at the FASID Research Seminar, Professors Hayami, Otsuka and Ohno for their valuable comments and suggestions on an earlier version of this paper. Financial assistance provided by FASID is acknowledged with thanks.

Appendix 1

Regression Coefficient of Variables Influencing Investor Decisions

Variables	*B*	*'t' statistics*
LDMNGR	−0.191483	−0.427
PROMCON	0.030138	0.450
BSENX	0.006623	3.746**
P/E	−1.850495	−4.172**
DER	0.574164	0.191
ISUZ	0.560054	2.912**
PROJCOST	−0.024996	−0.745
(Constant)	−10.234432	−1.321

** Significant at 1 per cent level F = 6.04515**

Appendix 2

Regression Coefficient of Variables Influencing Investor Decisions (Stepwise)

Variables	*B*	*'t' statistics*
BSENX	0.006724	3.905**
P/E	−1.751034	−4.116**
ISUZ	0.457738	3.306**
(Constant)	−10.108378	−1.528

** Significant at 1 per cent level F = 14.0029**

References

Aggarwal, Reena and Pietra Rivoli, (1990). "Fads in the Initial Public Offering Market?", *Financial Management*, Vol. 19, No. 4, 45-57.

Banerjee, Sreejata and Narasimhan M.S., (1999). "Pricing of Initial Public Offerings: A Multivariate Model for IPO Issuers to Reduce Underpricing Without Risking Under-subscription", *Working Paper No. 7* of IFMR.

Dawson, Steven M., (1987). "Secondary Stock Market Performance of Initial Public Offers in Hong Kong, Singapore and Malaysia: 1978-1984", *Journal of Business Finance and Accounting*, Vol. 14, No. 1 65-76.

Degeorge, F. and Zeckhauser R., (1993). "The Reverse Leveraged Buyouts Decision and Firm's Performance: Theory and Evidence", *Journal of Finance*, No.48, 1323-1348.

Ibbotson, R.G., (1975). "Price Performance of Common Stock New Issues", *Journal of Financial Economics*, Vol. 2, No. 3, 235-272

Jain, Bharat, and Kini, Omesh, (1994). "Post-Issue Operating Performance of IPO Firms", *The Journal of Finance*, Vol. 49, No. 5, Dec. 1699-1726.

Jensen, M.C. and Meckling, W., (1976). "Theory of the Firm: Managerial Behaviour Agency and Ownership Structure", *Journal of Financial Economics*, No. 3, 306-360.

Leland, H.E. and Pyle, D., (1977). "Informational Asymmetries, Financial Structure and Financial Intermediation", *Journal of Finance*, No. 42, 371-387.

Logue, Dennis E., (1973). "On the Pricing of Unseasoned Equity Issues: 1965-1969", *Journal of Financial and Quantitative Analysis*, Vol. 8, No. 1, 91-103.

Loughran, T. and Ritter, J.R., (1995). "The New Issues Puzzle", *Journal of Finance*, Vol 50, No.1, 23-51.

Machiraju, H.R., (1998). *Indian Financial System*, Vikas Publishing House, New Delhi.

Pardy, Robert, (1992). "Institutional Reform in Emerging Securities Markets", *WBPRWP*, No 907, World Bank, Washington, 1-2.

Ranganathan, M. and Subramanian, V., (1993). "Weak Form of Efficient Market Hypothesis: A Spectral Analytic Investigation", *Vikalpa*, Vol. 18, No. 2, 25-30.

————. (1993). "Long Term Dependence in Indian Stock Prices: An Empirical Test Using R/S Analysis," *Decision*, Vol. 20, No. 1, 45-50.

Reilly, Frank K., (1973). "Further Evidence on Short-Run Results for New Issues Investors", *Journal of Financial and Quantitative Analysis*, Vol. 8, No. 1, 83-90.

Ritter, J.R., (1984). "The 'Hot Issue' Market of 1980", *Journal of Business*, Vol. 57, No. 2 215-240.

————. (1991). "Signalling and the Valuation of Unseasoned New Issues: A Comment", *Journal of Finance* 1991, No. 39, 1231-1237,

Ross, Levine and Kunt, Asli Demirguc, (1995). "Stock Market Development and Financial Intermediaries: Stylised Facts", *WBPRWP*, Washington DC.

Subramanian,V., (1993). *"A Test of Weak-Form of Efficient Market Hypothesis under Indian Conditions"*, Unpublished Ph.D. Dissertation, University of Madras, Madras.

Vittas, D., (1992). "Financial Regulation: Changing the Rules of the Game", *World Bank Comparative Studies Series*, Economic Development Institute (E.D.I), World Bank, Washington DC.

11

Empowering the Indian Power Sector

A Road Map

R. HEMA

Efforts to revitalise the Indian power sector through a process of institutional restructuring and reforms, which started in the early nineties, have not yet begun to bear fruit. To make matters worse, the approach taken so far is raising serious concerns about whether the cure is worse than the ailment. Hence, it seems imperative to pause and take stock. It is important to ask 'Are we clear about where we want to head?', 'Are we *aware* of all possible ways of getting there and can we choose the best path, *given where we are located at present?*' This paper is an attempt in this direction. It tries to clearly spell out the destination, to understand the road map and to identify the best possible route to get there.

History

The Electricity Supply Act 1948 made electricity supply in India largely the monopoly responsibility of State Electricity Boards (SEBs), which were statutory, government-owned, quasi-autonomous entities. Some private generating or distributing companies that were in existence at that time were allowed to continue but no *new* generating or distributing companies could be started under private ownership. The respective state governments were basically given control over these SEBs. The objective was to ensure power development in a coordinated and efficient manner, realising all possible economies, and to ensure that output of this 'natural' monopoly industry was available to consumers at reasonable prices.

Most of the SEBs came into existence during the early fifties. The next two-and-a-half decades witnessed a phenomenal growth rate in the power sector and the SEBs were earning reasonable profits. However, things began to slide after the mid seventies. The SEBs began to fall prey to many of the typical ills that afflict State controlled monopolies. Performance inefficiencies went unpunished. Capacity expansions were financed through government budgetary allocations and through soft loans from government financial institutions, without any conditions on the financial performance of the entity. Political considerations encouraged overstaffing, *ad hoc* investment/pricing policies and unsustainable subsidies. The state governments, being in bad financial shape themselves, were defaulting on the promised subsidy payments to the SEBs. All these started pushing the SEBs deeper and deeper in the red. While artificially low prices fuelled the growth in demand the deteriorating financial status was making it increasingly difficult to mobilise sufficient resources for capacity expansion.

Reforms

In order to mobilise investment financing for new capacity and given the climate of structural reforms that were set in motion by the Government of India (GoI), the Electricity Supply Act was amended in 1991 to allow private sector participation in electricity generation. Independent Power Producers (IPP) could set up generating stations on the basis of Power Purchase Agreements (PPA) entered into with the concerned SEB. Attractive terms regarding foreign equity participation, debt-equity ratio and return on capital were offered to the IPPs to encourage investment. While there was an initial enthusiastic response from potential private investors, not all of this got translated into capacity realised. Given the financial ill-health of the SEBs and given that IPPs could not directly sell power to any other party, potential investors were uncertain about their revenue stream. Escrow accounts, guarantees for payment from the state governments and, given that even their finances were in bad shape, counter-guarantees from the GoI were demanded.

The lukewarm response from private investors and the widening gap between the demand for and supply of electricity encouraged a rethinking on the approach. It was realised that more fundamental reforms in the institutional arrangement were needed. The first efforts in this direction were undertaken in the state of Orissa. The Orissa

Electricity Reforms Act passed by the state government in 1995 paved the way for a total restructuring of the Orissa State Electricity Board and the formation of an independent regulatory commission. The following are the highlights of the restructuring process that followed: the vertically integrated OSEB was unbundled into smaller entities that separately dealt with the generating, transmitting and distributing functions. These were to operate on the basis of corporate principles. The unbundled entities were to initially continue under state ownership and were to eventually be privatised. These were to operate as licensees under the regulatory authority of the Orissa Electricity Regulatory Commission (OERC). The Regulatory Commission was charged with the responsibility of scrutinising and approving the tariff proposals submitted by the licensees, of regulating the quality of supply and of ensuring that anyone who wanted supply did have access to it. The Commission had to make sure that the tariffs approved "shall be just and reasonable and be such as to promote economic efficiency in the supply and consumption of electricity".

The Central Government passed The Electricity Regulatory Commissions Act in 1998 'for the establishment of a Central Electricity Regulatory Commission and State Electricity Regulatory Commissions, rationalisation of electricity tariffs, transparent policies regarding subsidies and promotion of efficient and environmentally benign policies'. This Act *required* the central government to set up an Electricity Regulatory Commission and specified that the state government may, *if it deems fit*, establish the State Electricity Regulatory Commission. Subsequently, the Central Electricity Regulatory Commission was set up and a few states took the initiative to set up state level Regulatory Commissions. Also, following the Orissa experiment, a few other SEBs (Haryana, Andhra Pradesh, Uttar Pradesh) started the unbundling process.

Outcome So Far

The results so far of all these efforts are far from desired and cause for concern. Some of the contracts entered into with IPPs are under dispute, some have been cancelled and some have been shelved. The controversies that were dogging the high profile contract for power purchase by the Maharashtra State Electricity Board from the Dabhol Power Company, set up by Enron and its subsidiaries to generate over

2000 MW of electricity based on combined cycle gas turbine technology, and the final closure of the generating stations after protracted legal battles and after the Central Government refused to honour its counter-guarantee commitment, is an important case in point. In Orissa, an international private company that took over one of the four distribution companies has found the transition problems insurmountable and has withdrawn. The government owned transmission company GRIDCO has had all the financial losses in the system, since unbundling, transferred on to it and is today facing staggering losses. The private distribution companies were finding it a Herculean task to instill the necessary meters, control theft and improve employees' efficiency within the time frame they had envisaged. Social and political tensions over all these have been mounting. The Orissa experience started slowing down the reforms process in other places like Haryana and Andhra Pradesh, which were adopting the same unbundling-privatising approach. While the SEBs have been unbundled and the Electricity Regulatory Commissions set in place the unbundled entities have not been privatised yet. In the case of Andhra Pradesh the performance efficiencies have been improved however but this is probably more due to the personal directions of its Chief Minister rather than due to the incentives provided by the institutional arrangement. There is a rethink on the whole process and informed opinion is now veering towards the idea that privatisation should probably start from the distribution end rather than the generation end. Some states like Delhi have embarked on this approach.

In the meantime, the usual funding for capacity expansion projects that was hitherto available from government budget allocations is being drastically reduced, mainly because the state finances are so bad that the funds are just not available and also in the expectation that significant private sector investments would materialise. This is worsening the power availability situation. Finally, all this flux is introducing considerable uncertainty regarding the shape of things to come, which is affecting investment decisions not only in the power sector but also in other sectors, particularly industry.

Evaluation of the Problem

It is clear that the above issues are not just teething troubles of a transitional process. Not only would these impose huge transaction costs that may outweigh benefits, they may also end up even derailing the reform process. The crux of the problem seems that the focus has been on addressing the symptom (investment resource constraint) without serious efforts to tackle the source of the malaise. Change of ownership from State to private would not automatically ensure increased efficiency. Nor would technical conversions of State-owned enterprises into 'corporations'. What is more important is to have strong competitive forces at play. To introduce and maintain these competitive forces it is imperative that an *independent and efficient* regulatory authority is in place that would have the legal and technical capability and the political will to design and enforce the needed regulatory mechanisms.

The *ad hoc* approach to reforms is due to the fact that the policies and management practices adopted by the SEBs over the past few decades have systematically encouraged some vested interests that would suffer from the redistributive implications of more fundamental reforms. Hence, it becomes politically very expensive and difficult to tackle. It is however not impossible to work out a smooth transition in a systematic and incremental fashion. What this requires is the genuine political will to attempt long-term solutions and this seems lacking. The alternative would be for the consumers who are currently paying a huge price, in terms of opportunity costs, for the inadequacies and inefficiencies of the existing system to organise themselves into bargaining groups and credibly demand more fundamental and long-term solutions.

The question then is what would be a possible strategy that would eventually make the power sector meet the needs of our growing economy in an efficient manner. In addressing this, it is important to take care that the transitional process is economically and politically feasible *and* sustainable and that the 'right' balance is found between performance efficiency and social equity considerations. I first discuss the economic rationale underlying the strong government role in this sector and the current restructuring efforts. We then look at lessons from other experiences in restructuring the electricity supply industry (ESI). Based on these, and taking into consideration the specific characteristics and constraints of the Indian power sector at present, a possible reform strategy is suggested.

Economic Rationale – A Brief Discussion

In every country the ESI has been and still is being subject to direct and specific government intervention. In most cases the ESI has, for the last many decades, been under public ownership. In other cases public and private ownership have coexisted with generally the publicly owned utilities playing a dominant role. In the US, utilities have largely been private investor owned subject to heavy public regulation, though about 24 per cent of generating capacity has been under public ownership. In all cases the governments have specific legislations for this sector that lay down the basic framework for the ownership pattern and regulatory control. These in turn have largely shaped the outcome in terms of investment decisions, pricing policies, growth rates, allocation of gains, and social costs and benefits.

The reason for such strong government intervention has been the special characteristics of the ESI that make it a strong candidate for a natural monopoly. These characteristics are: non-storability which means supply has to be instantaneous with demand; diverse patterns of demand that are also fluctuating; economies of scope in organising generation and supply in a coordinated manner through an interconnected network; and high degree of asset specificity combined with long asset life. These, in addition to the fact that electricity has become a crucial infrastructure input facing relatively inelastic demand, mean that the market may not automatically lend itself to a competitive framework. The potential for opportunism and 'hold-up' is quite high and hence may lead to considerable market power. Suppliers could exercise market power by charging prices much higher than marginal costs. It could also be that once the investments are made consumers exercise market power, with government support, and pay non-remunerative prices. Hence, if private investors are to feel confident about their revenue stream they need appropriate regulations to protect them. Similarly, consumers need to be protected from monopoly pricing. As a result the industry has been largely under public ownership or subject to heavy regulation.

In the case of state-owned monopolies, the roles of owner, supplier and regulator are all combined in one and rest with the Government. Given that ownership and regulation are not separate, slackness in performance is not penalised. Investment finances are available from government budget allocations or through soft loans and the utility is not subject to the financial discipline of a competitive market. Governments would tend to use policies concerning this sector as instruments to tackle macroeconomic issues (e.g., inflation, income distribution). Multiple objectives could be imposed on the sector some of which could be mutually conflicting. There is also considerable potential for rent seeking (e.g., irrational subsidies to build up vote banks, kickbacks). Very often the management is neither given the autonomy nor made accountable for the performance efficiency of the sector. All these would significantly raise the opportunity costs.

Most of the ongoing restructuring experiments are efforts to tackle the inefficiencies of state-owned utilities. In the process the natural monopoly argument has been reexamined. The feasibility of introducing competitive forces in some segments while isolating the natural monopoly segments and subjecting those to regulation has been explored and also been realised in some cases. A strong case has also been made for transferring the ownership to private investors so that the necessary incentives to minimise costs would be in place. The basic idea involved is as follows: the existing state-owned utility that carries out the generation, transmission and distribution functions in a vertically integrated manner can be broken up into a lot of smaller entities. The individual generating stations can be grouped into a certain number of generating companies. These companies could be made to compete to sell electricity to the grid. To ensure competition there has to be a sufficiently large number of generating companies. Distribution of electricity to final consumers involves two major aspects – building and maintaining the distribution network and supply *per se*, which refers to the actual selling of electricity, metering, billing, collecting payments and so on. It was envisaged that the supply function could be separated from the function of owning and operating the distribution network so that competition could be introduced in the supply segment. What this means is that consumers would be physically hooked on to their local distribution network but they would be free to contract with any supplier for purchase of electricity. These suppliers would have to pay for the use of the local distribution network. The distribution network would be a natural monopoly segment and hence needs to be regulated to monitor the quality of supply and the prices charged. The transmission network, which has to coordinate the operation of the various generating stations and the distribution networks, would also have natural monopoly characteristics. This segment could be under public ownership but compelling arguments have been made to keep it under private ownership but subject to regulation.

The integrated operation of the system, in terms of how the generating stations are scheduled and how the electricity gets allocated to distribution centres, would be based on the competitive bids for supply and demand. If the market is truly competitive, scheduling of generating capacity would be based on the short run marginal costs and capacity expansion would be based on the long run marginal costs. The challenge lies, however, in ensuring that the market is competitive and this depends largely on the efficacy of the regulator. Given the nature of the integrated operation of the system, market power could bring in considerable gains and there would be strong tendencies on the part of individual companies to gain market power. The regulator would have to effectively monitor these tendencies and design appropriate mechanisms to keep them in check. This would entail significant transaction costs.

Another alternative to the vertically integrated state-owned utility could be a vertically integrated private investor-owned utility subject to regulation. The US has a long history of such an arrangement. In this model, there is potential for a lot of X-inefficiency due to the fact that the entity has significant market power and there would be considerable information asymmetry between the regulator and the utility that would make it very difficult for the regulator to minimise the inefficiency.

Lessons from Other Experiments

The nineties have witnessed a spate of restructuring in the ESI of a large number of countries. A comprehensive comparative analysis of the institutional arrangements in the ESI of many countries and their implications for performance, giving due consideration to historical and political conditions, can be found in Gilbert and Kahn (1996). Chile was the first to embark on such a program, in 1982, by privatising its state-owned companies and introducing competitive forces. It was largely judged to be a success and became the source of motivation for experimentation in other countries. The Chilean approach was cautious and focused on creating shareholder confidence through legislation, prior to embarking on the privatisation process. The British experiment that started in 1990 has been one of the most dramatic and ambitious attempts at breaking up a vertically integrated state-owned monopoly into a number of smaller privately owned entities and introducing a spot market (Pool) for electricity. An independent, powerful and efficient regulatory authority was put in place and made responsible to oversee and ensure the competitive functioning of the system. Argentina, Colombia and Brazil have basically followed the same approach in terms of 'unbundling' the vertically integrated state-owned monopoly and privatising, though with some variant features.

Encouraged by the experience of liberalisation in the UK, the European Commission — anxious to tackle the issue of national monopoly electricity industries within its broader mission of creating a single market for goods and services — legislated through the 'Electricity Directive' that there should be a functional unbundling of generation from transmission and that at least 33 per cent of the supply market should be opened up so that eligible customers could *choose* their suppliers. (Newbery, 2002).

The Scandinavian countries, which have had a fairly successful experience with mixed ownership and voluntary cooperative mechanisms, started reforms primarily with the objective of introducing competition. Their earlier cooperative approach was characterised by self-regulation, price leadership by the bigger public-owned utilities and yardstick competition. The reform process sought to unbundle the system into separate entities for the generating, transmitting and distributing functions and to introduce competitive forces in their operation, without necessarily changing the ownership pattern. The main objective for this move was to take care of problems of excess capacity and low productive and allocative efficiencies.

In the United States, which has had a long history of both public utilities and regulated investor owned utilities, substantial pressure existed for introducing more competition. California started the liberalisation process in 2000 hoping to bring down high consumer prices. However, average wholesale prices in 2000 ended up being more than three times those in 1999 (Newbery, 2002), 2001 witnessed rolling blackouts and dangerously low reserve margins while the PG&E (the supplier) had to file for bankruptcy protection!

These large and increasing number of experiments in restructuring the ESI and their outcomes are providing a rich source of information that could help in better understanding the phenomenon. There have been quite a few in-depth studies (theoretical, empirical, and comparative institutional) that have compared the circumstances and outcomes of these experiments. These help us understand the general patterns, identify the most important issues, get a grasp on the prerequisites and indicate the likely effect of chosen strategies.

The dominant strategy seems to have been that of unbundling, privatising and introducing competition. The main problems of this approach have been to create and sustain adequate competition and to prevent market abuse. This calls for a truly independent, credible and efficient regulatory regime, which is effectively supported by a well functioning judicial system that provides an investor-friendly environment and builds shareholders confidence. The transaction costs of this strategy are fairly high and the more unfavourable the initial institutional circumstances the higher would these costs be. In fact, the empirical evidence is not conclusive as to whether the efficiency gains from unbundling and privatising are considerably higher than the transaction costs involved in ensuring that the market is competitive.

Restructuring has significant redistributive effects. Based on a social cost-benefit analysis of the British experiment, Newbery and Pollitt (1997) report that a permanent cost reduction of 5 per cent per year was achieved, but while producers gained more than the cost reduction consumers and the Government lost. In the case of Northern Ireland, Pollitt (1997) estimates that while a permanent cost reduction of 6 per cent per annum could be achieved, consumers would pay 4 per cent higher prices while the Government would realise £1.4 billion in net gains through the sale of assets and higher tax revenue. In Scotland, lack of competitive pressure in the restructured industry resulted in prices being higher by about 5 per cent after a decade of reforms. The very modest benefits of privatisation were entirely absorbed by the costs of restructuring and there were no net benefits. An analysis of the net social benefit of privatising Chilgener, which is one of a number of competing generators, and Enersis, which is a monopoly distribution company, is provided by Galal, as cited in Newbery 2002. Both these companies were created out of Chilectra, a former state-owned integrated entity in Chile. Chilgener had increased its profit and productivity. The net social gains were estimated to be about 4 billion Chilean dollars. Of this 2.7 billion went to foreign shareholders, which meant this was the amount of potential gains that the Government lost, 0.8 billion went to domestic shareholders, 0.1 billion to employees while the consumers got no share of these benefits. In the case of Enersis, most of the gains were captured domestically and some desirable redistribution from non-paying to paying customers resulted while it was costly for the government.

Restructuring would also significantly alter the incentives for investment decision-making. Brazil, which started its reform process in 1990 and intensified the momentum since 1994, is today facing an electricity crisis mainly because this dimension was not properly taken into account. The ESI in Brazil is predominantly hydro-based (over 90 per cent). Significant economies are realised in operating the hydro units in a coordinated fashion. Moreover, most of the dams are for multipurpose use and hence power dispatch has also to be coordinated with water use for irrigation and other requirements. Given the high degree of asset-specificity, the heavy investment costs and long asset life for these multi-use hydroelectric projects, that also need to be operated in a tightly coordinated fashion, the risks would definitely be very high for private investors. Hence, private owners prefer to go in for the Combined Cycle gas Turbine (CCGT) technology, which provides a low capital cost and flexible operations option. The network and market for gas supply in Brazil is relatively recent and immature. Given all this the long-run marginal cost of hydro investment is probably lower than that of CCGT in Brazil, in contrast to most other countries. The disquieting conclusion drawn from the Brazilian experience is that private ownership is unlikely to be an efficient way of financing and developing the generation sector here.

The Californian crisis was fomented by a climate of under-investment. This state had a long history of under-investment in generation, largely due to disputes about nuclear power plant costs and safety, due to environmental objections and due to some misconceived PPAs with Qualifying Facilities. The state was heavily depending on cheap hydroelectric power, imported from the Pacific Northwest. Also, while the wholesale market was deregulated, the distribution companies and the rates they charged to final consumers were heavily regulated. Moreover, there was a regulatory restraint on the distribution companies that they could not hedge by signing long-term contracts. The Californian crisis is a lesson on how inappropriately designed regulatory and political intervention can end up producing extremely unsatisfactory and 'costly' outcomes. (Newbery, 2002). It shows that, when reserve margin capacities in generation are low then volatile markets with high prices will be the outcome even in a fairly competitive market. This combined with unresponsive demand would end up giving the producers considerable market power. Also, a transition from a vertically integrated utility to an unbundled structure is bound to introduce price risks. The generators and suppliers would need contracts or other hedging instruments to insure themselves against unexpected and dramatic changes in the spot price, particularly because the prices in the final markets would be regulated. In an interconnected system that is operating under a variety of regulatory regimes and operational jurisdictions reserve capacity becomes a public good. In a decentralised market that also has a potentially energy-constrained hydroelectric system, it would be even harder to ensure adequate reserve capacity.

The most important lesson that emerges from all these is that reform strategies that appear to work well in some countries and under certain circumstances may not be easily transferable to countries facing different circumstances. "Choosing the right reform strategy is more challenging than early optimists claimed" (Newbery, 2002). The unbundling-privatisation-competition model has worked well in Britain mainly because it had adequate generating and transmitting capacity to start with. The fact that technical developments of the high efficiency CCGT reached maturity and that gas was becoming increasingly available at cheap prices just as Britain was restructuring has also been a major contributory factor. These were complemented by well designed regulatory mechanisms. Many other ESIs that have restructured fairly successfully have also all started with sufficient spare capacity.

Given all this, it is still not clear whether competitive markets can work as well in countries that are suffering from a shortage of capacity and hence requiring huge investments, having considerable excess demand, expecting rapid growth in demand and probably facing increasing long-run marginal costs for capacity expansion. The problem gets even more confounded if the existing system is corrupt, theft-prone and making huge losses. Arguments in favour of privatisation are made on the grounds that it would provide the necessary incentives for efficiency through cost minimisation. However, most of the studies indicate that privatisation alone would not necessarily improve efficiency. It has to be backed by good regulation that would ensure that the market is sufficiently competitive and that some of the gains from efficiency are passed on to consumers. On the other hand, public-owned utilities could also perform efficiently if provided the right incentives. Pollitt, (1997) in analysing ownership, costs and prices in electric utilities finds that the evidence from the US suggests that there is no difference in costs between private and publicly owned electric utilities. The Nuclear Electric Company in the UK, which continued to remain under public ownership even in the restructured regime, improved its productivity dramatically in the new regime. When considering restructuring options and strategics, it should also be borne in mind that privatisation itself is reversible at high external cost. Moreover, improperly designed privatisation can complicate subsequent reforms. It is also often hard and costly to reverse certain structural choices. Newbery, (2002) states that while making recommendations for restructuring "it is worth asking whether we are sufficiently familiar with the richer and longer history of US regulation or whether we are relying on standard competitive market doctrine of the kind normally written into competition law. The latter may be a weak reed on which to rely".

Suggested Strategy for India

The ESI in India is currently facing an excess demand situation, is financially deeply in the red, is characterised by poor technical efficiencies of performance, is burdened by unsustainable subsidies and is prone to corruption. It is undergoing reforms in some states. However, not only have these been unsuccessful in yielding any net benefits so far but they also seem to be in risk of derailing the whole process because of the socio-political and economic transaction costs they impose.

An alternative approach is suggested here to tackle the problem. It makes sense to still contemplate an alternative at this stage, at least for those states that have not yet set in motion restructuring efforts that are 'expensive' to reverse, because the legislations governing this issue fortunately allow for enough flexibility and multiplicity of approaches within certain broad parameters. The suggested strategy draws heavily on the fact that incentives have to be 'right' and that the appropriate institutional arrangement and its mechanisms should be designed so that they are incentive-compatible for all concerned groups. It emphasises the need to (a) separate ownership and regulation and (b) separate pricing decisions from subsidy decisions, in order to minimise the distortions caused by government interference and subsidies. It advocates keeping the utility vertically integrated rather than unbundling because given the present financial health of the SEBs economies of vertical integration could be efficiently tapped to nurse them back to good health. It is based on the recognition that while a competitive market would definitely be the best way to maximise efficiency, in a situation where the transaction costs of introducing and maintaining competition are likely to be very high an alternative might be desirable.

Institutional Changes

The existing SEB should be made a fully privately owned, vertically integrated, corporate entity that is subject to regulation. This Regulated Electric Utility (REU) would have monopoly rights and responsibilities for supply of electricity in the state and would be allowed to earn profits, provided it meets specified price and quality regulations. The REU may be given autonomy in terms of managing its internal organisational structure. For example, it could contract out any sections of its operations — building and operating generating stations, managing distribution systems, taking care of billing and payments etc. The management and staff of the REU should be given a share in the profits earned. This share and the proportion in which it is distributed to different categories of employees must be carefully worked out so that it would provide the best incentive for performance efficiencies. The profits distributed to the management should be in the form of shares in the company, with a condition that they cannot be sold for a reasonable length of time. This is to encourage management to take a long-term approach to efficiency. It may also be specified that the remaining profits be invested back into the REU for a certain length of time. In order to transfer control of the SEB to private investors in the restructured REU the existing capital assets will have to be appropriately evaluated. It is suggested that these capital assets be evaluated on the basis of their earning potential under the pricing regime allowed by the regulatory commission. This would be an appropriate indication of the opportunity cost of these assets. The written down value of these assets based on historical accounts may be an underestimate because they are based on accounting practices, income tax provisions for depreciation allowances and subsidised capital costs. The replacement value on the other hand would be an overestimate.

The State Electricity Regulatory Commission (SERC) established under the provisions of the Electricity Regulatory Commission Act 1998 could be the appropriate regulatory authority. However, it is very important to keep it totally independent and give it more powers. Towards these objectives it may be necessary to make suitable amendments to the ERC Act. The role of the state government in setting up the Selcction Committee to choose the Electricity Regulatory Commission (ERC) Members should be reduced and there should be greater representation from other sectors of the society. Moreover, the current approach focuses on legal and accounting expertise being represented in the ERC, going by the nature of appointments made so far. It is very important to include economic expertise also. The SERC should be responsible for ensuring that the REU supplies electricity to anyone in the state who demands it and is willing to pay for it and that the REU maintains quality standards and price ceilings as specified by it.

Regulatory Policy

Tariffs: It is suggested that the ERC adopt the 'price-cap' form of regulation. This would provide the maximum incentive for efficiency, since all the gains from cost-minimisation would go to the utility and in the Indian context improving performance efficiency is a priority now. The price cap estimated for the base year may then be allowed to increase each year by a percentage that is a bit less than the rise in the retail price index (RPI). This is the form of tariff regulation adopted in the UK for the unbundled natural monopoly segments. While the initial choice of the price ceiling would be a complicated exercise the information needed by the regulator to monitor subsequent price rises would be minimal and hence enforcement easier.

Estimating the Price-Cap: The initial price ceiling would have to be worked out with much care. Given the capital-intensive nature of electricity and given that creating the capital stock and utilisation of this capital stock involve different sets of parameters and related costs, it is important to work out the capital cost and energy cost separately. The concepts of Loss of Load Probability (LOLP) and the Value of Lost Load (VOLL) are made use of in working out the capacity cost of generation for the electricity sold to the British wholesale market (the Pool). These capture the opportunity cost of electricity that may be demanded but is not available. Estimating the opportunity cost in this manner would not be an advisable approach for the Indian context at present for the following reasons: there is considerable excess demand for electricity; many of the other markets are subject to administered prices and estimating the VOLL would be a complex exercise; and even if the value can be estimated it may be quite high to be immediately reflected in the tariff. Hence the following methodologies are suggested for estimating the capacity and energy costs.

Capacity Costs: The capital cost for the chosen reference year may be worked out as the weighted average of the cost of existing capacity and the average incremental cost (AIC) of planned capacity additions. The rationale for suggesting the weighted average of historical and incremental costs as a measure of the long run marginal cost of capacity is because the ESI is a network industry with a mix of capacities of different vintages and of different technologies that meets the total demand for any time period in a coordinated manner. The assets are highly specific and have asset lives extending much beyond the planning horizon for capacity additions. Hence, when an efficient integrated system is contemplating capacity expansion, the existing cost commitments and available capacities are taken as given and compared with potential capacity additions and their cost implications. The least cost option for expanding capacity is then chosen by retiring some existing high cost (including the opportunity costs of breakdown, repair etc.) capacity at the margin if necessary and adding low cost new capacity. Also, the capacity additions are generally a small proportion of existing capacity. If the new capacity were costlier than existing capacity then compensating all existing capacity at the higher rate would bring windfall gains for earlier investments and if new capacity were cheaper then infra-marginal investments would incur losses. This brings in a lot of uncertainty in terms of expected revenue streams and would adversely affect investments. In the unbundled electricity market of the UK, this problem is tackled by allowing the generating companies and distribution companies to sign long-term Contracts for Difference, which in effect helps the seller and buyer hedge against uncertainties in the revenue stream. In fact, it has been argued that the provision for hedging through such contracts has been largely responsible for the success of the British experiment. In an integrated system the weighted average of historical and incremental costs would serve the same purpose.

The methodology for estimating the costs of existing and incremental capacity for a reference year *t* is outlined here. The costs would have to be worked out separately for the generation, transmission and distribution categories. Investments in generation typically account for a higher proportion of capacity costs compared to transmission and distribution and also tends to be lumpy.

Generation: The capacity cost for generation is taken to be the sum of annuity charges corresponding to existing generating capacities and the annuity charges worked out for the average incremental capacity (AIC).

Suppose that there are E existing generating stations at time *t*. The existing plants taken into consideration should be net of any plants expected to be retired in the next five years. The annuity charge that would be assigned to year *t* from the eth generating station is denoted by $AG_{e,t}$

$$AG_{e,t} = [CCG_{e,y} (i_y) (1 + i_y)^{le}] / [(1 + i_y)^{le} - 1]$$

where, $CCG_{e,y}$ is the total capital cost (at the time of commissioning) of the eth generating station commissioned in year y; i_y is the opportunity cost of capital in year *y* and *le* is the life of the eth generating station. Typically coal-based thermal generating stations may take five to six years for construction and hydro stations would take longer, about seven to nine years. Hence, the total capital cost of the generating station at the time of commissioning should include the opportunity cost of capital expenses incurred during the earlier years of construction. In the above calculation the market interest rate for the entire period of the life of the asset is assumed constant and pegged at the interest rate at the time of commissioning the station. This can be fine-tuned if necessary and varying interest rates assumed, provided future interest rates could be anticipated with a reasonable degree of confidence. The total annuity charges relevant for time *t* for all the E existing generating stations would then be $AG_{E,t} = \Sigma AG_{e,t}$, the summation being over all $e = 1,2,...E$.

For estimating the capacity cost of AIC, suppose the planning horizon is taken to be five years as is currently followed by the SEBs. At time *t* we have information on the size, composition, estimated costs and expected year of commissioning of new capacity that is likely between *t* and *t*+5. All generating stations expected to be commissioned between *t* and *t*+5 are treated as incremental capacity. Depending on the expected year of commissioning, the expected total capital cost at the time of commissioning and the expected market rate of interest for that year, the annuity charges corresponding to each of the generating stations is worked out. The sum of these annuity charges corresponding to all new generating stations expected to be commissioned by the end of the planning horizon would be the capital cost corresponding to the AIC. Supposing N new generating stations are expected to be commissioned during the plan horizon and the capital cost corresponding to all this new capacity is denoted by $AG_{N,t}$, where $AG_{N,t} = \Sigma AG_{n,t}$ the summation being over all n = 1,2,...N. The total capital cost relating to generating capacity in time *t* would then be $AG_t = AG_{E,t} + AG_{N,t}$. In effect this method of calculation advances the capital cost relevant for time *t*+5 to time *t*. The total capital cost for generation is then converted into cost per MW of available peak capacity, which is the simultaneous maximum demand that the available generating capacity can handle.

Transmission and Distribution: In the case of transmission and distribution (T&D), investments are more of a regular stream over the years though occasional years may witness heavier investments. Moreover, most of the states already have a well established T&D network that would only need regular reinforcing and marginal expansions. Hence, in this case the capital expenses incurred each year in the T&D network could be annuitised over the typical life of T&D assets, probably 25 to 30 years. And the capacity costs relating to T&D assets that would be relevant for time *t* would be the sum of the annuity charges relating to all past investments that are assigned to year *t* plus the sum of the annuity charges relating to planned investments between *t* and *t*+5. Thus, if AT_t denotes the total capital cost relating to the transmission assets in time *t* then $AT_t = AT_{E,t} + AT_{N,t}$, where $AT_{E,t}$ would be the annuitised costs relating to existing transmission capacity and $AT_{N,t}$ the annuitised costs relating to new capacity. $AT_{E,t}$ is given by the formula $AT_{E,t} = \Sigma AT_{t-i}$, the summation being over all i = 1,2,....25 if the typical life of these assets is taken to be 25 years. AT_{t-i} is the annuitised cost of investments made in transmission at time period t-i. The capital cost relating to all incremental capacity planned in the transmission network for the next five years $AT_{N,t}$ is calculated in a similar fashion. The annuity costs relating to the distribution network is calculated exactly as suggested for the transmission network and AD_t could denote the total costs relating to distribution capacity that is relevant for time *t*.

The total capital cost is then the sum of the costs relating to the generation, transmission and distribution assets. If we denote it as CC_t then $CC_t = AG_t + AT_t + AD_t$. The capital cost can also be estimated per MW of available peak capacity separately for the generation, transmission and distribution levels taking into consideration the line losses at the transmission and distribution levels. The capital cost per MW at the generating level would be AG_t/AP, where AP is the available peak capacity at time t+5. The capital cost at the high voltage level would be $AG_t/AP + AT_t/[AP(1-t_l)]$, where t_l is the allowance for transmission losses specified by the SERC. The capital cost at the low voltage level would be $AG_t/AP + AT_t/[AP(1-t_l)] + AD_t/[AP(1-t_l-d_l)]$, where d_l is the allowance for distribution losses. It is assumed here that there is no significant mismatch between the generating capacity available to meet peak demand and the T&D capacity available to evacuate all this power.

If any such mismatch exists then necessary adjustments may have to be made to the estimated T&D costs or generation costs or both, probably based on suitable techno-economic studies. It must be noted that the capital costs are *not* expressed in constant prices. If they are expressed in constant prices then it amounts to considering the replacement costs of assets existing at time t. It is felt that this is unnecessary. If the utility has the advantage of utilising capacity invested at lower costs then these should accrue to the consumers. The basic rationale here is that investments made at any point of time should generate resources that are equal to the resources that can potentially be earned elsewhere in the economy for the period of time it is locked in this sector.

Energy Costs: The energy costs should be worked out assuming a merit-order dispatch of all available generating capacity to meet the total energy generation corresponding to an optimal system load factor for the reference year $t+5$. In other words, for the total available generating capacity, the energy generation potential can be worked out for a hypothetical system load factor. The SERC could decide on the optimal system load factor taking into consideration the available composition of generating capacity and the specific characteristics of existing demand patterns. The least cost strategy and the related operating costs for realising this energy potential during the year, given the composition of generating capacities, can be worked out. Merit-order planning (bringing generating plants on line based on increasing marginal costs, subject to any technical constraints) on an annual basis would of course provide only crude estimates as it cannot capture the day-to-day fine-tuning that would be needed. However, it would be good enough for the purpose of setting tariff limits and by erring on the 'safe' side, it could provide the necessary incentives to the utility to choose the least cost option. An important aspect in working out the energy costs is to address the issue of operating efficiencies. Some of the parameters that reflect operating efficiencies are plant load factor for each generating station (which is a measure of its capacity utilisation), plant availability factor (which depends on machine efficiencies, planned maintenance and potential breakdowns), auxiliary consumption, heat rates and fuel use efficiencies, technical T&D losses, reserve capacity and so on. It is crucial for the SERC to assume 'appropriate' norms for these parameters in working out the energy costs. These norms should take into consideration existing levels of operating inefficiencies in the system and a realistic time frame over which it would be economically feasible to eliminate them. In systems that have a significant proportion of hydro generating capacity the energy costs would depend on the water availability in the hydro stations and that would depend on the rainfall conditions for that year. It may hence be appropriate to work out the energy costs for a below-average rainfall year. This would provide a cushion for bad years and a little windfall for good years. The total energy costs relevant for reference year *t*, EC_t, is then worked out on the basis of all the above considerations. The energy costs can also be estimated separately at the generation, transmission and distribution levels by taking into consideration the line losses at each level as allowed by the SERC and the relevant variable costs at the transmission and distribution levels.

The Price Cap: The total capital cost CC_t relevant for the reference period *t* is converted into cost per MW of available peak capacity, i.e., CC_t/AP. This is then converted into a cost per kwhr of electricity, based on the optimal system load factor prescribed by the SERC. Similarly, the total energy costs estimated, EC_t, is also converted into energy cost per kwhr. The sum of these two would give the total cost TC_t per unit of electricity. In making these calculations, any existing power purchase agreements, either from the central sector generating stations or from independent power producers should also be taken into consideration for calculating the overall cost per unit. This cost per unit should be specified as the maximum price that the REU could earn per unit of electricity sold.

Regulatory Mechanisms: Some of the broad mechanisms that could be adopted by SERC to enforce the price ceiling, to encourage efficiencies, to ensure that the quality of supply meets the specifications and also to minimise the negative externalities from government intervention are suggested here.

Price Ceiling Enforcement: The SERC could rule that the overall price per unit charged by the REU for the reference period *t* should not exceed TC_t. It is enough that the SERC specifies the overall price per unit and not concern itself with the prices charged by the REU to its various consumer groups. The REU may be allowed the flexibility to devise the tariff structure for its different consumer categories. The idea is, given that the utility can earn profits subject to the price ceiling, the REU would be interested in designing the most efficient tariff structure based on its knowledge of the demand elasticities of its consumer categories. To prevent any cream skimming that may occur, where the monopoly utility does not adequately serve certain non-lucrative markets, the SERC should step in to ensure that no consumer who wants to have electricity is denied access to it as long as the consumer is willing to pay for it. The SERC should levy stiff penalties on the utility if found guilty of discriminating against certain consumers or consumer categories. In fact, the requirements to serve any non-lucrative markets should be clearly spelt out by the SERC and if the penalties for non-compliance were high enough then the incentive to default would be low. If any consumer or consumer group feels that the price charged is too high and unreasonable then they could represent the case to the SERC. The SERC has information on the cost of supply per unit at each voltage level. So given this cost and given the load factor of the consumer group, the SERC could judge whether unreasonably high prices have indeed been charged. The REU should be made to pay heavily, if found guilty, otherwise the complainant(s) should be penalised. The SERC need not also worry about the total revenue and hence profit earned by the REU as long the unit price does not exceed the level specified by it. If more demand is met by increasing efficiency and the system load factor the better it is for all concerned. The advantage of the above mechanism for enforcing the price ceiling is that the utility, which would have greater information about its markets and their consumption patterns as also about its own operating costs would be in a better position to devise a tariff that would yield the maximum surplus. And as long as a credible threat of steep penalties exists for discriminating against some consumers, the SERC can ensure that cream skimming is avoided.

This price ceiling may be allowed to rise with the rise in the retail price index of the economy less a certain percentage X. Thus if the retail price index between t and $t+1$ rises by RPI per cent then the electricity price ceiling may be allowed to rise by RPI – X. The X is to encourage the utility to improve its efficiency. In the Indian context, given the present level of inefficiencies, this X has to be carefully worked out. It may be worthwhile to keep the X low initially and then let it gradually rise each year to reach an optimum level. This would allow the REU the necessary time frame to bring up performance efficiencies to optimal levels. An additional adjustment of Z per cent may also be allowed in order to take care of any extraordinary circumstances or macroeconomic conditions. Thus the price ceiling could be allowed to rise by RPI – X + Z, where Z could be positive or negative. A time frame may be specified after which a major review could be undertaken and any changes needed in the regulatory decisions can be carried out.

Subsidies: Currently consumption by agriculturists for irrigation purposes and by low-income households is heavily subsidised by the SEBs, on instructions from the state governments. In fact, in the state of Tamil Nadu, electricity for irrigation is supplied totally free of any charge and their consumption is not even metered. This allows a lot of negative externalities to creep into the system. There is considerable theft of energy and this is all booked under agricultural consumption. Indiscriminate tapping of groundwater is being encouraged which is dangerously depleting the groundwater potential in many areas. This is giving rise to a lot of illegal markets for groundwater. Excessive flooding is also increasing the soil salinity in many places. The manner in which the subsidies are transferred by the state government to the SEB encourages considerable slackness in the SEB's financial discipline. The SEB typically would work out its total costs and total revenue earned for each year. The Electricity Supply Act requires the SEB to earn a 3 per cent return on its net fixed assets. Thus, the revenue required to earn this return is also calculated. Any difference between the revenue requirement and the actual revenue earned is treated as losses due to the subsidies and claimed from the Government. In fact, the costs of all these externalities would far outweigh the net benefits of subsidies and even these net benefits are misdirected away from really deserving groups.

It is therefore, very important that the SERC is given enough powers and is able to exercise its authority in minimising the negative externalities. In particular, the SERC should have the authority to decide both on the *magnitude* of subsidies offered and the *manner* in which they are offered. Of course, the SERC should be able to justify and defend its decisions. Regarding the manner in which the subsidies are provided, if the state government wishes to subsidise the consumption of any consumer group then the subsidy should be transferred to the consumers in the form of the Government paying a part of their bill. The REU works out the relevant tariff for the consumer group. Once the consumers' bills are made, based on their actual consumption, the Government could directly pay the REU a proportion of it. The individual consumer must pay the balance. It is important that each consumer be made to pay a proportion of the bill. This method would encourage energy use efficiency at the consumer end. It would also render the subsidy transfers totally transparent. The SERC should also have the authority to decide on the upper limit of the proportion of any bill that can be subsidised by the Government. Because, if the financial burden on the consumer is insignificant the opportunity costs of inefficient energy use may outweigh the net benefits to the consumers. Hundred per cent subsidies to any category of consumers are totally unjustifiable. However, given the present level of subsidies the situation cannot be changed drastically in the short run. Hence, the SERC should draw up a reasonable time plan over which the proportion of subsidies can be reduced and the size of the subsidised categories can also be reduced. The subsidy payment due from the Government based on these calculations may then be directly transferred to the utility. This would minimise the transaction costs of claiming the subsidies. The SERC should also monitor and ensure that the price charged by the REU to the subsidised categories is not unreasonably high, since the REU might have an incentive to pad up these prices.

One of the major problems that would be encountered in the short run is the existence of a sizeable section of consumers whose consumption is not metered. In Tamil Nadu, for example, there are about 16,00,000 agricultural consumers and about 14,00,000 low-income domestic consumers who get free supply and are not metered. Installing meters for all these consumers would take some time and would also involve significant costs. The costs could probably be met through subsidised World Bank loans or any other loans from international development agencies. As an interim measure to collect payments from these consumers the REU could probably require them to make payments based on their own assessment of their consumption. Once the meters are installed, if the self-assessed consumption is found to be too low compared with the metered consumption, without any valid reasons, then the consumer may be required to pay penalties. On the other hand, if the self-assessed consumption was higher the consumer may be offered some discounts.

Supply Quality: The SERC should also specify the technical quality of electricity supply in terms of voltage fluctuations, frequency cycles, power outages and power availability on demand and ensure that the utility meets these standards. One of the issues here would be the current timing restriction for certain consumer groups, particularly agricultural consumers. This cannot be removed immediately because the REU may not have enough generating and evacuating capacity if this entire load comes simultaneously on the system during peak hours. The SERC should work out a realistic time frame over which these restrictions in hours of supply can be gradually removed and start enforcing it. The REU should be made to find it worthwhile to encourage load management through appropriate pricing incentives rather than through administrative restrictions.

Legal Provisions

The Electricity Regulatory Commission Act (1998) may have to be amended to enable some of the suggestions made above. The flexibility accorded to the SERCs in the current Act in terms of the strategy they could follow for tariff regulation is not enough. The existing provisions strongly encourage the SERC to adopt the Rate-of-return form of regulation and given the lack of economic expertise represented in the ERCs so far this is being automatically adopted. The most important amendment should be in enabling the SERC to address the subsidies issue in a holistic manner. According to the present provisions the SERC shall allow the regulated utility to charge a subsidised price to any category of consumers that the Government may specify as long as the Government can make good the losses to the utility. This does not tackle the problem of the huge costs brought on by the negative externalities. Hence, it is important to give the SERC enough authority to be able to minimise these losses. The regulatory directives should also be given greater credibility by providing for heavy penalties when disobeyed.

Regulatory Evolution

The regulatory powers, policies and mechanisms suggested above can be periodically evaluated and modified as and when improvements are required. Once the financial health of the utilities are improved and stabilised and in the meantime if experiments with introducing competition prove its merits beyond doubt, the REUs could then be unbundled and the ESI could be subject to competitive forces. The regulatory mechanisms could then be altered to ensure that competition is maintained.

Conclusion

This paper emphasises the fact that the restructuring strategy adopted to address the present ills of the Indian power sector should be based on a sound understanding of the merits and disadvantages of available options especially in the context of where and how the sector is placed at present. It would greatly help to learn from others experiences and to try and avoid making the same mistakes. The transitional process, given all the related economic, social and political costs, needs to be planned carefully if the transaction costs are to be minimised.

It is felt that the conditions characterising the power sector in India today, particularly the supply shortages and the financial losses, are not conducive to adopting the unbundling-privatisation-competition route to reform. An alternative strategy of keeping the utility as a vertically integrated monopoly but at the same time creating the appropriate type of incentives, it is argued, would deliver better results. Moreover, this would be an incremental approach to restructuring so that costly reversions can be avoided. If necessary, in course of time it could still be unbundled and subject to competitive pressures if their merits are proven and achievable. The importance of separating ownership and regulation is stressed. The fact that both the magnitude of subsidies given and the manner in which they are distributed would have significant implications for efficiency through the signals they send has been highlighted. The philosophy underlying the regulatory approach outlined here is one of achieving maximum results with minimum direct interference. Hence, it is important that the regulatory regime is not itself required to make the major policy decisions for the REU. It should only ensure that the REU's decisions do not lead to 'unacceptable' price, quality and accessibility outcomes. This way, the 'costs' of regulatory intervention can also be minimised.

Two major questions still remain. First, what would be the incentive for state governments to embark on such a long-term reform process, especially when there is considerable potential for rent seeking in the existing arrangement or in attempting half-hearted reforms. To tackle this the pressures necessarily would have to come from outside, maybe from organised industry groups or consumer groups, maybe from funding agencies that are willing to provide the necessary funding for the reforms, may be from the Central Government by tying it up to central assistance for this sector and may be from the ESI itself. The second issue is what would ensure that the regulators would deliver and not become victims of regulatory capture. Here, it may be worthwhile to make regulatory power a contestable structure rather than a monopoly structure. If any aggrieved party, whether it is the REU, or a consumer or consumer group in a particular state feels that it is a victim of regulatory capture in its state then it should have the flexibility to take its case to any other SERC. This form of contestability may be superior to a hierarchical framework where the CERC alone addresses such problems. Moreover, as long as the penalties for flippant use of this option are kept exceedingly high, incentives to misuse the system would be minimised.

References

Andhra Pradesh Electricity Reform Act, 1998.

Gilbert, Richard J., (ed.) (1991). *Regulatory Choices,* University of California Press, Berkeley.

Gilbert, Richard J. and Kahn, Edward P., (eds.) (1996). *International Comparison of Electricity Regulation*, Cambridge University Press.

Hema, R., (1988). "An Optimum Rate Structure for Electricity in Tamil Nadu" unpublished Ph.D. thesis, University of Madras, Madras.

————. (1996). "Regulated Public Trust Utilities: a case for Restructuring the State Electricity Boards" in *Review of Development and Change,* 1&2, July-Dec.

Newbery, David M., (2002). "Issues and Options for Restructuring Electricity Supply Industries", University of Cambridge, Department of Applied Economics *Working Paper WP0210.*

Newbery, David M., and Pollitt, M.G., (1997). "The Restructuring and Privatisation of CEGB – Was it worth it", *Journal of Industrial Economics*, Vol XLV No. 3.

Orissa Electricity Reform Act, 1995.

Pollitt, M.G., (1997). "Ownership, Costs and Prices in Electric Utilities", *Oxford Energy Forum*, Issue 30, Aug.

————. (1997). "The Restructuring and Privatisation of Electricity in Northern Ireland – will it be worth it?", University of Cambridge, Department of Applied Economics *Discussion Paper No. 9701.*

Prayas, (2001/02). "India Power Sector Reforms Update Oct. 2001, Jan. 2002, May 2002, Sept. 2002".

Sankar, U., (1992). *Public Sector Pricing: Theory and Applications,* monograph published by the Indian Economic Association Trust for Research and Development, New Delhi.

Sankar, U. and Hema, R., (1992). "Economic Efficiency and Social Goals in Electricity Supply in Tamil Nadu", in S. Subramanian (ed.), *Themes in Development Economics,* Oxford University Press, New Delhi.

The Electricity Regulatory Commissions Act, 1998.

The Electricity Supply Act, 1948.

12

Institution of Collective Action for Pollution Abatement

The Common Effluent Treatment Plant

V. ANURADHA

INTRODUCTION

Collective approach by industries to control pollution is gaining importance as a viable option for environmental management. The presence of economies of scale in pollution abatement provides an opportunity for the industries to adopt these control measures in a collective way. These approaches also help to choose least-cost action to reduce pollution. But, these approaches are not always voluntary. They are taken sometimes under the threat of government regulation. One such approach for controlling industrial water pollution in India is the Common Effluent Treatment Plant (CETP). CETP is an institutional arrangement for small-scale water polluting units to treat the wastewater discharged by them and to meet the standards prescribed by the State Pollution Control Board. CETP as an institution provides a structure within which its members can co-operate. The evolution of CETP is due to the stringent enforcement measures adopted by the Government, resulting in the threat of closing down the units not adhering to the environmental standards.

Collective approach concept becomes important whenever the stand-alone cost of a project is higher compared to the share from a collective behaviour. Though the concept of collective action is contemporary to economics, it was neglected for a long period of time. It gained its prominence only after the pioneering work, 'The Logic of Collective Action' of Mancur Olson in mid-sixties. Thereafter, the concept of collective action has become an integral part of any policy evolution. It is being applied in politics (coalition government), in agriculture (cooperatives), in managing common pool resources (forest), in solving environmental problems among nations (global agreements) and recently in solving environmental problems in industries (CETP).

Against this background, this paper analyses the evolution of institutional arrangement for pollution control in tanneries and the conditions required to sustain such an arrangement. Section 2 gives a brief overview of the tanning industry and its pollution. Section 3 deals with the literature review on institutions and collective action. Section 4 discusses the evolution of CETP, the benefits and the conditions for sustaining the CETP in a cooperative game theoretic approach by considering a case study. Section 5 contains the summary and suggestions.

2. INDIAN LEATHER INDUSTRY: DEVELOPMENT *Vs.* ENVIRONMENT

Indian leather industry occupies a unique position as an industry characterised by its massive potential for development, employment and exports. The growth of this industry has been phenomenal during the last few decades, registering a remarkable growth in exports from US$ 746.34 million during 1986-87 to US$ 1589.11 million during 1997-98. This industry has a special status in the national economy as an important foreign exchange earner. But, in recent years, this industry is facing major environmental issues and threats. This section, thus, gives a brief overview of the industry's position in the economy and discusses the pollution problems, regulations and abatement options for the industry.

Brief Overview

The export potential of leather industry was recognised soon after independence and new policies that evolved helped the establishment of a number of small-scale units[1] in the fifties and sixties. The rapid expansion of the industry took place in the early

1. An industrial undertaking is defined as a small-scale unit if the investment in fixed assets in plant and machinery does not exceed Rs. 10 million.

seventies. The rising real wages and stringent environmental regulations in the developed countries resulted in a major relocation of this industry to developing countries due to relatively low wage and less pollution control regulations. With the comparative advantage of large raw material base, comparatively low wages and traditionally skilled work force, Indian leather industry expanded rapidly. A new method of tanning called chrome tanning method was introduced in the seventies to meet the export demand. The new method due to its advantages on the production front replaced the traditional vegetable tanning method, which was quite eco-friendly.

This industry is spread over different segments, namely, tanning, finishing, footwear and footwear components, leather garments, leather goods including saddlery and harness. The structure of the industry is apparently skewed towards the small-scale sector. A survey by the Central Leather Research Institute (CLRI) in 1986 revealed that out of 1083 units, 1008 were small-scale units. The survey also indicated that 62 per cent of the units in the small-scale sector were established after the major shift in the production process in 1973.

Production and Export Potential

The growth history of the industry shows that it has gained greater momentum during the last few decades. There has been a phenomenal growth in exports from Rs. 32 crore in 1965-66 to Rs. 5768 crore in 1996-97. But, the compound annual growth rate has been on the decline after 1992. The Murty Committee[2] (1992) suggested an export target of $ 6 billion for leather and leather products in 1999-2000, which is about 10 per cent of the world exports. In 1998, Ministry of Commerce announced a mid-term export policy for achieving an annual target of US$ 3.2 billion by 2000. But the actual export achievement for 2000-2001 was only US$ 1.97 billion. In 1996-97 and 1997-98 India's export recorded negative growth. This decline is attributed partly to the closure of tanneries in major production regions because of strict environmental regulations and partly to the growing competition

2. This Committee studied the measures of strengthening leather industry in India.

from other Asian countries. The growth rate has shown improvement after 1998. The export data for various segments are given in Table 12.1. Besides the foreign exchange earning capacity, this industry has tremendous potential for employment generation.

Table 12.1

Export of Leather and Leather Products

(Rs. in million)

Item	*1951-52*	*1971-72*	*1981-82*	*1991-92*	*1996-97*	*1998-99*
Raw hides and skins	82.4	6.6	4.4	—	—	—
Semi-tanned hides and skins	253.4	858.7	535.2	—	—	—
Finished leather	—	43.0	2264.0	7262.1	10594.1	11320
Leather footwear	—	85.8	300.5	4308.1	12080.2	12380
Leather footwear components	—	1.5	772.2	6633.5	7916.2	10400
Leather goods and garments	3.7	23.2	566.7	12558.6	24581.1	35460
Total	**339.5**	**1018.8**	**4443.0**	**30762.3**	**55171.6**	**69560**

Table 12.1 shows that there were significant changes in the composition of exports over the years. To begin with, India was a major exporter of hides and skins, but after 1970s India has been following the policy of adding value to its raw material before export. The share of leather products has increased from less than 1 per cent in 1971-72 to 80.8 per cent in 1996-97. The tanneries are mainly clustered in the states of Tamil Nadu and West Bengal. In the total exports, the contribution of Tamil Nadu alone is approximately 50 per cent. Thus, India's leather exports had a set back, when a substantial percentage of tanning units was closed in Tamil Nadu in view of environmental regulations.

Pollution from Tanneries

Tanning is a general term used for the various steps involved in converting hides and skins into leather. There are three major categories, namely: (a) converting raw hides and skins into semi-finished leather, (b) converting raw hides and skins into finished leather and (c) converting semi-finished leather to finished leather. Chrome tanning is the commonly used method. This process consumes large quantities of water and the wastewater discharged after the process contains toxic chromium, chlorides and other chemicals, which have severe impact on the environment. The effluent discharged from tanneries, due to the toxicity causes considerable damages to the receiving rivers, land and the health of the people. There are various options for controlling pollution from tanneries. They are: (i) reduction at source, that is, controlling pollution at the process level, by introducing clean technologies and (ii) end-of-pipe treatment, that is, treating the effluent before discharging. The first option requires the development of a new method of process, in which, the scope is limited and it can be done only in the long run. Thus, the immediate solution is end-of-pipe treatment. This can be undertaken either individually or jointly.

In end-of-pipe treatment, the wastewater from the tannery is collected and treated in the treatment plant before being discharged into the river or land. The decision to, either put up an individual effluent treatment plant (IETP) or become a member of a common effluent treatment plant (CETP) lies with the tannery, taking into account its capacity, financial conditions, available land area and the location of the unit. But, CETP emerged as a viable option for the units located in clusters, as 80 per cent of tanneries are small-scale units with land and financial constraints, and IETP as the solution for scattered units.

With this brief introduction on leather industry and its pollution problem, the following sections will focus on the institutional framework of collective approach to pollution control (the CETP), the major advantages of CETP and conditions for sustaining such a framework, besides providing a short review of literature on institutions for collective action.

3. INSTITUTIONS FOR COLLECTIVE ACTION - LITERATURE REVIEW

Collective action is important whenever the marginal benefit from joining a group is higher than that from acting alone. The theory of institutions is the backbone for theories of collective approaches. This section concisely discusses the core concepts and assumptions of the theory of institutions and the theories of collective action. 1930s and 40s witnessed the development of an economic discipline, often referred to as "old institutionalism". This school restricted its analysis to how resources are allocated in the market. But, the recent development called the "new institutional economics" focuses on how the markets themselves and other allocation mechanisms in society come into function (Anna Blomqvist, 1996). This section reviews the theory of institutions put forth by the new institutional school.

North (1990) defines institutions as '*the humanly devised constraints that structure political, economic and social interaction*'. They are the rules of the game in a society. Institutions may either be created or they simply evolve over time. The major role of institutions in a society is to reduce uncertainty by establishing a stable structure for human interaction. These uncertainties arise from incomplete information, with respect to the behaviour of the individuals. Institutions, with the standard constraints[3], determine the opportunities in a society. They provide the framework for exchange, which determine the cost of transacting and the cost of transformation.

Olson (1965) expresses the difficulty of getting individuals to pursue their joint welfare in contrast to their individual welfare in his Logic of Collective Action. Olson further states that, '*unless the number of individuals in a group is quite small, or unless there is coercion or some other special device to make individuals act in their common interest,* rational, self-interested individuals *will not act to achieve their common or group interests*' (p. 2). He challenges the assumption that the possibility of a benefit for a group would be sufficient enough to create collective action among the members to achieve the common goal.

In a recent study, Ostrom (1998) has pointed out the important components of design and evaluation of institutional arrangements for managing environmental problems. She states that, institutional analysis and development approach, provide a framework for designing institutions and focus on the action arena. Action arena is

---

3. Standard constraints could be informal like customs, tradition or formal constraints such as constitution, laws etc.

a set of variables, which includes the action situation, the actors, the community attributes, the rules and the physical and material conditions, which combine to determine the outcomes. In general, institutional analysts focus on rules and incentives and the effect of these on the outcome.

Ostrom's "Governing the Commons — The Evolution of Institutions for Collective Action", provides an institutional analysis to examine the different ways of governing the commons. She argues that, though both state control and privatisation of natural resources have been suggested as measures for governing the common pool resources (CPR), neither of them has been successful in solving CPR problems. Further, she has empirically illustrated that voluntary collective action, rather than a coercive action can sometimes solve the CPR problems. She attributes the success of these cases to appropriate institutional arrangements, that is, by defining a set of rules that often provides incentives to the individuals to govern resource use and to make contribution for preserving and/or expanding the resources.

A study by Misra and Murty (1995) explored the application of collective action concept in industrial water pollution abatement in India. This study found that, there are enough incentives for the polluters, affected parties, and the Government for achieving the required abatement through collective action. This study emphasises that, when fiscal instruments are less effective in the environmental pollution abatement, it is necessary to look for an alternative such as the institutional arrangement that facilitates collective action.

Given this background, the following section will deal with the development of an institution (the CETP) for pollution abatement in tanneries, identify the advantages of such an arrangement for small-scale units and elaborate the conditions for sustaining such a structure. The analysis is done in a cooperative game theoretic framework.

4. COLLECTIVE ACTION TO POLLUTION ABATEMENT — THE CETP FOR TANNERIES

Industries in India are generally classified under three categories; namely, *red, orange* and *green* based on the pollution intensity of the industry. The leather tanning industry, one of the key contributors to foreign exchange earnings of the country is classified under the *"red"* category, that is, *highly polluting industry.*

Most of the units in the leather tanning industry are small-scale units. The Government has been encouraging small-scale units, in order to reduce regional disparities in development and to generate employment opportunities. But now, the export prospects of leather and leather goods depend on the environmental sustainability of the tanning industry. At present, this industry faces environmental pressures both on the internal and external fronts. The internal pressure is from the local community (affected parties) who filed a case in the Supreme Court against the polluting industry. As a result, the court ordered closure of polluting units, which do not put up an individual treatment plant or become members of a CETP. The external pressure is due to the inclusion of environmental issues in the world trade agenda, which has forced the tanning industry to search for a cost-effective method of controlling environmental pollution.

Most of the tanning units are in the small-scale sector with land, financial and technical constraints to establish and run an effluent treatment plant individually. Thus, treating effluent collectively is considered to be the least cost solution. The presence of economies of scale in pollution abatement, location of units in a cluster and the Government subsidy, provide an opportunity for these units to adopt pollution control measures in a collective manner.

The evolution of CETP is thus attributed to environmental, social and economic factors (see Figure 12.1).

The process of evolution of CETP can be modeled as a three-stage game. In the first stage, the regulatory authority prescribes standards and provides a menu of treatment options. In the second stage, there is pressure from local community, threats from regulators and courts to close down the units if they do not become a member of CETP or put up an IETP or relocate the unit. In the third stage, the firm chooses one of the options (CETP or IETP or relocation or close down).

EVOLUTION OF CETP AS A THREE-STAGE GAME

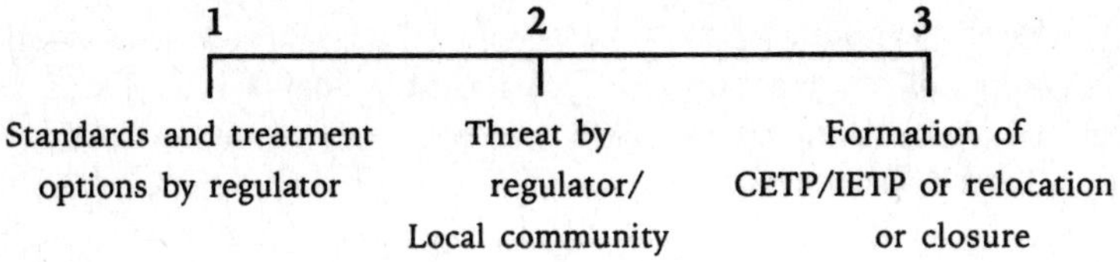

Figure 12.1

Evolution of CETP Institution

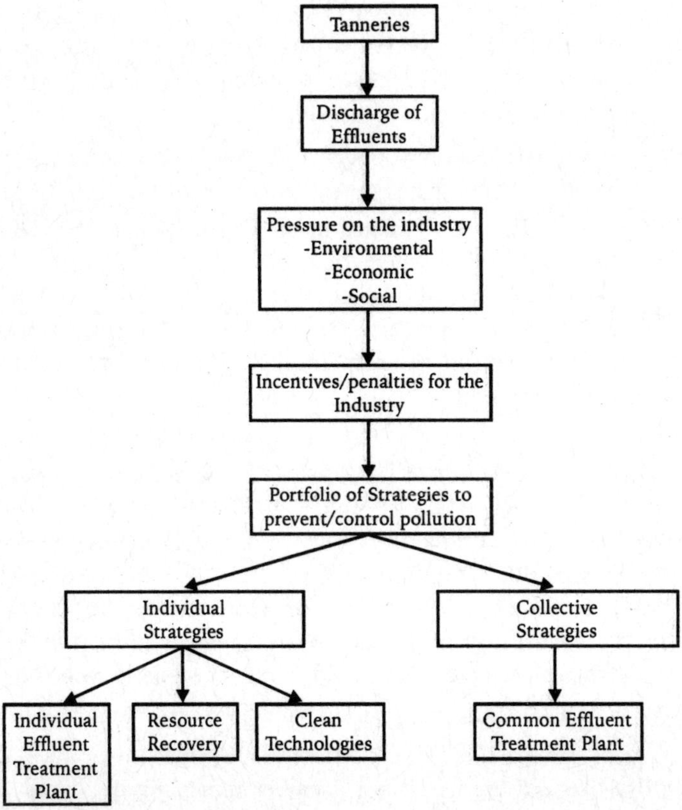

The main objective of CETP is to treat the effluent in a cost-effective way, in other words, to minimise the abatement cost for each unit. The formation of CETP, that is, the collective action takes place due to a threat from the regulators. Thus, CETP is not a pure voluntary collective action, but is a forced action.

The CETP Framework

The formation of CETP framework requires,

(i) the identification of wastewater discharging small-scale units located in an industrial estate or in a cluster, willing to cooperate;

(ii) decision about the ownership of CETP (to be a society or a company or to buy services from a private company);

(iii) designing an agreement, which specifies the nature of association of CETP with its member units and the rights and obligations of the member units;

(iv) estimation of the cost of installing and operating the CETP; and

(v) obtaining consent to operate the CETP and discharge the treated effluent.

As per government regulations, in the total project cost of CETP, 20 per cent is collected as equity from the members, 25 per cent (or Rs. 50 lakh, whichever is less) as subsidy from the state government, 25 per cent (or Rs. 50 lakh, whichever is less) as subsidy from the central government and the remaining is obtained as loan from financial institutions.

CETP as an institution, executes a contract with each of its member unit. This contract specifies the rules of the game. These rules or norms are designed after discussion with member units. Thus, communication before a contract leads to better cooperation among the members. The following are some of the incentives for the small-scale units to join the collective action of treating the wastewater.

(i) the cost share to be paid by the member unit in a CETP arrangement is less compared to the stand-alone (IETP) cost;

(ii) the CETP takes the financial and technical responsibilities and hence the members have less pressure;

(iii) by joining the CETP, the member units initially avoid the legal formalities and the threat of closure; and

(iv) the units satisfy the social obligation of keeping the environment clean.

CETP as a collective institution provides its members other gains besides cost savings. The most vital gain is the Government subsidy for establishing CETP, which is denied to IETP. CETP as a collective entity provides a platform to avail loans from financial institutions at reasonable rates. Also, CETP gets technical assistance from government and other agencies. The establishment of CETP also reduces monitoring and enforcement costs to the Government, because the monitoring can be done at the CETP level and not at the individual unit level. But, are these incentives sufficient to sustain this institutional arrangement is a crucial question. Thus, an attempt is made in this paper to find the conditions or incentives required for the sustainability of CETP.

Modeling CETP as a Game: A Step towards Sustainability

The institutional framework of CETP can be modelled as a cooperative game mainly because: (i) CETP is a cooperative behaviour; (ii) it provides opportunities to communicate and design agreements that are enforceable and (iii) its members have common knowledge, as information is available to all its members, i.e., they have information on treatment technology, cost sharing rules, pretreatment requirements etc.

It is generally assumed that, to induce cooperative behaviour, it is necessary to build sufficient incentive structure in the agreement. These incentives should be such that, they induce cooperative action and are able to sustain the action. In the case of CETP collective arrangement, the method of cost allocation among its members is very important for sustaining the agreement. But the prevailing method of cost allocation does not provide any incentive for the member units to stay in the coalition, as it treats all the units homogeneously. As CETP has members having different production capacities, using different raw materials, and using different tanning methods and thus different levels of concentration of pollutants, these factors have to be taken into account while sharing costs.

The cooperative game theoretic approach focuses primarily on the coalitions of players, stability of the coalition and its characteristic function. This theory mainly addresses the problem of allocation of cost or benefits among the players and the method of allocation. There are different methods of cost allocation such as Separating Cost Remaining Benefit (SCRB), Shapley Value and accounting methods. Shapley Value is an important method of cost allocation. It takes into account all possible coalitions. This method is applied to situations in which costs are allocated in parts or reallocated periodically. Thus to address the cost allocation problem in CETP, Shapley Value has been applied here. This value is defined as,

$$X_i = \sum_{S \subset N, i \in N} \frac{\{S-i\}!\{N-S\}!}{N!} C_i(S) \qquad i = 1, \ldots n$$

where, $\frac{\{S-i\}!\{N-S\}!}{N!}$ is probability of 'i' joining a coalition,

$C^i(S) = C(S) - C(S-\{i\})$ is the marginal cost of 'i' relative to S, where S is a subset of N, and the sum is over all subsets S containing 'i', and X_i is the share of 'i' in the total cost. This solution satisfies,

(i) Feasibility and Pareto-optimality condition, when $\Sigma X_i = C(N)$ = Cost of grand coalition;

(ii) Individual rationality condition, when $X_i < C\{i\}, i = 1,\ldots n$

(iii) Coalition rationality conditions and is in *Core*.[4]

This method is applied to find a solution to the cost-sharing problem in CETP, which is a crucial factor for sustaining CETP.

Data Analysis and Findings

To study the conditions for sustaining the CETP framework with a feasible size and to find a solution to its cost allocation problem in a game theoretic approach, VANITEC CETP located in the North Arcot District of Tamil Nadu is considered. This CETP was established in 1986 and started functioning from 1991 with 110 members. In order to model CETP as a game, these 110 units are grouped into four zones based on the terrain characteristics.

4. The first step in any cooperative game theoretic analysis is to check for the existence of core. Existence or non-emptiness of *core* is guaranteed only if 'C' is concave. 'C' is concave if and only if, for all 'i', the derivative of 'C' with respect to 'i' is a monotonically decreasing function of S, ($S \subset N$, where N is the grand coalition), that is, $S \subseteq S'$ implies, $C^i(S) \geq C^i(S')$, where $C^i(S) = C(S) - C(S-i)$ if $i \in S$ and $= C(S+i) - C(S)$ if $i \notin S$.

In order to find an incentive based cost allocation, the ex-ante options of various possible coalitions of zones are considered and the corresponding cost for each coalition is calculated based on the following assumptions. All costs are given in 1998-99 prices.

Table 12.2

Basic Characteristics of VANITEC CETP

Total Capacity of the Treatment Plant	2850 m^3/day
Total number of tanneries connected to the CETP	110
Total Processing capacity of all member units hides/skins/day	83600 kgs of
Tanning Process used by the units	Mainly Raw to Finish (R-F)
Nature of effluent treated by the plant	Chrome tanning effluent
Length of the sewer (one pipeline for soak liquor and one for combined effluent)	8 kms
Coverage of units by the CETP	Units located within 1.5 km radius (approximately)

Assumptions

The important assumptions here are:

(1) Zonal classification by the CETP is used for grouping the units (the possible coalitions).

(2) The capacity cost (excludes conveyance, pumping and land) is determined by engineering considerations and based on the formula:

$$\text{Capacity cost} = \text{Constant} * (\text{Capacity})^{\alpha}$$

where α is the elasticity of capital cost with respect to capacity. Here α is assumed to be 0.75 based on engineering economics, which gives a range of 0.6-0.8 for elasticity of capital cost with respect to volume of output.

(3) The length of the pipeline is measured from the individual zone maps and the conveyance cost is calculated for each coalition, taking into account the per kilometer cost of VANITEC CETP.

(4) The pumping cost for the coalitions, if any, is obtained from the per m^3 pump station cost of VANITEC CETP.

(5) The capital cost (excluding land) is taken as the sum of capacity cost, conveyance and pumping costs.

(6) The O&M cost for each coalition is calculated based on the various CETPs cost.

(7) The annualised capital cost for each coalition is obtained by dividing the capital cost after subsidy by the present value factor (assuming 20 years of life and 15 per cent discount rate) and the present value factor is 6.2613.[5]

(8) The total cost is the sum of annualised capital cost with subsidy and the O&M cost.

Table 12.3

Cost of Coalitions

(Rs. lakh)

*Coalition***	*Capital Cost (Excluding Land)*	*Capital Cost With Subsidy*	*Annualised Capital Cost (With Subsidy)**	*Operation & Maintenance Cost*	*Total Cost (With Subsidy for Capital)*
{I}	200.20	100.20	16.00	109	125.00
{II}	280.53	180.53	28.83	120	148.83
{III}	185.84	92.92	14.84	107	121.84
{IV}	141.16	70.58	11.27	69	80.27
{I II}	457.55	357.55	57.10	159	216.10
{I III}	363.33	263.33	42.06	140	182.06
{I IV}	341.09	241.09	38.50	124	162.50
{II III}	445.31	345.31	55.15	160	215.15
{II IV}	424.75	324.75	51.87	146	197.87
{III IV}	320.66	220.66	35.24	121	156.24
{I II III}	612.22	512.22	81.81	191	272.81
{I II IV}	582.06	482.06	76.99	176	252.99
{I III IV}	488.50	388.50	62.05	160	222.05
{II III IV}	570.13	470.13	75.09	179	254.09
{I II III IV}	733.44	633.44	101.17	208	309.17

** Coalition of firms in zones.

* Annualised capital cost (with subsidy) = (capital cost with subsidy/present value of capacity)

5. Present value = $[1/(1+r)]\ [(1-(1/(1+r))^t/(1-1/(1+r))]$; here $r = 0.15$ and $t = 20$ and hence the present value = 6.2613.

Cost subadditivity exists in this exercise, as the sum of costs of individual zones is greater than the cost of grand coalition (all zones combined). That is:

$$C(I) + C(II) + C(III) + C(IV) = 475.94 > C(N) = 309.17$$

which means, joining the grand coalition rather than acting alone benefits the zones (economies of scope). By applying Shapley Value method to this gives the cost allocation for the four zones as follows.

$$X_I = (1/4)\ (125) + (1/12)\ (67.27+60.22+82.23) + (1/12)\ (57.66+55.12+65.81) + (1/4)\ (55.08)$$

$\boxed{X_I = 77.38}$ for zone I;

$\boxed{X_{II} = 107.41}$ for zone II;

$\boxed{X_{III} = 75.49}$ for zone III; and

$\boxed{X_{IV} = 48.89}$ for zone IV.

and also, $\boxed{\Sigma X_i = 309.17}$ $\Rightarrow$ the cost is fully distributed.

The cost per KLD (excluding land) for each zone is calculated first by dividing the cost share for each zone by the designed capacity and then by 365 days (since CETP has to function throughout the year).

Table 12.4

Cost Sharing by Zones

Zone	*Approximate Volume of Effluent m³/day*	*Cost per KLD* (Excluding Land) (in Rs.)*
I	715	29.65
II	1100	26.75
III	655	31.58
IV	380	35.25

*KLD - Kilolitre per Day

The cost per KLD for all units combined (treating all zones equally) is Rs. 29.72 (excluding land). Comparing this with the

Shapley Value allocation indicates that, the units in other zones subsidise units in zones III and IV.

The Shapley Value allocation indicates that, the zone with largest need for capacity (Zone II in this case) has to pay less, and this will provide incentive for the largest zone to remain in the coalition, so that the other zones will also benefit from the coalition. Thus, the next large zone (here Zone I) will be paying slightly higher than the largest zone and so on. Hence, the incentive-based cost sharing mechanism is an efficient method, which takes into account possible heterogeneity in the characteristics of units for sharing the cost of treatment. This method provides incentives for units to control and reduce pollution and to stay in the coalition. In order to obtain these benefits the CETP should be of feasible size and thus, combining the four zones is very vital.

The second important factor is the cost of exit option. The threat of exit depends on the comparison of cost of continuing with the CETP and the stand-alone cost (SAC), that is, whether there are cost savings from exit. For this, the cost of exit must be compared with the SAC of each coalition. The exit cost includes the equity already paid to the CETP (sunk cost), and other committed costs (interest on debt and the cost of other contractual obligations) and the penalty for leaving the coalition, if any. But, at present, the exit option is not considered in the agreement and hence there is no reference about the penalty for leaving. That is, the sustainability of the collective action is assumed. But, when the SAC is less than the exit cost, there is a possibility of exit. Thus, in order to prevent post-contractual exit threats, it is necessary to design endogenous enforcement rules in the contract. That is, members and the CETP must define self-enforcing deterrence strategies to credibly punish any deviation from the cooperative strategy.

Let us assume that there is an exit option available to the member units. Let $M > 0$ be the exit option measured in monetary terms. In order to sustain the cooperative arrangement, M must be higher than the SAC and the punishment for exit shall be introduced in the contract.

The third important factor is enforcement. The enforcement of contracts must be effective for the success of CETP. Severe punishment must be enforced and incorporated in the contractual agreement. The rules must also provide ways for the CETP to levy high penalty for exit from the coalition. When there is a high penalty for exit, the incentive to leave the coalition will be less.

The last but not the least factor is the continuous compliance of CETP to the pollution standards. This is crucial to sustain the institutional set up. The guarantee of continuous compliance by the CETP with the standard provides an incentive for units to stay in the coalition.

Government's Role in Sustaining CETP Framework

Although government's role in sustaining the CETP arrangement is meager, it can be effective. For instance, the Government can discourage the units to break away from the coalition, by denying subsidy for these units to put up a new CETP. When there are no subsidies to install a treatment plant, the cost of exit option would be high and this would discourage the units to leave the collective action. Also, the Government should encourage CETP to follow an incentive-based cost sharing mechanism and it should provide adequate information about this mechanism to CETPs.

Moreover, the Government should insist that CETPs comply with the prescribed standards and it can also have some rewards (example, Certificate of Compliance) for those CETPs that are meeting the standards regularly. The member units connected to such a CETP can be given an ECO-LABEL for their products. This would encourage the member units as well as the CETP to undertake the treatment of effluents in an effective manner. Besides this, the Eco-label mark will provide incentive for the units to stay in the coalition.

The Government may allow the CETP to monitor and enforce the pollution control regulations on its member units so that the cost for the Government could be less. But, at the same time, Government should effectively monitor and enforce the rules on CETPs and it should provide an incentive/penalty system for effective environmental management.

5. SUMMARY AND SUGGESTIONS

Leather tanning industry is an important industry for the Indian economy. India has comparative advantage in the production of leather due to the strong raw material base, rich craftsmanship and relatively cheap labour. Small-scale units account for approximately 80 per cent of tanning units and the export prospects of leather and leather products depends on the environmental sustainability of the tanning industry. As most units are in the small-scale sector with financial, land and technical constraints, the CETP is the best option for the units located in a cluster. In order to manage the pollution problem from the tanning industry, the sustainability of CETP institution is very vital. The case study approach in this paper revealed that there are economies of scale in wastewater treatment, only when the CETP is of feasible size. Also, this study shows that, CETP framework can be sustained only when there is:

(a) an incentive-based cost sharing rule,

(b) the cost of exit option is high,

(c) the continuous compliance of CETP with the standards is guaranteed, and

(d) there is effective monitoring and enforcement of rules by CETP on its member units.

Thus, CETP can be made an efficient and sustainable institutional framework for collective action for pollution abatement by revamping the current cost-sharing mechanism, modifying some existing rules and by effective monitoring and enforcement of norms. CETP is an ideal institution for small-scale water polluting units to internalise their externalities and to meet the social obligation of keeping the environment clean by paying a price for it, i.e., to conform to the general 'Polluter Pays Principle', complemented with subsidy from the state and Central governments.

• Business Analyst, GE Capital International Services, New Delhi. The views expressed in the article are the personal views of the author and do not represent the views of the organisation with which she is associated.

References

Alston L.J., Eggerston T., and North, D.C., (Ed.) (1996). *Empirical Studies in Institutional Change*, Cambridge University Press.

Anna, Blomqvist, (1996). *Food and Fashion - Water Management and Collective Action among Irrigation Farmers and Textile Industrialists in South India*, Linkooping University.

Anuradha, V., (2000). "Economics of Collective Action and Cooperative Game Theoretic Approach to Analysis of Common Effluent Treatment Plant for Tanneries", Ph.D. thesis submitted to the University of Madras.

Central Leather Research Institute (CLRI) (1986). *The Fiscal Plan for Setting up Common Effluent Treatment Plants for Indian Tanning Industry*, Chennai.

Folmer, H., Landis, G. and Opschoor, (Ed.) (1995). *Principles of Environmental and Resource Economics - A Guide for Students and Decision-Makers*, Edward Elgar.

Kannan, V., (1996). "Case Studies - Consultancy on CETP", a paper presented at the *Programme on Appraisal of CETP for Tanneries in Tamil Nadu*, held at the Centre for Environmental Studies, Anna University.

Mehta, Mundle, and Sankar, (1997). *Controlling Pollution - Incentives and Regulations*, Sage Publications.

Murthy, E.N., (1992). *Report of Committee on Measures of Strengthening Leather Industry in India*, Ministry of Industry, Government of India.

National Environmental Engineering Research Institute, (1992). *Common Effluent Treatment Plants - State of the Art*, Nagpur.

North, D.C., (1990). *Institutions, Institutional Change and Economic Performance*, Cambridge University Press.

Oates, E. Wallace, (1999). *The RFF Reader in Environmental and Resource Management, Resources For the Future, USA.*

Olson, M. (1965). *The Logic of Collective Action*, University of Maryland, Department of Economics.

Ostrom, E., (1990). *Governing the Commons - The Evolution of Institutions for Collective Action*, Cambridge University Press.

Ostrom, E. and Walker, J., (1997). "Neither Markets Nor States: Linking Transformation Processes in Collective Action Arenas", in *Perspectives and Public Choice - A Handbook*, Edited by Dennis C. Mueller, Cambridge University Press.

Sankar, U., (1998). *Economic Analysis of Environmental Problems by Tanneries and Suggestions for Policy Action*, A Project Report submitted by Madras School of Economics to UNDP.

Smita, Misra, and M.N., Murty, (1995). *Collective Action in the Industrial Water Pollution Abatement: Conceptual Issues and Empirical Analysis*, Institute of Economic Growth, Delhi.

Williamson, Oliver, (1985). *The Economic Institutions of Capitalism - Firms, Markets, Relational Contracting*, The Free Press.

Young, Peyton, (ed.) (1985). *Cost Allocation – Principles, Methods, Applications*, Amsterdam, North Holland.